RESEARCH IN
THE LANGUAGE ARTS

RESEARCH IN THE LANGUAGE ARTS
Language and Schooling

Edited By
Victor Froese, Ph.D.
and
Stanley B. Straw, Ph.D.

Faculty of Education
The University of Manitoba

University Park Press
Baltimore

UNIVERSITY PARK PRESS
International Publishers in Science, Medicine, and Education
300 North Charles Street
Baltimore, Maryland 21201

Typeset by Maryland Composition Company, Inc.
Manufactured in the United States of America by
The Maple Press Company.

Library of Congress Cataloging in Publication Data

Main entry under title:

Research in the language arts.

Includes bibliographies and index.
1. Language arts—Addresses, essays, lectures.
I. Froese, Victor.   II. Straw, Stanley B.
LB1575.8.R463   428   80-20543
ISBN 0-8391-1609-8

CONTENTS

v

CONTRIBUTORS

Mark Aulls, Ed.D.
Educational Psychology Department
McGill University
3700 McTavish Street
Montreal, P.Q. H3A 1Y2
Canada

Diane V. Bewell, M.Ed.
Child Guidance Clinic of Greater
    Winnipeg
Winnipeg, Manitoba R3N OW5
Canada

Sandra Dahl, Ph.D.
University of Wisconsin-Madison
2902 Post Road
Madison, Wisconsin 53713

John Downing, Ph.D.
Faculty of Education
University of Victoria
P.O. Box 1700
Victoria, B.C. V8W 2Y2
Canada

Victor Froese, Ph.D.
Faculty of Education, Curriculum:
    Humanities & Social Sciences
University of Manitoba
Winnipeg, Manitoba R3T 2N2
Canada

Elaine Graham, M.Sc.
Speech and Language Pathologist
Speech and Hearing Clinic
Children's Centre
Winnipeg, Manitoba R3E 0W1
Canada

Richard E. Hodges, Ed.D.
School of Education
University of Puget Sound
Tacoma, Washington 98416

Carol J. Hopkins, Ph.D.
Department of Education
Purdue University
West Layfayette, Indiana 47907

John M. Kean, Ph.D.
Department of Curriculum and
    Instruction
University of Wisconsin-Madison
225 N. Mills Street
Madison, Wisconsin 53706

Bernard R. Klassen, Ph.D.
Faculty of Education, Curriculum:
    Humanities & Social Sciences
University of Manitoba
Winnipeg, Manitoba R3T 2N2
Canada

P. David Pearson, Ph.D.
Center for the Study of Reading
51 Gerty Drive
University of Illinois at Urbana
   Champaign
Champaign, Illinois 61820

Timothy C. Standal, Ph.D.
College of Education
University of Washington
Seattle, Washington 98195

Stanley B. Straw, Ph.D.
Faculty of Education, Curriculum:
   Humanities & Social Sciences
University of Manitoba
Winnipeg, Manitoba R3T 2N2
Canada

Judith S. Youngers, Ph.D.
136-A Burton Hall
178 Pillsbury Drive S.E.
University of Minnesota
Minneapolis, Minnesota 55455

Inez Striemer, M.Ed.
Resource Teacher—St. James-
   Assiniboia School Division
Winnipeg, Manitoba R3J 2C6
Canada

PREFACE

My interest in linguistic questions is ultimately an "applied" one, a concern with language in relation to the process and experience of education.

M. A. K. Halliday (1978)

As the title of this volume suggests, our concern is with language in relationship to schooling, and in that context the term *language arts* is perhaps the most appropriate label to use. Teachers normally use language arts to connote the two productive activities—speaking and writing—and the receptive processes—listening and reading. Writers have also identified the importance of cognition to the language arts, and we have considered it an essential element.

Within the school setting, speaking, writing, listening, and reading are further divided into "subject" areas such as spelling, composition, and literature.

Our position is that the current educational, psychological, and linguistic paradigms interact and influence the teaching of the language arts within the school setting. However, it is perhaps unrealistic to expect the classroom teacher to be well acquainted with the plethora of literature from such diverse fields. In response to this, we have engaged a group of professionals from a variety of psychological, educational, and language areas to address a number of identifiable issues. In this way we hope to acquaint teachers with some of the major trends in language and language arts. These issues are of various types; some represent areas of concern without a clear focus, some summarize vast stores of findings, and some challenge the current paradigms. All are written to encourage thought-provoking discussions.

This book is not intended to be a comprehensive treatise on the language arts; it is intended to address currently unresolved issues of importance to the field. It should be a welcome reference source in language arts classes both at the undergraduate level and the graduate level. At the undergraduate level, it can provide useful and up-to-date summaries in the major areas of language arts, thoughtful interpretations of research, and suggestions for classroom teaching. For the graduate class, it can provide a valuable source of questions for colloquia and seminars. For the clinicians, resource teachers, and those in the helping professions (i.e., psychologists, speech and hearing specialists, nurses, etc.), it should provide a realistic and current look at the study of language within the school setting. We have attempted to identify useful research topics for both the beginning and the advanced researcher. It is hoped that the volume will provide for all a source of "great debate."

The contributing authors were given complete autonomy in how they interpreted their particular issues. They were requested to summarize and synthesize the literature in their particular area. Even though we may not agree with every point of view, we do respect the contributors' professional judgment and opinion.

The contributors were also asked to take a position with regard to their particular issue and to support their stand through reason, professional judgment, research, and/or practice. The difficulty of this task will be appreciated by other professionals, since it necessitates the melding of research from at least three broad sources: linguistics, education, and psychology. Each is a challenge in itself.

A third task given to the authors was to make suggestions for the classroom and for research purposes. Because it is not always easy or efficient to separate interpretation and research, these issues are at times treated in the context of a general discussion.

Considerable latitude was allowed for the method of presentation, both to let authors use their own preferred style and to provide variety for the reader.

This volume is organized generally within a communication framework. Communication occurs through the oral mode if a listener is present (or is intended, as in prerecorded messages) and vice versa. We have labeled the discussion of these processes, which comprises the first section of the book, *oracy*. Our language has not always had a term for the joint processes of speaking and listening; this is a recent term (Wilkinson, 1965) to fill that void. Communication occurs through writing if a reader is present (or is intended, as in a book) and vice versa. This set of processes, considered in Part II, is labeled *literacy*.

Posed as questions, the issues would take the following form:

Oracy Chapters

1. How can knowledge about language acquisition help us to plan oral language activities in the classroom?
2. What is communicative competency and how does it relate to first and second language learning?
3. How is oral language evaluated both in research and in the classroom?
4. What do language tests, especially imitation tests, tell us for clinical diagnosis and remediation?
5. How are creative dramatics, language, and cognition interrelated?
6. How does conscious knowledge about language affect language learning?
7. What is meant by listening instruction and in what direction is current research taking us?

Literacy Chapters

8. Is written composition best taught through analytic or synthetic processes?
9. What is grammar and what is its utility in the curriculum?
10. How can written composition be evaluated and what do the results mean for the classroom teacher?
11. How has psycholinguistics influenced spelling instruction?
12. What has happened to handwriting in the past 60 years?

13. How do children recognize printed words?
14. What have we learned about reading comprehension in the last decade?
15. How do contextual constraints influence the construction and reconstruction of meaning?
16. What can we learn from international reading research?

These are the key questions only; many more are raised in turn by the various authors. The reader is invited to participate in this dialogue. The editors have already enjoyed the challenge.

A great amount of work and energy was necessary to complete each chapter within this book, and we appreciate the dedication displayed by each contributing author in making this volume a reality.

REFERENCES

Halliday, M. A. K. *Language as a social semiotic*. Baltimore: University Park Press, 1978, p. 5.

Wilkinson, A. *Spoken English*. Edgbaston, Birmingham: University of Birmingham, 1965, p. 14.

RESEARCH IN
THE LANGUAGE ARTS

PART I ⎩ ORACY

The term we suggest for general ability in the oral skills is *oracy*; one who has these skills is *orate*, one without them *inorate*. An educated person should be numerate, orate, and literate. These are the NOL skills; NOL are to our age what the Three Rs were to the nineteenth century, fundamental objects of educational effort.

> from Wilkinson, A. *Spoken English*. Edgbaston, Birmingham: University of Birmingham, 1965, p. 14.

Any training in oracy must involve both production and reception. The task of the teacher of English can be summed up by a variation of three words. He is to encourage the *verbalisation of experience* and the *experience of verbalisation*. His focus is on the language used.

> from Wilkinson, A. "The implications of oracy," in *The Place of Language*, Educational Review, 20 (February, 1968), p. 126.

This change [an increasing concern with oracy] implies that oral language has been neglected in the past. This neglect is shown most vividly, perhaps, by the absence in English of a term that distinctly and uniquely refers to the ability to use the skills of speaking and listening.

> from Groff, P. "What's new in the Language Arts: Oral Language," ERIC Document ED 096671, 1974, p. 1.

1 Oral Language and Its Relationship to Success in Reading

Sandra Dahl

The creative, spontaneous use of language by young children has fascinated researchers from broad areas of study. Fundamental questions that have guided research investigations have included: 1) How does a child learn language? 2) What does a child need to learn in order to speak? 3) Is there a developmental sequence to language learning? Answers to questions such as these have produced a vast amount of research data on child language acquisition. Researchers have been motivated, in part, by the feeling that if more can be learned about how children learn language, more will be understood about how learning in general takes place. The first purpose of this chapter is to present a summary of the relevant thinking and research on oral language acquisition.

As a child nears school age, those concerned with academic success begin to raise questions on the issues related to readiness to learn in the school environment. One aspect of the research centers on the relationship between a child's oral language ability and reading achievement. The literature raises questions such as: 1) What does the child need to master in order to learn to read? 2) What is the relationship between a child's oral language skill and achievement in reading? The second purpose of this chapter is to look at some recent evidence on issues surrounding reading acquisition with specific focus given to the oral language-reading achievement issue.

Implications of the research on oral language development and the topic of oral language and reading achievement are presented at the end of the chapter.

ORAL LANGUAGE DEVELOPMENT

How Does a Child Learn Language?

Linguists, psycholinguists, educators, and representatives from other fields have shown an interest in the study of children's language.

3

Although the development of child language study can be traced to the eighteenth and nineteenth centuries, most of the research has accumulated over the past 15 years. Currently, explanations of language learning take the form of theories because no one school of thought is capable of explaining all facets of the acquisition process. However, one thing is certain: children learn the intricacies of language on their own. They are not taught language as they are taught reading, writing, arithmetic, or other skills. Existing theories of how the discovery process takes place have been grouped into three categories: 1) behavioristic, 2) nativistic, and 3) cognitive.

Behavioristic Theory   All normal children do learn the language of the society in which they live. The sounds, word elements, and sentences that a child uses reflect the ones he has heard used in his environment. Therefore, say behaviorists, the principles of imitation, reinforcement, and conditioning must play a major role in language learning. The child hears language used in his environment, is rewarded for responses that are increasingly similar to those of mature speakers, and is, thus, motivated to learn more. Certainly, the young child must develop and use the skill of imitation, and the value of positive reinforcement in human learning cannot be denied. However, behavioristic theory fails to explain the creative aspect of language. For example, what permits a toddler to produce elements which he has never heard modeled in his linguistic environment, such as "allgone juice" or "no want Timmy cereal"? In addition, the behaviorist position becomes questionable when one considers the vast number of possible sentences that could occur in any language. Butler (1971) quotes Gough's claim that ". . . for a 15 word sentence there are 10^{45} possible different ways to construct it, a formidable task if one were to memorize each structure" (p. 70). Although behavioristic principles may account for a portion of the acquisition process, answers to several questions still remain beyond the grasp of this school of thought.

Nativistic Theory   A nativist views the parameters of language as innate or biologically based, species-specific abstractions that are far from being understood. Chomsky (1968) based his nativistic position on Humbolt's theory of speech perception where finite linguistic rules govern the generation of an infinite number of acceptable sentence structures. The human being is equipped with an innate capacity for processing linguistic data in the environment, sorting the data, establishing a structured set of rules, and then using the set of rules to generate an infinite number of creative sentences. Errors that children produce demonstrate that rules are in the process of developing, but are, at that moment, being overgeneralized.

Lenneberg (1967) and McNeill (1970), proponents of the nativistic belief, use the issue of linguistic universals to substantiate their theory. Language universals, or commonalities shared by all natural language, include ". . . the same universal principles of semantics, syntax, and phonology. Each language has words for relationships, objects, feelings, and qualities, and any human can learn any language of the world" (Lenneberg, 1967).

Cognitive Theory   Those who adhere to the cognitive theory of language acquisition believe that children are innately equipped with the ability to process cognitive information in general. Cognitive theorists are concerned with the roles played by concept formation, memory systems, attention, decision making, information processing, and understanding. Cognitive process mechanisms are used to handle incoming and outgoing linguistic data. Language ability develops as children actively attend to language in their environment, process the information they receive, and develop a personal theory of how language works. An unsettled issue in the cognitive arena concerns the relationship between language and thought. Does language guide the thinking processes? Do cognitive abilities precede language abilities? the interested reader is referred to McNeill (1970), Kagan (1971), Cazden (1972), Vygotsky (1973), and Sinclair-de Zwart (1973).

The three major theories of language acquisition have all made a contribution to our understanding of how human beings come to learn their language. No one theory can explain the process fully. As theorists in each camp gather and analyze more data, perhaps a more precise statement will be made available to all those concerned with how a child's language is acquired.

What Does a Child Need to Learn about Language?

Learning to comprehend and use language is indeed a miraculous accomplishment. Interest in the content of oral language learning has been documented by a large number of investigations carried out over the past years. McCarthy's study entitled *The Language Development of the Preschool Child* (1930) was one of the forerunners of the vast number of research studies currently available.[1] The question "What does a child need to learn?" can best be answered by focusing on two aspects of language: 1) the content of language learning, and 2) the functions of language learning.

What has a child learned when he is able to communicate in the language of his culture? Overall, the child has acquired *linguistic competency*, that is, he has acquired a knowledge of his native language including the

---

[1] The interested reader/researcher is referred to Abrahamsen (1977) for an excellent annotated bibliography of past and current literature in the field.

finite system of rules needed to enable him to understand and produce an infinite number of creative sentences. Unconsciously acquired rules govern the use of phonology, morphology, and syntax in the child's communications.

Phonology   Phonology is the study of the sounds of a human language. Knowing the phonology of a language means that one can recognize individual phonemes (distinctive sounds) and the system or pattern of allowable combinations of sounds in the language. The language learner must learn that the distinctive qualities of phonemes signal meaning change. *Tim* and *Jim*, *ball* and *bill*, *bean* and *bead* each differ from one another by one sound. In each pair of words, there is a difference in form and meaning signalled by the change in phoneme. The distinguishing phoneme is termed a *distinctive sound* in the English language. Not all features are distinctive in a language. In English, for example, aspirated and unaspirated qualities do not change meaning; that is, the *p* in pit and the *p* in spill are said to record the same sound. In learning the phonology of a language, a child must pay attention to features that make a difference in meaning.

In addition to knowing the sounds of a language, speakers must learn that phonemes are strung together in a predetermined order. Phonological rules determined which phonemes can appear initially, medially, or at the end of a word. Certain strings are permissible, others are not. For example, the sound sequence recorded by KBLOGP is not and never would be a word in English because it violates the sequencing restrictions placed on phonemes. Phonological rules allow the speaker to add, change, delete, transpose, or switch segments within strings of phonemes. Part of acquiring language includes learning to manipulate and understand these predictable sound changes.[2]

Morphology   Not only does a child learn to use the sounds of his language, he also learns that the sounds and meanings of words are inseparable (Fromkin and Rodman, 1978). Although the union between sound and meaning is arbitrary, the child's task is to build a mental dictionary of terms categorized by sound features and meaning features. A lexical entry must also include a syntactic feature that marks it as a noun, verb, adjective, etc.

As the child's linguistic competency increases, he adds to his lexicon in the form of free and bound morphemes. Free morphemes, morphemes that can "stand alone" such as *bake*, *bus*, and *turn*, are learned along with bound forms (prefixes and suffixes) such as *-er* (baker), *-es* (buses),

---

[2] See Chapter 8 in Dale (1976), Section 1 in Morehead and Morehead (1976), and Chapter 5 in Fromkin and Rodman (1978) for more complete discussion and research on the phonology of English.

and *re-* (return). Words in the child's developing lexicon are composed of one or more morphemes or meaning-bearing units.

Every language has a set of morphological rules that guide the language user in how to combine morphemes to form acceptable words. As noted in the previous section, patterns and structures are fundamental in language acquisition. Morphological rules are *productive rules*. For example, some derivational morphemes change words from one class to another by forming new words:

1. (verb)   *like*   + (suffix) *-able* = (adjective) *likeable*
2. (noun)   *girl*   + (suffix) *-ish* = (adjective) *girlish*
3. (verb)   *dance* + (suffix)   *-er* = (noun)   *dancer*
4. (adjective) *soft*   + (suffix)   *-ly* = (adverb)   *softly*

Compound words, words composed of two or more morphemes, appear in several combinations in English. A few examples include adjective + adjective as in *bittersweet*, noun + noun as in *boyfriend*, verb + verb as in *sleepwalk*, and preposition + preposition as in *into*. The meanings of many compounds must be learned as if they were independent lexical items because the meaning of the individual morphemes is often lost in the compounding process. Whereas *birdhouse* is a home for birds, *firehouse* is not a home for fires.

Inflections become a part of children's morphological competence quite early. Inflectional morphemes are bound forms which function as grammatical markers to change the form and meaning of existing morphemes without altering the syntactic value of the base word. Tense, number, gender, and possessives are grammatical changes performed by the addition of inflectional morphemes.

The acquisition of morphemes in language includes learning word meanings or acquiring a semantic knowledge of the language. The accumulation of semantic properties or features gives lexical items their unique meanings (Clark, 1973). No two words mean exactly the same thing. Clark's hypothesis is that words enter a child's lexicon with incomplete semantic features (or meanings). As the child hears a word used in natural settings, additional features are acquired.

As discussed thus far, knowing a language means acquiring a phonological and morphological competency, or simply knowing the permissible ways to pronounce meaningful units of language. The next section demonstrates an additional task of a language learner: putting words together to express meaning.

Syntax   In order to communicate with others in his environment, the child learns to combine morphemic units together into phrase constituents and, eventually, completely formed sentences. Once again, the child's task is to learn to conform to a finite set of rules; in this case the rules determine how grammatical sentences in his native language may be formed. When combinations of morphemes follow the syntactic rules of language, grammatical sentences are formed (Tim wanted Eric to jump first.). However, violation of these rules, or the improper shifting of morphemes renders an ungrammatical product (First to jump Eric wanted Tim.).

Ambiguity often occurs in completely grammatical sentences, as in the two classic examples:

1. They are eating apples.
2. Visiting professors can be boring.

Multiple meaning results from the structure of the sentence; a reader is not certain of the grammatical relations of constituent parts of the above samples. Syntactic rules also allow meanings to be expressed in synonymous forms.

1. Tim hid his bicycle. (simple, active, declarative)
2. The bicycle was hidden by Tim. (passive)

Ambiguous and synonymous forms of sentences have led some scholars to postulate that language users possess and use both deep and surface structures of lingustic data (Chomsky, 1968). At the deep structural level, meanings are clearly apparent to the speaker/hearer. However, surface structure forms may cause confusion unless they are spoken and are in an appropriate contextual setting.

What does the child need to learn in order to form grammatical sentences and relate to ambiguous and synonymous sentence forms in a meaningful way? At an early stage of linguistic growth the child learns that the linear order of words in sentences is an essential ingredient. Sentences are made up of words grouped into constituent structures belonging to specific syntactic categories. For example, a noun phrase (NP) and verb phrase (VP) constituent could be joined to form a simple sentence:

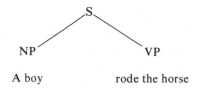

Constituents can be drawn from many other syntactic categories as a means of elaborating the above sentence. As an example, note the phrase structure tree below:

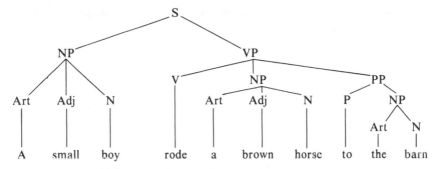

As part of language learning, the child inductively appears to learn phrase structure rules that allow him to join constituents together in a variety of appropriate ways to form complete thoughts. At the same time, the child gradually learns the lexical-insertion rules which allow him to put appropriate words into slots in the grammatical structure. Expressive/receptive grammar grows as the child masters transformational rules that delete, add, and rearrange elements within one or between two or more phrase structures.[3]

Function of Language   In an attempt to outine *what* children learn about language, the fact that their acquisition includes learning the functions of language or how language is used in communication in a variety of ways cannot be ignored. Halliday (1975) says that a child acquiring language "learns how to mean" and that part of that learning includes mastery of seven universal functions of language:

1. *Instrumental Language*—"I want . . . ." or "I need . . . ." Language is used to satisfy needs or desires. It often takes the form of a request.
2. *Regulatory Language*—"Do this" or "Get out of here." Language is used to control the behavior of other people.
3. *Interactional Language*—"Let's play together." Language is used to establish or define social relationships or for participating in social activities.
4. *Personal Language*—"I am going to be a doctor." or "Here I am." Expressions of individuality are included; personal opinions are expressed.
5. *Imaginative Language*—"Once upon a time . . . ." "A long time ago . . . ." The speaker uses language to create a fantasy or a personal world.

---

[3] For an elaboration of the brief summary of syntax given above, see Jacobs and Rosenbaum (1971), Dale (1976), and Fromkin and Rodman (1978).

6. *Heuristic Language*—"I wonder if . . . ." "Why does . . . ." Language is a tool for exploring the world, asking questions, seeking information.
7. *Informative Language*—"I've got something to tell you." Language is used to convey information to others.

Along with learning the basic communicative elements and functional uses of language, sociolinguists remind us that children also learn to use variations in their speech. *Register* is a word used to describe varieties of language we use in specific social settings. Children learn that it is appropriate, or perhaps more comfortable, in some situations to alter the phonology, lexical items, or syntax of their language. DeStefano (1978) offers the following example of register switching:

> *Teacher to unruly student:* "If you don't be quiet, you'll have to stay in from recess," or "Be quiet, Tommy."
> *Teacher to friend in teacher's lounge:* "That kid's yackity-yaking is driving me nuts."
> *Teacher to principal:* "Tommy is disruptive in class and a behavior problem at times."
> *Teacher to parents:* "Tommy has a tendency to be noisy in class." (p. 99)

DeStefano hypothesizes that children acquire a set of rules that govern the use of registers.

In sum, children learn the rules governing the phonology, morphology, and syntax of their native language. When one examines the data and hypotheses of linguists, the complexity of this cognitive task is overwhelming; yet all normal children master the vast amount of learning without special training. Acquisition of language also includes learning how to use language in communication with others. It has been noted that elements of language change in unique social settings.

What Is the Sequence of Language Development?

Children learn a great deal as they progress toward acquiring mature communication ability. The process of language learning is a gradual climb that is charted into stages in the literature.

The Babbling Stage   The first stage of language acquisition, the babbling stage, is a time of passive acquisition often referred to as part of the prelinguistic era. During the early months of life, a baby's babbling includes sounds of all human languages. Intonation patterns of pitch, stress and rhythm are practiced, making some segments of babbling sound similar to true speech. No one is certain what role babbling plays in language acquisition (Sanders, 1969). The traditional view is that as a child babbles sounds at random he will inevitably babble sounds that are recognized and reinforced by his parents. Others believe that parents or caregivers model the native language sounds; these sounds are picked up and imitated by the baby (Mowrer, 1958). Sounds that are not reinforced by people in the child's environment atrophy.

Although a baby's babbling may offer him an opportunity to practice sound production, true phonological development begins to develop when the child uses phonemes to convey meaning (Cazden, 1972). However, it is extremely difficult to mark the onset of this meaning-bearing stage. Roman Jakobson (1971) developed a theory of phonemic acquisition based on the concept that as true phonemic development begins, the child's random babbling dissipates and the vocalizations that accrue are maximally contrasted sounds. The child consciously recognizes and produces distinctive contrasts such as the front consonant /p/ and the back vowel /a/. Gradually finer and finer contrasts are made until all phonemes of the language are in the child's repertoire and can be used to communicate meaning. Research investigations of the future will, perhaps, substantiate or refute Jakobson's theoretical position of the emergence of sounds in language.

The Holophrastic Stage The active stage of language acquisition begins at about 1 year of age when children begin to use combinations of sounds to communicate meaning. These "one-word" expressions are called holophrases and the presence of this powerful linguistic unit ushers in the initial stage of syntactic acquisition. The child's holophrase may have no similarity to a morphemic unit in the parents' language; however, the utterance is clearly meaningful to the child. For example, my own son used the holophrase "bebreke" whenever he wanted ice cream as a treat. A holophrastic utterance can refer to one word as "bebreke" did or the phrase can take the place of an entire sentence. "Daddy" along with the appropriate intonation and situational context could communicate:

1. A command: "Come here, Daddy."
2. A request: "Daddy, I want a drink."
3. A question: "Where is my Daddy?"
4. Information: "This is my Daddy's coat."

Holophrastic speech develops and permits the child to use language for social purposes. Words accumulating in the child's lexicon soon resemble those modeled in the environment.

The Telegraphic Stage Syntactic acquisition continues as the youngster systematically begins to combine two or more holophrases. Utterances at this stage of development, at about 2 years of age, are likely to be devoid of function words. Illustrations from this era, drawn from my own personal records include:

Utterance	Approximate meaning
"Timmy truck"	This is my truck.
"Allgone juice"	My juice cup is empty.
"No want doggy"	I don't want the dog to lick my face.

Note that the above examples are similar to messages adults would send via telegraph. Constructions consist of content words strung together in an acceptable grammatical sequence; much of the meaning depends on intonation and the context of the utterance.

On to Mature Syntax   As the child's language develops, telephrases expand to form sentences that are less dependent on the context of the utterance. In their classic study of the development of syntax, Brown and Bellugi (1964) stated that by the age of 3 years some children produce all of the major varieties of simple English syntax. Theory holds that children take in structures modeled in their natural language environment. The child processes the structures and formulates a rule system which permits him to produce similar types of sentences. Early syntactic productions are constrained in length so the child's utterances include only the essential elements.

As the child gains the ability to produce longer utterances, researchers note that more words are used and more syntactic classes are represented. Inflectional and derivational morphemes emerge according to a scheduled sequence (Berko, 1958). The child appears to learn how to expand constituents of basic phrase structures. Studies of the emergence of two syntactic forms, negation and the question form, have been reported by Klima and Bellugi (1971) and by Cazden (1972).

Increasingly complex transformational rules are developed during the preschool years. Menyuk (1969) reports that "certain structures not only appear before others but are used with much greater frequency than are others" (p. 106). Menyuk's subjects used all of the basic structures of English syntax. However, the structures did not always appear in complete form; according to Menyuk grammatical development continues for some children beyond the age of 7. Chomsky (1969) concluded that school-age children have not yet mastered the entire set of syntactic rules of English. Research by Fox (1972) also pointed to a developmental trend in syntactic maturity.

Most school-age children, then, are at a mature state of language acquisition. Some will need to acquire a few complex syntactic patterns. Morphological rules may be in need of refining. Much of the remainder of the acquisition process involves the expansion of a lexicon. Semantic growth will be a life-long pursuit as the language user learns not only new word meanings but also learns how those words can be used in existing syntactic formats.

Language development, which begins in infancy, is a never-ending learning task. Theorists cannot fully explain how the acquisition process occurs. There does appear to be a sequence in the acquisition of phonology, morphology and syntax. Rate of acquisition, however, varies among individual children (Chomsky, 1969; DeStefano, 1978). Because children differ in what they know about and can do with language, they will exhibit unique characteristics and needs as they are introduced to another form of language, the written language.

WRITTEN LANGUAGE ACQUISITION

Reseachers have been interested in providing a model that explains what people do when they read. To date, no group of scholars has been successful in describing the reading act completely. One of the more popular theories of reading, the psycholinguistic theory, draws heavily on the role played by language ability as the reader meets the printed page. Communication, the main goal of a reading act, occurs when a reader successfully decodes the meaning an author has expressed in print. If a reader is to be successful at discovering an author's meaning, it seems to be essential that the language of the reader and the language of the author be closely matched. A review of the positions taken by Kenneth Goodman and by Frank Smith explains the psycholinguistic definition more fully.

What Do People Do When They Read?

Goodman (1973) states that "reading is a psycholinguistic process by which the reader (a language user) reconstructs, as best he can, a message which has been encoded by the writer as a graphic display" (p. 22). During the beginning stages of reading, a child may rely on recoding techniques prior to decoding meanings from the graphic display. As children gain experience with written language, they appear to process graphemes and aural equivalents of the graphic items at the same time. The child's unconscious awareness of intonation patterns of his native language aid him in decoding meaning from the structures he is processing. As proficiency increases, Goodman (1974) hypothesizes that recoding and decoding occur together so that ". . . the reader is virtually decoding meaning directly from graphic input" (p. 18).

There are several cognitive processing mechanisms that help the reader decode meaning from the graphic input. These agents of receptive language allow a reader to sample features from the visual stimuli, predict possible structure, test the structure against the meaningful information he has gathered, and confirm hypotheses through further sampling (Goodman, 1973). Thus, the reading process makes use of some combination of perceptual and linguistic information. The information is decoded by higher-level cognitive processing agents.

Specific perceptual and linguistic cue systems have been outlined in Goodman's theory. These systems can be labeled as graphophonic, syntactic, and semantic (Goodman, 1973). Graphophonic sequences within (English) word boundaries primarily aid the reader in recoding written language. These sequences refer more to morphophonemic (spelling patterns) relationships than to singular letter-sound correspondences. At the structural level, syntactic cues operate. Here the redundant features of language, markers (noun, verb, etc.), and inflectional forms help the reader formulate a structure that will ease his search for meaning. Finally, Goodman's model relies on a semantic framework supplied by the reader. In order to complete the decoding process, the reader must be able to draw on his experiential and conceptual background. Goodman believes that the three cue systems are used simultaneously and interdependently. If the reader makes sufficient use of syntactic and semantic cues, he may rely very little on the graphic stimuli to predict the content of written messages.

Frank Smith (1971, 1975) proposes a feature analytic theory of reading. At the outset, his theory holds that reading is the reduction of uncertainty. Cognitive agents search for visual and nonvisual cues in order to decode underlying meaning. Features of the graphic stimuli, along with linguistic structures (lexical, syntactic, semantic) present varying amounts of information that reduces the uncertainty of the author's message. For example, a reader uses his knowledge of the patterning of syntax to predict the meaning of the cloze sentence: The child put on his shoes and his _____. The reader's syntactic information predicts that a noun or noun substitute must occur in the open slot; semantic background would help him select a noun such as "socks." Smith posits that in fluent reading, a reader constantly makes hypotheses about the author's meaning and uses just enough cues to accept or reject the hypotheses. Redundancy provided by the patterns found in our written language provides cues that help the reader limit possible predictions. We know that letters and words are limited in distribution by rules of structure.

As linguistic input enters the processing system, syntactic and semantic constraints operate to aid in predicting and then testing possible meanings. In the act of reading, then, Smith feels that a person samples just enough visual information to categorize units of language. At the same time, relationships between units are being established and the passage is understood. The more syntactic and semantic information a reader can make use of, the less visual information is required. In short, Smith sees reading as a process of sampling bits of information sufficient to test and confirm hypotheses about the meaning of a written message.

Up to this point, two components of the language arts have been explored: 1) the development of spoken language, and 2) the reading process. Children bring a tremendous amount of language with them when they come to school. As reading has been defined here, the child will need to draw extensively on his background language skills in order to learn to read. If children do exhibit differences in their ability to understand and use spoken language, it is probable that these differences would be reflected as they encounter instructional programs in reading. As stated by Pearson and Johnson (1978), ". . . the closer the match between the syntactic and semantic information on a page of print and syntactic and semantic information in our heads, the greater the likelihood we will understand the text" (p. 12).

What Is the Relationship between
Oral Language and Reading Achievement?

The integration of language arts skills in the elementary curriculum has been an issue for some time (Tiedt, 1974; Smith, 1979). Smith (1979) terms the usual separation of categories (listening, speaking, reading, and writing) as ". . . arbitrary and artificial; they do not refer to exclusive kinds of knowledge or activity in the human brain" (p. 118). From the beginning, children learn to use language in meaningful settings as part of an attempt to understand and relate to the world around them. Smith's major argument, like that of Halliday (1975), is that children try to make sense out of language they hear used in their environment. Reading is a language-based skill and children expect that the written word will make sense or carry meaning.

Anastasiow (1971) looks at the relationship between oral language and reading as a two-phase process. First, to "learn" the relationship of spoken speech to the written symbol system, the child must discover the regularities of print and come to develop a decoding system consistent with the code. Second, the child's previous ability to comprehend and decode speech auditorily is critical to decoding print. If he is to reconstruct print, he must be able to match the regularities of print with regularities of his stored auditory perceptions; that is, he has to recognize the printed words as ones he already knows.

Anastasiow's comments account for the beginning reader's task as well as that of the mature reader. The child's task must be first to form hypotheses about the relationships between speech and print. The visual images, letters and words, must come to represent sounds and meanings stored in the child's brain. It would seem, then, that comprehension of written passages would be higher if the passages were similar to the child's oral language patterns.

Several research reports have examined children's syntactic ability to determine its relationship to success in reading. Strickland (1962) and Loban (1970) provided extensive background data that spurred numerous investigations. Ruddell (1965) studied the relationship of fourth grade children's reading comprehension to the syntactic structures of written material. Using cloze procedures, children responded to sentences written in common and uncommon syntactic patterns that Strickland had identified. Ruddell reported that higher scores were achieved on written passages which contained high-frequency syntactic patterns. When Tatham (1970) expanded and elaborated on Ruddell's research idea, similar results were achieved. Infrequent language patterns caused problems in reading comprehension, especially for Tatham's second grade subjects. As a result of her study, Tatham stated that, "For beginning readers, it is logical and in keeping with linguistic knowledge to use children's patterns of language structure in written material to facilitate learning the concept that spoken and written language are related" (p. 24).

More recently, Morrow (1978) examined the syntactic complexity of oral language samples collected from 6-, 7-, and 8-year-old children. Language protocols were analyzed using the Botel, Dawkins, and Granowsky (1972) formula for syntactic complexity. A definite developmental trend in linguistic fluency was noted. Morrow urged that the syntax of children's textbooks should ". . . not exceed that of children's language to any great deal" (p. 147).

A number of research efforts have been directed toward the prediction of reading achievement through language measures. Bougere (1969) collected and analyzed the language output of 60 first grade children in an effort: 1) to specify oral language factors related to reading achievement, and 2) to examine the ability of language variables to increase the predictive value of the *Metropolitan Readiness Test*. Although language variables were not as accurate as the MRT in predicting reading achievement, the predictive value of the subtests for Word Recognition and Comprehension was increased by adding certain language measures.

Shepherd (1974) designed a study to examine the relationship of length of utterance, amount of language, and select syntactic patterns to reading readiness as measured by the *Metropolitan Readiness Test*. Positive relationships were found to exist between reading readiness and three language variables: total number of words, total number of sentences, and the total number of words used in sentences.

Vogel (1974) investigated the syntactic ability of normal and dyslexic children. Her major hypothesis was that dyslexic children demonstrated deficiencies or immaturity in oral syntax. Dyslexic children proved to be deficient in seven of Vogel's nine syntactic variables. Vogel urged further assessment of oral syntax in cases of reading disability.

Dahl (1975) conducted a thorough search through the literature that resulted in the identification of seven language variables related to success in beginning reading. Dahl and Johnson (1978) collected oral language data from first, second, and third grade children. Oral language ability was significantly correlated with reading achievement scores at all three grade levels. Fluency variables were shown to be most valuable in predicting reading achievement.

The oral language of 100 subjects was used by Hopkins (1976) in her search to determine the relationship between oral language and reading achievement at the first grade level. Among other findings, Hopkins reported that significant correlations existed between five selected language variables and reading comprehension scores.

Does all of the accumulated research evidence point to a positive relationship between oral language and reading? The answer is a definitive *no*. Groff (1977) surveyed past and present positions and researches on the oral language/reading topic and reported that the literature contains numerous studies that show little relationship between the two variables. Groff says ". . . this topic remains one of the most unsettled to be found in reading instruction" (p. 75).

One thing is clear: Further empirical research is needed to explore the language/reading issue. Implications for that research are stated at the end of this chapter.

Implications for Oral Language Development

Oral language is basic to the development of other communication skills. Since school-age children are still in the process of acquiring language, classroom teachers need to provide opportunities for children's language to grow. What kinds of experiences can be provided for children? It seems that many implications could be drawn from what is known about early childhood language acquisition. The hypothesis accepted in this paper is that children learn their language by listening to models in their environment who are using language in meaningful ways. Sounds, word meanings, and sentence patterns are discovered, practiced and, in time, used in a mature fashion. There are innumerable activities which classroom teachers can plan to encourage the growth of language in natural settings.

The most important requirement for growth in language skill is that the teacher and other adults take the time to thoughtfully interact with children. Conversations with an adult provide an excellent avenue of language input for the child. Teachers are encouraged to use every possible opportunity to listen to their children and to interact with them in a personal manner. A positive, supportive climate where children know that their speech will be accepted is of utmost importance. They need to feel free to talk and not be afraid to make "errors." Extensions of children's speech provide the best means of encouraging growth (Cazden, 1972). For instance:

> Child: "I ain't gonna go out."
> Teacher: "Well, if you aren't going to play outside, let's find
>   something interesting to do in the playcorner."

Extensions are simply comments that react to a child's utterance. Schwartz (1975) says that positive teacher attitude is important during pupil-teacher interactions. Language strategies that build a child's potential include:

a. Engaging in real communication (a two-way process) as opposed to a teacher monologue. This means valuing and really listening to what the child says, responding honestly and humanely.
b. Encouraging child-child communication as well as child-teacher communication.
c. Being certain that teacher responses are clear and focused; that information is embedded in a meaningful context.
d. Involving children in activities which stimulate verbal interaction. (Activities which involve active manipulation of materials are especially good for this.)
e. Developing questioning strategies which go beyond the simple fact retrieval or literal comprehension level, and which challenge children to think.
f. Sharing with children the best of our literary heritage through story and poetry reading; encouraging children to dictate their own prose and poetry efforts.
g. Playing the games, singing the songs, and sharing in the kinds of choral speaking which help children to pattern standard dialect without coercion.
h. Modeling by the teacher of the standard school dialect. (p. 35)

The language used in the classroom serves as a model for future growth and development. Some examples of specific types of activities that encourage language growth in the classroom follow.

One strategy for encouraging children to converse with one another is to give them time to play in stimulating settings. Creative play items can be gathered from homes of teachers and pupils with no cost at all. Dress-up clothes can turn a 6-year-old into Superman, The Green Lantern, a teacher, a nurse, or a farmer. Large packing crates from appliance stores become the homes of any character the children care to portray. Poster paint, construction paper, and magic markers can be used to decorate the crates. The teacher can encourage special types of play activities by equipping the play corner with numerous types of diverse items. A taped story of any favorite fairytale along with appropriate hats may encourage the creation of a spontaneous drama. A collection of miniature dolls or cars and trucks could attract the attention of children and encourage role-playing.

Reading quality literature, both prose and poetry, to children is a superb way to expand their language competency. Listening to the words and sentences used by expert writers is a great experience for children; however, listening is not enough. Children should be encouraged to respond to literature in creative ways. Creative drama, discussions, choral reading of select passages, story retelling, or puppetry all encourage the child to use the author's language. Using words in meaningful situations will help children expand their vocabulary and retain the words for future conversational use. Teachers should be aware of words that need explanation and discussion such as "Jack be *nimble*, Jack be quick" or "Upstairs and downstairs and in my *lady's chamber*." Explanatory comments are often needed to help children understand the textual content of portions of a story. Explanations or expansions can increase the child's perception of an author's intent.

Some teachers expand the learning environment by establishing interest centers in the classroom. Activities in the centers can be designed to build skill in both receptive and expressive language through any curricular area. A science center could display collections of caterpillars along with books, slides, and charts covering the life cycle of butterflies and moths. Children can be given time to explore information in the science center and to share what they have learned in teacher-directed discussion groups. A listening center, equipped with tapes, records, and tape/book combinations, could be used to help children improve their language ability through increasing their listening comprehension skills. Retelling a taped fairytale, drawing pictures, and then explaining the taped message; following a set of directions in a specific manner; and listening to a poem in order to create a new title are examples of a few good listening center activities. Opportunities for planning listening activities are unlimited.

The few ideas here are samples of the types of activities teachers could incorporate into their language arts lesson plans. Children need to see a real purpose in their oral communication and to be actively involved in discovering more and more about language. Building experiences in oral language will provide the child with more stored information to use when he attacks reading and writing skills.

Implications for Reading Development

All reading instruction must be made relevant to the child. Reading must be taught in such a way that the child realizes that the written language is just another form of language used to communicate with others in his world. The language experience approach to beginning reading instruction offers an excellent opportunity to help children discover the principles of written language. Language experience activities, drawn from the experiences and interests of the child, provide a superb transition between oral and written language skill.

During the reading readiness era, songs, poems, and chart stories developed by groups of children provide an opportunity for individuals to learn all kinds of things about the written language. A few examples include:

1. Language can be recorded permanently. We can read our stories over and over again. Each time our stories sound the same.
2. Ideas are recorded using letters of the alphabet. Twenty-six letters are used over and over again in groups to form words. White spaces separate one word from another.
3. Written language is recorded from left to right and from the top of a page toward the bottom.
4. Words that look the same are usually pronounced the same.
5. Words that start with the same letter usually have the same beginning sound.

In other words, recording meaningful language with children allows them to make discoveries about the way their written language works.

As formal reading instruction begins, language experience activities provide an excellent means of developing skills of word recognition, comprehension, and fluency. As children study the stories they have created, sight vocabulary develops, phonic skills emerge, structural elements become apparent, and beginning dictionary skills accrue. Reading comprehension involves an awareness of how words work together to express ideas. Language experience activities deal with this aspect of learning on a daily basis. Fluency skills develop as children read their creations silently to themselves and orally to the teacher or to groups of other children.

Language experience activities draw on the child's existing oral language skill; however, an essential ingredient in any language experience lesson is to foster growth in oral communication. Allen (1976) proposes that language experience lessons begin with ample opportunies for children to experience communication. Singing songs and creative new ones, reciting familiar poetry, hearing a story, moving to the rhythm of music, or discussing an experience are all examples of activities that promote children's language learning. Meanings of new words can be developed as children experience them. Complex sentences are modeled so that children can discover how they are used to communicate ideas.

Futhering growth in oral langauge is a essential ingredient in any language experience activity plan.

Once children have experienced language, they are ready to record their experiences. Recorded songs, poems, and stories provide the material needed to study consistencies and inconsistencies of the written language. Sight vocabulary is developed as content words, selected as key vocabulary items (Veatch et al., 1975), are accumulated by children. Function words, which are guaranteed to appear as natural language is recorded, develop through constant use and exposure. Groups of recorded stories can be skimmed by the teacher for items to use in planning introductory and review lessons on any needed word attack skill. Comprehension lessons may include sentence expansion activities; children may be encouraged to add descriptive words or phrases, add action words, or expand their sentences in other ways.

Building oral language skills in natural settings and using natural language to promote early reading skills are two implications that can be drawn from the research presented earlier in this chapter. The final paragraphs turn to a discussion of implications for the researcher.

IMPLICATIONS FOR RESEARCH

Classroom instruction should be based on the results of careful research rather than on assumptions or intuitions. It seems appropriate to suggest that classroom teachers themselves become involved in research with their pupils. Much research has been carried out on the topic of language acquisition. It has been hypothesized that language growth can best be fostered by providing natural, yet challenging, settings that encourage the child to expand language knowledge and to use it in performance-type activities. Classroom teachers could design programs of this nature, administer the programs and, finally, evaluate and report the products of their efforts. Perhaps teams of teachers could corraborate on a plan to determine the most effective methods of promoting oral language growth. Research studies designed to measure the effects of instruction could be carried out.

We need research to develop and to perfect instruments or tools for teachers to use in language assessment. Questions that need to be asked include: Which elements within a child's growing language storehouse should be selected for testing? How can the teacher gather accurate data on children's level of language achievement? What are some accurate and convenient analytic tools or procedures that teachers can use? Is it feasible to develop a valid, reliable group achievement test that probes language performance skills? Dale (1976) offers some information on testing that may prove helpful to researchers.

Currently, the professional literature provides many studies of the reading process; psycholinguistic models predominate. There is a great need to translate the theoretical research into classroom practices. Does increased oral language activity have a positive effect on learning to read? How should early reading be presented to children? What role should the teaching of skills play in early reading program?

The effect of language experience teaching is a area that needs to be explored more fully. Again, it seems that classroom teachers should be involved in the research. Language experience activities within a group of classrooms could be designed and carried out in similar fashion to lend control to the experiments. Language experience approaches have been compared to alternative methods of reading instruction; however, language experience activities and techniques vary greatly from one teacher to another. It would be possible for teams of teachers to devise long- and short-term activities, to use the activities with children, to keep careful records, and then to use the data to make judgments of the value of the language experience lessons. Practical/applied research questions might include: What activities are most useful in helping children retain key vocabulary items? Do children recall the vocabulary of stories written over a 2-month period of time? Are word attack skills developing at an acceptable rate? Are children able to read words they have recorded in their "invented" phonetic spelling patterns? Can children transfer reading ability from stories they write or dictate to easy textbooks or library books? What are some efficient record-keeping techniques and evaluation tools the teacher might use?

The research implications listed here are aimed at the practitioner. Researchers in language development and reading have accumulated much theoretical information over the past years. The time has come to apply the new ideas in practical settings in attempts to improve learning possibilities for children.

FOR DISCUSSION

1. Dahl has identified three broad theories of language acquisition. How does acceptance of a belief in any one of these theories affect the way a teacher organizes a classroom or teaches language arts?
2. Dahl has identified several areas of language learning. Within these areas, what competencies do most children bring to school and how do they affect the content and approach in language arts curricula?
3. Why do you think the correlations between oral language perform-

ance and subsequent reading performance are so low? Does this mean that they are unrelated? Why or why not?

4. Dahl suggests a "language experience" reading program. How does this differ from the "skills" approach and what justification is there for the "language experience" approach?

REFERENCES

Abrahamsen, A. A. *Child language: An interdisciplinary guide to theory and research*. Baltimore: University Park Press, 1977.

Allen, R. V. *Language experiences in communication*. Boston: Houghton Mifflin, 1976.

Anastasiow, N. *Oral language: Expression of thought*. Newark, Delaware: International Reading Association, 1971.

Athey, I. J. Language models and reading. *Reading Research Quarterly*, Fall 1971, *7*, 16–110.

Berko, J. The child's learning of English morphology. *Word*, 1958, *14*, 150–177.

Bloom, L. M. *Language development: Form and function in emerging grammar*. Cambridge, Massachusetts: MIT Press, 1972.

Botel, M., Dawkins, J., and Granowsky, A. *Syntactic complexity: Analyzing it and measuring it*. Philadelphia: University of Pennsylvania, 1972.

Bougere, M. B. Selected factors in oral language related to first grade reading achievement. *Reading Research Quarterly*, Fall 1969, *5*, 30–57.

Brown, R., Cazden, C., and Bellugi, U. The child's grammar from I to III. In R. O. Brown (Ed.), *Psycholinguistics*. New York: Free Press, 1970.

Brown, R., and Bellugi, U. Three processes in the child's acquisition of syntax. In E. H. Lenneberg (Ed.), *New directions in the study of language*. Cambridge, Massachusetts: MIT Press, 1964.

Butler, L. G. Language acquisition of young children: major theories and sequences. *Elementary English*, November 1971, *51*, 1120–3+.

Cazden, C. B. *Child language and education*. New York: Holt, Rinehart and Winston, 1972.

Chomsky, C. *The acquisition of syntax in children from 5 to 10*. Cambridge, Massachusetts: MIT Press, 1969.

Chomsky, N. Language and the mind. *Psychology Today*, 1968, *I*(9), 48–51, 66–68.

Clark, E. J. What's in a word? On the child's acquisition of semantics in his first language. In T. E. Moore (Ed.), *Cognitive development and the acquisition of language*. New York: Academic Press, 1973.

Dahl, S. S. *An identification of language variables related to success in beginning reading*. Unpublished doctoral disseration, University of Wisconsin-Madison, 1975.

Dahl, S. S., and Johnson, D. D. *The relationship between children's oral language and reading achievement*. Working Paper No. 242, Wisconsin Research and Development Center for Individualized Schooling: The University of Wisconsin, November 1978.

Dale, P. S. *Language development: Form and function*. New York: Holt, Rinehart and Winston, 1976.

DeStefano, J. S. *Language, the learner and the school.* New York: John Wiley and Sons, 1978.

Fox, S. E. Syntactic maturity and vocabulary diversity in the oral language of kindergarten and primary school children. *Elementary English,* April 1972, *49,* 489–496.

Fromkin, V., and Rodman, R. *An introduction to language* (2nd ed.). New York: Holt, Rinehart & Winston, 1978.

Goodman, K. Psycholinguistic universals in the reading process. In F. Smith (Ed.), *Psycholinguistics and reading.* New York: Holt, Rinehart and Winston, 1973.

Goodman, K. *The psycholinguistic nature of the reading process.* Detroit: Wayne State University Press, 1974.

Gibson, E. J., and Levin, H. *The psychology of reading.* Cambridge, Massachusetts: MIT Press, 1975.

Groff, P. "Oral language and reading. *Reading world.* October 1977, *17,* 71–75.

Halliday, M. A. K. *Learning how to mean—Explorations in the development of language.* London: Edward Arnold Ltd., 1975.

Hopkins, C. J. *An investigation of the relationship of selected oral language measures and first-grade reading achievement.* Unpublished doctoral dissertation, Purdue University, 1976.

Jacobs, R. A., and Rosenbaum, P. S. *Transformations, style and meaning.* Waltham, Massachusetts: Xerox College Publishing, 1971.

Jakobson, R. The sound laws of child language and their place in general phonology. In A. Bar-Adon and W. Leopold (Eds.), *Child language: A book of reading.* Englewood Cliffs, New Jersey: Prentice-Hall, 1971.

Kagan, J. *Understanding children: Behavior, motives, and thought.* New York: Harcourt, Brace and Jovanovich, 1971.

Klima, E. S., and Bellugi, U. Syntactic regularities in the speech of children. In A. Bar-Adon and W. Leopold (Eds.), *Child language: A book of reading.* Englewood Cliffs, New Jersey: Prentice-Hall, 1971.

Lenneberg, E. H. *Biological foundations of language.* New York: John Wiley and Sons, 1967.

Leopold, W. F. The study of child language and infant bilingualism. In A. Bar-Adon and W. Leopold (Eds.), *Child language: A book of readings.* Englewood Cliffs, New Jersey: Prentice-Hall, 1971.

Loban, W. Stages, velocity, and prediction of language development: Kindergarten through grade twelve: Final report. Arlington, Virginia: Computer Microfilm International Corporation, March 1970. (ERIC Document Reproduction Service No. 040198)

Lutz, J. Some comments of psycholinguistics research and education. *The Reading Teacher,* 1974, *28,* 36–39.

McCarthy, D. The language development of the preschool child. *Institute of Child Welfare Monograph Series,* 1930, (No. 4).

McNeill, D. *The acquisition of langauge.* New York: Harper and Row, 1970.

Menyuk, P. *Sentences children use.* Cambridge, Massachusetts: MIT Press, 1969.

Morehead, D. M. and Morehead, A. E. *Normal and deficient child language.* Baltimore: University Park Press, 1976.

Morrow, L. M. Analysis of syntax of six- seven- and eight-year-old children. *Research in the Teaching of English,* May 1978, *12,* 143–148.

Mowrer, O. Hearing and speaking: An analysis of language learning. *Journal of Speech and Hearing Disorders,* 1958, *23,* 143–152.

Pearson, D. P., and Johnson, D. D. *Teaching reading comprehension*. New York: Holt, Rinehart and Winston, 1978.

Pinnell, G. S. Language in primary classrooms. In M. L. King (Ed.), *Theory into Practice*, December 1975, *XIV*(5), 318–327.

Ruddell, R. B. Effects of the similarity of oral and written patterns of language structure on reading comprehension. *Elementary English*, April 1965, *42*, 403–410.

Sanders, E. K. How significant is a baby's babbling? *Elementary English*, January 1969, *46*, 80–84.

Schwartz, J. I. Teacher talk and pupil talk. *The Education Digest*, December 1975, *41*, 34–35.

Shepherd, R. C. Oral language performance and reading instruction. *Elementary English*, April 1974, *51*, 544–546.

Sinclair-de Zwart, H. Language acquisition and cognitive development. In T. E. Moore (Ed.), *Cognitive development and the acquisition of language*. New York: Academic Press, 1973.

Smith, F. *Comprehension and learning*. New York: Holt, Rinehart and Winston, 1975.

Smith, F. *Understanding reading*. New York: Holt, Rinehart and Winston, 1971.

Smith, F. The language arts and the learner's mind. *Language Arts*, February 1979, *56*(2), 118–125+.

Strickland, R. G. The language of elementary school children—Its relationship to the language of reading textbooks and quality of reading of selected children. Arlington, Virginia: Computer Microfilm International Corporation, July 1962. (ERIC Document Reproduction Service No. ED002970)

Tatham, S. M. Reading comprehension of materials written with select oral language patterns: A study at grades two and four. *Reading Research Quarterly*, Spring 1970, *5*(3), 402–426.

Tiedt, I. Input. *Elementary English*, September 1974, *51*, 757.

Tovey, D. R. Language acquisition. A key to effective language instruction. *Language Arts*, November/December 1976, *53*(8), 868–873.

Veatch, J. et. al. *Key words to reading: The language experience approach begins*. Columbus, Ohio: Merrill, 1975.

Vogel, S. A. Syntactic abilities in normal and dyslexic children. *Journal of Learning Disabilities*, February 1974, (7), 103–109.

Vygotsky, L. S. *Thought and language*. Cambridge, Massachusetts: MIT Press, 1973.

Wanat, S. Language acquisition: Basic issues. *The Reading Teacher*, November 1971, pp. 141–147.

2 | Communicative Competence and Second Language Learning

Bernard R. Klassen

Recent research in second language learning has increasingly pointed to a necessary shift in emphasis in devising and implementing instruction to coincide with theoretical assumptions (Dulay and Burt, 1973, 1975; Oller and Richards, 1973; Paulston and Bruder, 1976; Wood, 1977; Alatis and Crymes, 1977; Wolfgang, 1979). Giving primary attention to analytical approaches to language forms has been replaced by addressing the sociocultural dimensions first. Meanings embedded in the nonverbal code of the target culture and language comprise the essential communicative signals required by a newcomer.

The importance of this assumption is critical for second language teachers. Their understanding and teaching of a student population is complicated by the overriding importance of understanding a modality of communication that is submerged and inadvertently hidden to them. Each culture has developed its own unique meanings for its accustomed speech acts. With the recent advances made in our knowledge of other cultures, teachers have begun to realize the importance of multicultural dimensions for teaching and curriculum development.

Teachers of English as a Second Language (ESL) need to be aware of this new emphasis. An important first step for them is to become familiar with the culture that is native to their students. With this knowledge they will be better prepared to formulate a curriculum that is acceptable and motivating for their students. They need to be aware of the attitudes that are ingrained about their own language and culture, as well as the linguistic and cultural prejudices held by the students and their parents. It is also essential to have an awareness of greeting formulas, the meaning of typical gestures, acceptable interpersonal distance, parameters of touch and eye contact, the relative importance of time constraints, and status-formality considerations. These nonverbal parameters, so easily taken for granted by the native speaker, need to be made explicit to the second language learner. If these factors are given consideration at the beginning stages of a second language program, a comfortable orientation can be achieved. Students will then be prepared psychologically and socially to move on to more complicated stages of language and culture acquisition. If integrative motivation can be achieved in this way from the beginning of the language learning experience, the teacher can more realistically expect to "trigger" success- ful language and culture acquisition in both children and adults.

THEORETICAL ASSUMPTIONS

Theories underlying the assumptions of language learning and teaching have traditionally been drawn from educational psychology, linguistics, and anthropology. More recently, psycholinguistics and sociology have dominated the field with major revolutionary assertions relating to the process and context of second language learning. Furthermore, John Oller's (1973) definition of pragmatics has helped educators to focus on the emerging trend "away from language as a self-contained system toward language as a medium of communication."

The popular term "communicative competence" implies an ability in human learners to intuit the grammar of a language when exposed to it in meaningful contexts. Human beings appear to have the mental predisposition to acquire a natural language. This enables them to internalize the rules that govern the production and comprehension of meaningful utterances in their native language. The "creative construc- tion hypothesis" posited by Dulay and Burt (1975) further explicates the manner by which children and adults follow a natural, predetermined sequence of language acquisition which is activated by exposure to natural language in meaningful contexts. In earlier studies of children's language acquisition, Dulay and Burt (1973) asserted that what is more important than explicit teaching of syntax, especially to children, is the messages rather than to their form. Richard Tucker (in Alatis, 1977) makes a similar assertion about adult learners when he ascribes the process of language learning to be "incidental to the task of communica- tion with someone, about something which is inherently interesting to the student."

These new hypotheses should free the classroom teacher from exten- sive drilling, repetition, and memorization of non-contextualized gram- matical paradigms or syntactical patterns in an attempt to induce rote learning of a language. Instead, students are exposed to meaningful situa- tions which prompt them to formulate messages that emanate from real experiences. The "language act" rather than the sentence becomes the basic unit for analysis and practice and this requires the inclusion of social acts and human interactions. Paulston and Bruder (1976) suggest activities which give second language students opportunities to engage in meaningful dialogues using social formulas, interaction activities, community-oriented tasks, role playing of real-life interactions, and problem-solving activities. These activities require an interpersonal responsiveness to social context and an awareness of when, how, and to whom different levels of the language code are appropriate and effective.

EXTRALINGUISTIC FACTORS IN COMMUNICATION

The impact of the major shift in linguistic and anthropological research that made speech a tenable area for scientific investigation in the early twenties has extended the scope of linguistics into another exciting new domain in the last decade. It is now recognized that speech cannot be studied in its entirety as an isolated linguistic corpus, but that is must be seen as an interactional process with the context in which it occurs. Dell Hymes (Fishman, 1968) refers to this as the "ethnography of speaking," emphasizing that its concern is with "the situation and uses, the patterns and functions of speaking as an activity in its own right."

This shift has finally accorded the study of sociolinguistics the respectability that attracts linguists, psychologists, educators, sociologists, anthropologists, psychiatrists, as well as other non-professional researchers to investigate a wide range of communicative behavior such as paralinguistics (pitch, pause, and stress of an utterance), kinesics (gestures), proxemics (physical distance between communicators), haptics (touch), aromatics (smell), and chronemics (time) (Birdswhistell, 1952; Hall, 1966; Harrison, 1974). These modalities of communication provide a convenient framework on which to examine the cross-cultural variations of coding experience.

PEDAGOGICAL APPLICATIONS

The implications of these new designations of communicative acts are particularly pertinent to second language teaching methodology. The importance of understanding the culture of a target population has been acknowledged for many years but has not been applied systematically to the interpretation of cross-cultural contexts. If it is true, as Mehrabian (1972) claims, that the predominant carriers of meaning in interpersonal communication are the nonverbal channels, then these parameters should receive special attention in the initial stages of second language learning. Furthermore, they could serve as motivational and integrative functions. Recognition and understanding of the nonverbal features of communication and language are less critical to foreign language learners within their native culture than for those who are learning a new language in a target culture.

A CROSS-CULTURAL EXHIBIT

It might prove useful to focus directly on a foreign linguio-cultural setting in order to delineate its characteristic codes of communication. We might thus be sensitized to our own characteristic nonverbal patterns of communication and consequently be better able to overtly teach second language learners the culturally acceptable concomitants of verbal communication.

Although I grew up in a minority culture and taught public school in several different cross-cultural communities, I became aware of the dynamics of cross-cultural communication most acutely while teaching English as a second language to Arab boys in a preparatory school. The extralinguistic modalities of communication I observed there as a foreigner tended to sensitize me to the potential problems that immigrant children and adults encounter when they are faced with learning a new language and a nonverbal code that is often not taught overtly but is critical for unambiguous communication. A delineation of the Palestinian Arabic (PA) speech events in various social settings should throw light on some of the parameters that have to be considered in cross-cultural communication. It should also make us aware of our characteristic modes of nonverbal communication which we tend to take for granted and too easily ignore in our language curricula.

Attitudes

It is essential first to know the basic attitudes that the Palestinian Arab has toward his own language. Though his attitudes are based on the "linguistic folklore" of his community and are not based on fact, they are, nevertheless, real and held to with some conviction.

The Arabic language is revered by Arabs; it is the language of the sacred Koran. To speak its superposed form well is to be held in high esteem in an Arab culture. Native speakers consider their language to be grammatically symmetrical and logically structured (Chejne, 1969). In public speeches, the art of cultivated rhetoric is popular and highly respected. Furthermore, the Arabesque decorative writing enshrined in mottoes and Koranic inscriptions on mosques and monuments make it easy for the common man to exalt Arabic script by associating it with divinity. This high regard is not limited to the classical Arabic of the Koran or the modern literary Arabic of the educated. Each colloquial dialect, e.g., Palestinian, Syrian, Lebanese, Egyptian, is considered by its native speakers as the closest to the classical and, therefore, the best.

In view of these attitudes it would be very unwise to make amused comments, even in jest, about Arabic writing moving in the wrong direction. Arab sensitivities toward their language have to be taken seriously and respected. Arabic has a proud linguistic heritage; the foreigner would do well to imbibe this attitude. Much respect can be gained by learning to speak and write their language. The difficulties encountered will support the popular perception that Arabic is complex and unique.

Greetings

Learning a foreign language often begins with memorizing the common greetings. Book-learning of Arabic greetings has little value because what is most significant in the less formal greetings of everyday life in a PA community is not the semantic content of the greeting, but rather the nonverbal and paralinguistic concomitants of a given greeting in a given context.

One of the first things to be noticed about PA greetings in the community is their length. A simple "hello" occasion generally calls for a voluble "Peace to you, and the blessing and mercy of God be upon you and your family . . . " which is only the beginning of a lengthy exchange of polite solicitude for each other's families.

Not only are PA greetings lengthy, they are also stereotyped rituals which conform to a dialogue set by convention. A foreigner can easily memorize these greeting dialogues, but it will take careful and perceptive observation to learn to use the channels that carry the real message. The discursive content is of little importance beyond that it conforms to the norms of traditional utterances. What the native speaker attends to are the more subtle variations of tone, pitch, and melody which are interpreted according to the culturally defined meanings. The stereotyped dialogue is a kind of "phatic communion" which carries important messages through the nonverbal modalities other than the syntactic and semantic components. What is communicated by opening talk about the weather or other small talk in an American setting in fulfilled in the PA setting by the elaborate, ritualized greetings, on which interpersonal, affective messages can be improvised nonverbally.

It is, therefore, important to learn all the significant modalities of communication. Some of the major parameters that can be identified are paralinguistics, kinesics, proxemics, haptics, and to some extent olfactory according to E. T. Hall (1966). These parameters have to be viewed with reference to the varying social dimensions in which speech events are observed—domain, status, attitude, and function.

Arab hospitality, motivated initially by traditional norms, accentuates the need for the foreigner to be all the more discerning about the actual relationship that exists between him and his host. This can be done best by learning the nonverbal cues that accompany greetings and invitations. Hymes (1964) asserts that "the contextual frames must be sought not in the usual linguistic corpus but in the behavioral situations." Put another way, listening with a third ear is essential.

The greeting of a stranger in a shop with the "salaam" greeting may be said with overt show of feeling, but there are important nonverbal cues added when using the same greeting with a casual acquaintance, a neighbor, an official, a dignitary, a close friend, or an enemy. The uninitiated are apt to misconstrue the real meaning or message contained in the greeting.

In order to gain useful information about the dynamics of greetings within the social domain of the PA culture, the observer should distinguish between the informal, intimate context within the family and the neighborhood and the more formal exchange with people holding power and authority in the city and government.

The "marhaba" (welcome) greeting is perhaps the first Arabic greeting the newcomer will hear. It is the closest approximation to the English "hello" and, like it, has a very wide range of appropriate usage. It can serve as a perfunctory greeting between people passing each other on the street, in which case the reply would simply be "marhabateen" (twice welcome). Eye contact would be brief and no attempt would be made to approach each other. This greeting indicates simply, if used in casual passing, that they recognize each other: absence of the exchange could imply some hostility. The tone is, therefore, quite matter-of-fact and impersonal. It provides an opening, however, if either party should like to continue the engagement. If the parties are neighbors or friends, this same greeting could be used, but it would be intensified by paralinguistic, proxemic, and haptic features. Adults of the same sex would shake hands vigorously and the greeting would be uttered slowly at a slightly higher pitch with heavy stress on the last syllable. The reply would have a terminal contour that suggests nonterminality (Schegloff, 1968). The conversation has to continue for another "stroke" (Berne, 1964). While disengaging the handshake, another exchange of wishes of good health can terminate the greeting. If friends meet often in this context and want to avoid a sentimental exchange, they can transform the first reply into a humorous "marhabateen wa nus" (welcome two and a half times). However, serious-minded adults will normally continue the exchange in the traditional way. If there is evidence of reciprocal concern and friendliness in the nonverbal concomitants of the greeting dialogue, they can now separate or continue with discussions of mutual interest. The nonverbal cues would include intense eye contact, interpersonal distance of about a foot, active hand gestures, and animated facial expressions. If the encounter takes place in a home, the host or hostess may carry on the exchange while receiving the guest and getting him comfortably seated while beginning to prepare coffee.

Adolescent boys or young men who are real "buddies" may use the "marhaba" greeting as a mere filler while approaching to within hand-shaking reach; then both would raise their right hands and while looking directly at each other's eyes, slap their hands together with unerring aim and resounding smack while simultaneously uttering "kaafe" (palm). Frequently this handshake would continue in a kind of hand-holding while the two friends animatedly converse and walk hand in hand or arm in arm along the street. The palm slapping in analogous to the back-slapping and shoulder-jabbing of North American young men, as is the use of epithets like "ya zilimii" (old chap) or "ya ahii" (brother) that often accompanies the greeting of close friends.

The only other public greeting that includes so much physical contact is the meeting of relatives after long separation. The closer the relationship, the longer and more intense the greeting. The conventional embracing followed by a kiss on both cheeks is appropriate between relatives; between very close relatives like a parent and child, the greeting ritual is repeated several times. Fathers will grasp their son's head firmly with both hands and kiss both cheeks in turn, sometimes kissing him on the lips as well. The son's role is more restricted and requires a handshake and a light kiss on the father's cheek. The mother is allowed more informality and may pinch the boy's cheeks and tousle his hair while uttering motherly endearments not unlike those she used when he was a baby. Emotions are not repressed and all parties will often openly weep with joy.

Babies are greeted with endearing epithets like "ya habiibtii" (sweetheart), "shelabee" (beautiful), accompanied by pinches on their cheeks and sharp slaps on the backs of their hands. A stranger who admires a baby or draws attention to it must end his greeting with a wish for God's protection of the baby. If this is forgotten, the mother of the baby will hastily add the omitted expression. (Ancient tradition prescribed this invocation in order to avert the "evil eye" from focusing on an innocent child because of undue attention given to it.)

These greetings occurring in the family setting have been characterized by an intensity of interpersonal contact in which the nonverbal modalities rather than the syntactic-semantic component carry the significant message contained in the greeting or the event.

Within the more formal social settings, however, a quite different function is evident in the modalities that dominate the less formal events.

The PA culture attaches great significance to status differentials. The nature of the greetings tends to support and perpetuate the established social strata. Any visitor is greeted with "ahlan wa sachlan" (Hearty welcome, i.e., You have met your family and come upon a smooth path.) If the visitor is an honored person (mayor, politician, sheik, lawyer, doctor, headmaster, etc.), the greeting dialogue emphasizes the status differential of the participants. Aside from a welcoming handshake, no further physical contact is made; formal distance is maintained and a deferential attitude and tone are cultivated by the lower status person toward the higher status individual who in turn is polite and somewhat patronizing.

Similar formality is evident in greetings that are messages of salutation and congratulation. Such greetings range from formal greetings to mayors at their annual levees on special feast days, to congratulatory messages extended upon the birth of a baby boy, upon someone's return from a pilgrimage, upon the completion of a building, upon the purchase of an important appliance or car, or to a person who has just had a haircut or shave. The greetings appropriate to these occasions are known to all and become a part of the formal event that requires them. The personal element is subordinated to the formality of ritualized greetings.

For the foreigner in a PA culture, a careful observation of the customs associated with the formal and informal greetings can serve as a vignette of the subtle nonverbal parameters of communication.

Gestures

Arabic speech is accompanied by a great deal of gesticulation. Very seldom do Arabs communicate interpersonally without elaborate gestures and body movements to add to their verbal expression.

Proxemics

The North American who is used to a recognized 2-foot bubble of privacy when engaged in normal communication will find the 1-foot norm of the Arabs somewhat pushy and threatening. However, greater proxemic distance is construed by Arabs as apathy or coldness.

Territory

Another potential cause of "culture shock" for the North American alien in the Arab world is the concept of territoriality and privacy in public. The "first-come-first-served" dictum of Western society is not heeded and the behavior of Arabs in organized queues appears to be pushy and chaotic. In buses and public waiting rooms people tend to sit together on double seats or couches, unlike the tendancy of North Americans to choose the vacant seat and to sit alone if at all possible. Hall (1966) observes that priority is given to fast movement and assertiveness in claiming territory. Even so, once settled the claim can still be challenged with impunity.

Haptics

The discussion of greeting behavior indicates its dependence on interpersonal touch. Haptics is an important feature in Arab society, not only among small children but also in the adult world of communication events. Jabbing, pushing, slapping, pinching, and caressing are normal and expected concomitants of animated interpersonal communication.

Smell

The olfactory sense is also considered an important modality of communication among Arabs. Hall (1966) states that Arabs can perceive personality characteristics through the sense of smell. They tend to label certain individuals as "nervous" or temperamental on the basis of body odor. Perhaps this accounts for the tendency of young men to use perfumes and lotions fairly readily. It is not uncommon to hear someone warn a friend not to stand too close while visiting because of a "sour stomach." Compatibility of "smell" was traditionally an important feature to be considered when marriage partners were selected. The rationale was that different temperaments could be detected and compatibility could be assured by judicious matching of body odor.

Time

With the rapid urbanization of Arab society, time constraints are becoming increasingly more important. Traditionally, with a largely rural population dependent on seasonal occupations like gardening and herding, daily work and leisure activities were not tightly scheduled. Now, with many rural people commuting to factory jobs and places of business, buses run on time and people at all levels of society are expected to arrive on time for appointments.

Implications for ESL Instruction

The extralinguistic characteristics of a target population can give the ESL teacher important clues as to optimum strategies to be used in second language instruction.

The facility with which Jordanian boys learned English can be largely attributed to the positive attitude they held towards Americans and American culture as they knew it through films, tourists, and correspondence with their American friends. It is not uncommon to hear English expressions and complete English sentences interspersing animated discussions among young people on the streets, in shops, and at the cinemas. American and Canadian tourists in Jordan are eagerly entertained, not just in the hope of generous handouts, but as a source of information about a people and land their hosts admire and envy. Most extended families have numerous relatives living in North America, and once in America the Jordanians integrate very rapidly, learn the language quickly, and all too often abandon their own mother tongue. Integrative motivation (Lambert, 1969) toward the American way of life for the Arab emigrants and Arab nationals who are fascinated by the Western World seems to expedite their rapid acquisition of English. In Jordan it is facilitated by the strong desire of the people to imitate the American way of life. Their seemingly boundless self-confidence and their pride in their own language and culture helps them to embrace a foreign language and culture with such alacrity.

This attitudinal orientation to an English-speaking culture affects the implementation of teaching strategies for any ESL program involving such highly motivated learners. In fact, almost any method is bound to succeed. The present generation of secondary students is just now being weaned from a long entrenched memoritor system of learning in the schools. This has conditioned them to memorization. Audio-lingual methodology with its emphasis on the oral mode has proved very successful in the Arab world. The more recent emphasis on contextualized, realistic, and "meaningful" language production is even more compatible with their penchant for drama, rhetoric, and verbality. This inclination for talk and play-acting provides a convenient vehicle for the ESL teacher to plan skits and simulations which focus on the nonverbal modalities of the target culture. Skits and mini-dramas written and directed by the teacher but dramatized and discussed by the students could depict vignettes of American social interactions and the characteristic kinesic, proxemic, and haptic codes that accompany typical speech events. Seelye's (1975) culture "capsules" and "mini-exposés" could be adapted to highlight further language instruction.

A CONTRASTING EXHIBIT

Experience with Cree Indian children in Northern Manitoba provided me with a decisive contrast in cross-cultural accommodation and the effect of quite different orientations on cultural assimilation and second language learning.

Unlike the talk-oriented Arab society in which an audiolingual, talk-oriented ESL program seemed so appropriate, this Canadian Indian population revealed a decided aversion toward vocal participation of students. Talk within a competitive classroom setting violated the cultural norms of the native Canadian society. The presence of an alien white teacher further inhibited talk. This situation, coupled with a loss of self-confidence in the face of an aggressive, talk-oriented, encroaching white culture, complicated the teaching of ESL. Audiolingual methodology proved incompatible with this cultural milieu. What further militated against its success was the ingrained non-competitiveness of North American native culture. There was one exception: team competition was accepted in sports activities. This fact might be a useful clue for teachers in similar situations to devise teaching strategies that capitalize on team rather than individual competition.

It appears from my own experience with Cree Indian children and from accounts of Vera John (Cazden, 1972) with Navajo children and Robert Dumont (Cazden, 1972) with Sioux Indian children that "silence" is the major obstacle to successful conventional classroom activities that depend on competitive verbal interaction. Group work in which the teacher stays in the background and acts as a resource person and allows for a maximum of peer planning and peer cooperation in small groups appears to be the clue for productive language activities. Susan Philips (Cazden, 1972) reports some success using this strategy with American Indian children.

Group work need not be confined to the classroom. Dumont (Cazden, 1972) found that while Sioux and Cherokee Indian children tended to be "monosyllabic" inside the classroom, outside they were "noisy, bold, daring, insatiably curious." The Rough Rock Demonstration School as reported by John (Cazden, 1972) experienced its most successful curriculum innovations when children were allowed to schedule their lessons outside in a natural setting.

Strategies for successful ESL programs for native Canadian children would also have to take characteristic nonverbal modalities of their culture into account. Unlike the integrative motivation displayed by the Arab children, the native Canadian Indian children do not aspire to adopt the alien culture of the white majority.

The Rough Rock School in Arizona has led the way in offering English as a Second Language programs to Navajo children alongside primary instruction given in their native language. During the first 6 years of school, a gradual shift takes place as more and more English is used after children are fluent and literate to their native language. Manitoba has initiated a similar experiment in some of its native Indian communities and seems to be resolving some of the cross-cultural problems as the Indian communities develop their own bilingual educational programs. Members of the community participate in the instruction of their children and provide accounts of traditional folklore and historical events in the native language.

Whereas the optimum strategies for second language teaching to Arabs were in the direction of extroverted activities and talk, a contrasting approach is necessary with native Canadian Indian populations. New ways of teaching English without undue emphasis on oral techniques will have to be developed to suit the sociological parameters of a silent, noncompetitive culture. Gattegno's Silent Way (1972) may well be a method that could succeed within their curriculum.

It appears, even from a cursory observation of the Arab and Canadian Indian target ESL populations, that the nonverbal modalities need to be considered very seriously in the planning of beginning phases of second language programs. In the case of the Palestinian Arabs it is largely a matter of capitalizing on their verbal exuberance and integrative motivation, and perhaps ironically, teaching them consciously to restrain their accustomed kinesic, proxemic, and haptic behavior. The native Canadian culture, on the other hand, will have to be shown greater understanding and respect for their own language and culture. As they are given opportunity to build up their confidence and pride in their rich heritage and culture in their own way, they will enrich the existing multi-cultural mosaic in a bilingual context.

IMPLICATIONS FOR INSTRUCTION

The new knowledge that we now have about communicative competence and language learning should facilitate the development of curricular innovations to promote language development in both first and second language learning. Green (1971) suggests the need for gesture inventories to be developed and incorporated into materials of instruction. He recommends an undergraduate course that will provide teacher trainees with sufficient knowledge and experience with "foreign culture" to enable them to "internalize the nonverbal system of the target culture." Tucker (in Alatis and Crymes, 1977) suggests the necessity for a "new and dynamic partnershp between the ESL specialist and the content-area teacher. The ESL teacher must be prepared to understand, to systematize, and to integrate into her ESL lessons information about her students' language performance from other classes or realistic communication situations." Wood (1977) suggests that the language teacher must be concerned with developing communicative competence by "putting language to work" for her students in the following ways: "enlarging their *repertoire* of communication acts; *selecting* criteria for making choices from the repertoire; *implementing* the communication acts chosen; and *evaluating* the effectiveness of communication employed."

Another area of research that is gaining momentum and is supplying important practical pedagogical innovations is that of *sentence-combining*. Frank O'Hare (1975) is leading the way with curriculum materials designed to facilitate syntactic growth and fluency through graduated exercises of sentence-combining. Klassen (1976) has tested this technique with ESL populations and found that sentence-combining exercises can be dramatically effective in expediting linguistic fluency in ESL students at an intermediate level of language development, i.e., after students have acquired the ability to read the write in a target language. Language development materials based on this research are now being tested in Manitoba schools and reports from students and teachers involved in this program are enthusiastic. It holds a great deal of promise in that students are highly motivated by seeing how they can extend their syntactic growth by putting short sentences into meaningful and correct combinations that come closer to approximating the language development achieved in their native language.

More research is needed to point teachers to those language-learning activities that are productive. Of particular importance is an accelerated pursuit of the new trends that encourage the development of communicative competence with due regard for cross-cultural sensitivities and second language learning proclivities.

FOR DISCUSSION

1. Klassen discusses briefly both communicative context and the importance of a meaning-based language education. How do his views compare with Aulls' (Chapter 15) view of context and Pearson's (Chapter 14) view of prior experience?
2. Klassen seems to be supporting an inductive approach to language learning. Is there a role for deductive instruction in his curriculum? Does age affect the applicability of such programs?
3. How would Klassen define communicative competence?
4. What implications do Klassen's remarks on second language learning have for teachers of first language?

REFERENCES

Alatis, J. E., and Crymes, R. (Eds.). *The human factors in ESL*. Washington D.C.: Teachers of English to Speakers of Other Languages, 1977.

Berne, E. *Games people play*. New York: Grove Press, 1964.

Birdswhistell, R. *Introduction to kinesics*. Washington, D.C.: Dept. of Stats, Foreign Service Institute, 1952.

Cazden, C. B. et al. *Functions of language in the classroom*. New York: Teachers College, 1972.

Chejne, A. *The arabic language: Its role in history*. Minneapolis: University of Minnesota Press, 1969.

Dulay, H., and Burt, M. "Should we teach children syntax?" *Language Learning*, 1973, *23*(2), 245–257.

Dulay, H., and Burt, M. Creative construction in second language learning. In M. Burt and H. Dulay (Eds.), *New directions in second language learning, teaching and bilingual education*, Washington, D.C. TESOL, 1975.

Fishman, J. (Ed.). *Readings in the sociology of language*. The Hague: Mouton, 1968.

Gardner, R. C., and Lambert, W. E. "Motivational variables in second-language acquisition." *Canadian Journal of Psychology*, December, 1959, *13*, 266–272.

Gattegno, D. *Teaching foreign languages in schools: The silent way*. New York: Educational Solutions Inc., 1972.

Goffman, E. *Behavior in public places*. New York: Doubleday, 1966.

Green, J. R. "A focus report: kinesics in the foreign-language classroom." *Foreign Language Annals*, 1971, *5*(1), 132–143.

Hall, E. T. *The hidden dimension*. New York: Doubleday, 1966.

Haddad, E., and Irany, J. *Standard colloquial arabic*. Jerusalem, 1955.

Harrison, R. P. *Beyond words*. Englewood Cliffs, N.J.: Prentice-Hall, 1974.

Hymes, D. *Language in culture and society*. New York: Harper and Row, 1964.

Klassen, B. R. *Sentence-combining exercises as an aid to expediting syntactic fluency in learning english as a second language*. Unpublished, doctoral dissertation, University of Minnesota, 1976.

Mehrabian, A. *Nonverbal communication*. Chicago: Aldine-Atherton, 1972.

O'Hare, F. *Sentencecraft: An elective course in writing*. Lexington, Massachusetts: Ginn and Co., 1975.

Oller, J. W., and Richards, J. C. (Eds.). *Focus on the learner: Pragmatic perspectives for the language teacher*. Rowley, Massachusetts: Newbury House Publishers, 1973.

Paulston, C., and Bruder, M. *Teaching english as a second language: Techniques and procedures*. Cambridge, Massachusetts: Winthrop Publishers, 1976.

Schegloff, E. Sequencing in conventional openings. *American Anthropologist*, 1968, *70*, 1075–1095.

Sebeok, T. (Ed.). *Approaches to semiotics*. The Hague: Mouton, 1964.

Seelye, H. *Teaching culture: Strategies for foreign language educators*. Skokie, Illinois: National Textbook Co. with ACTFL, 1975.

Wolfgang, A. (Ed.). *Nonverbal behavior: Applications and cultural implications*. New York: Academic Press, 1979.

Wood, B. S. (Ed.). *Development of functional communication competencies: Grades 7–12*. ERIC Clearinghouse on Reading and Communication Skills, 1111 Kenyon Rd., Urbana, Illinois, 1977.

3 | Evaluating Children's Oral Language

Carol J. Hopkins

The purpose of this chapter is to review the literature on the topic of the evaluation of children's oral language. Studies are categorized within a historical framework spanning the traditional, structural, and transformational grammar eras. This review is followed by a discussion of the measures that have been used to evaluate children's language and focuses on problems involved in deciding *which* variables should be included and *how* they should be evaluated as well as basic problems involved in eliciting language samples. Implications for classroom instruction are considered.

Prior to the late 1920s and early 1930s, most oral language investigations were studies concerned with the acquisition of vocabulary. These "baby biographies," as they have been termed, were approached through a diary method. For example, the Whipples (1909) recorded each word that they heard their son use in sentences for 10 days prior to his third birthday. Mr. and Mrs. Bush (1914) recorded all of the words that they heard their daughter use from age 2½ until her third birthday and then made comparisons of the words she used with the words used by the Whipple's son. Similar studies were conducted by Brandenburg (1915) and Nice (1915), who recorded their own children's speech; Langenbeck (1915), who listed the words used by a precocious child; and Stern (1924), who gathered data about the language of his three children from his wife's diary. Criticism was leveled against these early investigators by researchers in favor of testing and scientific research who claimed the biographical approach lacked systematic data gathering and employed inadequate sampling procedures.

Since the middle 1920s, 3 eras of research may be identified (Fox, 1970). First are the investigations conducted during the scientific period which utilized the traditional Latin-based grammar constructs. Next, research inquiries designed to investigate structural grammar theory were reported. Finally, studies based on transformational grammar were conducted. These eras provide the organization for the literature review.

ORAL LANGUAGE RESEARCH BASED
ON TRADITIONAL GRAMMAR CONCEPTS

The rules of syntax imposed on the English language by eighteenth century grammarians form the basis of traditional grammar, a prescriptive set of rules employed by speakers and writers of English. Pre-1960 studies of children's oral language development derived their methods from traditional grammar components and focused on charactertistics of: 1) length of total response, 2) sentence length, 3) frequency tabulations of simple, compound, complex, and incomplete sentences, 4) distribution of declarative, imperative, interrogative, and exclamatory sentences, 5) kinds of subordinate clauses and their ratios to each other as well as to main clauses, 6) the relative frequencies of the eight parts of speech, often with special attention to verb phrases and verb types, and 7) the tabulation and cataloging of morphological and syntactic "errors."

McCarthy's (1930) investigation of the oral language of 20 children at each of seven ½-year age levels from 18 to 54 months has often been cited as having the greatest influence in the establishment of stimuli and the methodological and analytical procedures for oral language research during the traditional period. In her study, 50 consecutive verbalizations were elicted and recorded while each subject played with a collection of toys and picture books. These 7,000 responses were analyzed according to length of verbalization, parts of speech used, and their grammatical structure—incomplete, simple, simple with phrases, and the number of compound, complex, and elaborated sentences.

Among the investigators who, with minor individual modifications, adopted McCarthy's methods of collecting and analyzing oral language samples were Day (1932), Davis (1937), Shire (1945), Templin (1957), and Sampson (1956, 1959, 1962). Similar schemes for classifying oral responses within a traditional grammar framework were developed by Smith (1926), Williams (1937), Carroll (1939), Gibbons (1941), Yedinak (1946), Hahn (1948), Milver (1951), Martin (1955), Winter (1957), and Morrison (1962). The results of these studies in the traditional era indicated that, within groupings of higher chronological age, mental age, and parental occupation, children produced increasingly longer utterances, spoke more words, and used more different words. Furthermore, sentence length and the number of different words spoken were accepted as reliable measures of language maturity (DeStefano and Fox, 1974). For the various language factors studied, girls' language appeared to develop at a slightly faster rate than did boys' although statistically significant sex differences were not often observed.

ORAL LANGUAGE RESEARCH BASED
ON STRUCTURAL GRAMMAR CONCEPTS

The major thrust of the investigations based on structural grammar concepts was toward a detailed description of the overt structure of language, that is, the ways in which phonological, morphological, and syntactic units were patterned in speech. Rather than classifying words as parts of speech as was characteristic of the traditional grammar era, words were categorized according to the way they were used in sentences. The influence of structural grammar on oral language research resulted in studies which examined children's language using more refined and detailed systems than had previously been employed.

For example, Strickland (1962) analyzed the oral language structure of 575 elementary school children in grades one through six according to the syntactic structure of sentences, frequency of specific syntactic patterns, amount and kind of subordination, length of sentences, and flow of language. She reported that subjects at all grade levels could expand and elaborate their sentences through the use of movables, i.e., words, phrases, or clauses with no fixed position in the sentence, and subordinating elements. Significant relationships were found between the use of movables and subordination patterns and the variables of intelligence, mental age, and parental education and occupational status. A wide range of language patterns, five or six of which were distinct favorites used by subjects at all grade levels, led Strickland to conclude that children acquire basic language structures at an early age.

Another classic investigation of this era was Loban's (1963, 1976) longitudinal study of the language growth of 338 students from kindergarten through high school to determine whether language growth followed a predictable sequence and whether definite stages could be identified. In addition to employing some of the same linguistic analyses developed by Strickland, Loban devised the "communication unit," the grammatical independent clause with any of its modifiers. Loban reported an increase in the toal number of words spoken, number of communication units, and average number of words spoken in communication units with chronological age. Conversely, the number of mazes and number of words spoken in mazes decreased with age. Therefore, he concluded that communication units and mazes were promising measures of language development because they could be independently verified.

Strang and Hocker (1965) applied Strickland's methods to examine syntactic structures in 2,500 phonological units of first grade children and found that of the 331 different sentence patterns used, only three of them occurred more than 100 times. Concurring with Loban, they concluded that the most significant aspect of language development was flexibility within sentences. Other investigations which followed the Strickland and Loban procedures and reached similar conclusions were conducted by Riling (1965) and Shepherd (1974).

In summary, studies conducted during the structural grammar era reported conflicting evidence as to the usefulness of sentence length as a measure of language maturity. The investigators concluded that linguistic maturity could be better measured by examining flexibility within structural patterns and the occurrence of mazes. Research of this era has since been criticized (MacGinitie, 1969) for the lack of information reported concerning the specific grammatical structures examined. Few studies used this format, however, for by the time it was employed in educational research, the validity of structural grammar was being contested by a new theory known as transformational grammar.

ORAL LANGUAGE STUDIES BASED ON TRANSFORMATIONAL GRAMMAR CONCEPTS

The focus of transformational generative grammar was to explain the ways in which speakers generate sentences and to formulate a system of rules governing sentence production. Researchers strongly influenced by the transformational approach to language study attempted to measure the syntactic ability of their subjects at different age levels by determining how many and what types of transformations were effected in sentence production. There are three basic types of transformation rules. One accounts for the proper combination of elements that have been separately identified in a string, yet in an order not acceptable in actual language. Another type provides options for converting kernel sentences into different sentence types. Finally, there are transformations that join two strings or embed one in the other.

Menyuk (1963, 1964) was the first to report a study of a transformational analysis of children's language when she described the oral language of nursery school and first grade children in terms of what appeared to be the rules that generated utterances which conformed to standard adult usage and those which deviated from it.

Slobin (1967) examined the behavior of kindergarten, second, fourth, sixth grade, and college students when presented with the task of evaluating various kinds of sentences or retelling stories that involved specific structures. He found evidence to suggest a rough, but not thoroughly systematic, correspondence between the transformational complexity of sentences and the subjects' difficulty in comprehending them.

Perhaps the most influential study of the transformational grammar era in terms of providing insights into measures of grammatical complexity was Hunt's (1965) study of written language which resulted in the development of the Minimal Terminable Unit. Commonly called the T-unit, it is an objective, quantitative measure of response defined as a syntactic unit consisting of one main clause expanded at any of a number of different points by structures that are modifiers, complements, or substitutes for words in the main clause. The purpose of Hunt's study was two-fold. The first was to provide a coherent, systematic, broad, reliable method for the quantitative study of syntactic structures and the second was to search for developmental trends in the frequency of various grammatical structures in the writing of fourth, eighth, and twelfth grade students. A 1000-word writing sample from each student was analyzed for variables of sentence length, clause length, subordination ratios, kinds of subordinate clauses, and structures within a clause (coordinated structures, nominals, the verb auxiliary, main verbs and complements, modifiers of verbs, and predicate adjectives). Hunt found that of the four indices he examined to determine the best indication of a student's grade level, the T-unit was the most accurate, followed by clause length, subordination ratio, and sentence length. He identified two factors, the formation of subordinate clauses and modifiers and coordination within the clause, as underlying the increased growth in T-unit length across the grade levels. Hunt concluded that the T-unit was a promising index of maturity since the average main clause written by successively older students had more subordinate clauses attached to it and the clauses themselves increased in length.

O'Donnell, Griffin, and Norris (1967) extended Hunt's research in their investigation designed to discover more about the use of syntactic units and structures from a series of analyses applied to the oral and written language samples of children from kindergarten through seventh grade. Their purpose was to examine the validity of certain indices purported to be reliable, easily observable, and objective measures of children's development of syntactic control. The most frequent increases from grade level to grade level were the subjects' use of coordinate constructions within clauses, of sub-clausal adverbial constructions, and of nominal constructions containing adjectives, participles, and prepositional phrases. The greatest developmental progress in oral language occurred in the time spans between kindergarten and the end of first grade and between the end of fifth grade and the end of seventh grade. The research team concluded that the T-unit was a valid measure of syntactic development.

Fox (1970) replicated a portion of the O'Donnell, Griffin, and Norris study as she explored the developmental trends of syntactic maturity and vocabulary diversity in the oral language of kindergarten, first, second, and third grade children. The subjects' oral responses to stimulus films were analyzed for their syntactic maturity as measured by the total number of words in T-units, the total number of T-units, the mean word length of T-units and number of words in garbles. Vocabulary diversity was measured by the number of different words and a corrected type-token ratio. Fox concluded that a developmental pattern of syntactic maturity existed for all of the measures of syntactic maturity except for garbles and that the growth between kindergarten and first grade was significant on all three syntactic measures. The developmental trend in syntactic maturity measured by mean word length in T-units found by O'Donnell, Griffin, and Norris were partially confirmed in her results.

Another major study employing the T-unit as a measure of syntactic maturity was conducted by Bougere (1968), who performed a linguistic analysis of the verbal output of 60 first graders in an attempt to specify oral language factors which were related to beginning reading achievement. A second purpose of her study was to demonstrate that selected language measures could enhance the predictive value of a standardized readiness test. The linguistic predictors studied were number of T-units spoken, mean length of T-unit, ratio of sentence-combining transformations to T-units, ratio of subordinate clause length to T-unit length, percentage of words at frequency levels one and two on the Thorndike-Lorge list, percentage of words at frequency levels three through five on the same list, and type-token ratio. Results of her study indicated that none of the language measures predicted reading achievement as accurately as the readiness test, but that the predictive value of the test for word recognition and comprehension could be increased by adding some of the language measures alone and in combinations. Other results indicated high intercorrelations among syntactic measures, few significant relationships between language scores and the variables of sex, intelligence, or socioeconomic status, continued need for reliable language measures, and a need for reevaluation of the adequacy of standardized measures of first grade reading achievement.

Other studies which employed T-units as a measure of syntactic maturity across a variety of age, grade, and socioeconomic levels were conducted by Calvert (1971), Stewart (1972), Hensley (1973), Ciani (1974), Pope (1974), Morrow (1975) and Hopkins (1976).

METHODOLOGICAL CONSIDERATIONS

Oral language research, regardless of the era in which it was conducted, has been hampered by methodological difficulties of eliciting, analyzing, and quantifying language data. This problem leads to consideration of two important areas: 1) eliciting and recording language samples, and 2) determining measures to be used to evaluate the language samples.

Eliciting and Recording Language Samples

There are two basic approaches to language assessment. One is analyzing spontaneous speech and the other is the use of highly structured situations, i.e., tests (see Chapter 4 by Striemer, Graham, and Froese). Because both methods have merits and limitations, the two approaches should be viewed more as complementary rather than mutually exclusive. The primary advantages of using spontaneous speech are that, because research on oral language development has focused most intensively on spontaneous speech, a larger body of normative data exists. Also, any testing situation is, to some extent, artificial and constraining, whereas spontaneous conversations are less so (Dale, 1976). Prutting, Gallagher, and Mulac (1975) illustrated this by comparing results on the Northwestern Syntax Screening Test to an analysis of the spontaneous speech of 4- and 5-year-old children. The investigators found that 30 percent of the structures children failed to name on the test were correctly produced in their spontaneous speech.

Anderson, Messick, and Hartshorne (1972) offered the following suggestions in an Educational Testing Service task force report:

> The decision to use either natural or contrived settings often appears to be a matter of the investigator's taste, when it should depend on the proposed use of the "scores" in subsequent analyses. If the observational measures are to serve as dependent variables, they should be derived from standardized situations. If they are to serve as independent variables, describing the program or treatment, they may be derived from naturalistic settings, although valuable predictive (independent variable) information can also stem from standardized situations. . . . (p. 32)

There is obviously no perfect solution to the problem of language sampling. One of the most common sources of uncertainty in the interpretation and comparison of reports made on children's language is the diversity of conditions under which the language being investigated was produced. A pertinent question in the discussion of sampling problems arises. Does the absence of an item from a child's speech mean that the child cannot produce it or merely that, in the given situation, the child has not found it necessary? One of the implications of this dilemma is that sizable samples are necessary for analysis, which leads to the question, how sizable? Much clinical work is based on samples of 50 to 100 utterances. Dale (1976) claims that the most informative research in language development has been based on samples of at least 300 to 800 utterances and, in some cases, even more.

The context in which language samples have been drawn has varied widely in oral language investigations. Many language collections such as those of McCarthy (1930), Day (1932), Davis (1937), Templin (1957), Strickland (1962) and Riling (1965) were gathered by the interviewers as they attempted to stimulate conversation with the aid of books, toys, pictures, and other objects. An alternative method of collection employed by Menyuk (1963, 1964) and numerous other researchers was to record speech heard in a variety of situations.

There have been many investigations of the variables affecting language performance (Helsabeck, 1971). Various effects of social setting have been investigated by Smith (1935), Joos (1962), Goffman (1964), Labov, Cohen, and Lewis (1968), Labov (1970), Williams and Legum (1970), Kline (1971), and Longhurst and Grubb (1974). Most of these studies demonstrated that the child's language performance varied according to the interpersonal relationships of the individuals in the interview situation, the number of participants, and the formality of the situation.

The effects of the type of task and the degree of structure within it have also been shown to be related to language performance (Lawton, 1968; Heider, Cazden, and Brown, 1968; Williams and Naremore, 1969; Boehnker, 1973). Many of these researchers concluded that some groups of children were able to display more abstract and elaborative language in the more highly structured tasks.

Results of studies conducted by Berlyne and Frommer (1966), Cowe (1967), Cowan et al. (1967), Strandberg and Griffith (1968), and Lawton (1968) suggested that the particular topic used to elicit language also influenced the language sample obtained from children. Other investigators (Strandberg, 1969; Drdek, 1970; Duquette, 1971; Ahmed, 1973; Smith, 1974; Hopkins, Moe, and Stephens, 1975) have directly measured the effect of stimulus variation upon the language samples produced by their subjects.

Given all the variables which may affect language performance, one final area to consider is the actual recording of the samples, regardless of the elicitation or collection procedures used. The earliest language studies relied on someone writing down the child's speech without the aid of recording devices. The recorder's speed and accuracy in capturing the subject's speech on paper became a large source of error. This problem, soon solved by the availability of recording instruments, was to be replaced by the possibility of inaccurate or inconsistent transcriptions.

Evaluating Language Samples

Once decisions have been made as to how to elicit language which is believed to be representative of the child's oral performance, questions of what features to analyze and how to measure them become paramount. Not surprisingly, the measurement of language features has proved to be an extremely difficult task. Linguistic tools for observing and categorizing oral responses have either not been available or they have been too complex for the volume of data to be examined. According to Cazden

(1972), writing a grammar for each child's oral language would be the most complete description possible. Unfortunately, because of the time and expertise required, this task would be possible for only a few experts in the field of language development. Thus, researchers have tried to devise their own methods of evaluating language samples. Almost all these methods may be viewed as attempts to quantify identifiable language characteristics and can be categorized as measures of vocabulary diversity or syntactic complexity.

Measures of Vocabulary Diversity   The initial and most frequently employed measures of vocabulary diversity consisted of a count of different words spoken (Horn, 1925; Gates, 1926, 1935; Child Study Committee of the International Kindergarten Union, 1928; Murphy, 1957). Comparisons of different frequency lists were difficult because of inconsistencies in basic considerations of what constituted a word and how different forms and multiple meanings of words should be counted (Hopkins, 1979).

Researchers in the area of quantitative linguistics have long struggled with the development of a formula to indicate vocabulary diversity or word frequency distributions. One such measure which is often used for comparing diversity over time or among children is the type-token ratio developed by Carroll (1939, 1964). He discussed language complexity in terms of vocabulary diversity as measured in a word frequency distribution and stated that this distribution, however it was analyzed, reflected a relationship between the number of types (different words) in a language sample and the number of tokens (total words). The type-token ratio, obtained by dividing the number of different words by the total number of words, was then used as a measure of the richness or diversity of vocabulary in a language sample. However, it was noted by Chotlos (1944) and Johnson (1944) that the type-token ratio decreased as the size of the sample increased because fewer and fewer of the words did not occur in the sample already counted. To overcome this problem, Carroll (1964) proposed that a measure of vocabulary diversity independent of sample size, the corrected type-token ratio, could be obtained by dividing the number of different words by the square root of twice the number of words in the sample. This measure is still employed in oral language research (Hopkins, 1976; Moe and Rush, 1977).

Zipf (1935), Herdan (1960, 1962), Carroll (1970), and Kidder (1974) are among those who have examined the implications of statistics and calculus on the vagaries of lexical distribution. One of the constraints that has affected their work is the statistically unusual curve of vocabulary usage; high frequency words are used with high frequencies and words of subsequent frequencies follow a sudden drop (Kidder, 1974). Unfortunately, none of these measures, no matter how simple or complex their derivations may be, give more than a numerical index or score. No provision is made for qualitative analyses.

Syntactic Complexity A traditional measure employed in much child language research is the mean length of utterance (MLU), computed by counting the number of morphemes (not words) found in a sample of 50 to 100 utterances (Slobin, 1967). Language researchers have found this measure useful not because utterance length itself is important, but because an increase in utterance length is an index of increasing linguistic complexity. Because it has been confirmed that MLU increases with age and that there is a correspondence between the mean length of utterances and the emergence of specific grammatical features up to age 4, MLU has been accepted as a valid measure of language complexity (Cazden, 1972).

A similar and probably more common language measure in educational research is the average sentence or utterance length. Determined by the natural break in the child's verbalizations, the utterance or sentence is considered to be finished when the child comes to a stop, letting the voice fall, giving interrogatory or exclamatory inflections, or indicating that there is no intent to complete the sentence.

The major criticism of measures like MLU or average sentence length is that all morphemes or words are assigned equal value. No provision is made for difficult or unusual vocabulary or sentence structure, nor is the existence of extraneous word or word sequence revisions, sometimes referred to as garbles or mazes, accounted for. Cazden (1972) summarized the problem well when she stated, "The trouble with length is that one counts units as if they were beads on a string and all alike."

As researchers realized the need for quantifying syntactic structures as an indication of increasing language complexity, attempts to develop objective, reliable indices increased. A popular outcome was weighted scales. One of the earlier attempts reported by Miner (1969) described a length complexity index computed by assessing MLU and performance on noun phrase and verb scales. Shortly after, Frank and Osser (1970) proposed a scale that allowed quantitative and qualitative analyses of complete utterances. Utterances were categorized as simple or complex according to the types of transformations used. The number of sentence elements and the number of transformations required were also counted and compared. Calvert's (1971) K-Ratio (Kernel Structure) Index was another attempt to quantify syntactic complexity. His ratio was computed by dividing the number of T-units in a language sample by the number of kernel structures embedded in each T-unit.

In an attempt to overcome inadequacies in measures of syntactic complexity which focused on only a few syntactic structures correlated with reading complexity, Botel and Granowsky (1972) developed the

Syntactic Complexity Formula (SCF). Their formula was based on notions from transformational grammar theory which suggest that complex sentences are derived from processes of changing and combining underlying structures. To apply the SCF, sentences in a selected passage are assigned complexity ratings by comparing them to the structures described and illustrated in the instrument. The basic structure of the main clause of the sentence is assigned a count of zero, and one, two, or three additional features or structures are added to this. The sentence ratings are then averaged to obtain a complexity rating for the entire passage. The SCF has been employed in studies conducted by Miller and Hintzman (1975), Morrow (1975), and Glazer and Morrow (1978).

Endicott (1973) proposed a system for determining the syntactic complexity of language within T-units. By weighting co-memes (basic units of complexity) which he categorized as base co-memes, syntactic co-memes, compression co-memes, and morphemic co-memes, a complexity ratio of the number of co-memes per number of words could be obtained. In a critique of this measure, O'Donnell (1976) stated that while Endicott's scale had the ability to discriminate one structure from another, it was not clear that it would always favor the more complex constructions.

The Syntactic Density Score (SDS) developed by Golub and Kidder (1974) represents another approach to developing a single quantitative index of syntactic complexity. The SDS is based on the ten linguistic structures of words per T-unit, subordinate clauses per T-unit, words per main clause, words per subordinate clause, number of modals, number of *be* and *have* forms in the auxiliary, number of prepositional phrases, number of possessive nouns and pronouns, number of adverbs of time, and number of gerunds, participles, and absolute phrases. Each item is assigned a loading which is then multiplied by its frequency of occurrence and the resulting products are summed and divided by the total number of T-units. The quotient is the SDS and can be converted to a grade level equivalent. The tabulation of the SDS has been programmed for computer analyses and has been used to assess written and oral language samples (Kidder, 1974; Hopkins, 1976). The arbitrary assignment of item loadings, the lack of precision in converting the SDS to grade level equivalents, and the likelihood that some items would occur more frequently in one mode of discourse than in others have been cited (O'Donnell, 1976) as limitations of the SDS. However, in a summary of his critique of Endicott's and Golub's measures, O'Donnell concluded:

> In spite of the limitations cited above, however, there is little doubt that if the language sample is large enough and diverse enough both Golub's and Endicott's measures will reveal developmental differences in syntactic complexity of language. Since both of them involve rather complex and exten-

sive procedures of analysis, however, it seems appropriate to raise the question of how much better they are than the grosser measures of T-unit length, clause length, and number of subordinate clauses. (p. 38)

Finally, Lee and Canter (1971) and Lee (1974) developed a comprehensive scheme for measuring the complexity of sentences called Developmental Sentence Analysis. Based on normative data obtained from 200 children between the ages of 2 years and 6 years, 11 months, the Developmental Sentence Scoring procedure (DSS) quantifies eight aspects of sentences—indefinite pronouns and noun modifiers, personal pronouns, main verbs, secondary verbs, negatives, conjunctions, interrogative reversals, and Wh-questions—to provide an overall assessment of grammatical structures in children's spontaneous speech. The mean score for 50 complete sentences constitutes the Developmental Sentence Score.

ISSUES IN ORAL LANGUAGE EVALUATION

In addition to dealing with questions of which language measures to use, individuals interested in studying children's language have had to consider several other issues. One major concern, referred to earlier in this chapter, is that of competence versus performance. In all language investigations, results and conclusions are based on observed speech, that is, the child's language performance in a limited speech sample. It is not possible to determine whether words or constructions are missing because the child is unable to produce them or merely because the child finds it unnecessary to do so to convey a particular message. Thus, one is never certain how closely the child's oral performance approximates or reflects linguistic competence. Then, too, we often do not know what a word or grammatical structure means to a child even if it is used appropriately in a sentence. This is an important consideration in light of the widespread belief that children can understand or comprehend much more than they can or choose to produce at any given stage in their language development. The only solution to this unresolved problem would be to develop procedures to obtain more information about the child's competence than is presently obtainable from observations of oral productions.

Another issue associated with evaluating children's oral language are questions concerning the validity and reliability of available measures of language complexity. For the majority of measures these data are not available. This may be due, in part, to the limited use made of many measures. Many are developed for use in a single study, often the author's doctoral research, and then abandoned. Speaking to this issue, Chun et al. (1973) stated, "About 70 percent of all measures once published are never used again, even by the authors themselves" (p. 593).

A final issue to be considered is the lack of predictive validity for most language measures. Many of the measures were developed to enable educators to predict success in reading. It was rationalized that oral language was a prerequisite for learning to read and was the foundation of later growth and development in reading. While this notion may be intuitively appealing, there is little evidence in the research literature to support the belief that fluency in using language is a predictor of reading achievement. For related reviews of this large body of literature, see Chapter 1 in this book, Hopkins (1976) and Groff (1977).

IMPLICATIONS FOR INSTRUCTION

In view of the fact that it is so time consuming to elicit and evaluate language samples using existing measures and procedures, it is the opinion of this writer that it is probably not worth the classroom teacher's time to undertake such analyses. Moreover, there is no support for using these language complexity measures for diagnostic purposes or for curriculum evaluation. This is not to say that the goal of developing children's oral language skills is unimportant. It *is* important to increase children's communicative abilities. But these skills should be emphasized for the sake of broadening oral language in and of itself and not for purposes of developing "prerequisite" skills for success in other academic areas. It is suggested that teachers provide a rich language environment in the classroom that is closely related to children's interests and that encourages the use of oral language in a variety of situations.

FOR DISCUSSION

1. What is the problem with the evaluation of children's oral language that use only a syntactic analysis?
2. What alternative to the procedures outlined by Hopkins could a teacher use to evaluate student growth in oral language?
3. What roles do home environment and background experience play in oral language development?
4. How do the measures outlined by Hopkins compare with the measures of written composition outlined by Straw in Chapter 10?

REFERENCES

Ahmed, S. E. *Linguistic analysis of children's speech: Effects of stimulus media on elicited samples.* Unpublished masters report, Kansas State University, 1973.
Anderson, S., Messick, S., and Hartshorne, N. *Priorities and directions for*

research and development related to measurement of young children. Princeton, N.J.: Educational Testing Service, 1972.

Berlyne, D. E., and Frommer, F. D. Some determinants of the incidence and content of children's questions. *Child Development*, 1966, *37*, 177–189.

Boehnker, D. M. A study of the effects of student-taken photographic essays on the length and complexity of oral language production in primary-aged children. (Doctoral dissertation, Indiana University, 1973). *Dissertation Abstracts International*, 1973, *34*, 08-A, 4978.

Botel, M., and Granowsky, A. A formula for measuring syntactic complexity: A directional effort. *Elementary English*, 1972, *49*, 513–516.

Bougere, M. B. *Selected factors in oral language related to first grade reading achievement.* Unpublished doctoral dissertation, University of Chicago, 1968.

Brandenburg, G. C. The language of a three-year-old child. *Pedagogical Seminary*, 1915, *22*, 89–120.

Bush, A. D. The vocabulary of a three-year-old girl. *Pedagogical Seminary*, 1914, *21*, 125–142.

Calvert, K. C. H. An investigation of relationships between the syntactic maturity of oral language and reading comprehension scores. (Doctoral dissertation, University of Alabama, 1971). *Dissertation Abstracts International*, 1971, *32*, 09-A, 4828.

Carroll, J. B. Determining and numerating adjectives in children's speech. *Child Development*, 1939, *10*, 215–229.

Carroll, J. B. *Language and thought.* Englewood Cliffs, New Jersey: Prentice-Hall, 1964.

Carroll, J. B. The nature of the reading process. In H. Singer and R. Ruddell (Eds.), *Theoretical models and processes of reading.* Newark, Delaware: International Reading Association, 1970.

Cazden, C. B. *Child language and education.* New York: Holt, Rinehart and Winston, 1972.

Child Study Committee of the International Kindergarten Union. *A study of the vocabulary of children before entering the first grade.* Baltimore, Maryland: The International Kindergarten Union, 1928.

Chotlos, J. W. Studies in language behavior: IV. A statistical and comparative analysis of individual written language samples. *Psychological Monographs*, 1944, *56*, 95–111.

Chun, K., Cobb, S., French, J., and Seashore, S. Storage and retrieval of information on psychological measures. *American Psychologist*, 1973, *28*, 592–599.

Ciani, A. J. *Syntactic maturity and vocabulary diversity in the oral language of first, second, and third grade children.* Unpublished doctoral dissertation, Indiana University, 1974.

Cowan, P. A., and others. Mean length of spoken response as a function of stimulus, experimenter, and subject. *Child Development*, 1967, *38*, 191–203.

Cowe, E. G. *A study of kindergarten activities for language development.* Unpublished doctoral dissertation, Columbia University, 1967.

Dale, P. S. *Language development: Structure and function* (2nd ed.). New York: Holt, Rinehart and Winston, 1976.

Davis, E. A. The development of linguistic skill in twins, singletons with siblings, and only children from age five to ten years. *Institute of Child Welfare Monograph Series*, 1937 (No. 14).

Day, E. J. The development of language in twins I. A comparison of twins and single children. *Child Development*, 1932, *3*, 179–199.

DeStefano, J. S., and Fox, S. E. Children's oral language development: The literature and its implications for teachers. In J. S. DeStefano and S. E. Fox (Eds.), *Language and the Language Arts*. Boston: Little, Brown, 1974.

Drdek, R. E. Stimulating oral expression with pre-school children. *English Record*, 1970, *21*, 53–63.

Duquette, D. A. The effect of stimuli on the measurement of oral language responses of second and fifth grade children. (Doctoral dissertation, Arizona State University, 1971). *Dissertation Abstracts International*, 1971, *32*, 03-A, 1183.

Endicott, A. L. A proposed scale for syntactic complexity. *Research in the Teaching of English*, Spring 1973, *7*, 5–12.

Fox, S. E. *Syntactic maturity and vocabulary diversity in the oral language of kindergarten and primary school children.* Unpublished doctoral dissertation, Indiana University, 1970.

Frank, S. M., and Osser, H. A psycholinguistic model of syntactic complexity. *Language and Speech*, 1970, *13*, 38–53.

Gates, A. I. *A reading vocabulary for the primary grades*. New York: Bureau of Publications, Teachers College, Columbia University, 1926.

Gates, A. I. *A reading vocabulary for the primary grades, revised and enlarged.* New York: Bureau of Publications, Teachers College, Columbia University, 1935.

Gibbons, H. D. Reading and sentence elements. *Elementary English Review*, February 1941, *18*, 42–46.

Glazer, S. M., and Morrow, L. M. The Syntactic complexity of primary grade children's oral language and primary grade reading materials: A comparative analysis. *Journal of Reading Behavior*, 1978, *10*, 200–203.

Goffman, E. The neglected situation. In J. Gumperz and D. Hymes (Eds.), *The ethnography of communication*. American Anthropologist Special Publication, 1964, *6*.

Golub, L. S., and Kidder, C. Syntactic density and the computer. *Elementary English*, November/December 1974, *51*, 1128–1131.

Groff, P. Oral language and reading. *Reading World*, October 1977, *17*, 71–78.

Hahn, E. Analysis of the content and form of the speech of first grade children. *Quarterly Journal of Speech*, October 1948, *XXXIV*, 361–366.

Heider, E. R., Cazden, C. B., and Brown, R. *Social class differences in the effectiveness and style of children's coding ability* (Project Literacy Reports, No. 9). Ithaca, New York: Cornell University, 1968.

Helsabeck, M. V. *Effects of mode of stimulus presentation on oral language performance in kindergarten children.* Unpublished doctoral dissertation, Indiana University, 1971.

Hensley, B. E. The relationship of selected oral language, perceptual, demographic, and intellectual factors to the reading achievement of good, average, and poor first-grade reading groups. (Doctoral dissertation, University of Southern Mississippi, 1973). *Dissertation Abstracts International*, 1973, *34*, 08-A, 4562.

Herdan, G. *The calculus of linguistic observations*. The Hague: Mouton, 1962.

Herdan, G. *Type-token mathematics*. The Hague: Mouton, 1960.

Hopkins, C. J., Moe, A. J., and Stephens, M. I. *A comparison of four oral lan-

guage elicitation probes used with kindergarten, first- and second-grade children. Paper presented at the meeting of the Midwest Association for the Education of Young Children, April 1975, Madison, Wisconsin.

Hopkins, C. J. *An investigation of the relationship of selected oral language measures and first-grade reading achievement.* Unpublished doctoral dissertation, Purdue University, 1976.

Hopkins, C. J. The spontaneous oral vocabulary of children in grade 1. *Elementary School Journal,* 1979, *79,* 240–249.

Horn, E. Appropriate materials for instruction in reading. In G. M. Whipple (Ed.), *Report of the National Committee on Reading, Twenty-Fourth Yearbook of the National Society for the Study of Education, Part I.* Bloomington, Illinois: Public School Publishing Company, 1925, 185–199.

Hunt, K. W. *Grammatical structures written at three grade levels.* Champaign, Illinois: National Council of Teachers of English, 1965.

Johnson, W. Studies in language behavior: I. A program of research. *Psychological Monographs,* 1944, *56,* 1–15.

Joos, M. The five clocks. Supplement to *International Journal of American Linguistics,* 1962, *20,* 13.

Kidder, C. L. *Using the computer to measure syntactic density and vocabulary intensity in the writing of elementary school children.* Unpublished doctoral dissertation, Pennsylvania State University, 1974.

Kline, C. R. *A comparison of language sampling techniques using second grade children.* Unpublished doctoral dissertation, University of North Carolina, 1971.

Labov, W. The logic of nonstandard English. In F. Williams (Ed.), *Language and Poverty.* Chicago: Markam, 1970.

Labov, W., Cohen, P., Lewis, J. A study of non-standard English of Negro and Puerto Rican speakers in New York City. In United States Office of Education Cooperative Research Project No. 3288 *Final Report* (Vols. 1, 2). New York: Columbia University, 1968. (Mimeographed)

Langenbeck, M. A study of a five-year-old child. *Pedagogical Seminary,* 1915, *22,* 65–88.

Lawton, D. *Social class, language and education.* New York: Schocken, 1968.

Lee, L. L. *Developmental sentence analysis.* Evanston, Illinois: Northwestern University Press, 1974.

Lee, L. L., and Canter, S. M. Developmental sentence scoring: A clinical procedure for estimating syntactic development in children's spontaneous speech. *Journal of Speech and Hearing Disorders,* August 1971, *36,* 315–340.

Loban, W. D. *The language of elementary school children.* Champaign, Illinois: National Council of Teachers of English, 1963.

Loban, W. D. *Language development: Kindergarten through grade twelve.* Urbana, Illinois: National Council of Teachers of English, 1976.

Longhurst, T. M., and Grubb, S. A comparison of language samples collected in four situations. *Language Speech and Hearing Services in Schools,* April 1974, *5,* 71–78.

MacGinitie, W. H. Language development. In R. L. Ebel (Ed.), *Encyclopedia of educational research* (4th ed.). Toronto, Ontario: Macmillan, 1969.

Martin, C. Developmental interrelationships among language variables in children of the first grade. *Elementary English,* March 1955, *XXXII,* 167–171.

McCarthy, D. A. The language development of the preschool child. *Institute of Child Welfare Monograph Series,* 1930 (4).

Menyuk, P. Syntactic structures in the language of children. *Child Development*, 1963, *34*, 407–422.

Menyuk, P. Syntactic rules used by children from preschool through first grade. *Child Development*, 1964, *35*, 533–546.

Miller, J. W., and Hintzman, C. A. Syntactic complexity of Newbery Award winning books. *Reading Teacher*, 1975, *28*, 750–756.

Milver, E. A study of the relationship between reading readiness in grade one school children and patterns of parent-child interaction. *Child Development*, 1951, *22*, 95–112.

Miner, L. E. Scoring procedures for the length-complexity index: A preliminary report. *Journal of Communication Disorders*, *1919*, *2*, 224–240.

Moe, A. J., and Rush, R. T. Predicting first-grade reading achievement from selected measures of oral language performance. Paper presented at the annual meeting of the National Reading Conference, 1977, New Orleans, Louisiana.

Morrison, I. E. The relation of reading readiness to certain language factors. In J. A. Figurel (Ed.), International Reading Association Conference Proceedings, *Challenge and Experiment in Reading*. New York: Scholastic Magazines, 1962.

Morrow, L. M. An analysis of syntax in the language of elementary school children. (Doctoral dissertation, Fordham University, 1975). *Dissertation Abstracts International*, *36*, 03-A, 1351.

Murphy, H. The spontaneous speaking vocabulary of children in primary grades. *Journal of Education*, December 1957, *140*, 3–106.

Nice, M. M. The development of a child's vocabulary in relation to environment. *Pedagogical Seminary*, 1915, *22*, 35–64.

O'Donnell, R. C. A critique of some indices of syntactic maturity. *Research in the Teaching of English*, Spring 1976, *10*, 31–38.

O'Donnell, R. C., Griffin, W. J., and Norris, R. C. *Syntax of kindergarten and elementary school children: A transformational analysis*. Champaign, Illinois: National Council of Teachers of English, 1967.

Pope, M. The syntax of fourth graders' narrative and explanatory speech. *Research in the Teaching of English*, Summer 1974, *8*, 219–227.

Prutting, C. A., Gallagher, T. M., and Mulac, A. The expression portion of the NSST compared to a spontaneous language sample. *Journal of Speech and Hearing Disorders*, 1975, *40*, 40–48.

Riling, M. E. *Oral and written language of children in grades four and six compared with the language of their textbooks*. Report to the United States Office of Education Cooperative Research Project No. 2410, 1965.

Sampson, O. C. A study of speech development in children of 18–30 months. *British Journal of Educational Psychology*, November 1956, *XXVI*, 196–201.

Sampson, O. C. The speech and language development of five-year-old children. *British Journal of Educational Psychology*, November 1959, *XXIX*, 217–222.

Sampson, O. C. Reading skill at eight years in relation to speech and other factors. *British Journal of Educational Psychology*, February 1962, *XXXII*, 12–17.

Shepherd, R. C. Oral language performance and reading instruction. *Elementary English*, April 1974, *51*, 544–546; 560.

Shire, M. L. *The relation of certain linguistic factors to reading achievement in first-grade children*. Unpublished doctoral dissertation, Fordham University, 1945.

Slobin, D. I. *A field manual for cross-cultural study of the acquisition of com-*

municative competence. Berkeley, California: University of California, 1967.

Smith, C. T. The relationship between the type of questions, stimuli, and the oral language production of children. (Doctoral dissertation, University of California, Berkeley, 1974). *Dissertation Abstracts International,* 1974, *35,* 01-A, 177.

Smith, M. E. An investigation of the development of the sentence and the extent of vocabulary in young children. *University of Iowa Studies in Child Welfare,* 1926, *3*(5).

Smith, M. E. A study of some factors influencing the development of the sentence in preschool children. *Journal of Genetic Psychology,* 1935, *46,* 182–212.

Stern, W. *Psychology of early childhood up to the sixth year of age.* New York: Holt, 1924.

Stewart, R. D. *The Oral Language of the Inner City Black Child: Syntactic Maturity and Vocabulary Diversity.* Unpublished doctoral dissertation, Indiana University, 1972.

Strandberg, T. E. *An evaluation of three stimulus media for evoking verbalization from preschool children.* Unpublished masters thesis, Eastern Illinois University, 1969.

Strandberg, T. E., and Griffith, J. A study of the effects of training in visual literacy on verbal language behavior. Unpublished manuscript, Eastern Illinois University, 1968. (Cited in Cazden, 1972.)

Strang, R., and Hocker, M. E. First-grade children's language patterns. *Elementary English,* 1965, *42,* 38–41.

Strickland, R. G. The language of elementary school children: Its relationship to the language of reading textbooks and the quality of reading of selected children. *Bulletin of the College of Education.* (Vol. 38). Bloomington, Indiana: Indiana University, 1962.

Templin, M. C. Certain language skills in children: Their development and inter-relationships. *Institute of Child Welfare Monograph Series* (No. 26). Minneapolis: University of Minnesota Press, 1957.

Whipple, G. M., and Whipple, (Mrs.) G. M. The vocabulary of a three-year-old boy with some interpretive comments. *Pedagogical Seminary,* 1909, *16,* 1–22.

Williams, C. E., and Legum, S. E. *On recording samples of informal speech from elementary school children.* Southwest Regional Education Lab Report, May 1970. (ED 057 203)

Williams, F., and Naremore, R. C. On the functional analysis of social class differences in modes of speech. *Speech Monographs,* 1969, *36,* 77–102.

Williams, H. M. An analytical study of language achievement in preschool children. *University of Iowa Studies in Child Welfare,* 1937, *XIII* (Part I).

Winter, C. Interrelationships among language variables in children of the first and second grades. *Elementary English,* 1957, *34,* 108–113.

Yedinak, J. G. A study of the linguistic functioning of children with articulation and reading disabilities. *Journal of Genetic Psychology,* January 1946, *LXXIV,* 23–59.

Zipf, G. K. *The psycho-biology of language.* Boston: Houghton Mifflin, 1935.

4

A Comparison of Three Sentence Imitation Tests for Clinical Use

Inez Striemer, Elaine Graham,
and Victor Froese

A major problem in assessing a child's language is that of obtaining a sample representative of the child's productive, receptive, and integrative language capabilities. The last decade has seen a revision of the venerable Illinois Test of Psycholinguistic Ability (ITPA, 1969) and the spawning of the Northwestern Syntax Screening Test (NSST, 1969), the Carrow Elicited Language Inventory (CELI, 1974), and the Test of Language Development (TOLD, 1977).

These instruments present a dilemma for the clinician. In an already burdensome diagnostic profile, how can the clinician fit yet another measure? What information does each test provide? How do the instruments compare in intent or in the actual components that they claim to assess? How good are the tests?

The purpose of this chapter is to address these questions. More specifically the chapter raises four concerns with respect to three of these tests (NSST, CELI, TOLD); presents descriptions of the instruments along with specific user information; and suggests some sources of additional materials related to current language paradigms. The ITPA is included more or less as a criterion variable already known to most clinicians and hence not dealt with in great detail here.

CONCERNS AND ISSUES

The major concern the clinician has with any instrument, whether recent or well established, is knowing whether it is valid and reliable. While hundreds of studies have involved the use of the ITPA, Newcomer and Hammill (1975, 1976) concluded that "the test should not be used for the purposes of (1) determining the cause of academic failure, (2) devising strategies for the remediation of academic problems, (3) selecting instructional programs designed to match a child's psycholinguistic characteristics, and (4) screening individual children to locate those who have a high probability of failing basic school subjects."

When a well established instrument such as the ITPA is open to such criticism, it is easy to be skeptical about instruments such as the NSST, CELI, and TOLD without some sort of "track record." However, some information is accumulating and some reviews have appeared in Buros (1978). Dailey and Boxx (1979) compared the NSST, the CELI, the Menyuk Sentences, and a spontaneous language sample, and they found rather marked differences for the NSST. Their findings are in accord with Prutting, Gallagher, and Mulac (1975) who concur in recommending the NSST as a screening instrument only (its stated purpose) because it did not evaluate specific syntactic structures reliably.

A second concern deals with the dependence of an utterance on its *context* and *intent*. Bloom and Lahey (1978) cite instances where spontaneous speaking ability exceeded the ability to imitate. Since imitation and comprehension tasks often lack context or intent for the subject, some serious reservations must be made when such responses are taken as evidence of competence.

A third concern is Menyuk's (1969) finding that deviant-speaking children differ from normal-speaking children. Since clinical cases often fall into the category of "deviant speaking," the validity of elicited imitation tests needs careful examination.

A fourth concern is with the unique aspects of the NSST, the CELI, and the TOLD. What do they measure that other language tests do not measure? Do they add sufficient information to a profile to warrant the time required in analyzing the results? How do the results compare to spontaneous language samples? Which instrument is best for which information? How are these instruments different from the ITPA? A comparison of these tests appears in Table 1.

Since the NSST, the CELI, and the TOLD all contain elicited imitation tasks, it becomes essential to review the literature concerning language production and how it relates to elicited sentence imitation.

ELICITED SENTENCE IMITATION AND LANGUAGE PRODUCTION

Because elicited sentence imitation is influenced by a variety of performance factors such as short-term memory and the comprehension and production of speech, its relationship to competent language production is not clear. Frazer, Bellugi, and Brown (1963) found that in a situation where children were asked to imitate sentences of grammatical contrasts, they could repeat sentences which they could not comprehend. This led

Table 1.   A comparison of language tasks

Test or subtest by task description	CELI	NSST	TOLD	ITPA[a]	PPVT
1. Sentence Imitation					
Sentence Imitation	X		X		
Expression		X			
2. Auditory Comprehension					
Grammatic Understanding			X		
Reception		X			
3. Receptive Vocabulary					
Picture Vocabulary			X		X
4. Expressive Vocabulary					
Verbal Expression				X	
Oral Vocabulary			X		
5. Closure					
Grammatic Completion			X		
Grammatic Closure				X	
6. Association					
Auditory-Vocal Association				X	
Test age range	3;0–7;11	3;0–7;11	4;0–8;11	2;0–10;0	2;9–18;5

[a] Only four subtests of the ITPA are considered here: Auditory Reception, Auditory-Vocal, Verbal Expression, and Grammatic Closure. The remaining eight subtests do not have comparable tasks.

them to conclude that imitation is a perceptual-motor skill not associated with comprehension and production. Menyuk (1969) found ". . . that repetition was dependent on structure rather than just imitation up to the limits of memory capacity. With sentences up to nine words in length, the length of the sentence was not the factor which determined successful repetition even for children as young as 3 years" (p. 113). Mostly, children's reproductions included the structural descriptions found in their own production rather than those in the sentences given. Thus, the utterances which they produced seemed to accurately represent their grammatical competence. However, in some instances children were able to exceed the level of competency displayed in their spontaneous production. Because these structures occurred in the spontaneous production of older children, Menyuk attributed their occurrence to the possibility that they were structures that children were in the process of acquiring. But Bloom, Hood, and Lightbown (1974) and Slobin and Welsh (1973) have presented evidence that spontaneous speaking ability exceeded elicited imitation.

    In examining the language production of deviant-speaking children, Menyuk found that their repetitions were limited both by the length and the complexity of the sentences. While normal-speaking children could replicate certain structures which they did not produce spontaneously, the deviant-speaking children repeated with less structural complexity than was found in their spontaneous production. The elicited response of the deviant-speaking children nearly matched but did not exceed the grammatical competence shown in their spontaneous utterances. These findings suggest that elicited language imitations probably should be viewed differently for normal-speaking and deviant-speaking children. The memory aid of the presented sentences may allow some normal-speaking children to exceed the level of competence displayed in their spontaneous productions, while deviant-speaking children may be hampered by the short-term memory load, causing them to use less structural complexity than is found in their spontaneous productions.

Ervin-Tripp (1964) found that although there were some instances in which children imitated structures which they spontaneously produced at a later time, and some instances when children spontaneously produced structures which they imitated at a later time, most children appeared to imitate only those utterances which they could produce spontaneously.

Berry-Luterman and Bar (1971) proposed using elicited sentence repetitions as a diagnostic tool. Following Menyuk's (1964) procedure, they assessed performance of four language-impaired subjects on elicited sentence repetition tasks under the following three conditions: 1) the repetition of grammatically incorrect sentences taken from the child's own production, 2) the repetition of correct versions of these sentences, and 3) the repetition of the reversed word order of the grammatically correct versions. Findings of this research suggest that the performance of language-impaired children differs from normal children in developmental sequence and operational complexity since "... the rules for formulating some of the individual structures seem to be different from normal at each level of the grammar." Lee (1966) reached similar conclusions. Berry-Luterman and Bar suggest that theoretical implications of these findings would involve an analysis of errors to develop an individual scale of developmental complexity for each child to indicate which language structures should be taught in a therapy program.

Slobin and Welsh (1973) examined approximately 1,000 elicited imitations of a 2-year-old child and found that the rules of the child's grammar affected the repetition of an utterance. Like Menyuk and Ervin-Tripp, they found that in some cases children could spontaneously utter sentences which they could not imitate and repeat imitations of model sentences which exceeded their spontaneous productions, indicating that elicited imitations may not fully estimate a child's linguistic competence. Ungrammatical sentences were repeated perfectly when they were short enough to hold in short-term memory, revealing an important relationship between sentence development and memory span. Slobin and Welsh suggest that aspects of a child's theory of syntax can be discovered through an analysis of elicited imitations but that these imitations should be used together with an analysis of spontaneous speech.

Smith (1973) found that is is easier for children to repeat grammatical structures than ungrammatical structures. Grammatical responses to ungrammatical stimuli suggest that children impose structure on sentences, and the difficulty of repeating more difficult ungrammatical structures appears to be due to storage and production difficulties rather than identification.

In his study of delayed recall and imitation, Thieman (1975) found that while adults and older children tended to recall sentences in deleted forms, regardless of input forms, the youngest child retained and repeated full syntactic forms even when presented in deleted form. These results lend some support to Slobin and Welsh's (1973) findings that children will produce the full form of optionally deletable linguistic forms when they are first gaining control of syntax.

Prutting, Gallagher, and Mulac (1975) compared the spontaneous language performance of language-delayed children to their elicited repetitions of test sentences in Lee's (1969) Northwestern Syntax Screening Test. They found that 30 percent of the structures which were incorrectly produced on the NSST were correctly produced in samples of spontaneous language. While an immediate imitation task has been shown to provide useful information (Menyuk, 1969; Berry-Luterman and Bar, 1971), delayed imitation procedures such as those used in the NSST do not provide an accurate productive language sample when used with language-delayed children. The data of this study supports previous research evidence (Ervin-Tripp, 1964; Slobin and Welsh, 1973) which indicates that elicited sentence imitation may underestimate a child's communicative skills.

There appears to be a general consensus of opinion that elicited sentence imitation may be a useful assessment technique in determining productive capacities of children although the test results must be viewed with some caution. Two advantages of elicited sentence imitations are the ease of administration and the convenience of presenting a large number of model sentences in a short period of time, some of which may not frequently occur in children's spontaneous productions. Limitations of elicited repetitions include the possibility that productive capacities of some children may be underestimated and the further possibility that they would not be useful in assessing the productive language capacities of children with a weak attention span, listening problems, or auditory memory deficits.

TEST DESCRIPTIONS AND USER REPORTS

This section presents descriptions of three instruments, the TOLD, CELI, and NSST, as well as a brief description of the ITPA for those not particularly familiar with it. After the description of each instrument, brief user reports are presented to aid the prospective user to acquire a better "feel" for the instrument. These reports are not composites nor should they be taken to be representative of a particular group.

TEST OF LANGUAGE DEVELOPMENT

Publisher:	Empiric Press, Austin, Texas
Date:	1977
Developers:	Newcomer, P. L. and Hammill, D. D.

Description of the TOLD

Theoretical Base   According to the authors, the TOLD is based on a linguistic model focusing on specific components of language structure which are identified as phonology, syntax, and semantics. Reference is made to the ideas of Jakobson, Font, and Halle (1963) regarding the learning of phonological rules, to C. Chomsky's (1969) research in children's mastery of syntax, to De Vito's (1970) hypothesis that a child's semantic development proceeds from general to more specific categories, and to N. Chomsky's theory (1957, 1965, 1971) which synthesizes all three components to describe a child's underlying knowledge of linguistic rules as reflecting both competence and performance. Competence reflects a child's knowledge of underlying linguistic rules while performance refers to a child's vocalizations of what he understands.

The TOLD is described as adhering to a 2-dimensional model of language structure: 1) the primary dimension encompasses the major components of linguistics: phonology, syntax, and semantics, and 2) the secondary dimension is comprised of expressive and receptive skills. For this test the primary dimensional terms are defined as follows: 1) phonology involves the ability to hear the difference in sounds associated with certain words and the ability to articulate critical speech sounds; 2) the semantic label denotes the child's ability to define vocabulary words and recognize pictures which represent vocabulary words; and 3) syntax refers to tasks involving the ability to imitate sentences, associate sentences with representative pictures, and to complete sentences by supplying the correct form of certain words. One expressive and one receptive test is used to measure each of the phonological, syntactic, and semantic skills.

Test Purpose   The TOLD is designed to identify broad areas of language inadequacy by providing a convenient means of obtaining information about a child's language development. The test results provide the examiner with a comparative index of a child's specific strengths and weaknesses among the seven skills which it measures. Conversion of the subtest scores to age equivalents and standard scores allows the examiner to compare a child's functional competencies in relation to those of his peers. A low score in a specific skill does not necessarily suggest a language disability.

The authors present somewhat contradictory views concerning diagnostic interpretations of the students. They state in the Test Manual: "While the subtest total scores may be interpreted diagnostically, the TOLD subtest items were not specifically designed for such a purpose" (p. 15). They suggest that a poor performance on a particular subtest indicates a general deficit in that area which may then be followed by indepth assessment and remedial training. Since subtest items do not encompass all the abilities in any given linguistic area, inspection of subtest items will not denote particular language skills which a child may lack.

Test Design   The TOLD consists of seven subtests. The basic formats of the tests are not the authors' own creations. A brief description of the subtests follows.

1. *Picture and Oral Vocabulary.*   Fifty words for each of the two vocabulary tests were selected from those classified as AA and A on the Thorndike and Lorge (1944) list. A certain amount of grammatic and semantic equivalence was maintained between the forms, e.g., Picture subtest: ear; Oral subtest: finger, reflecting the same grammatic form (noun) and the same semantic category (body part). The tests developed by Van Alystine (1961), Ammons and Ammons (1958), and Dunn (1965) served as a model for estimating a child's receptive vocabulary as measured by these subtests.

2. *Grammatic Understanding.*   This subtest is designed to measure a child's ability to understand certain syntactic aspects of language. It is similar in format to Carrow's (1973) *Test for Auditory Comprehension of Language.* The child listens to the stimuli as presented by the examiner and selects a picture to match it. Only complete sentences are used in this subtest and commands to find a particular item are avoided. The pictures are designed so that a child's ability to select the correct response depends upon a child's knowledge of the grammatical element in the sentence rather than on understanding of context word meaning. A deliberate selection of complex grammatic forms is intended to challenge older students. There are 25 items on the test.

3. *Sentence Imitation.*   The underlying rationale of this subtest is that

a child's ability to imitate sentences reveals one aspect of his syntactic usage. It is based on studies which support the idea that young children cannot imitate sentence forms which are not part of their spontaneous speech production (Slobin and Welsh, 1967; Ervin-Tripp, 1964; Menyuk, 1969). The basic sentence types selected were developed by Stockwell (1963) and modified by Clay (1971). The six basic active, affirmative, and declarative sentence types all begin with a noun phrase followed by a verb phrase. There are a total of 30 sentences, ranging 5 to 12 words in length.

4. *Grammatic Completion.* This subtest is intended to measure a child's ability to use common morphological forms. It incorporates many of the morphological features selected by Berko (1958) from Rinsland's (1945) vocabulary list for first grade children. The Grammatic Completion subtest closely resembles the Grammatic Closure subtest of the ITPA and Berko's *Test of Morphology* (1958). The test consists of 30 items, is verbal in format, and utilizes a cloze technique which requires the child to supply the final word of sentences read by the examiner.

5. *Word Discrimination.* This test, like that of Wepman (1968) and Templin and Darley (1960) uses the word-pair principle which requires a "same-different" response. There are 20 items on the test, including 6 "foils" (identical word pairs), which are scored separately.

6. *Word Articulation.* Words containing the most difficult sounds in the speech of preschool and elementary children (as determined by Van Riper, 1972; Egland, 1970; and Irwin, 1972) were selected using the Thorndike-Lorge (1944) word lists and the Wepman-Haas (1969) spoken list as guides. The test consists of 20 items utilizing stimulus pictures to encourage the child to make spontaneous utterances. Imitation is resorted to only when a child fails to give a spontaneous response.

Age Group   Although it is not specifically stated what ages the test is designed for, scaled score equivalents for raw scores are provided for children ages 4 years, 0 months (4;0) to 8 years, 11 months (8;11), which suggests that the test is designed for children of these ages.

Test Reliability   Because this test was published in 1977, no reports were available in Buros' *Eighth Mental Measurements Yearbook* (1978) or Hoepfner's *CSE Elementary Test Evaluations* (1970). The internal consistency of the TOLD and its subtests was estimated by two studies involving the split-half procedure with a random selection of subjects and one study involving children with oral communication problems. Except for the Picture Vocabulary and Grammatic Understanding subtests, coefficients of 0.80 or greater were associated with the subtests at all age levels. Stability reliability was established by testing 21 children twice with an intervening period of 5 days. Reliability coefficients exceeded 0.80 in every case.

Test Validity   The authors describe the content validity of the TOLD as follows: "To ensure that the TOLD subtests would have adequate content validity, special care was taken to select items which were representative of the subject matter being assessed" (Hammill and Newcomer, 1977, p. 25). This was carried out through field testing and item analysis of experimental versions of each subtest before a final selection of items was made.

Concurrent validity, i.e., comparing the test with existing criteria, was established by administering the seven subtests and eight criterion tests (two for the Sentence Imitation subtest) to the same 114 children who participated in the two split-half procedure studies. The tests selected as criterion measures for each TOLD subtest are as follows:

1. Picture Vocabulary: *Peabody Picture Vocabulary Test* (Dunn, 1965)
2. Oral Vocabulary: *Wechsler Intelligence Scale for Children* (Wechsler, 1949)
3. Grammatic Understanding: The Receptive subtest of the *Northwestern Syntax Screening Test* (Lee, 1969)
4. Sentence Imitation: The Expressive subtests of the *Northwestern Syntax Screening Test* (Lee, 1969) and the Auditory Span for Related Syllables subtest from the *Detroit Tests of Learning Aptitude* (Baker and Leland, 1959)
5. Grammatic Completion: The Grammatic Closure subtest from the *Illinois Test of Psycholinguistic Abilities* (Kirk, McCarthy, and Kirk, 1968)
6. Word Discrimination: *Auditory Discrimination Test* (Wepman, 1968)
7. Word Articulation: *Templin-Darley Tests of Articulation* (Templin and Darley, 1960)

The TOLD total score was also correlated with the *Test for Auditory Comprehension of Language* (Carrow, 1973). There was a substantial relationship between the two tests with correlation coefficients of 0.63, 0.72, and 0.73 at the 4-, 6-, and 8-year-old levels respectively. Except for the Grammatic Understanding subtest, correlation coefficients were so high that the authors suggest the TOLD subtest could be used interchangeably with the criterion tests. However, this judgment may be somewhat premature on the basis of one study and one comparison for each subtest.

Construct validity (the degree to which the TOLD reflects the theoretical model on which it is based) was investigated by means of a factor analysis using the criterion measures. There were two factors with eight values greater than IQ. They were the phonology factor comprised of the Word Discrimination and Word Articulation subtests and the general linguistic factor which included all the other subtests. Because the two phonological subtests did not load with the other subtests, they were treated as supplemental tests on the battery. According to the authors, linguistic abilities are highly intercorrelated, and, therefore, subtests measuring the various aspects of language will tend to load on a common factor, suggesting that the TOLD subtests do in fact measure components of linguistics. Thus, factor analysis supports validity of the TOLD subtests as measures of language.

Diagnostic validity was established by comparing the TOLD subtest scores obtained by a group of deviant-speaking children with those obtained by a group of standard-English-speaking children. Findings indicated that the TOLD subtests successfully differentiated children with language problems from normal-speaking children.

Test Administration and Scoring   The Word Discrimination and Word Articulation subtests are supplemental and not usually used for children over the age of 6 years, 0 months (6;0) because they are too easy for older children.

The TOLD is easy to administer and score. Administration time for the complete battery is approximately 20 minutes. Testing in each subtest is discontinued after five consecutive failures except for the Word Discrimination and Word Articulation subtests.

Language ages (LAs) may be derived from the raw scores and a Language Quotient may be obtained by summing the scaled scores of the five principal subtests.

User Report of the TOLD

The test was administered to a boy in kindergarten age 5 years, 5 months. He was receiving speech therapy and therefore the language age (LA) of 4;3 on the Word Articulation subtest was not unexpected. He had some difficulty in pronouncing the following sounds: *sh*, *th*, *r*, *j*, and *l*. Jeff's Language Quotient for the five principal subtests was 104 which was interpreted as average. On three of the five subtests, Jeff's LAs ranged from 7;0 to 8;9, which were well above his chronological age (CA) of 5;5.

Jeff experienced difficulty with two subtests, Sentence Imitation and Grammatic Completion. It appears that he had some difficulty in understanding this test as shown by the following examples:

"Rob is a man. Bill is a man. Bob and Bill are two (*men*)."
(Jeff's reply: *friends*.)
"John likes to throw a ball everyday. Yesterday he (*threw*)."
(Jeff's reply: *played*.)

Before beginning the subtest, the subject is presented with one example, but ". . . accuracy of the child's response to the example is not important. The demonstration item serves only to convey the procedure, i.e., that the subject must supply the missing words" (Test Manual, p. 36). If the subject fails to respond, the examiner presents another item and then proceeds with the test regardless of the subject's response. The example is:

"Bill is a boy and John is a (_____)."

In my opinion, this is rather a poor example because the word ending does not change, while in subsequent test items, endings or whole words do change. Under these conditions the test may be administered to a subject who does not fully understand what is expected. In comparison, the example for the Grammatic Closure subtest of the ITPA is as follows:

Using a picture the experimenter says: "Here is a bed. Here are two (beds)."

If the subject responds incorrectly, the examiner repeats the item and, if necessary, gives further demonstrations. The two tests differ in that the Grammatic Closure subtest (ITPA) items are accompanied by pictures which portray the content of the verbal expressions while the Grammatic Completion subtest (TOLD) does not. The method of presentation used in the ITPA subtest seems to avoid the confusion encountered in the TOLD subtest. The Grammatic Closure subtest (ITPA) was later administered to Jeff and he obtained a psycholinguistic age (PA) of 6;8 as compared to an LA of 5;3 on the TOLD. One could then conclude that Jeff has little difficulty in this language area.

Further difficulties were encountered in administering the Sentence Imitation subtest. Jeff was only able to repeat one sentence. The chief difficulty seemed to be encountered in remembering the sentences. Because the examiner had previous experience in using the Carrow Elicited Language Inventory (CELI), this test was administered in an effort to gather further information, although a full diagnostic analysis of the CELI was not made. On the TOLD Jeff correctly repeated only one of the 30 sentences in the test. The sentences range in length from 5 to 12 words. On the CELI he correctly repeated 22 of the 52 sentences in the test. Here, the sentences range in length from 2 to 9 words. Many of the sentences were scored as errors because Jeff says "a" for "the." Since he has difficulty in making the "th" sound, these may be articulation errors, although he did pronounce "the" correctly on a few occasions.

Jeff was unable to remember and repeat sentences of more than 7 words in length; therefore, most of the sentences on the TOLD were too long for him to repeat correctly. It appears that sentence length may be a more important factor than sentence structure in determining whether a child is able to repeat the sentence or not. Some examples are:

> CELI: "The children don't play, do they?"
> TOLD: "Monkeys don't eat bananas by the
>   dozen, do they?" and "Our dog chased
>   a cat a mile, didn't he?"
>
> CELI: "Bring me the car that is on the chair."
> TOLD: "They gave the lion who had become
>   very dangerous to the zoo."

The majority of Jeff's errors were verb errors, in which an auxiliary was omitted such as "(has) been," "would (have) liked," and in verb endings such as "seed" for "see." While the TOLD correctly indicates that Jeff has some difficulty with certain sentence structures, it does not provide any relevant diagnostic information.

Dunn's *Peabody Picture Vocabulary Test* was also administered to Jeff (for purposes of comparison only). His score on this test was a mental age (MA) of 7;8 as compared to an LA of 7;0 on the TOLD Picture Vocabulary subtest. Here, there is not as much discrepancy between test scores on the two tests as there was in either Grammatic Completion or Sentence Imitation.

The TOLD may prove to be a useful instrument in determining a child's strengths and weaknesses among the language skills which it measures, but more comparisons of children's performances on the TOLD and on other tests which measure similar skills are necessary before this test can be used with confidence. In using the TOLD as a language assessment instrument, I found that it successfully identified two areas of language inadequacy, articulation and mastery of syntax in oral communication. Another area identified as weak by the TOLD (grammatic closure) was verified when subsequently tested with a comparable ITPA subtest. These results agree with the TOLD authors' suggestion that a low score in a specific skill does not necessarily suggest a language disability. For some educators, the TOLD may be a convenient instrument to use if a general assessment of language development is desired in the areas which the subtests measure. However, the results must be interpreted cautiously and further assessment may be required. For others, who have access to the well-known criterion tests used to establish concurrent validity of the TOLD, there may be little or no advantage to using the TOLD.

CARROW ELICITED LANGUAGE INVENTORY

> Publisher: Learning Concepts, Austin, Texas
> Date: 1974
> Developer: Carrow, E.

Description of the CELI

Test Purpose   The author states that the purpose of the Carrow Elicited Language Inventory (CELI) is to provide a means for measuring a child's productive control of grammar. It is based on the technique of eliciting imitations of a sequence of sentences that have been systematically developed to include basic sentence types and specific grammatical morphemes. In addition to identifying children with language problems, it may be used as a diagnostic test to determine which linguistic structures may be contributing to a child's inadequate linguistic performance.

Test Design   The CELI consists of 51 sentences and 1 phrase ranging in length from 2 to 10 words. Forty-seven sentences are in the active voice and 4 in the passive voice; 37 are affirmative and 14 are negative; 37 are declarative, 12 are interrogative, and 2 are imperative. The grammatical categories include: articles, adjectives, nouns, noun plurals, pronouns, verbs, negatives, contractions, adverbs, prepositions, demonstratives, and conjunctions.

Test Review   Since the Carrow Elicited Language Inventory was published in 1974, only one review, by Courtney Cazden, was found in Buros' (1978) *Eighth Mental Measurement Yearbook*. Cazden pointed out four areas of concern. First, she noted that the CELI does not include complex structures (embeddings and coordinated sentences) which would make it more useful for older children. Second, she suggested that the types of questions asked may be confusing since the subject may be torn between *answering* the question and *repeating* the question. A third concern dealt with dangers of generalizing from elicited to spontaneous speech (a problem addressed earlier in this chapter). Finally, Cazden was concerned with the difficulties encountered when the test is used with non-standard English speakers. The clinician needs to be aware of limitations such as these before interpreting and generalizing from CELI findings.

Theoretical Base   According to Carrow (1974), the CELI is based on the following assumptions:

1. Sentence imitation has been found to be a fruitful source of information relative to the development of language comprehension and expression in children (Menyuk, 1964, 1969; Lenneberg, 1967; McNeill, 1970).
2. Children will reproduce a sentence using the rules they know, filtering it through their own productive system (McNeill, 1970).
3. Imitation of structured sentences will reveal aspects of the child's theory of syntax only if the stimuli are chosen to put stress on immediate memory, . . . but must be within the child's level of comprehension (Smith, 1973; Slobin and Welsh, 1973).
4. Structures that are clearly beyond the child's competency are treated as word lists (Slobin and Welsh, 1973).

5. A fine-grained analysis of imitations of systematically-varied model sentences can determine the child's knowledge of transformational rules and the syntactic and semantic markers born by lexical items (Slobin and Welsh, 1973).
6. Imitation has been used to study language-disordered children (Menyuk, 1964; Berry-Luterman and Bar, 1971) (p. 2).

From the references cited by Carrow, four of the studies have examined elicited imitation and, except for Menyuk's study, they are concerned with rather small numbers of subjects. The subjects in the Luterman and Bar study were 4 language disordered children ranging in ages from 5;2 to 13;5 years. Smith examined 18 children from 3 to 4 years of age and Slobin and Welsh studied the development of 1 child, age 2 years, for 2 months. It appears that Carrow has based the CELI mainly on Menyuk's study since she uses the same procedure in presenting sentences for imitation; however, the grammatical features and categories vary from those used by Menyuk. Menyuk's subjects were 14 nursery school children between the ages 2;0 and 3;8 and 50 kindergarten children ranging in age from 4;9 to 6;1. Menyuk (1969) found ". . . that repetition was dependent on structure rather than just imitation up to the limits of memory capacity. With sentences up to nine words in length, the length of the sentence was not the factor which determined successful repetition even for children as young as 3 years" (pp. 113–114). Carrow appears to have followed these findings in constructing her test sentences, which range in length from 2 to 10 words.

Carrow's reference to Lenneburg and McNeill is to books which they have authored rather than to specific studies. McNeill (1970) states:

There is a strong tendency among children to include nothing in the surface structures of sentences that cannot be related to deep structures—i.e., nothing for which there is no transformational derivation known. The principle encompasses spontaneous speech as well as imitation. If a child does not yet include the progressive inflection -ing in his speech, he will not imitate -ing in the speech of adults, particularly if the adult model is long relative to memory span . . . . It is for this reason that imitation can be used as a test of children's productive capacities . . . . (p. 106)

Another study cited by Carrow and also referred to by Newcomer and Hammill (1977) is that of Ervin-Tripp (1964), who found the grammatical organization of children's spontaneously occurring free speech was identical to that of their spontaneously occurring imitations. Slobin and Welsh (1973) report further studies of imitation by 2- and 3-year-olds conducted by Brown and Fraser (1973) and Fraser, Bellugi, and Brown (1963).

It is interesting to note that another recently developed test by Newcomber and Hammill (1977), The Test of Language Development (TOLD), also includes a Sentence Imitation subtest. The authors use the same rationale as Carrow for developing their test, also referring to the studies by Slobin and Welsh and Menyuk as well as to that of Ervin-Tripp. Although empirical support for using elicited sentence imitation to assess children's oral language production may be somewhat limited, it may prove to be a useful tool. Further study as to the validity of tests such as these is necessary.

Test Reliability   Reliability data given for the CELI are test-retest reliability and inter-examiner reliability. To determine test-retest reliability, 25 children (5 at each of the age levels from 3 through 7) were selected at random and were tested and then retested after a 2-week period. The same examiner administered and scored the test results, obtaining a product-moment correlation coefficient of 0.98. Two measures of inter-examiner reliability were obtained. One measure was obtained by having two examiners score 10 randomly selected tapes and the other was obtained by having two examiners administer and score the CELI on 20 children, 10 of whom were diagnosed as language disordered. Coefficient correlations of 0.98 and 0.99 respectively were obtained. These somewhat meager results are encouraging, but both the number of children and the number of examiners are too small to confirm reliability of this test.

Validity   Little congruent validity is available for the CELI. According to the author, the CELI was compared by Cornelius (1974) to the Developmental Sentence Scoring (DSS) by Lee and Cantor (1971) as to its ability to reflect the severity of language disorders that had been independently determined by external clinical judgment. A rank order correlation between the rank of the children by clinical judgment and the CELI was 0.77 and the correlation between the CELI and the DSS was -0.79, leading Carrow to declare that the CELI has congruent validity. Carrow suggests that further evidence of congruent validity is provided by the fact that the test reflects a change in performance of children as they increase in chronological age since language has been shown to be a developmental phenomenon, and that the test correctly classifies individuals as reported in a study by Cornelius (1974) who used the CELI to separate language-disordered children from normal children. While the CELI may prove to be a useful instrument for assessing children's oral language production, it requires further study and comparison with other language measures involving other groups of children to provide further evidence of validity.

Test Administration and Scoring   Children are tested individually. The examiner presents the stimulus sentences in a live voice. The child repeats these sentences, with the responses being recorded on tape. The test takes approximately 10 minutes to administer.

The scoring procedure involves three tasks: 1) listening to the tape and recording the child's errors on each sentence, 2) recording the errors on a grid in order to tally the number of errors made in each grammatical category (article, noun, verb, etc.) as well as five categories of error types (substitutions, omissions, additions, transpositions, and reversals), and 3) completing a separate verb analysis (for children falling below the tenth percentile for their age) to classify verbs according to type, i.e., modal, auxiliary, copula, main verb, infinitive, and gerund as well as by tense, person, and number.

User Report of the CELI

The test was easy to administer and the student whom I tested performed the task quite well. There were a few instances when it appeared that either sentence length, sentence complexity, or both were taxing his memory. One false start was made, but after a pause he was able to begin again and repeat the sentence. Near the end of the test it also appeared that the student was experiencing a little difficulty in attending, but this did not hinder successful completion of the test.

The scoring, at least at first, is rather time consuming, but it provides a thorough analysis of errors. The directions for the main scoring form are adequate and could be followed without difficulty, but those for the verb analysis form are rather difficult to follow.

The test does not specifically state for what ages it is designed, but the norm group was 475 white children ages 3;0 to 7;11 from a middle socioeconomic level in Houston, Texas. The tables for converting raw scores to percentile ranks and stanines are given for each year: 3;0 to 3;11, 4;1 to 4;11, 5;0 to 5;11, 6;0 to 6;11, and 7;0 to 7;11. Thus, one assumes the test is intended for children ages 3;0 to 7;11.

The test appears to have good potential in assessing children's oral language production. Easy administration and the short time in which it can be administered are advantages, and it seems to provide a fairly thorough assessment of language production. The student whom I tested has experienced great difficulty in developing facility in oral language and at age 7, his development is still far below that of most children his age. The CELI appears to have assessed his oral linguistic performance quite well.

Carrow suggests that the CELI may not be useful for children having problems with severe misarticulations causing speech to interfere with intelligibility, severe jargon speech, and severe echolalia. In my opinion the test may also not be useful for children with listening problems, weak attention span, or auditory memory deficits.

The CELI could be useful as an additional tool in gathering oral language samples because it is often difficult to obtain enough samples of spontaneous speech to provide a clear picture of a child's oral language. Personally, I would use the test if it is appropriate to a case, but I would view the results rather cautiously until I could evaluate them in the light of other measurement techniques, i.e., how do the results compare with information obtained by other methods such as spontaneous speech samples or other tests. I believe that the CELI merits further investigation and cross-validation. To date, our findings indicate that the relationship of the CELI to spontaneous language samples is lower than the Carrow Comprehension Test, which had a rank-order correlation of 0.728 ($N = 15$) with a spontaneous language sample.

THE NORTHWESTERN SYNTAX SCREENING TEST

Publisher:	Northwestern University Press
Date:	1969
Developer:	Lee, L.

Description of the NSST

Test Purpose   The Northwestern Syntax Screening Test is designed to be a screening instrument only. It is useful in screening large numbers of children for an estimation of syntactic development, but for diagnostic purposes, it should be used in conjunction with other language tests.

Test Design and Administration   NSST measures both receptive and expressive language abilities using identical linguistic structures in both parts of the test. The test itself consists of pictures and a recording form. In order to test receptive abilities, the child is requested to look at a page consisting of four pictures while the examiner reads sentences describing two of the pictures. The examiner then repeats one of the sentences and the child is required to point to the appropriate picture. In total, there are 40 test sentences that are supposedly in order of increasing syntactic difficulty. The second part of the test superimposes the task of expression onto the task of reception. The expressive test also consists of 40 test sentences. There are, however, only 2 test pictures on each page. The examiner reads the sentence pairs, points to one of the pictures and requests that the child repeat that sentence. The NSST differs from the CELI in that responses in the expressive subtest are delayed until after the two stimulus sentences have been presented.

All test pictures have been randomized for their location on the page. The sentences in each pair have also been randomized for the order in which the child is asked to point to them.

Test Scoring   Norms were established by administering the test to 344 children between the ages of 3;0 and 7;11. The children were from nursery school or public school classes and were presumed to have no conditions which would contribute to difficulties in language development.

Two charts showing the progression of receptive and expressive scores according to 1-year age groups are included. Raw scores are converted into percentile ranking for each group. An individual child's performance can then be compared with his age group. Children whose scores fall between the 10th percentile line and the second standard deviation line may be considered as low-normal in syntactic development. It is emphasized, however, that other language tests should be administered to substantiate these findings.

Test Review   Buros' (1978) *Eighth Mental Measurement Yearbook* contained three reviews of the NSST. From the reviewers comments several concerns may be gleaned. First, a question is raised about the expressive section: Is it testing the child's expressive syntactic ability or the child's imitative ability? Second, the scoring system utilized for the expressive syntactic items is somewhat subjective, since the types of grammatical distinctions being tested are not identified. A third concern is with the lack of documented validity. A fourth criticism is directed at the emphasis on syntactic screening at the expense of semantic data. If these items are of concern to the clinician, then the NSST must be used with caution.

User Report of the NSST

The test was administered to a boy in second grade, age 7 years, 10 months. He was receiving language therapy. His expressive and receptive subtest scores on the NSST, which placed him more than two standard deviations below the mean in both areas, clearly reflected his poor language abilities.

Tom experienced greatest difficulty on the Expressive Subtest particularly as the sentences became more complex toward the end of appeared to encounter difficulty with more complex language structures

1. *Item:*   "The boy pulls the girl."
   Tom: "The boy pulls the girls."
2. *Item:*   "The boy is pulled by the girl."
   Tom: "The girl pulled the boy."
3. *Item:*   Mother says, "Where is the boy?"
   Tom: Mother says, "Where is the boy?"
4. *Item:*   "Is the car in the garage?"
   Tom: "The car isn't in the garage?"

Generally, the expressive subtest results indicated that Tom appeared to encounter difficulty with more complex language structures including reflexives, passives, interrogatives, and correct use of the verb "to have." These structures were usually only tested with one or two items and supplemental testing to determine the accuracy of these findings would be necessary. It is clearly stated in the NSST manual that the test results require support from additional testing before a decision regarding therapy can be made.

The Carrow Elicited Language Inventory (CELI) was also administered to determine Tom's expressive language abilities. The administration of this test differs in that the child simply repeats a sentence after the examiner. The NSST, however, in addition to using pictures, also requires that the child listen to the oral presentation of two sentences. The child must first repeat one sentence while the examiner points to the picture and then the child repeats the second sentence as the examiner points to the second picture. Results of testing utilizing the CELI placed Tom at the 10th percentile for children of his age range. These findings would substantiate the need for language therapy.

The CELI also differs from the NSST in that interpretation involves a detailed analysis of errors breaking them down into percentile rank of total raw score, percentile ranks of grammar subscores, and percentile ranks of subscores (substitutions, omissions, additions, transpositions, and reversals). The NSST interpretation involves only a percentile rank of the raw score. Further analysis of Tom's CELI scores indicated a verb grammar subscore at the 22.5 percentile, which accounted for most of his errors. Most errors involved substitutions of forms of the verb "to have." Reversals involving passive forms were also noted.

One can conclude, then, that the NSST is valuable as a screening device. The test indicated some expressive language structures which Tom appeared to have difficulty with and these findings were substantiated by additional language testing utilizing the CELI. It should be stressed, however, that the test cannot be used exclusively for diagnosis of language disorders and that it does not provide an indepth analysis of results which could be used as a means for determining goals of therapy.

THE ILLINOIS TEST OF PSYCHOLINGUISTIC ABILITIES

> Publisher: University of Illinois Press, Urbana, Illinois
> Date: 1969
> Developers: Paraskevopoulos, J. N. and Kirk, S. A.

Description of ITPA

Test Purpose The ITPA deals with psycholinguistic functions which operate in the communication activities of an individual. It is a diagnostic test of specific cognitive abilities. Its purpose is to delineate specific abilities and disabilities in communication, to specify their relationships, and to provide a framework for observing and evaluating a child in order to plan remedial measures.

Theoretical Base   Paraskevopoulos and Kirk (1969) based the ITPA on a psycholinguistic model ". . . which attempts to relate those functions whereby the intentions of one individual are transmitted (verbally or nonverbally) to another individual, and, reciprocally, functions whereby the environment or the intentions of another individual are received and interpreted" (p. 11). It is a 3-dimensional model and contains 1) the channels of communication which include auditory and visual input and verbal and motor response; 2) the psycholinguistic processes of reception (association and expression); and 3) the levels of organization (the degree to which habits of communication have been developed within an individual) which include the representational and automatic levels.

Test Design   The ITPA contains twelve tests, six at the representational level and six at the automatic level.

I. *Functions Tested at the Representational Level*
    A. *The Receptive Process (Decoding)*
        There are two tests at this level which assess the child's ability to comprehend symbols:
        1. *Auditory Reception (Auditory Decoding).* This test assesses the ability of a child to derive meaning from verbally presented material. The test contains 50 short, direct questions. Responses are kept at a simple level of "yes" or "no" or a nod or shake of the head. The response remains at a 2-year level but the vocabulary becomes more difficult. Only one sentence form is used throughout to minimize the automatic functions of determining meaning from syntax. Examples are: "Do dogs eat?" "Do carpenters kneel?"
        2. *Visual Reception (Visual Decoding).* This test is comparable to the Auditory Reception Test but utilizes the visual sense modality. There are 40 picture items, each consisting of a stimulus picture on one page and four response pictures on a second page. The child is shown the stimulus picture for 3 seconds with the directions, "See this?" Then the page of response pictures is presented with the directions, "Find one here."
    B. *The Organizing Process (Association)*
        At the representational level, Paraskevopoulos and Kirk view this process as the ability to relate, organize, and manipulate visual or auditory symbols in a meaningful way. There are two tests to assess association.

1. *Auditory-Vocal Association.* This test examines a child's ability to relate concepts presented orally. The organizing process of manipulating linguistic symbols in a meaningful way is tested by verbal analogues of increasing difficulty while the requirements of the receptive process and vocal expressive process are minimal. A sentence completion technique is used. One statement is presented followed by an incomplete analogous statement which the child completes. There are 42 analogies which are presented orally. Example: "I cut with a saw; I pound with a _____."

2. *Visual-Motor Association.* In this channel the organizing process is examined by means of a picture association test which assesses a child's ability to relate concepts presented visually. The test consists of 20 items of a simple form at the lower level and 22 visual analogies at the upper level. At the lower level the child is presented with a single stimulus picture surrounded by four optional pictures, one of which is associated with the stimulus picture. The examiner first points to the stimulus picture and asks, "What goes with this?" and then points to the four optional pictures asking, "Which one of these?" The child must choose one picture most closely related to the stimulus picture. At the upper level the test provides visual analogies comparable to the auditory analogies. The examiner points to a preliminary pair of pictures and asks, "If this goes with this, then what goes with this?" (pointing to the central picture).

C. *The Expressive Process (Encoding)*

At the representational level this process involves the child's ability to use verbal or manual symbols to express an idea. There are two tests, one requiring vocal responses and the other manual responses.

1. *Verbal Expression (Vocal Encoding).* This test assesses a child's ability to express his own concepts vocally. The child is shown four familiar objects, one at a time (ball, block, envelope, and button) and is asked, "Tell me about this."

2. *Manual Expression (Motor Encoding).* This test examines a child's ability to express ideas manually. The child is shown 15 pictures of common objects and is asked to, "Show me what we do with a _____." The child is required to pantomine the appropriate action, such as dialing a telephone.

II. *Functions Tested at the Automatic Level*

At this level the tests are designed to measure a child's ability to perform automatic, nonsymbolic tasks. The two abilities that are measured are closure (auditory and visual) and short-term sequential memory (auditory and visual).

A. *Closure.* The child's ability to fill in the missing parts is assessed by means of a grammatic closure test (including two supplementary tests) and a visual closure test.

1. *Grammatic Closure.* The task elicits a child's ability to respond automatically to often-repeated verbal expressions of standard American speech while the conceptual difficulty is kept low. The test measures the form of the missing word. There are 33 orally presented items accompanied by pictures portraying the content of the verbal expressions. Example: "Here is a dog; here are two _____."

a) *Supplementary Test 1, Auditory Closure.* This test assesses a child's ability to fill in the missing parts of an auditory presentation in completing a word such as *bo/le*. There are 30 items ranging from easy to more difficult words.

b) *Supplementary Test 2, Sound Blending.* In this test the sounds of a word are spoken singly at half-second intervals, and the child is asked to tell what the word is. There are 32 items.

2. *Visual Closure.* This test assesses a child's ability to identify a common object from an incomplete visual presentation. Four scenes are presented separately, each containing 14 or 15 examples of a specified object. The objects are presented in varying degrees of concealment. The child is asked to point to all examples of a particular object within the time limit of 30 seconds for each scene.

B. *Sequential Memory.* There are two tests, one to assess a child's ability to reproduce a sequence of auditory stimuli and one to assess the ability to reproduce visual stimuli.

1. *Auditory Sequential Memory.* In this test the child is asked to reproduce from memory sequences of digits increasing in length from two to eight digits. The digits are presented at the rate of 2 per second and the child is allowed a second trial if he fails on the first presentation.

2. *Visual Sequential Memory.* This test measures a child's ability to reproduce nonmeaningful figures from memory. The child is shown a sequence of figures for 5 seconds and

then is asked to put corresponding chips of figures in the same order. Each sentence of figures is shown for 5 seconds, and the child is allowed two trials on each sequence.

SUMMARY AND CONCLUSIONS

Imitation can be considered as but one of three processes involved in language acquisition, the other two being rule learning and advancement in the comprehension of adult speech (Ervin-Tripp, 1964). While Fraser, Bellugi, and Brown (1963) considered imitation to be a perceptual-motor skill not dependent on comprehension, Slobin and Welsh (1973) found some recoding in elicited imitation. It is, consequently, important to distinguish between *elicited* and *spontaneous* imitation.

It has also been demonstrated that at times imitation may be less advanced than spontaneous language (Bloom, Hood, and Lightbown, 1974; Slobin and Welsh, 1973) and hence the assumption that *production* follows *comprehension* may no longer be warranted.

In considering elicited imitation it must be recognized that *intention*, *context*, and *topic* are important considerations since they are eliminated as sources of information and the subject relies largely on linguistic knowledge (Bloom and Lahey, 1978; Bransford and Johnson, 1972).

While the three instruments discussed (TOLD, CELI, NSST) are similar in that they include an *elicited imitation* task, they also vary considerably in the other dimensions assessed.

Generally speaking, the instruments are seen as useful adjuncts to clinical assessment, although it is recognized that they may underestimate productive language capabilities and that they may be unduly affected by auditory memory. The authors' experience with these measures indicates that they are not heavily loaded on the intelligence factor. However, the validity data are still being accumulated and cautious use of these tests is recommended in the meantime. At present the CELI appears to be favored by clinicians, but not without a spontaneous language sample to accompany it.

The three tests (TOLD, CELI, NSST) are useful for subjects between ages 3 and 8, but because children with deviant-language abilities may perform differently on elicited imitation tasks (Lee, 1966; Menyuk, 1969; Berry-Luterman and Bar, 1971), great caution must be recommended in using these subtests.

In conclusion, these instruments have a theoretical base with a "linguistic" flavor and may be indicative of a changing paradigm in psycholinguistic and educational assessment. The clinician may wish to examine the books, kits, and materials listed in the appendix for remedial activities to follow up on the diagnosis made on the basis of the TOLD, the CELI, and the NSST.

FOR DISCUSSION

1. How do the procedures outlined in this chapter differ from those explained by Hopkins in Chapter 3?
2. Of what use to the classroom teacher are the tests outlined here?
3. Is it possible to validly assess student performance in oral language using an elicited response test? How could these measurements be adjusted or changed for classroom or group use?

REFERENCES

Ammons, R., and Ammons, H. *Full-range picture vocabulary test.* Missoula, Montana: Psychological Test Specialists, 1958.

Baker, H. J., and Leland, B. *Detroit tests of learning aptitude.* Indianapolis: Test Division of Bobbs-Merrill, 1959.

Berko, J. The child's learning of morphology. *Word,* 1958, *14,* 150–177.

Berry-Luterman, L., and Bar, A. The diagnostic significance of sentence repetition for language-impaired children. *Journal of Speech and Hearing Disorders,* 1971, *36,* 29–39.

Bloom, L., Hood, L., and Lightbown, P. Imitation in language development: If, when, and why. *Cognitive Psychology,* 1974, *6,* 380–420.

Bloom, L., and Lahey, M. *Language development and language disorders.* New York: John Wiley and Sons, 1978.

Bransford, J., and Johnson, M. Contextual prerequisites for understanding: Some investigations of comprehension and recall. *Journal of Verbal Learning and Verbal Behavior,* 1972, *11,* 717–726.

Brown, R., and Fraser, C. The acquisition of syntax. In C. Ferguson and D. C. Slobin (Eds.), *Studies of child language development.* New York: Holt, Rinehart and Winston, 1973.

Buros, O. K. (Ed.). *Seventh mental measurement yearbook.* Highland Park, New Jersey: Gryphon Press, 1975.

Buros, O.K. (Ed.). *Eighth mental measurement yearbook.* Highland Park, New Jersey: Gryphon Press, 1978.

Carrow, E. *Test for auditory comprehension of language.* Austin, Texas: Learning Concepts, 1973.

Carrow, E. *Carrow elicited language inventory.* Austin, Texas: Learning Concepts, 1974.

Cazden, C. B. *Child language and education.* New York: Holt, Rinehart and Winston, 1972.

Chomsky, C. *The acquisition of syntax in children from 5 to 10.* Cambridge, Massachusetts: MIT Press, 1969.

Chomsky, N. *Syntactic structures.* The Hague: Mouton, 1957.

Chomsky, N. *Aspects of theory of syntax.* Cambridge, Massachusetts: MIT Press, 1965.

Chomsky, N. Deep structure, surface structure, and semantic representation. In D. Steinberg and L. A. Jakobovits (Eds.), *Semantics: An interdisciplinary reader in philosophy, linguistics, and psychology.* Cambridge, England: Cambridge University Press, 1971.

Clay, M. Sentence repetition: Elicited imitation of a controlled set of syntactic structures by four language groups. *Monograph of the Society for Research in Child Development*, 1971, Vol. 36, No. 3, Serial No. 143.

Cornelius, S. *A comparison of the elicited language inventory with the developmental syntax scoring procedure in assessing language disorders in children.* Unpublished masters thesis, University of Texas, Austin, 1974.

Dale, P. S. *Language development, structure and function* (2nd ed.). New York: Holt, Rinehart and Winston, 1976.

Dailey, K. and Boxx, J. R. A comparison of three imitation tests of expressive language and spontaneous language sample. *Language, Speech, and Hearing Services in Schools*, 1979, *10*, 6–13.

De Vito, J. A. *The psychology of speech and language: An introduction to psycholinguistics.* New York: Random House, 1970.

Dunn, L. *Peabody picture vocabulary test.* Minneapolis: American Guidance Service, 1965.

Egland, G. D. *Speech and language problems.* Englewood Cliffs, New Jersey: Prentice-Hall, 1970.

Ervin-Tripp, S. M. Imitation and structural change in children's language. In E. H. Lenneberg (Ed.), *New directions in the study of language.* Cambridge, Massachusetts: MIT Press, 1964.

Frazer, C., Bellugi, U., and Brown, R. Control of grammar in imitation, comprehension and production. *Journal of Verbal Learning and Verbal Behavior*, 1963, *2*, 121–135.

Hammill, D. D., and Newcomer, P. L. *Construction and statistical characteristics of the test of language development.* Austin, Texas: Empiric Press, 1977.

Hoepfner, R. (Ed.). *CSE elementary school test evaluations.* Los Angeles: Center for the Study of Evaluation, UCLA Grauate School of Education, 1970.

Irwin, O. C. *Communication variables of cerebral palsied and mentally retarded children.* Springfield, Illinois: Charles C Thomas, 1972.

Jakobson, R., Font, C., and Halle, M. *Preliminaries to speech analysis.* Cambridge, Massachusetts: MIT Press, 1963.

Kirk, S., McCarthy, J., and Kirk, W. *The Illinois test of psycholinguistic abilities* (Rev. ed.). Urbana, Illinois: University of Illinois Press, 1968.

Lee, L. Developmental sentence types: A method for comparing normal and deviant syntactic development. *Journal of Speech and Hearing Disorders*, 1966, *31*, 311–330.

Lee, L. *The Northwestern syntax screening test.* Evanston, Illinois: Northwestern University, 1969.

Lee, L., and Cantor, S. Developmental scoring: A clinical procedure for estimating syntactic development in children's spontaneous speech. *Journal of Speech and Hearing Disorders*, 1971, *36*, 315–340.

Lenneberg, E. H. *Biological foundations of language.* New York: Wiley, 1967.

McNeill, D. *The acquisition of language, the study of developmental psycholinguistics.* New York: Harper and Row, 1970.

Menyuk, P. A preliminary evaluation of grammatical capacity in children. *Journal of Verbal Learning and Verbal Behavior*, 1963, *2*, 429–439.

Menyuk, P. Comparison of grammar of children with functionally deviant and normal speech. *Journal of Speech and Hearing Research*, 1964, *7*, 109–121.

Menyuk, P. *Sentences children use*. Cambridge, Massachusetts: MIT Press, 1969.

Newcomer, P. L., and Hammill, D. D. ITPA and academic achievement: A survey. *Reading Teacher*, 1975, *28*, 731–741.

Newcomer, P. L., and Hammill, D. D. *Psycholinguistics in the schools*. Columbus, Ohio: Merrill, 1976.

Newcomer, P. L., and Hammill, D. D. *Test of language development*. Austin, Texas: Empiric Press, 1977.

Paraskevopoulos, J. N., and Kirk, S. A. *The development and psychometric characteristics of the revised Illinois test of psycholinguistic abilities*. Urbana, Illinois: The University of Illinois Press, 1969.

Prutting, C. A., Gallagher, T. M., and Mulac, A. The expressive portion of the NSST compared to a spontaneous language sample. *Journal of Speech and Hearing Disorders*, 1975, *40*, 40–48.

Rinsland, H. D. *A basic vocabulary of elementary school children*. New York: Macmillan, 1945.

Slobin, D. L., and Welsh, C. A. Elicited imitation as a research tool in developmental psycholinguistics. In C. Ferguson and D. Slobin (Eds.), *Studies of child language development*. New York: Holt, Rinehart and Winston, 1973.

Smith, C. S. An experimental approach to children's linguistic competence. In C. Ferguson and D. Slobin (Eds.), *Studies of child language development*. New York: Holt, Rinehart and Winston, 1973.

Stockwell, R. P. The transformational model of generative or predictive grammar. In P. L. Garvin (Ed.), *Natural language and the computer*. New York: McGraw-Hill, 1963.

Templin, M., and Darley, F. *The Templin-Darley tests of articulation*. Iowa City: Bureau of Educational Research, State University of Iowa, 1960.

Thieman, T. J. Imitation and recall of optionally deletable sentences by young children. *Journal of Child Language*, 1975, *2*, 261–269.

Thorndike, E. I., and Lorge, I. *A teacher's word book of 30,000 words*. New York: Bureau of Publications, Teachers College, Columbia University, 1944.

Van Alystine, D. *Van Alystine picture vocabulary test*. New York: Harcourt, Brace, and World, 1961.

Van Riper, C. *Speech correction*. Englewood Cliffs, New Jersey: Prentice-Hall, 1972.

Wechsler, D. *The Wechsler intelligence test for children*. New York: The Psychological Corporation, 1949.

Wepman, J. *Auditory discrimination test*. Chicago: Language Research Associates, 1968.

Wepman, J., and Haas, W. A. *A spoken word count*. Chicago: Language Research Associates, 1969.

APPENDIX: LINGUISTICALLY ORIENTED TEACHING MATERIALS

Books

Braun, C., and Froese, V. *An experience-based approach to language and reading*. Baltimore: University Park Press, 1977.

Cramer, R. L. *Writing, reading, and language growth*. Columbus, Ohio: Merrill, 1978.

Ives, J. P. et al. *Word identification techniques*. Chicago: Rand McNally, 1979.

Markoff, A. M. *Teaching low-achieving children reading, spelling, and handwriting*. Springfield, Illinois: Charles C Thomas, 1976.

Pearson, P. D., and Johnson, D. D. *Teaching reading comprehension*. New York: Holt, Rinehart and Winston, 1978.

Pflaum-Connor, S. *The development of language and reading in young children*. Columbus, Ohio: Merrill, 1978.

Ransom, G. A. Teaching linguistic comprehension skills. Chapter 10 in *Preparing to teach reading*. Boston: Little, Brown, 1978.

Kits and Materials

Auditory Discrimination in Depth. Boston: Teaching Resources Corporation.

Before and After Sequential Cards. Niles, Illinois: Developmental Learning Materials.

Breakthrough to Literacy. Don Mills, Ontario: Thomas Nelson & Sons Ltd.

Developmental Syntax by Coughran & Liles. Austin, Texas: Learning Concepts.

Emerging Language by John Hallen, Tracy Goman, Carole Lent. Tucson, Arizona: Communication Skill Builders Inc.

Folkes Sentence Builder. Boston: Teaching Resources Corporation.

Folkes Sentence Builder Expanded. Boston: Teaching Resources Corporation.

Goal Language Development Kit, I & II. Springfield, Massachusetts: Milton Bradley.

Goldman-Lynch Sounds and Symbols Kit. Willowdale, Ontario: Psycan Limited.

Learning Language at Home Kits I & II by Merle Karnes. Reston, Virginia: Council for Exceptional Children.

Opposites Flip Book. St. Paul, Minnesota: Trend Enterprises, Inc.

Peabody Early Experience Kit. Markham, Ontario: Psycan.

Peabody Language Development Kit P, I, II, III. Circle Pines, Minnesota: American Guidance Service.

Ready Steps Resource Kit. Boston: Houghton Mifflin.

Scrabble Sentence Building. Bay Shore, New York: Selchow & Righter Co.

Sentence Building Sequential Cards. Niles, Illinois: Developmental Learning Materials.

Sound Order Sense Level 1 by Eleanor Semel. Chicago: Follett Publishing Company.

Sound Order Sense Level 2 by Eleanor Semel. Chicago: Follett Publishing Company.

Syntax One. Tucson, Arizona: Communication Skill Builders Inc.

Wilson Expanded Syntax Program by Mary Sweig Wilson. Cambridge, Massachusetts: Educators Publishing Service Inc.

Wilson Initial Syntax Program by Mary Sweig Wilson. Cambridge, Massachusetts: Educators Publishing Service Inc.

Working With Meaning: A Language Patterns Book by J. Trischuk. Toronto, Ontario: Holt, Rinehart (Winston Press in U.S.A.).

5 | The Process and Potential of Creative Dramatics for Enhancing Linguistic and Cognitive Development

Judith S. Youngers

The holistic development of individuals—this is the goal of creative dramatics.

No doubt this statement has a familiar ring, for it has been reiterated in countless books and professional articles on creative dramatics. Because it corresponds to a cardinal purpose of education, who would deny the worthiness of this ultimate goal?

True believers can choose to remain at lofty levels proclaiming such admirable but amorphous values for creative dramatics, as has been done for over a 60-year period. However, by doing so, proponents will not convince fellow educators nor the public of a rationale for the inclusion of creative drama into school curricula. By not making more definitive efforts toward supplying concrete research evidence to support long-held claims of both holistic and particular benefits to be derived from dramatics experiences, creative drama will remain in a disembodied state, a state of unrecognized potential that has characterized it since its inception.

The challenge before us "is not to define the frontiers of a subject where no frontiers exist, but to establish clearly the contribution of dramatics activity to the growth and education of children" (Great Britain Department of Education and Science, 1967).

Confronting this challenge seems especially important in an era when school personnel are expected to demonstrate economic and educational accountability and when public concern for the acquisition of basic skills is voiced in a cry for a return to "the basics."

The intent of this discussion is to respond to the challenge by: 1) making an assessment of the state of the art, 2) positing a multidimensional development model of creative drama focused particularly on cognitive and linguistic aspects, 3) identifying supportive theoretical and empirical research, and 4) suggesting implications of such a model for classroom practice and for further research.

It should be noted immediately that creative dramatics as it is conceived of here is distinctly different in both purpose and technique from theatrical drama. While the words "theater" and "drama" are often used interchangeably, their origins indicate a basic difference. *Theater* is derived from a Greek word meaning "to see, to view"; *drama* comes from the Greek root meaning "to do or live through." Theater's greater focus on product and communication between actors and audiences contrasts with the participant and process centeredness of creative dramatics. Spontaneity is characteristic of creative dramatics, and dialogue, if any, is improvised by participants, regardless of whether the content evolves out of literature or is an original plot. Writing down of stories by participants and subsequent enactment may occur, but the dialogue is likely to be everchanging with each playing, as the form remains essentially scriptless drama. Talent is not required, nor is playing to an audience. Creative dramatics, then, may be seen as an inclusive term designating a variety of forms of informal dramatic activities involving symbolic representation, such as movement and sensory exercises, mime, improvisation, story dramatization, and any other kind of extemporaneous drama created by the participants themselves.

A CONTEXT FOR CREATIVE DRAMATICS IN SCHOOLS

One can trace the history of creative dramatics in American school programs through educational thought, events, and programming relevant to creative expression back to Edward Sheldon's "object lessons" in the late nineteenth century. On occasion, striking parallels between propositions expressed in the current literature and those set forth in much earlier writings can be noted. For example, over 50 years ago Harold Rugg and Ann Shumaker (1928) in their well-known book, *The Child-Centered School*, claimed enthusiastically:

> Drama more than any other single art, represents an integration of all the processes of self-expression. It is at once the most completely personal, individualistic, and intimate, as well as the most highly socialized art. Rich in content, it represents also an effective union of intellect and emotion. (p. 294)

Thirty years later Philip Coggin (1958) in *Uses of Drama* echoed a similar justification for drama when he said:

> Creative drama is "the doing of life." . . . It is a great integrating force. It helps the personality to self-realization by educating the emotions, stimulating the intellect, and co-ordinating movement and gesture to the wishes of the mind and spirit. (p. 293)

In 1975 these recurrent claims for creative dramatics' integrative potential again surfaced, this time in an article by Ann Shaw. She averred:

> ... It is reasonable to state that improvisational drama promotes the development and integration of the child's cognitive abilities (his ability to think) with his subjective life (what he feels and intuits) with his affective growth (his internalization of attitudes and values) with his capacity to create. (p. 88)

Thus, for over a 50-year period, the multidimensional and developmental nature of creative dramatics has been theorized, and advocacy for continued and expanded use of creative dramatics at all levels in school programs has been enthusiastic.

Yet the third-quarter mark in the twentieth century has now passed, and educators remain unsure of the nature of creative dramatics, its role in school programs, and the benefits, goals, appropriate methodology, and developmental process connected with it. As the climate of creative expression has shifted from a concern with practical outcomes to an affirmation of intrinsic purposes, from an advocacy of creative expression for some to a belief in the values of imaginative effort for all, the idea of creative dramatics has taken root, gone through sporadic periods of growth and taken several different forms in keeping with the times to evolve into a vague entity whose potential has been largely untapped and undemonstrated. Duke (1974) quite accurately described the current state of diverse practices and philosophies when he noted that, at times, creative dramatics is "used as an educational technique; at other times it is seen solely as a theatre art. In some situations, it is considered a separate academic subject, and on still other occasions it is viewed as a personality development strategy" (p. 55). In light of the debate over whether creative dramatics should be seen as justifiable in its own right, as an art, or as an effective instructional tool, a compromise viewpoint is suggested here, that is, viewing creative drama as an art which can be utilized as an instructional tool.

Attendance at conference and workshop sessions devoted to creative drama indicates continuing and increasing interest in the topic. Publications suggest that creative dramatics is becoming more widely implemented in some form in schools. An ERIC Reading and Communication Skills report (Reed, 1974) noted that since 1969, "more curriculum guides than ever have recommended dramatic activities and more English teachers than ever have experimented with role playing, improvisation and dramatic games" (p. 105). The 1977 report of the American Council for the Arts in Education: Arts, Education, and Americans Panel, chaired by David Rockefeller, Jr., made the following claims:

The use of creative dramatics is growing in importance.

In the last ten years, there has been an increase in the number of universities offering in-service and pre-service courses in creative dramatics for teachers.

A few states have ruled that creative dramatics must be part of the elementary school day, along with music, art, and physical education. This has made a significant difference, and teachers have shown greater interest in its use.

There is more demand for drama specialists who are used as resources for the classroom teacher. (p. 69)

Despite clear indications in the literature of increased interest, creative drama is far from being accepted as integral to the curriculum on a widespread basis on either side of the Atlantic. Brian Way indicated in 1975 that while there were over 150 teachers colleges in Great Britain offering drama courses and 60 national drama advisors to schools, only 5%–7.5% of the schools are doing drama on a regular, sustained basis. In a recent survey (Littig, 1975) of 346 classroom teachers in the United States, 75% reported that they favored creative drama in the classroom, but less than 25% actually did drama on a regular basis.

Two major reasons have been posited for this current lack of inclusion in school programs. First, creative drama has not been clearly identified as a discipline. Writings are needed which provide a focused rationale for drama, a sound theoretical or philosophical examination of its nature, and/or descriptions of the structure of the discipline. Second, claims for the particular benefits or the development of the "whole" person through creative dramatic activities have not been empirically well-documented (Wright, 1972; Stewig, 1976).

In assessing the total scope of activity in the field, one is forced to agree with Dwight Burton's conclusion based on a review of the literature up to 1973:

Lavish claims by the proponents with little or no empirical substantiation necessarily must be the scholarly summary to date of the value of dramatic activities in the classroom, though the furor may be more in print than in practice, especially on the American side of the Atlantic. (p. 184)

Research reports are far outweighed by the number of articles directed at the practitioner. The latter rely chiefly on the voice of experience and they characteristically present anecdotal reports of methods and activities used by teachers. Frequently there is little consistency of basic creative dramatics procedures shown within these works, to say nothing of any recognition of findings accepted in the social sciences. While serving a beneficial purpose as an idea resource, these works are of questionable value in producing long-term evidence to support curricular decisions.

The few reported experimental studies dealing with creative dramatics tend to suffer from one of more of the three types of problems identified by Koziol (1973):

1. Narrowness of focus, serious (sometimes unavoidable) design problems, and treatment periods too short to produce conclusive results. (For example, Karioth, 1970, had unavoidable teacher and group effects; experimentals had multiple enrichment in Hartshorn and Brantley, 1973.)
2. Inappropriate measurement criteria and instruments.
3. Nonreplicability because of inadequate description of procedures and dramatic method (Irwin, 1975, for example) and/or inconsistency in definition and use of terms.

Several years ago, Geraldine Siks (1977), a recognized leader in creative dramatics, posed a number of critical questions still largely unanswered: What is the precise distinctive contribution made by creative dramatics which justifies its inclusion in language arts curricula? What difference does creative dramatics make, if any? Are students different in identifiable ways as a result of regular experiences in such dramatics?

One problem evident in much of the empirical research in drama is that the particular and diverse dependent measures used lean toward assessing the secondary impact of creative dramatics, the impact of dramatic methods of teaching some subject matter. It seems logical that prior to studying the effects of drama as a teaching method on secondary variables such as learning and retention of content in social studies, for example, we need to more effectively study the processes of creative dramatics and therefore the effects on those linguistic, cognitive, personal, or social attributes which are affected by participation in drama itself. Identifying a starting point is in order.

IN SEARCH OF A MULTIDIMENSIONAL
MODEL OF CREATIVE DRAMATICS

Because oral language and body movement have been identified as two of the most vital symbolic tools available to humans in their attempts to bring order and reason to their personal worlds, several researchers (Hendricks, 1973; McGregor, 1973; Irwin, 1975; Shaw, 1975; Stewig, 1976) have endorsed strongly the provision of improvisational drama activities in school programs on a regular basis. They have viewed this kind of drama, which calls for immediate action with no extensive preparation time and for spontaneous languaging at the point of utterance, as ideal for the stimulation of internal mental structuring involving symbolic transformations, for the stimulation of ideational fluency or associative flow, and for verbal fluency.

Opportunities are inherent in creative dramatics for the symbolizing behavior involved in both language and creative thinking processes that Susanne Langer (1957) and others have pointed out is a primary need for both children and adults in all civilizations, a need which is insufficiently recognized in the culture of Western society and its educational system. A capsule description of this role of drama has been provided by Furner (1978) in her explanation of the personal growth model of English:

> Through roletaking, the child, in keeping with man's need to use processes of symbolism to make reality from experience, is able to re-experience an important event to understand it more fully, prepare for an experience by anticipation, or come to know another's role without having to actually experience it. (p. 113)

Contribution of Theory and Research in Play

Several theorists and researchers from diverse fields have discussed the importance of the symbolic process in the development of the intellect from the standpoint of the early manifestations of drama in young children's behaviors. Among the many who have tied cognitive and linguistic growth processes to dramatic play are Anastasiow (1971), Courtney (1974), El'Konin (1957), J. N. Lieberman (1965), Luria and Yudovich (1959), Piaget (1962), J. Singer (1972), Sutton-Smith (1967), and Vygotsky (1962). Evidence reported by Singer (1972) shows that fantasy and imaginative play significantly facilitate not only children's divergent thinking abilities but their cognitive development as well. He also believes that "role playing involved in imaginative play lends itself to more verbal communication and increased vocabularies as well as spontaneity, inventiveness, and practice in responding to cues of others." One conclusion drawn by Jerome Kagan (1971) based on this line of research is that "Thought (trial action), language, and intelligence are . . . inextricably interwoven, as language promotes the elaboration of play, and both play and language help to restructure further the child's cognitive processes" (p. 82).

According to this view, individuals develop the capacity for creative symbolism in infancy as they initiate self-exploration through play and verbal experimentation. Shaw (1975) emphasized in this growth process the overt enactment of the "as if," the symbolic transformation of experimental data which is essential to the development of human intelligence and a fundamental way of meaning making. Piaget (1962) also referred to the value of play for "as if" thinking. He suggests that make-believe in particular enables the child to think in symbols about things not actually present and to recognize causal relationships between events. In *Play, Dreams, and Imitation in Childhood*, Piaget developed at length his theory on the relationship between play and intelligence. In fact, the three general developmental stages of play frequently identified by child development experts closely parallel Piaget's stages of cognitive development.

Considerable experimental or quasi-experimental research has focused on the second developmental level of play, that of symbolic or sociodramatic play. It should be recognized that the process of sociodramatic play is much like the process of creative dramatics, except that it is on a simpler level and generally involves younger children in a voluntary social play situation. While this research is not reviewed here, a substantial number of studies have confirmed a positive relationship between the development of play and cognitive and linguistic development and have investigated the effect of adult intervention in play situations to facilitate maturation. Pertinent studies reported elsewhere include Luria and Yudovich (1959), Lieberman (1965), Smilansky (1968), Rosen (1972), Lewis (1972), Feitelson and Ross (1973), Lovinger (1974), Sachs and Devin (1975), and Martlew, Connolly, and McCleod (1976).

Repeatedly then, both the theoretical and empirical literature in the areas of creativity, play, language development, and cognitive development have linked imaginative play to various forms of cognitive and linguistic growth, including problem solving, abstract thinking, vocabulary growth, and more mature, organized, and fluent language.

Theory of Creative Dramatics Processes

Questions of whether the interrelationships found between play and cognitive and linguistic growth are also found in creative dramatics are not yet well answered. Again, theory abounds. In speculating about possible connections, Piaget (1962) and others have observed that for the child from 6 to 12 years of age, fantasy apparently goes "underground" and is increasingly less visible both verbally and behaviorally in play. Menyuk (1970) reported on intriguing co-occurrence in children's semantic development. Children from preschool years through the first grade have been observed to explore actively the inherent potential in language for creating new words by changing syntactic classes and adding appropriate grammatical markers or by creating entirely unique words, "He is 'grouching,'" "He is a 'bugiebooer.'" (p. 182). The frequency of these semantic inventions, however, has been reported to decline sharply after the preschool period and to disappear almost entirely after first grade. This corresponds to the age at which a decline in fantasy and spontaneous dramatic play was first reported as significant. Adult support at the elementary school years may be necessary for spontaneous dramatic play to develop and for linguistic inventiveness to be extended.

Those who have advocated creative dramatics as a valuable way to extend the gains that researchers like Smilansky (1968) and Singer (1972) saw as inherent in dramatic play situations include Irwin (1975) and McGregor (1973). McGregor has developed an interesting and logical theoretical construct which supports creative drama because of the cognitive growth it engenders. "It has the advantage of being more structured than children's random play," she noted, "yet much of the same freedom is present" (p. 225). McGregor identified and illustrated four aspects of the child's cognitive growth which have been verified as psychologically significant.

The first aspect identified by McGregor is inter- and intra-individual communication, intra-individual communication being what Lewis (1963) has termed "synpractic language," or talking to oneself, which becomes inner speech in adults. Along with inter-individual communication or social speech, that is, speaking to others, intra-individual communication has been viewed as vital to the development of perceptual and conceptual thinking as well as affective development. A second aspect of cognitive development fostered by creative dramatics is identified as *differentiation*, an important step in semantic development particularly. Third is *categorization*, which McGregor discusses in terms of arrriving at groupings by way of consensus. It is felt to be important in building perception, concept formation, judgment, memory, problem solving, inventive thinking, and aesthetics. The fourth and final aspect of cognitive development discussed by McGregor is termed *constructive alternativism*, postulated to have broad implications for a child's adaptive ability or personal awareness of alternative ways of viewing the world and solving problems. Others, including Flavell (1974), have expanded on the Piagetian view of the effect of egocentrism and young children's inability to assume other points of view on communicative competence. Flavell's work does support McGregor's notion and shows how children develop four role-taking or inference-making skills. The body of literature now available on egocentrism, role-taking, and audience awareness relative to oral and written composing is certainly of pertinence in considering the potential of creative dramatics. The reader is referred to Britton et al. (1975) and Kroll (1977).

That creative dramatics might enhance not only cognitive development but also linguistic growth, both in a syntactic and semantic sense, is a natural extension of the recognition that both linguistic and creative thinking processes involve symbolizing behaviors. The same elements described as operative in creative self-discovery and symbolizing processes, namely, associative thinking, child-generated language in response to a need, and shaping at the point of utterance, have been identified as key factors in children's semantic and syntactic productions and development. The question, "How do children express ideas?" cannot be readily and neatly separated from the question, "What kind of ideas do children have to express?" Rosen and Rosen (1973) note, "Firstly, a child must have experience of language; secondly, he must have experience of the world (i.e. non-linguistic experience); thirdly, he must be able to organize his thinking so that he makes sense of both kinds of experience" (p. 41). Drama affords a unique opportunity for capitalizing in several ways on the tripartite interaction of language, other experience, and thought.

A Formative Model

Since the central concern here is with creative dramatics as it relates to the development of language and thinking, the involvement of these specific processes in drama requires focus. Obvious sources to draw upon in developing a model are psychological and linguistic studies in child development, yet to expect that a ready-made model would emerge from this literature is naive. However, research in creative problem-solving processes and recent work in linguistic composing processes and theories of discourse specifically prove to be very useful.

The strategies an individual uses in creative dramatics result necessarily from a set of interrelated variables that arise from the dramatic context, socially determined and personal experiential frameworks, and both linguistic and non-linguistic resources that he or she brings to the dramatic situation. Way (1967) has identified the personal resources as the senses, imagination, physical self, language, emotion, intellect, and at the root of all the others, concentration. Recognizing that the player is an individual with both unique and socially determined experiences, attitudes, and expectations, improvising may be self-initiated and shaped, or, as is more typical in school situations, dramatization occurs within the constraints of a teacher-structured task. The player either acquires ownership of this task and makes it his own or the player perfunctorily fulfills his notion of what is demanded. Superficial playing would be typical of the latter approach. The player's level of involvement and choices related to the strategies that are used are likely to vary from experience to experience, dependent on the day and task; yet, there are processes common to players and elements common to the creative dramatics experience.

Dramatic Context   Like other purposeful oral composition in the classroom, the stimulus or starting point for creative dramatics may range from children's shared experience, that is, immediate real-life sensory and emotional experience, or memories and imagination, sparked frequently by a teacher-proposed topic, or works of literature. One dimension of difference across dramatic contexts is the concreteness

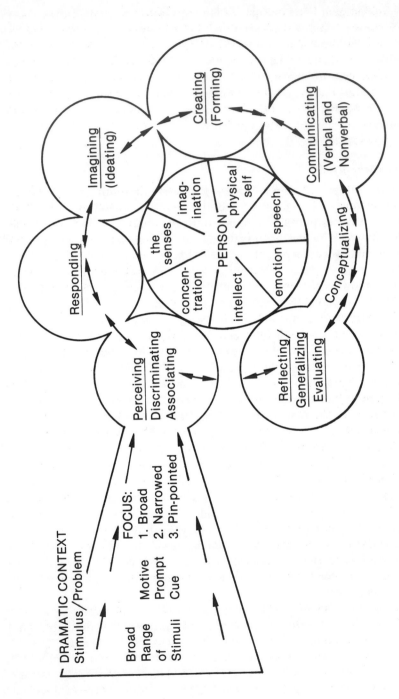

Figure 1.   A multidimensional model of creative dramatics.

or immediacy of the material, hence the distance between the player and the stimulus or focal concept. In a "re-creating" experience, to make a shared experience more meaningful, the material is relatively concrete and close. This closeness would also be typical of sociodramatic play or role-play seen as "rehearsal" experiences. The distance is greater with "what if" material which has more fantasy elements. A work of literature might offer material which the players, by themselves, would never imagine.

The degree and level of dramatic engagement with the material or concept suggest a related dimension and continuum. Dramatic involvement with a piece of literature, for instance, will vary dependent on whether players remain on its periphery or get inside of it. Peripheral dramatic engagement would be a literal interpretation of a story, oral reading of a play, or rote presentation of an adult-scripted play. Inside engagement would be when the story, character(s), and/or situations are used as a base, but participants extend and expand by creating their own characters, dialogue, and events. A work of literature, then, might be seen as a voice contributing to the drama, and the drama in its turn, as helping children to interpret what the voices have to say by providing a personally meaningful context. To what extent does the action remain a literal representation or achieve personal meaningfulness or symbolic value in the course of the drama? Response to media—still pictures, films, tapes, television—also might provide the dramatic context. Again, whether literal interpretation of this material or symbolic transformation involving personal meaning making occurs depends upon the dramatic use of the material.

Dramatic Processes   Within this dramatic context, a number of different mental, linguistic, and physical processes or activities occur. In examining them, it is helpful to keep in mind that creative dramatics fits a definition of problem solving which is more characteristic of the arts than the sciences. In drama, the execution, discovery by doing, rather than the conceptualization receives the focus. Here, as is true with other arts, one is continually redefining and refining one's goals by manipulating the medium.

In part, the processes may be seen as cumulative, each encasing the other, and as having a natural progression. The processes generate one another and are intertwined, but a strict linear progression is inaccurate. One process does not uniformly precede or follow another in the sequence outlined in the multidimensional model shown in Figure 1 and in the ensuing discussion. Yet there are many occasions when the processes are tapped sequentially as in a full blown exploration of a topic or problem. For instance, Furner (1973) recommends a drama planning procedure that corresponds to a more general creative problem-solving progression in terms of processes involved:

1. Preparatory warm-up exercises involving physical, relaxation, concentration, and sensory processes
2. Expressive activities (verbal and non-verbal) ranging from imitative to more interactive and less outer-directed
3. Improvisation activities where participants become self-generating in creating and collaborating on responses to stimuli
4. Reflection; conceptualizing in the sense of extending awarenesses, communicating the significance of what occurred, and generalizing to universals; and evaluation

Such a problem-solving sequence would be more typical of children who have reached a level of development in drama that is conducive to sustained involvement.

At times, however, particularly when children are just being introduced to dramatic elements, processes may be experienced singly or in clusters. Geraldine Siks (1977) supplies the example of initial exploration of the concepts of tension and release in relaxation. Here children would use only the processes of responding and perceiving. Whatever the experience, the processes should be seen as overlapping and without distinctive boundaries. Thus, the isolating of the individual processes in the model in Figure 1 is somewhat artificial, but it serves to bring them into sharper focus. If we can better describe these individual processes, activities, and elements and establish the dynamics of their interrelationships, we may be able to describe the totality of drama processes.

Perceiving We apprehend the world through our senses—sight, sound, smell, taste, touch—or through sensory perceptions. In attending to certain stimuli the individual selects and sorts, discriminates among, and matches what is sensed to frames of reference stored in memory. In drama, perceiving may be at as low a level as listening to sounds heard within a room. Or it may be more demanding, as with the dramatic task of creating an action narrative based on a series of sounds heard. In the latter instance, perceiving and identifying auditory stimuli is again involved; but, in addition, auditory sequential memory is involved, that is, interpreting the sounds in the sense of a coherent sequence of events plausible sources of the sounds, which demands recalling stored frames of reference, and, finally, establishing sensory associations with physical movement in an imagined context. This process is not directly observable; it is assessed in drama by observing behavioral responses made to stimuli.

Responding Response in drama may be individual or collaborative; imitative or improvised; physical or verbal; a single statement or sustained dialogue; or participation in numerous other ways. To encourage personal response in this enactive mode, a stimulus must: 1) be sufficiently distinct for a player to attach a response to it, 2) be presented in such a way that the player is inclined to attend to and receive it, and 3) generate a response that is within the player's cognitive, experiential, and physical capabilities. For example, if children are expected to collaborate in constructing a dramatic plot involving a given object or character, they must know basic elements of plot construction.

Imagining (*Ideating*)   As Shaw (1975) has observed, "Behaving 'as if' is the bedrock of symbolic behavior and fundamental to learning in any intellectual discipline. Drama is the field that is most specifically and literally derived from this human capacity" (p. 81). At the core of the creative dramatic process, then, is imagining, the process by which humans form mental pictures of what is not present, what has never been experienced personally, what might happen, or what never could occur. It may also be seen as the process of forming associative links, the combining of diverse images and experiences. Ideating has been defined as conceptualization in the sense of using labels, relations, generalizations, etc., to shape ideas and to form abstractions. However, this creative symbolization process should not be viewed as controllable or manageable by intellect alone. It is proposed that when the child relaxes personal efforts to accommodate reality, the child is then able to form relationships and associations among objects, actions, and ideas which may be typically unrelated. Intuitive flashes, Gestaltic leaps, the "A ha!" phenomenon have all been associated with the imagining phase in which solutions to a problem or organization of an experience begin to take shape. In a creative problem-solving conception of drama, a participant imagines individually or, at times, collaboratively in brainstorming fashion, in order to formulate original solutions for a wide range of problems. Still, it is in the creative enactment that full exploration of ideas is prominent, that discoveries occur, solutions gel, and symbolic realization happens.

Creating (*Forming or Improvising*)   Obviously, creating pervades the entire range of processes involved in forming drama. Although creation is, in one sense, an individual, subjective process in drama, the action of dramatic creation often demands collaboration between two or more persons. Participants learn to select, to synthesize, to use others' ideas and experiences as springboards, to reformulate, and to elaborate in order to achieve an artistic whole. Here conscious choice and manipulation of patterns of ideas, of language, or of activity to suit specific purposes occurs.

Communicating   Crucial to informal dramatics processes is the involvement of individuals from a variety of communicative and expressive stances. As drama participants plan; collaborate; try out various ideas and personae, both singly and in response to each other; and, finally, as they reflect upon shared experiences, abundant opportunities arise for both participatory and spectatorial language. Other pertinent characteristics of creative dramatics that suggest its potential for stimulating children's conceptual and linguistic growth stem from its holistic and interactive nature. In a typical creative dramatics experience, there is frequent simultaneous involvement of all participants in both voiced and unvoiced expression. While the languaging is receptive in part, greater focus is usually put on expressive aspects of language and on movement. Nonverbal forms of dramatic expression are seen as particularly growth inducing because students can be challenged to explore meanings and ways of sharing them fully without relying on language customarily used to label and thus to shape experiences. Specifically, students learn to communicate nonverbally through gesture, action, and expressive body movement and to use a variety of elements unique to drama. These elements include light, color, shape, sound, and space.

In considering the oral composing processes in drama, the differences between talk and drama deserve attention. Barnes (1968) identified three points of variance:

> Movement and gesture play a larger part [in drama] in the expression of meaning; a group working together upon an improvisation needs more deliberately and consciously to collaborate; the narrative framework allows for repetition and provides a unity that enables the action more easily to take on symbolic status—to have meaning beyond the immediate situation in which it occurs. (p. 8)

Dramatic Process Research

What confirmation of the model of creative dramatics presented here or of any proposed model exists? Psychological processes involved in drama are not well understood, one obvious problem being the necessity of making inferences from overt behaviors. To date, very little systematic direct observation of drama participants in action has been reported.

Two nonempirical studies exemplify foundational efforts. In order to describe in analytic fashion the nature of creative dramatics as a discipline, Ann Shaw (1970) attempted to identify and classify in taxonomical form the cognitive and affective behaviors expected of participants in creative dramatics experiences. Using the Bloom and Krathwohl (Shaw, 1970) taxonomies as a base, Shaw accomplished the organization of the many objectives of creative drama propounded in scattered descriptions of techniques and activities by using a simple-to-difficult sequence. Little subsequent effort has been made to verify this progression of objectives with children, although Koziol (1973) did make a more modest analysis of the intellectual processes required of students in drama classes at the secondary school level.

In an effort to describe the actual behavior of children during creative dramatics sessions, Ayllon and Snyder (1969) attempted to measure
the effectiveness of two specific procedures on the overt responses of five
first grade children. In an initial experiment, the children were given on
an individual basis a series of prompts, which were primarily verbal (questions or directions), but visual and tactile as well. A positive relationship
was observed between the number of prompts given and the number of
motor and verbal responses elicited from the child. A second experiment
involved groups of children watching a model (another child) respond to
verbal prompts. The high or low score of the model was found to relate
positively to the dramatic response scores given the children who subsequently responded to prompts. Not only did both experiments indicate
that child participants in dramatics situations are influenced by stimuli
presented them, but also that responses are categorizable. Two broad
categories, sensory and activity, were used. Responses were further
broken down according to the topic of the drama situation into groups
such as: sensory—visual, emotional manifestations, play, and vocal;
activity—walking and running, movement in place, and facial gesture.
Any interpretation of the findings, however, must account in two ways
for the deviance of the experimental situation from typical creative dramatics experiences: the use of isolated individual work by children and
the use of models for children to follow.

Lazier and Sutton-Smith (1970) carried on further research on creative dramatics procedures and processes. Their initial efforts were aimed
at formulating a method of rating dramatic involvement of child participants as well as describing systematically the techniques utilized by
the teacher-leaders. Subsequent procedures were aimed at describing
developmental characteristics of differing age levels of children engaged in
carrying out three sequentially more difficult improvisational tasks on an
individual basis. Analysis of videotyped data samples revealed that some
age differences in specified, observable behaviors did exist. It was reported
that the improvisations of the younger subjects (6;0 to 8;5 years) were
episodic, stylized, and freer. Comparatively, those of the older children
(9;0 to 12;0 years) were Scribean, that is, formulized; more unified, more
specific, localized in time, place, and action; and more conforming. The
ultimate construction of an Inventory of Dramatic Behavior (IDB) did
provide a vehicle for potentially accurate recording of incidences of
specific observable dramatic behaviors and minimization of subjective
judgments of quality or appropriateness (Lazier, 1971). Variables
measured included time; space traversed; number of stops; dramatic
incidents created within each scene; novel incidents; repeated acts; and
characters created (pp. 158–159). The value of this numeric data,

however, insofar as it actually describes the nature of dramatic processes, both verbal and nonverbal, is open to question. The inventory at least represents an initial effort to obtain systematic observational data upon which pedagogical assumptions might be based and indicates the possibility of making more sophisticated systematic comparisons of developmental behavior in creative dramatics.

Research in dramatic processes can be likened to other research in composing. It is, by necessity, less scientific than technological research because complicated human functions are involved. However, as Barritt and Kroll (1978) point out, it should be recognized that the alternative, "reduction of complexity by forcing statements into behavioral objectives—will lead to an understanding not of the original concepts, but of the behavioral ones—and they are often not the same" (p. 57). It is obvious that these studies tap on a superficial level selected aspects of children's overt behaviors in a drama session. The holistic model of creative dramatics processes described here is far from substantiated.

FOR DISCUSSION

1. Why do researchers believe that creative drama can affect cognitive and language development?
2. Youngers discusses creative dramatics as employing symbolic tools. What other kinds of activities could be integrated into the language arts curriculum that would serve similar purposes?
3. How does the model presented by Youngers compare to the traditional models of language which have elements of listening, speaking, reading, and writing?
4. Is it possible that ability in creative dramatics may be the *result* of cognitive or linguistic development and is not an appropriate method for enhancing cognitive or linguistic development?
5. Differentiate between cognitive processing and affective processing. How do they interact?

REFERENCES

Ayllon, M., and Synder, S. Behavioral objectives in creative dramatics. *Journal of Educational Research*, 1969, *62*, 355–359.

American Council for the Arts in Education: Arts, Education and Americans Panel. *Coming to our senses*. New York: McGraw-Hill, 1977.

Anastasiow, N. *Oral language: Expression of thought*. Newark, Del.: International Reading Association, 1971.

Barnes, D. (Ed.). *Drama in the English classroom*. (The Dartmouth Seminar Papers.) Champaign, Illinois: National Council of Teachers of English, 1968.

Barritt, L., and Kroll, B. Some implications of cognitive-developmental psychology for research in composing. In C. Cooper and L. Odell (Eds.),

Research on composing. Urbana, Illinois: National Council of Teachers of English, 1978.

Britton, J., Burgess, T., Martin, N., McLeod, A., and Rosen, H. *The development of writing abilities (11–18).* (Schools Council Publications.) London: Macmillan Education Ltd., 1975.

Burton, D. Research in the teaching of English: The troubled dream. *Research in the Teaching of English,* 1973, *2,* 160–189.

Coggin, P. *Uses of drama.* London: Thames and Hudson, 1958.

Courtney, R. *Play, drama and thought: The intellectual background to drama in education* (3rd ed.). New York: Drama Book Specialists, 1974.

Duke, C. *Creative dramatics and English teacher.* Urbana: National Council of Teachers of English, 1974.

El'Konin, D. Ob uslovnykh refleksakh na slozhnye slovesnye razdrazhiteli u shkol'nikov. [On conditioned reflexes to complex verbal stimuli in children of school age.] In *Materialy Soveshchaniya po Psikhologii.* Moscow: Akao Pedag. Nauk RSFSR, 1957, pp. 371–379.

Feitelson, D., and Ross, G. The neglected factor—play. *Human Development,* 1973, *16,* 202–223.

Flavell, J. H. The development of inferences about others. In T. Mischel (Ed.), *Understanding other persons.* Oxford: Blackwell, 1974.

Furner, B. A. Creative writing through creative dramatics. *Elementary English,* March 1978, pp. 405–408; 416.

Great Britain Department of Education and Science. *Drama* (Education Survey 2). London: Her Majesty's Stationery Office, 1967.

Hartshorn, E., and Brantley, J. Effects of dramatic play on classroom problem-solving ability. *Journal of Educational Research,* February 1973, 243–246.

Hendricks, B. L. Mythmaking with children through improvisation. *Speech Teacher,* 1973, *22,* 226–230.

Irwin, E. C. Facilitating children's language development through play. *Speech Teacher,* 1975, *24,* 15–23.

Kagan, J. *Understanding children: Behavior, motives and thought.* New York: Harcourt, Brace, Jovanovich, 1971.

Karioth, J. Creative drama as an aid in developing creative thinking abilities. *Speech Teacher,* November 1970, *19,* 301–309.

Koziol, S. Dramatization and educational objectives. *English Journal* November 1973, *1,* 167–1; 170.

Kroll, B. M. *Cognitive egocentrism and written discourse.* Unpublished doctoral dissertation, University of Michigan, 1977.

Langer, S. *Philosophy in a new key.* Cambridge, Massachusetts: Harvard University Press, 1957.

Lazier, G. A systematic analysis of developmental differences in dramatic improvisational behavior. *Speech Monographs,* August 1971, *38,* 156–165.

Lazier, G., and Sutton-Smith, B. *Assessment of role induction and role involvement in creative drama.* (Final Report of Project No. 90032). Washington, D.C.: United States Department of Health, Education, and Welfare, 1970.

Lewis, M. M. *Language, thought, and personality in infancy and childhood.* New York: Basic Books, 1963.

Lewis, P. H. *The relationship of sociodramatic play to various cognitive abilities in kindergarten children.* Unpublished doctoral dissertation, Ohio State University, 1972.

Lieberman, J. N. Playfulness and divergent thinking: An investigation of their relationship at the kindergarten level. *Journal of Genetic Psychology*, 1965, *107*, 219–224.

Littig, E. *Drama as an important classroom tool.* (Project Overview). Green Bay Northeast Wisconsin In-School Television Project, August 1975.

Lovinger, S. L. Socio-dramatic play and language development in preschool disadvantaged children. *Psychology in the Schools*, 1974, *11*, 313–320.

Luria, A. R., and Yudovich, F. I. *Speech and the development of mental processes in the child.* New York: Humanities Press, 1959.

Martlew, M., Connolly, K., and McCleod, C. Language use, role and context in a five-year old. *Child Language*, 1976, *5*, 81–99.

McGregor, M. Cognitive development through creative dramatics. *Speech Teacher*, 1973, *22*, 220–225.

Menyuk, P. C. *The acquisition and development of language.* Englewood Cliffs, New Jersey: Prentice Hall, 1970.

Piaget, J. *Play, dreams, and imitation in childhood.* New York: Norton, 1962.

Reed, L. Creative drama in the language arts program, or "Catch that crab before he finds a hole!" (ERIC/RCS Report). *Elementary English*, January 1974), *51*, 103–110.

Rosen, C. The effects of sociodramatic play on problem-solving behavior among culturally disadvantaged preschool children. (Doctoral dissertation, University of Georgia, 1972). *University Microfilms (Ann Arbor) Dissertation Abstracts*, 72, 2536.

Rosen, C., and Rosen, H. *The language of primary school children.* Harmondsworth, Middlesex, England: Penguin Education for the Schools Council, 1973.

Rugg, H., and Shumaker, A. *The child-centered school.* New York: World Book, 1928.

Sachs, J., and Devin, J. Young children's use of age-appropriate speech styles in social interaction and role-playing. *Journal of Child Language*, 1975, *3*, 81–98.

Shaw, A. M. A taxonomical study of the nature and behavioral objectives of creative dramatics. *Educational Theatre Journal*, December 1970, *22*, 361–372.

Shaw, A. M. Co-respondents: The child and drama. In N. McCaslin (Ed.), *Children and drama.* New York: David McKay, 1975.

Siks, G. B. *Drama with children.* New York: Harper & Row, 1977.

Singer, J. *The child's world of make believe.* New York: Academic Press, 1972.

Smilansky, S. *The effects of sociodramatic play on disadvantaged pre-school children.* New York: John Wiley and Sons, 1968.

Stewig, J. W. What do we really know about creative drama? *Annual Conference on Language Arts Education*, 1976, *2*, 1–12.

Sutton-Smith, B. The role of play in cognitive development. *Young Children*, 1967, *22*, 361–370.

Vygotsky, L. F. *Thought and language.* Cambridge, Massachusetts, MIT Press, 1962.

Way, B. *Development through drama.* New York: Humanities Press, 1967.

Way, B. *Drama in education.* Presentation at the Educational Arts Association National Conference, Seattle, June 25, 1975.

Wright, M. E. S. The effects of creative drama on person perception. Doctoral dissertation, University of Minnesota, Minneapolis, 1972.

6 | Metalinguistic Awareness, Cognitive Development, and Language Learning

Diane V. Bewell and
Stanley B. Straw

Since the early 1920s educators have debated the question of the appropriate time for children to begin reading instruction. Until recently this issue has been approached from a narrow point of view, but currently the perspective is being broadened as consideration is given to the relationship between cognitive and linguistic development and the impact of this relationship on development in the language arts in general. The question of whether cognitive and linguistic development come together to result in metalinguistic awareness is an issue of importance not only as it concerns readiness for reading instruction, but also as it concerns readiness for instruction at all levels and in all areas of the language arts. In terms of this concept of readiness, children must come to regard language from a relatively objective point of view, analyzing it in terms of phonology, syntax, and semantics. That is, children must have developed metalinguistic awareness, an awareness of language as a thing that can be analyzed.

The purpose of this chapter is to examine the relationships between metalinguistic awareness and competence in the language arts as well as the issues raised by these relationships. The first issue seems to center on learning readiness as it relates to cognitive and metalinguistic development. It has been suggested that the attainment of progressively higher levels of metalinguistic awareness is paralleled by corresponding levels of cognitive development. Cazden (1972) emphasizes that metalinguistic awareness makes special demands and Robeck (1978) asserts that the use of language is one way in which cognitive development is expressed. She relates this cognitive/linguistic development to competence in one area of the language arts, success in beginning reading. This is significant because, if increasing levels of linguistic awareness are dependent upon cognitive development, it is important for the classroom teacher to expand the concept of "readiness" to include psychological or cognitive, as well as linguistic, readiness.

A second issue concerns the relationship of the development of metalinguistic awareness to the development of competence in the language arts. It would seem that the development of degrees of metalinguistic awareness provides essential levels of readiness for growth in language learning. If such a relationship can be substantiated, then metalinguistic awareness should be taken into consideration by developers of curricula, and its significance should be understood by classroom teachers.

Intimately connected with this issue of readiness is the third issue, the relationship between linguistic experience and metalinguistic development and the particular linguistic experiences that promote metalinguistic awareness. If higher levels of metalinguistic development and cognition are related, and if the development of metalinguistic awareness parallels cognitive development, then students should be assessed for their linguistic experiences and should receive appropriate experiences and instruction to enhance metalinguistic awareness.

DEFINITION OF METALINGUISTIC AWARENESS

In order to deal with the issue raised here it is important to establish as specifically as possible what is meant by metalinguistic awareness. Authors have varied somewhat in the definition and use of this term; however, they appear to be in general agreement as to its meaning. Bateson (1976) calls it "those explicit or implicit messages where the subject of discourse is the language" (p. 120). Dale (1976) defines it as "the ability to think about language and to comment on it, as well as to produce and comprehend it" (p. 127). Cazden (1974) calls it "the ability to make language forms opaque and to attend to them in and for themselves" (p. 13). Blachowicz (1978) says it is "awareness of language and linguistic concepts" (p. 875), and Fowles and Glanz (1977) say it is "the ability to manipulate language as an object" (p. 432).

Frequently authors have used other terms which appear to be synonomous with metalinguistic awareness. Mattingly (1972) talks about "linguistic awareness" and Downing (1971) and Robeck (1978) use the term "linguistic concepts." Downing (1969a) also contrasts Vernon's "cognitive confusion" with "cognitive clarity relative to concepts of language." "Cognitive clarity" would seem to be the equivalent of metalinguistic awareness. Evans (1975) uses the term "metalinguistic competence" and cites Karpova's definition as the "ability to separate the message of a sentence from its format and to think objectively about language" (p. 170).

As these authors use the concept, it would appear that metalinguistic awareness or competence requires an ability to go beyond linguistic competence and to judge linguistic performance at an abstract level in one's self and others.

A complicating factor in defining the concept of metalinguistic awareness is that there seems to be a progression in levels of awareness. Miller (1972) theorized the following: "I can conceive of some level of linguistic processing being accessible, in the sense that special transformations, like spelling or versification, could take advantage of it, yet it might not be describable at the level of conscious awareness." Cazden (1974) calls the ability to take advantage of linguistic processing the level of accessibility and the ability to describe such processing, the level of conscious awareness.

There appear to be different types of metalinguistic awareness as well: phonological, semantic, and syntactic. One of the purposes of this article is to investigate whether facility with these types of awareness may reflect both the cognitive development and the linguistic performance of the child. Not only may there be different types of metalinguistic awareness, but within each type there may be varying degrees of awareness.

METALINGUISTIC AWARENESS AND COGNITION

The exact relationship between metalinguistic awareness and cognitive development seems unclear. Little research to date has specifically approached this topic. However, it seems that major events in linguistic development do parallel Piaget's stages of cognitive development. During the sensorimotor stage, the early development of metalinguistic awareness at the phonological level is evident as the young child plays with the sounds of language. Weir (1970), following an intensive analysis of her son's pre-sleep utterances, concluded that the metalingual function is characteristic of young children, as shown by the child's preoccupation with practicing the sounds of language, starting with babbling in the crib. This continues through nursery rhymes and tongue twisters, and is important in the development of an understanding of the language at the phonological level.

According to Dale (1976) syntactic awareness develops at around age 5. This would be during Piaget's preoperational stage, at about the time when the child is moving from the preconceptual to the intuitive stage. Dale cites studies by Gleitman, Gleitman, and Shipley, and de Villiers and de Villers who have investigated the emergence of grammatical awareness in young children. The very young child seems to display the linguistic competence to follow a rule before he can judge grammatical and ungrammatical sentences and before he can state the rule. From these studies, it would seem that the level of syntactic aware-ness achieved by children at around age 5 may be that of accessibility rather than conscious awareness.

In a study which was concerned with metalinguistic functioning in the area of syntactic development, Kail and Segui (1977) attempted to study the development with age of linguistic and cognitive abilities. An analysis of their results suggested that the development of progressively higher levels of metalinguistic awareness enabled the subject to consider the words in the stimulus groups as different parts of speech, that is, to perceive words as fulfilling different roles in different sentences. This study seems to suggest that in order to perform the task presented, the child must have a concept of the word as divorced from the speech stream and must have some concept of the privileges of occurrence.

The concept of privileges of occurrence leads to a consideration of the development of semantic awareness. This does not appear until the child reaches the concrete operational stage, for it is not until then that he masters the distinction between words as symbols and the things they symbolize.

Cazden (1972) suggested that a clue to the development of semantic awareness may lie in the syntagmatic/paradigmatic shift which takes place sometime during the early elementary school years. This is also the period during which children are moving from the preoperational to the concrete operational stage of cognitive development.

Following the report of his work on the syntagmatic/paradigmatic shift, Anglin (1970) asks the following question, which suggests that metalinguistic awareness at the semantic level may develop concurrently with the shift:

> . . . within the child's own body of utterances there exists a potential indi-cant of the most abstract semantic relations among words. . . . Moreover, in his spontaneous speech the child does treat the members of a grammatical class as equivalent by respecting their privileges of occurrence. How does one reconcile this ability with his apparent inability to treat them as equivalent in our other tasks? (p. 101)

He then goes on to hypothesize that this ability to treat members of a grammatical class as equivalent in spontaneous speech may parallel the fact that the use of the rules of grammar in spontaneous speech appears much earlier than the ability to describe these rules, that is, competence precedes awareness.

A study by Bigaj, Dinnan, and Crable (1977) may provide some insight into the relationship between semantic awareness and cognitive development. In this study, the *Peabody Picture Vocabulary Test* and the *Paradigmatic/Syntagmatic Inventory* were given to subjects at the end of first grade. The subjects were identified by their teachers as being either good or poor readers. It was found that there was a significant difference in favor of the good readers in the measure of paradigmatic behavior. A significant correlation was also found between the *PPVT* and the *P/S Inventory*. One might hypothesize that the poor readers had not reached the level of concrete operations and that this was reflected in both their poor reading success and their tendency to associate syntagmaticly.

It would seem, therefore, that the types of metalinguistic awareness are acquired in a particular order: first phonological, then syntactic, and finally semantic. It would further seem that this acquisition parallels the stages of cognitive development identified by Piaget.

A study carried out by Markman (1977), although not dealing with linguistic processing per se, may give some indication of the relationship between metalinguistic awareness and cognitive development. She investigated the development of children's awareness of their own misunderstanding. She suggested that current work in cognitive development indicates that individuals develop an awareness of reasoning which allows them to assess their cognitive processes because they come to take an active, self-directive role in certain areas of cognition. She hypothesized that children's initial lack of awareness of their own failure to comprehend is due to their failure to engage in constructive processes which operate on the original input. Two studies involving first through third graders were undertaken. It was found that the first graders were more likely to become aware of their deficient understanding when they had to enact the procedure, the enacting forcing them to process more thoroughly the information they had heard. It would seem that older children can engage in metamemorial activities. They have an awareness of what it is to remember and consciously engage in activities which facilitate remembering. It may be that listening to instructions requires an analysis of the linguistic input and an awareness of the discrepancies in linguistic cues translatable into action, that is, a degree of metalinguistic awareness.

Christie's study (1977) of age-related increases in memory also investigated metamemorial activities. The constructive processes considered were deliberate mnemonic strategies to retain meaningful prose passages. The subjects, 40 first grade children, listened to a tape-recorded passage. Only half the subjects were told there would be a memory task and only half were presented with contextual information necessary for discerning high order relations in the passage. The results suggested that increase in memory for prose was age-related, due in part to the development of mnemonic strategies, a kind of awareness of the structure of the stimuli. That the older children used deliberate mnemonic strategies may be indicative of an awareness of the need to manipulate the information in order to store it.

Although it is not clear whether one is causal of the other, there appears to be at least a parallel relationship between the development of metalinguistic awareness and cognition. Phonological awareness may have its roots in the sensorimotor stage, syntactic awareness in the pre-operational stage, and semantic awareness in the concrete operational stage. However, there is a paucity of empirical research in this area. Nonetheless, what evidence there is suggests that the issue of an understanding of the concept of metalinguistic readiness and its relationship to cognitive development is of importance to the classroom teacher.

METALINGUISTIC AWARENESS AND LANGUAGE LEARNING

When considering the issue of the development of metalinguistic awareness as it relates to the development of competence in the language arts, two names occur repeatedly in the research reports, Piaget and Vygotsky.

Piaget (1959) noted that children use certain words appropriately in the stream of speech and yet cannot understand them when they are considered as single words. He concluded that children are aware of the sentence before they become aware of individual words. This degree of awareness would appear to have implications in terms of readiness for reading and writing because the child who is not aware of words as individual entities will have difficulty comprehending the purpose of much beginning reading instruction. For example, the learning of sight words will be a mechanical rather than a meaningful experience.

Vygotsky (1962) made a powerful statement regarding written language that has had an impact on the investigations regarding metalinguistic awareness and the language arts, particularly reading:

> Written speech is a separate linguistic function, differing from oral speech in both structure and mode of functioning. Even its minimal development requires a high level of abstraction. . . . Our studies show that it is the abstract quality of written language that is the main stumbling block, not the under-development of small muscles or any other mechanical obstacles. (pp. 98–99)

One implication of Vygotsky's statement is that in order to cope with the abstract quality of written language, the child must have reached a level of cognitive and linguistic development that will allow him to understand the concept of the word.

Reading Instruction

Following the work of Piaget and Vygotsky, researchers have produced a series of studies, generally related to beginning reading instruction, which have investigated the young child's awareness of words as entities in and of themselves and of the abstract terminology related to language and early reading instruction. These studies have investigated the degree of metalinguistic awareness in young children of individual constituents in a stream of language. They have studied the young child's ability to discriminate among the graphic representation of letters, words, and sentences, and to distinguish among orally produced phonemes, syllables, words, and sentences. Many of these studies have also attempted to determine the child's understanding of such words as *letter*, *number*, *word*, *sentence*, and *sound*.

Reid (1966) was a pioneer in this area, and her work seems to have greatly influenced subsequent investigations. From her analysis of answers to questions collected in an initial set of interviews conducted with children in their first year of school, she concluded that children have a very imprecise idea of the elements involved in the reading act. She attributed this to their total lack of ability to reflect on the essentials of their own spoken language. Her analysis of subsequent interviews showed that awareness was not easily or swiftly obtained, and she pointed out the need for research investigating the effect of instruction on the development of metalinguistic awareness.

One researcher whose work has been greatly influenced by the Reid study is Downing (1969a, 1969b, 1970, 1971), who was prompted to undertake studies which were in part a replication and in part an extension of Reid's.

Downing's replicated interviews produced results similar to those of Reid. Downing (1969a) surmised that the three approaches (interview, concrete stimuli, and experimental methods) used in the study, taken together, confirm Reid's original conclusions that young beginners have difficulty in understanding the *purpose* of written language, and that they have only a vague idea of how people read and have a special difficulty in understanding the *abstract* terms.

The children in this study made slow progress through the course of the year in linguistic awareness, none of them coming to an adult-like categorization of "a word." Downing (1971) infers that it is only after considerable experience with the written word that children come to a solid understanding of the concept of a word. Downing (1969a) states:

> 'The spaces stop the words from getting stuck together' might be the typical first real insight of the child. At the same time, in analyzing his own speech for the purpose of writing, he may learn to isolate the words and separate them in their written representation by larger spaces then those between the letters within words. (p. 18)

Similar conclusions, that metalinguistic awareness is developed through the act of learning to read and write, occurred as well in the work of other researchers like Francis (1973) and Evans (1975).

A study which appears to have been developed without reference to Reid or Downing but which contains interesting parallels is that of Meltzer and Herse (1969). This investigation relied on purely visual stimuli and attempted to investigate to what extent 39 children in the third month of the first grade were able to discriminate the boundaries of written words. The results indicated that the subjects experienced what Downing has called "cognitive confusion." Meltzer and Herse further concluded that the development of concepts of word boundaries is sequential and developmental and that reading requires children to regard language from a new point of view, analyzing it in terms of structure. That is, children must have developed an awareness of language as a thing which can be analyzed, a kind of metalinguistic awareness, before mastering the act of reading.

Francis (1973) set out to trace children's comprehension of instructional terms and their abilities to identify units in written and spoken language as they learned to read.

In her discussion, Francis agreed that her results confirm Reid's and Downing's findings that children's understanding of such technical terminology as *word*, *letter*, *number*, and *name*, is unclear. She disagreed with Downing's conclusion that the concepts are abstract, and felt, rather, that the problem was that the concepts overlap in their application and are somewhat ill-defined. She did not quarrel with Vygotsky's view that the abstract nature of written language is a problem for children, but she did not believe that this was the same thing as the question of the type of terminology used in teaching.

Francis' results tend to confirm the theory that learning to read has a positive effect on the development of metalinguistic awareness.

> It was as though the children have never thought to analyze speech, but in learning to read had been forced to recognize units and sub-divisions. . . . Young children lack a consciously analytic approach to speech and their notions of units of language appear to be derived from analysis of written forms as they learn to read. (pp. 22–23)

In an investigation using children from a different cultural background (Canadian rather than British) Downing and Oliver (1974) continued to examine the development of the child's awareness of what constitutes spoken sounds and words. The results tended to confirm the findings of Downing's previous study. They state:

> Young children do not have an adequate concept of what constitutes the spoken "word," and the results extend these findings to a culturally different population of children. In addition, the present findings tend to show that as children grow older, their concept of what constitutes the spoken "word" improves. (p. 580)

Downing and Oliver attributed this to cognitive confusion, a state in which many young children begin school. As the child matures, cognitive clarity in basic concepts of language is gained which reflects a degree of metalinguistic awareness.

In an investigation which was exploratory in nature, Holden and MacGinitie (1972) studied kindergarten children's concepts of word boundaries in both speech and print. They also attempted to discover if there was a correspondence between concepts of spoken and written word boundaries. The children were discerned to have difficulty in isolating function words from content words. It would appear that this group of children had not arrived at a level of awareness at which they could accurately segment all the individual words in an utterance. Furthermore, they seemed to have better developed concepts of content words than of function words.

In the second phase of the investigation Holden and MacGinitie asked the subjects to identify, from a choice of four 1-line sentences printed on a card, the line which had the same number of words as he had just counted in the tape-recorded sentence. From this data, it was concluded that the subjects did not divide utterances into units that corresponded to conventional printed words and that "a first-grade teacher cannot take for granted that children will understand her when she talks about 'words' and their printed representation. Nor can she assume that the concepts can be quickly and easily taught, since printed word units do not correspond to the way the child thinks the utterance should be divided" (p. 556). These results seem to confirm earlier conclusions that young children lack a clear concept of words as adults define them and that they do not segment speech according to adult conventions.

Evan's (1975) work derives from Karpova, whom she credits with suggesting that metalinguistic "competence" can be measured by a sentence segmentation task. Evans tested kindergarten and grade one children in September and December. She found that there had been improvement in sentence segmentation ability in both grade level groups, but particularly in the grade one group, over a 3-month period. She did not feel that her results suggested that sentence segmentation ability was predictive of differential success in beginning reading, but she stated that the first grade children appeared to have acquired an understanding of how to deal with words apart from their meanings as they were being introduced to reading. She suggested that the act of learning to read may enable children to attend to the structure of the sentence rather than simply to process it in meaning units. This lends support to Downing's (1971) suggestion that metalinguistic awareness is strengthened through the act of learning to read and write.

Another study which seems to support the impact of reading instruction on metalinguistic awareness is the first of three experiments reported by Pick et al. (1978). The results indicated that these children did have some accurate knowledge of the characteristics of printed words before they began to read and that this knowledge increased with age. Pick et al. also credited reading instruction with gains made in awareness of the word. "Obviously, during the course of learning to read, they [the students] acquire a great deal of new knowledge about what words are" (p. 613). The fact that even the younger subjects had some knowledge of what words are is not discussed by Pick et al., but the results may be affected by the high socioeconomic status of the group.

Begy and Cahill (1978) attempted to determine if the completion of a "Modified Rebus Reading Readiness Program" would enable kindergarten children to segment oral language into words significantly better than a control group which had not been exposed to such a program. Posttreatment tests indicated that the experimental group was significantly better at segmenting oral language than the control group. This lends support to the thesis that the act of learning to read assists in the development of cognitive clarity or metalinguistic awareness. The authors interpreted their findings as supportive of the idea that the Modified Rebus Reading Readiness Program provides experiences and activities which promote cognitive clarity.

An additional area of interest, which specifically concerns reading, is the influence of syntactic awareness on comprehension. Weber (1970) studied early readers' use of context and attempted to assess the grammatical dimension of their reading performance, that is, their sensitivity to grammatical structure. She found that weaker readers do not differ from better readers in their use of grammatical constraints for the identification of words in a string. However, when ungrammatical errors were made, only the better readers consistently corrected themselves. This may indicate a difference in the level of awareness in better and poorer readers. Perhaps poor readers have the tacit ability to recognize grammatical constraints, but when grammatical constraints are violated, it is the better readers who have the level of awareness sufficient to correct the violation.

Writing

Another area in the language arts in which some research related to metalinguistics awareness is available is spelling. Early spelling development depends heavily on awareness at the phonological level and it is only when a more sophisticated level of metalinguistic awareness is attained that the child is able to make use of abstract spelling strategies.

Read (1971) studied the spelling of 20 early writers and found that they had consistently developed a letter-name-based spelling system founded on their knowledge of English phonology. It would appear that the young child, in developing an initial spelling system, is operating at a purely phonemic level, giving no consideration to the morphology of the language.

Beers, Beers, and Grant (1977) wondered if this letter-name spelling strategy remained a basic tool of students as they entered school and encountered formal instruction. The results of their study indicated that there continued to be a heavy reliance on letter names to represent vowel sounds. It also showed that children used more advanced strategies for high frequency words but reverted to less advanced strategies for low frequency words. The authors interpreted this as an indication that "formal spelling instruction may not be appropriate until children have had ample time to develop an understanding of word-attack principles" (p. 242). This implies that until the child reaches a cognitive level appropriate for the comprehension of the abstract nature of word-attack principles, little is gained from such instruction. Students require a level of metalinguistic awareness beyond the phonological level which will allow them to apply the abstract principles needed in becoming a competent speller.

Zutell (1979) was interested in extending the investigation of children's spelling strategies as they relate to certain aspects of Piagetian cognitive development. The researcher constructed a test of 36 words to measure spelling ability and a battery of tests to measure a child's ability to decenter. Results indicated that as grade level increased, so did the use of sophisticated spelling strategies. Performance on the decentration battery and levels of spelling strategies were significantly correlated and Zutell concluded from this that learning to spell was not simply a matter of enough drill work and/or rote memorization, but that the development of spelling proficiency seemed to involve both cognitive and linguistic awareness. Perhaps as the child grows cognitively and is able to decenter, he becomes aware of aspects of the language which enable him to use more abstract or sophisticated spelling strategies.

An exploratory study by Hall, Moretz, and Statom (1976) investigated both spelling and writing in the earliest stages of writing development. The definition of early writing as used by Hall, Moretz, and Statom was relatively broad:

> To be classified as an early writer a child's efforts at writing should contain legible (distinct) letter and/or word forms, and it should be evident that the child is trying to communicate or represent specific letters, words, or ideas through writing. (p. 583)

They pointed out that ability in writing and spelling often precedes early reading, and they set out to investigate environmental factors which might contribute to the development of early writing. The researchers identified certain environmental traits which could be influential in the development of early writing. Most of the parents were college graduates; parents or siblings frequently engaged in writing activities; writing materials were easily accessible; books and other print materials were available; the children frequently were read to or observed other family members reading. The authors suggested that since early writing often precedes early reading, "comparison studies of children's concepts of language might reveal contributions of writing to cognitive clarity about language" (p. 585). By implication they seem to be suggesting that early writing and the home experiences that appear to contribute to early writing may also develop metalinguistic awareness.

One area of the language arts in which one would expect to find many investigations of the influence of metalinguistic awareness is written composition. Vygotsky (1962) stated:

> All these traits of written speech explain why its development in the school-child falls far behind that of oral speech. The discrepancy is caused by the child's proficiency in spontaneous, unconscious activity and his lack of skill in abstract, deliberate activity. As our studies showed, the psychological functions on which written speech is based have not even begun to develop in the proper sense when instruction in writing starts. It must build on barely emerging, rudimentary processes. (pp. 100–101)

When one looks for research in this field, however, very little can be found. In fact, as recently as 1975 Britton et al. stated:

> It seems likely that a writer draws upon his linguistic experience both as a speaker and as a writer/reader in order to write. In what relation do the two processes stand, and does the relationship vary with individuals? We would certainly suppose that the internalizing process—say of the forms of the written language met in reading—will have selective laws of its own. . . . Recent studies of reading have stressed "linguistic awareness" as something essential to reading and extra to competence in speech: there is clearly an area of common interest here that we need to pursue. (p. 200)

LINGUISTIC EXPERIENCE

In addition to the relationship between instruction in the language arts and growth in metalinguistic awareness, there appears to be a relation between the quality and quantity of linguistic experiences and metalinguistic awareness. A number of studies already reported have implications related to linguistic experience and metalinguistic awareness. Downing (1971), Francis (1973), Gleitman and Rozin (1973), Evans (1975), Begy and Cahill (1978), and Pick et al. (1978) all found a relationship between developing metalinguistic awareness and reading instruction. Hall et al. (1976) indicated that there may be a relationship between early writing and linguistic experiences in the home.

Recently, several studies have indicated that culturally influenced linguistic experiences may have a bearing on the development of metalinguistic awareness. A research study aimed at discovering linguistic experiences which influence cognitive clarity was undertaken by Downing, Ollila, and Oliver (1975). Their stated aim was to obtain further evidence of the effects of different home backgrounds on the development of concepts of language and writing in children.

The authors suggested that the results indicated that metalinguistic awareness as related to literacy was correlated with sociocultural factors. They expressed concern that current teacher training in linguistics may not be sufficient to enable teachers of beginning reading to determine the level of linguistic development children required for initial success.

Downing, Ollila, and Oliver (1977) continued to investigate the influence of linguistic experience on the development of language concepts in a study designed to determine whether students from higher socioeconomic neighborhoods would have better developed concepts of language than children from lower socioeconomic neighborhoods.

The findings reported that high socioeconomic children had significantly superior initial scores on the cognitive tests (Orientation to Literacy, Understanding Literacy Behavior, and Technical Language of Literacy) than the middle or low socioeconomic students, but that after a period of kindergarten experience these differences disappeared on all but Technical Language of Literacy. There was a high correlation between the Technical Language of Literacy test and the perceptual test (word matching, letter recognition, and initial phonemes). There was a significant general improvement in scores on the conceptual tests from initial test to retest. The authors conclude:

> These findings seem to support the view that the child's development of concepts of language is related to experiences of speech and writing or printing at home and in kindergarten. Awareness of the functions of forms of language and consciousness of linguistic categories are fostered in richer home backgrounds, and the teacher's concern with language in kindergarten also stimulates conceptual development in this area. (p. 280)

They suggest that it would be interesting to discover what kinds of experiences bring about differences in the child's development of language concepts or metalinguistic awareness.

CONCLUSIONS AND IMPLICATIONS

There is strong evidence to suggest that a relationship exists between the development of metalinguistic awareness and language learning. It seems that readiness for beginning reading instruction is related to a certain level of metalinguistic awareness, which, in turn, seems to reflect cognitive development. This level of awareness is related to prior linguistic experiences. A child coming to school from an environment which has provided little in the way of linguistic experiences should be recognized by the teacher in order that the student can be provided with appropriate opportunities to develop linguistically and cognitively. If the teacher in structuring instructional activities is aware of the implications of the concept of metalinguistic awareness, then it would seem that both cognitive and linguistic growth could be facilitated, leading to increased ability or performance in language arts.

Teachers need to be knowledgeable in the areas of linguistic and cognitive development in order to assess the psychological readiness of their students for language arts instruction in the classroom. They should be aware of Downing's (1977) observation that new levels of metalinguistic competence may "occur over and over again throughout all years of education as new concepts of language are encountered by the pupil" (p. 38).

Teachers of beginning reading should be able to assess the level of metalinguistic awareness in their students in terms of their concepts of the purposes of reading and writing; words as units in the stream of speech; and words, syllables, and phonemes and their relationships.

All language arts teachers need to be aware of the prior linguistic experiences of their pupils and the influence that it may have had on metalinguistic development and, subsequently, on language learning. Following from this, teachers also need to provide opportunities and to design classroom experiences to aid in the development of metalinguistic awareness.

The fact that the literature in metalinguistic awareness is obviously incomplete and, at times, only implicative, points up a need for additional research in the area. A number of questions bear investigation, including:

1. Is it possible to influence cognitive development through instruction which enhances metalinguistic awareness?
2. Is it possible to aid growth in language processing performance through metalinguistic awareness?
3. What is the effect of increased linguistic experiences on growth in metalinguistic awareness?
4. What impact does teacher ability to identify metalinguistic awareness have on the linguistic growth and success of students?

The concept of metalinguistic awareness in young children is new and, at times, confusing. It seems that language learning and cognitive development are closely related, but the exact nature of that relationship is unclear. One of the ways in which the two may be related is through the construct of metalinguistic awareness. If this is the case, then additional research needs to be done so that the construct can be clearly identified and instructional methods developed for incorporating the development of metalinguistic awareness into the goals of a complete language arts curriculum.

FOR DISCUSSION

1. Is knowledge of formal grammatical rules a kind of metalinguistic awareness? If it is, how does the research outlined by Bewell and Straw relate to Straw's conclusions in Chapter 8?
2. The relationships between thought and language have always seemed unclear. What assumptions about those relationships are made by Bewell and Straw?
3. How do Bewell and Straw perceive readiness for learning? What factors beyond those mentioned in this chapter may affect readiness? How might those same factors affect development of metalinguistic awareness?
4. Dahl in Chapter 1 outlines areas of language learning. How do these relate to Bewell and Straw's levels of metalinguistic awareness?

REFERENCES

Anglin, J. M. *The growth of word meaning.* Cambridge, Massachusetts: MIT Press, 1970.

Bateson, G. A theory of play and fantasy. In J. Bruner and K. Jolly (Eds.), *Play—Its role in development and evolution.* New York: Basic Books, 1976.

Beers, J. W., Beers, C. S., and Grant, K. The logic behind children's spelling. *Elementary School Journal,* 1977, *77,* 238–242.

Begy, G. L., and Cahill, K. The ability of kindergarten children having completed a Modified Rebus Reading Program to segment oral language into words. *Reading World,* 1978, *18,* 27–32.

Bigaj, J. J., Dinnan, J. A., and Crable, E. Word contrasts: beginning readers' responses. *Reading Improvement,* 1977, *14,* 209–211.

Blachowicz, C. L. Z. Metalinguistic awareness and the beginning reader. *The Reading Teacher,* 1978, *31,* 875–6.

Britton, J., Burgess, T., Martin, N., McLeod, A., and Rosen, H. *The development of writing abilities (11–18).* London: Macmillan Education, Ltd., 1975.

Cazden, C. B. *Child language and education.* New York: Holt, Rinehart and Winston, 1972.

Cazden, C. B. Play with language and metalinguistic awareness: One dimension of language experience. *OMEP,* 1974, *6,* 12–24.

Christie, D. J. *Memory for prose: Development of mnemonic strategies and use of high order relations.* Unpublished paper delivered at the Biennial Meeting of the Society for Research in Child Development, 1977.

Dale, P. S. *Language development: Structure and function.* New York: Holt, Rinehart and Winston, 1976.

Downing, J. How children think about reading. *The Reading Teacher*, 1969, *23*, 217–230. (a)

Downing, J. The perception of linguistic structure in learning to read. *The British Journal of Educational Psychology*, 1969, *39*, 267–271. (b)

Downing, J. Children's concepts of language in learning to read. *Educational Research*, 1970, *12*, 106–112.

Downing, J. The development of linguistic concepts in children's thinking. *Research in the Teaching of English*, 1971, *4*, 5–19.

Downing, J. Linguistics for infants. *Reading*, 1977, *11*, 36–45.

Downing, J., and Oliver, P. The child's concept of a word. *Reading Research Quarterly*, 1973–74, *9*, 568–582.

Downing, J., Ollila, L., and Oliver, P. Cultural differences in children's concepts of reading and writing. *British Journal of Educational Psychology*, 1975, *45*(3), 312–316.

Downing, J., Ollila, L., and Oliver, P. Concepts of language in children from differing socio-economic backgrounds. *The Journal of Educational Research*, 1977, *70*(5), 277–81.

Evans, M. C. Children's ability to segment sentences into individual words. In G. H. McNinch and W. D. Miller (Eds.), *Reading: Convention and inquiry*. Clemson, South Carolina: National Reading Conference, 1975, 177–180.

Fowles, I., and Glanz, M. E. Competence and talent in verbal riddle comprehension. *Journal of Child Language*, 1977, *4*, 433–452.

Francis, H. Children's experience of reading and notions in units in language. *The British Journal of Educational Psychology*, 1973, *43*, 17–23.

Gleitman, L. R., and Rozin, P. Teaching children by use of a syllabary. *Reading Research Quarterly*, 1973, *8*, 447–483.

Hall, M. A., Moretz, C. A., and Statom, J. Writing before grade one—A study of early writers. *Language Arts*, 1976, *53*, 582–585.

Holden, M. H., and MacGinitie, W. H. Children's conceptions of word boundaries in speech and print. *Journal of Educational Psychology*, 1972, *63*, 551–557.

Kail, M., and Segui, J. Developmental production of utterances from a series of lexemes. *Child Language*, 1977, *5*, 251–260.

Markman, E. M. Realizing that you don't understand: A preliminary investigation. *Child Development*, 1977, *48*, 986–982.

Mattingly, I. G. Reading, the linguistic process, and linguistic awareness. In J. F. Kavanagh and I. G. Mattingly (Eds.), *Language by ear and by eye*. Cambridge, Massachusetts: MIT Press, 1972.

Meltzer, N. S., and Herse, R. The boundaries of written words as seen by first graders. *Journal of Reading Behavior*, 1969, *1*, 3–14.

Miller, G. A. Reflections on the conference. In J. F. Kavanagh and I. G. Mattingly (Eds.), *Language by ear and by eye*. Cambridge, Massachusetts: MIT Press, 1972.

Piaget, J. *The language and thought of the child*. London: Routledge and Kegan Paul Ltd., 1959.

Pick, A. D., Unze, M. G., Brownell, C. A., Drozday, J. C., and Hopmann, M. R. Young children's knowledge of word structure. *Child Development*, 1978, *49*, 669–80.

Read, C. Preschool children's knowledge of English phonology. *Harvard Educational Review*, 1971, *41*, 1–34.

Reid, J. F. Learning to think about reading. *Educational Research*, 1966, *9*, 56–62.

Robeck, C. P. Linguistic concepts and beginning reading. *Reading World*, 1978, *17*, 210–219.

Vygotsky, L. *Thought and language*. Cambridge, Massachusetts: MIT Press, 1962.

Weber, R. First-graders' use of grammatical context in reading. In H. Levin and J. P. Williams (Eds.), *Basic studies on reading*, New York: Basic Books, 1970.

Weir, R. H. *Language in the crib*. The Hague: Mouton, 1970.

Zutell, J. Spelling strategies of primary school children and their relationship to Piaget's concept of decentration. *Research in the Teaching of English*, 1979, *13*(1), 69–80.

7 | Hearing/Listening/Auding: Auditory Processing

Victor Froese

A recent newspaper headline announced: "Doctors learning to listen to patient." The article went on to state that "now and then, a patient feels a doctor is listening with only half an ear, treating the patient as a body rather than a person" (Winnipeg Tribune, 1979). Industry, too, is becoming aware of the importance of listening. A bank newsletter entitled "The Act of Listening" claimed that "only half of the oral messages passed around in the course of a day's work are fully understood" (Royal Bank of Canada, 1979). A *Childhood Education* article suggests that "we need teachers who can hear and respond" (Trubowitz, 1975).

The three references deal with differing connotations to the communication process of "listening" or auditory processing (AP). Intuitively one may subcategorize this process into the physiological act of *hearing*, the perceptual act of *listening*, and the comprehending act of *auding* (adapted from Brown, 1954). Typically the literature related to "listening" fails to make these distinctions; hence, it becomes difficult to know what is being discussed.

The purpose of this chapter is to interpret current research and practice related to the broader receptive communication skill of auditory processing. The narrower terms, *hearing*, *listening*, and *auding*, are used for organizational purposes.

Specifically, the following issues are addressed:

1. Auditory processing models and theories are still primitive in the technical sense (Travers, 1970).
2. "Listening comprehension" as used in much of the literature is analogous to "reading comprehension." The commonly listed "skills" are not skills in the psychological sense; they are labels for the kinds of exercises and questions teachers devise.

3. Hearing is a physiological process; listening is a perceptual process; auding is a comprehension process.
4. A number of useful, theory-based training approaches are emerging from the research literature.

This chapter focuses on research and practice related to continuous discourse rather than that related to isolated speech and word perception. It also eliminates most references to dialect variations and second language learning, although an extensive literature was found in this area. Most references to the handicapped, hearing impaired, and other anomalous conditions are kept to a minimum.

AUDITORY PROCESSING MODELS AND CONSTRUCTS

Oracy is important to most activities in which people interact. The auditory component of oracy has been defined broadly as "the process by which spoken language is converted to meaning in the mind" (Lundsteen, 1979, p. 1). This is obviously an important activity both in school and in the world of work. Rankin (1928) estimated that adults spent approximately 45% of their time in "listening" (AP); in a study by Wilt (1950) it was found that elementary school children were required to "listen" (AP) approximately 58% of the time they were in the classroom.

In the preface to the revised edition of *Listening*, Lundsteen (1979) suggests that "little about listening methodology is supported by reliable and replicable research findings." However, a reasonable amount of theoretical and speculative work abounds in the literature. A number of attempts at clarifying the process of auditory processing are reviewed here in order to let the reader form his own opinions.

The first three models (the term is used very loosely here) are from publications intended for teachers. Figure 1 illustrates a two-dimensional example of an auditory processing model. On the vertical axis we find

	CONTENT	EMOTIONS	AESTHETICS
Attention	1	4	7
Understanding	2	5	8
Evaluation	3	6	9

Figure 1. Example of a two-dimensional auditory processing model. (From Friedman, 1978; reprinted by permission.)

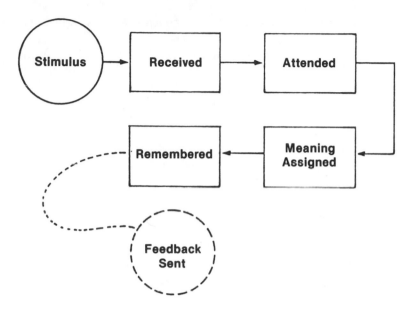

Figure 2. Wolvin and Coakley's model of auditory processing. (From Wolvin and Coakley, 1979. Permission granted by the ERIC Clearinghouse on Reading and Communication Skills.)

points on the "how" continuum beginning with attention, progressing to the mid-point, understanding, and continuing to the far end of the continuum, evaluation. These three states may be viewed as occurring "sequentially, cumulatively, and often almost concurrently" (Friedman, 1978, p. 6). The horizontal axis represents the "what" dimension, the type of message being received. A message may represent content, emotions, aesthetic impact, or some combination of these. Obviously, this model is based on the assumption that the physiological process of hearing is operating normally. Friedman also assumes that categorizing auditory activities according to this model will enhance the instructional process, and he gives examples of each of the nine cells in the model.

In Figure 2 we find Wolvin and Coakley's (1979) model of auditory processing which involves four separate but interrelated components: receiving, attending, assigning meaning, and remembering. It is intended to be a decoding model only and we are told that "memory is probably involved in all aspects of listening" (p. 4). The authors present a series of 38 exercises directed toward each of the four identified components. This model has the potential of recognizing the receiver(s) of the message as an influence on the listening process, but it does not differentiate the types of message being received. Furthermore, the role of memory is not clear. Presumably, working on the components will result in improved auditory processing.

Figure 3 summarizes Lundsteen's (1979) ten steps of proficient listening (AP). Lundsteen cautions that this model is not technically precise, that it is not sequential, that the steps are not entirely independent, and that "most statements based on this framework are tenuous; they are made solely to provide a basis of definition and later objectives" (p. 46). The intent of this model is to assist the teacher in identifying the components of auditory processing so that they will not be overlooked in the classroom. The model is also intended to act as an organizational framework for instructional activities. While this model is more inclusive than the previous two, it does not clearly show how exclusive the components are to listening. Except for steps 1 and 2, the remainder could easily account for the processing of visual, tactile, or other sensory stimuli. The following information processing models indicate somewhat more clearly the central auditory processing roles.

The Mackworth model shown in Figure 4 obviously has broader application than to the reading process. Since it also accounts for auditory input, it may also be applied to auditory processing. A real advantage that this model has over the previous ones is that it shows commonality in the processing mechanisms, beginning with "coding." In curricular terms that implies that auditory processing and reading have similar underlying processes and are different mainly in terms of input stimuli. Many activities affecting auditory processing should affect visual processing of reading.

That is not to say that the Mackworth model is complete and above criticism. For example, the "Echo Box" in listening is considered somewhat analogous to the sensory store in reading, but Lindsay and Norman (1927) consider the Echo Box to be part of short-term memory. Obviously the omission of one stage in the model would give serious problems to its explanatory power. Also, Smith (1971) points out that there are at least six neural relays between a visual input and the brain. While less is probably known about the human auditory system, there is some evidence that a variety of different neural excitations are received by the auditory cortex as well (Whitfield, 1967). Obviously this model does not explain what is happening at those various decision points.

Figure 5 illustrates Sticht, Beck, and Hauke's (1974) developmental model of auding and reading. While the diagram alone does not explain the model adequately, it does show some important aspects of auditory processing that none of the foregoing models have. Particularly noteworthy is the recognition that languaging acts as a bridge between the human's environment and the cognitive system (the arrows in Figure 5 appear to indicate that the bridging is a two-way one). Sticht, Beck,

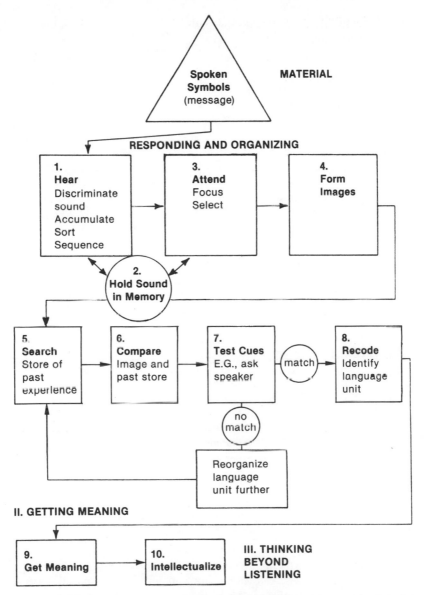

Figure 3.   Flowchart of the steps a proficient listener may take. (From Lundsteen, 1979. Permission granted by the ERIC Clearinghouse on Reading and Communication Skills.)

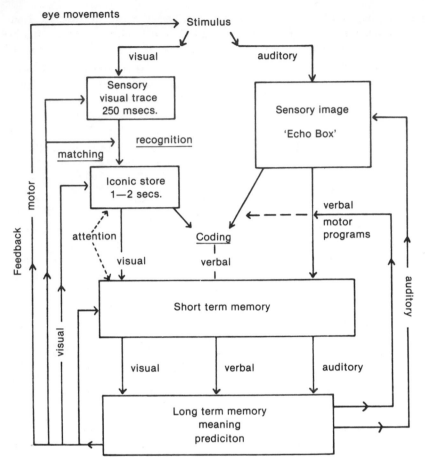

Model of Reading Process

Figure 4.   Mackworth information processing model. (Reprinted from *The Psychology of Reading* by E. J. Gibson and H. Levin by permission of The MIT Press, Cambridge, Massachusetts. Copyright © 1975 by the Massachusetts Institute of Technology.)

and Hanke further explain that conceptualizing is "outside the language itself" (p. 19). That is, one must first acquire a conceptual base and experience in conceptualizing. Then one can learn a sign system by which to communicate with others either through auding or speaking or through reading or writing. This model also distinguishes between hearing, a reflexive process, and auding, an actively controlled and conscious process.

Sticht, Beck, and Hauke (1974) intend this model to be an "ideational scaffolding" on which other more detailed models, such as Mackworth's, may be built. In addition they have compiled data to support four hypotheses predicted by this model: auding and reading become equally effective around the seventh or eighth grade; the relationship between auding and reading increases up to the fourth grade and then stabilizes; the rate of comprehending is very similar between auding and reading; and, there is a reasonable transfer effect between auding and reading.

In summary, then, this section briefly illustrates some commonly found analogies, or models, of auditory processing. The first three models were essentially intended to clarify the process of auditory processing for the teacher; the last two for the researcher. All are based on the synthesis of previous research and practice; only limited research that is based on and generated by the models can be found in the literature. Because of the paucity of substantiating research, these models are best viewed as the precursors of theories in a developmental state. Another indicator of a developing theory is the lack of precision with which terminology is used. Words such as hearing, listening, and auding are not systematically differentiated as used in the literature. Con-

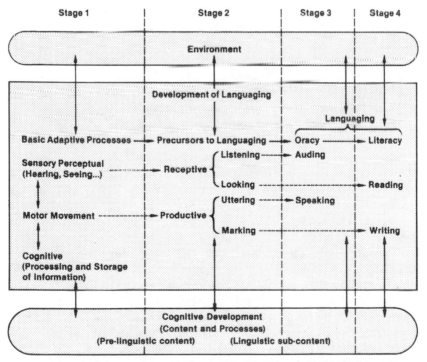

Figure 5.   Developmental model of auding and reading. (From Sticht, Beck, and Hauke, 1974; reprinted by permission.)

sequently, it is difficult to communicate what we do know in a precise manner.

Of even greater importance is the realization that these models indicate very little that is unique to auditory processing. They do not suggest to the teacher or researcher what can be done to enhance auditory processing; they do not lead us to a list of skills unique to auditory processing; and they do not help us in generating curricular information. Also, the models do not consider the non-verbal aspects of oracy or the fact that communication is a two-way process. Further, they fail to say anything about spontaneous speech and how it differs from writing that is read orally. The models are "primitive" in a technical sense and need considerable research and development before they may be relied on.

SKILLS

Words are wise men's counters, they do but reckon with them, but they are the money of fools.

Thomas Hobbes (1588–1679)

Philosophically, the establishment of what constitutes an auditory skill is an important epistemological concern. Words are but counters in this endeavor.

On a more pragmatic level, it is possible to take the tack facetiously suggested by Devine (1978): Define listening skills as what listening tests measure. Or one might follow his second, more serious approach, that is, to ask professionals to judge which are important skills.

Another procedure is to consult lists of objectives compiled by curriculum committees (Edmonton Public School System, 1979) or by other professionals (Lazarus and Knudson, 1967; Flannegan et al., 1971). Often related to these lists are commercial instructional materials such as *Listening Strategies* (Thorn and Richmond, 1970) which provide a series of lessons to develop listening skills.

Yet a different approach may be taken, an approach often labeled "systems technology" (Canada and Lynch, 1975) or "task-analysis." This is essentially the approach of Wilkinson, Stratta, and Dudley (1974), who concluded that the elements of auding were content, contextual constraint, phonology, register, and relationship.

Factor analysis, a complex statistical procedure used to identify commonalities, is another method of identifying skills unique to auditory processing. Spearritt (1962), for example, identified an auding factor which was highly related to verbal comprehension, memory span, and inductive reasoning. Verbal comprehension and redundancy utilization were factors found to be moderately related to auditory processing by

Weaver (1977). Unfortunately, this method cannot go beyond the measures or tests used in the factor analysis and the procedures are rather involved if used for other than experimental purposes.

One of the first attempts to classify and organize auditory processes in a corporate manner was made by the Commission on the English Curriculum of the National Council of Teachers of English (1952), which outlined purposeful, accurate, critical, and responsive or appreciative auditory activities. Two years later (1954) a similarly commissioned group outlined passive or marginal, appreciative, attentive, and analytic auditory processing.

Russell and Russell (1959) compiled a book of 190 aids classified as either *listening*—perception of sounds and words—or *auding*—listening with comprehension. We note here the first systematic attempt to use the terms "listening" and "auding" when addressing teachers.

Because auditory processing and reading are both receptive processes, much of the commercial material has adopted the skills so common to the reading series. Consequently we find skills such as following sequence, finding main ideas, and making inferences identified as auditory skills (Thorn and Richmond, 1970; Burdick and Collins, 1968; Educational Progress Corporation, 1971) In many ways this is an unfortunate turn of events because these long lists of skills have not been supported by research in reading either (Davis, 1968; Froese, 1971).

The most recent attempts at compiling taxonomies of auditory processing skills have been made by Kellogg (1972) and Lundsteen (1979). Both lists are patterned after Bloom's *Taxonomy of Educational Objectives* (1956) and use the recall, translation, application, analysis, synthesis, evaluation breakdown. To some extent the size of language unit (word, sentence, paragraph) is taken into consideration. Lundsteen presents separate hierarchies for general and critical listening; Kellogg groups skills as either getting information or as critical listening.

A slightly different but related hierarchy of auditory processing skills is presented by Weaver and Rutherford (1974). They also acknowledge that "in the absence of research to indicate a specific sequence for auditory abilities, the order was derived from current programs and theories of development of auditory abilities drawn from the review of the literature" (p. 1148). The list proceeds from pre-natal to sixth grade and is organized under environmental, discrimination, and comprehension skills.

These compiled lists of skills are as far as we have progressed in the educational field of auditory processing. Even a cursory inspection can detect overlap, contradiction, and poor logic. For example, how is the identification of a main idea different from making an inference (assuming the main idea is not directly stated)? It is perhaps more accurate to say that these skills are labels for the kinds of exercises and questions teachers can ask rather than being a set of underlying abilities. This situation could well be a case of confusing "money" and "counters" as expressed by Hobbes.

HEARING, LISTENING, AUDING

"We need teachers who can hear and respond" is one of the statements that is quoted at the beginning of this chapter. Implied, of course, is that one can hear and not respond. The difficulty with a developing field is that the terminology is not precise and that intuitive terms may take on specialized functions.

Initially the reader was alerted to the multiple use of the term "listening." It may refer to the physiological process of *hearing*, the perceptual act of *listening*, or the comprehending act of *auding*. In order to clarify this range of meanings, each aspect is elaborated in the following pages.

Hearing

Normally we receive sounds conducted through the air or through our bones. We have little control over most of these sounds and we may not even be consciously aware of them. The human ear is usually thought to be able to detect sounds in the range of 20–20,000 cycles per second or Hertz (Hz), the internationally standardized unit for measuring frequency. The sound range for speech communication is 250 to 3000 Hz. The loudness of sound is measured in decibels (dB), a 55-dB sound being faint speech and an 85-dB sound being very loud conversation. Incidence of hearing impairment in the school population is estimated as between 5% and 10% (Phillips, 1975).

Taylor (1964) suggests that four factors influence hearing: auditory acuity, masking, auditory fatigue, and binaural hearing. These aspects naturally should be known by the teacher.

The aspects of hearing discussed here are only occasionally referred to in auditory processing studies, but they are basic neurophysiological aspects that need careful consideration. For example, Larson and Petersen (1978) reported that results of a study which indicated that 5–6-year-old subjects performed 10% poorer than 20–26-year-old subjects under a +20 signal-to-noise ratio, and 20% poorer under a +10 signal-to-noise ratio (a signal-to-noise ratio of +20 and +10 means that the signal was 20 dB or 10 dB louder than the background noise). The task was to discriminate words in the presence of interfering noise. Although this was a clinical experiment, the results might be considered in the context of self-contained and open area classrooms. Similar findings in terms of younger and older subjects were reported by Hedrick and Kunze (1974).

From a more theoretical perspective, hearing may be conceptualized as the first step in auditory information processing. Massaro (1975) hypothesizes an auditory feature detection and storage function which stores completed sound patterns in the preperceptual auditory storage where it may remain for 250 msec. These components of Massaro's model do not draw on long-term memory and are thereby distinguished from the following processing stages.

It appears, then, that the term *hearing* might be a useful one when speaking about oracy because fairly distinctive measurable and theoretical constructs may be assigned to it.

Listening

"Listen my children and you shall hear..." wrote Longfellow. And indeed one is *hearing* when one *listens*. However, in the sense in which the terms are used here, the quotation would need to be reversed. "Listening" is defined here as a perceptual process which is preceded by the neurophysiological act of hearing described in the previous section.

Gibson (1975) succinctly summarized perceptual learning when she stated that it is "learning to extract relevant information from the manifold available stimulation ... an increase of specificity of discrimination to stimulus input, an increase in differentiation of stimulus information. It is extraction or 'pulling out' rather than adding on. The modification is in *what* is perceived" (p. 13). Gibson goes on to say that perceptual learning is adaptive, active, selective, and progressively differentiating. "Listening" is perceptual learning through the auditory modality. Listening is one aspect of auditory processing which may be conceptualized as involving hearing but preceding auding (which is defined in the following section).

Listening is somewhat akin to Massaro's (1975) primary recognition stage which accounts for the detection of information but without attendant meaning. In the Sticht, Beck, and Hauke (1974) model, listening falls in the "languaging" stage, but "languaging" is somewhat more inclusive. Phonological rules and other sequential constraints operate at the listening level to assist in recognizing auditory information. For example, one is able to recognize what a "sentence" is or that a particular speech is in French or Spanish. In reading it is analogous to "word calling," that is, language processing without processing meaning.

Listening deals with perceptual information processing on the basis of information in the perceptual storage and short- and long-term memory.

A number of common classroom-level factors influence listening. These are mental set, rate of input, distracting associations, knowledge about language (see Chapter 6 by Bewell and Straw on metalinguistic awareness), concentration, and attention. Perhaps it would be more appropriate to say: Hear my children and you may listen.

Auding

Sticht, Beck, and Hauke (1974) suggest that "auding" is the joint occurrence of languaging and listening processes: reading is the joint occurrence of looking and languaging" (p. 17). This analogy aptly points out the dilemma of our current terminology with respect to auditory and visual processing. If teachers can discuss whether or not a student has "read" or "listened" with understanding, then "reading with comprehension" or "listening with comprehension" identify separable and identifiable components of information processing.

Auding is auditory processing with comprehension or with languaging. If we capitalize on Gibson's definition of perception, we also get a glimpse of what comprehension might be. She stated that perception was a "pulling out" of information, not an "adding on." Auding, then, is listening as defined here plus the "added on" notion of comprehension.

Actually this does not yet define auding, because we do not know what comprehension (or languaging in Sticht's analogy) is. Sticht, Beck, and Hauke (1974) define languaging as the "representation of conceptualizations by properly ordered sequence of signs" (p. 19). The conceptualizations are seen to exist outside the language itself. This is a useful way of thinking about auding. It is somewhat analogous to a carrier wave with a message superimposed on it. That is, the message of a communication is separable from the medium by which it is conveyed—a parody and allegory are obvious examples. In auding, as in reading with comprehension, there is much that is implicit and, therefore, not directly conveyed by the auditory or visual stimuli. The inferential nature of comprehension is currently the subject of many investigations (Bransford and Johnson, 1972 and others).

Auding is dependent on hearing and listening as defined earlier. It involves perception, but in addition it requires an integration with the existing form of the individual's knowledge base. The reader undoubtedly will see the relationship of the previous statement to Piaget's assimilation and accommodation notion.

Auding is explained at least partially by Massaro's (1975) conception of secondary recognition in auditory processing, since he states that "the goal of the secondary recognition process is to transfer this perceptual information into conceptual information" (p. 12). Secondary recognition may involve the use of context, syntactic and semantic knowledge, and episodic information.

At a more prosaic level, auding is influenced by assigning relative value to new information, comparing it to the known, noting organization, register, imaging, imagining, and appreciating. Auding is one end point of the auditory processing continuum, hearing is the other end, or, as Trabasso (1972) has put it: "[comprehension] is viewed as a set of psychological processes consisting of a series of mental operations which process linguistic information from its receipt until an overt decision [is made]" (p. 113).

RECENT APPROACHES TO AUDITORY PROCESSING

Research, testing, and the practice in auditory processing historically dealt primarily with skills similar to reading skills (Devine, 1978; Wilkinson, Stratta, and Dudley, 1974). As alluded to earlier, this is not a particularly productive approach because it does not take into account factors that are unique to auditory processing. However, that approach is understandable since there is a moderate correlation (0.58–0.60) among reading and auditory processing tests as reported by Sticht, Beck, and Hauke (1974). The relationship between reading and auditory processing is at least partially due to the similarity of the test items and partly due to the similar underlying cognitive processes (Kintsch and Kozminsky, 1977). It is difficult, if not impossible, to establish whether the majority of educational studies were dealing with hearing, listening, or auding. This criterion is not particularly applicable to studies in speech pathology and clinical experiments but these studies may have other inherent limiting factors. The intent here is to familiarize the reader with some aspects of auditory processing discussed in the educational literature of the 1970s.

One aspect of auditory processing almost completely lacking in the earlier research is the differentiation between spontaneous oral language and written language that is read orally. Spontaneous speech typically contains more mazes, pauses, and fillers and hence is less precise compared to edited prose. Therefore, Walker (1974–75) compared written accounts based on the same information given both ways. He concluded that spontaneous speech resulted in more distorted and added information in the recall protocols. This result was attributed to the hypothesized variables of *cue sampling* (selecting information from an array of sensory stimuli) and *message reconstruction* (recreation of the author's meaning).

Wilkinson, Stratta, and Dudley (1974) were also concerned with the ecological validity of the message being communicated and hence suggested five aspects to be considered in the evaluation of auditory processing: 1) contextual constraints—grammatical, stylistic, semantic, collocational, and phonological, 2) *content*—like traditional comprehension questions, 3) phonological—effect of intonation, 4) *register*—switching of registers (written to spoken, technical to non-technical, etc.), and 5) *relationships*—the communicative interaction between people (covert and overt) which signal relationships such as intimate-distance, superior-inferior, etc. A test based on these aspects and designed for British students (ages 10–18) was later published (Wilkinson, Stratta, and Dudley, 1976).

A new perspective on an old problem is provided by the propositional analysis and schema theory of Kintsch (1974) and Rumelhart (1975). Story comprehension based on these theories was investigated by Stein and Glenn (1975) who found that "when the story recalls were broken down and categorized according to the seven primary categories (major setting, direct consequence, initiating event, attempt, reaction, minor setting, internal response) occurring in an episode, developmental differences were consistently found in the internal response category. Fifth grade children recalled significantly more internal response statements than first grade children in all four stories" (p. 43). While this type of work has extremely limited generalizability, it does seem to point to some more refined systems of classifying comprehension variables. It is, however, very likely that the *proposition* and *schema* analysis are common to auditory and visual processing.

A related line of research deals with the effect of *prior context* and *advance organizers* on the text to follow. This work is related to that on story comprehension (discussed in the paragraph above) because it focuses on the structure of the textual stimuli. Studies by Christie and Schumacher (1976), Arnold and Brooks (1976), and Luderer (1976) addressed the effectiveness of advance organizers when prose was presented orally. The organizers were of a higher level of generality or inclusiveness than the "stories" on which they were based and there were slight procedural differences in the three studies. The first and the third studies stressed "main ideas" information and both found no significant differences for the presence or absence of the organizers. The Arnold and Brooks study, however, stressed "relationships" among ideas and consequently found an effect due to the advance organizers. A study by McLeod (1979) could help to clarify this situation. McLeod found that when subjects were tested on orally presented literary narrative, science, or social studies materials, they comprehended the science material best because the ideas were presented in a linear relationship, whereas the other subject matter presented the ideas in branching or spiral relationships. Furthermore, Riding, Van der Will, and Lambourne (1977) found syntactic predictability to enhance recall. One may conclude from these studies that advance organizers, whether verbal or pictorial, do not produce a *simple* facilitating effect for comprehension through auditory processing. Instead, the facilitating effect appears to be produced by advance knowledge of the structural organization of the materials to be processed. Swinney and Hakes (1976) refer to this as the "prior decision hypothesis" and acknowledge the limiting effect of such a strategy. By focusing on structural organization the listener may well ignore other important information; this may explain why subjects in the Christie and Schumacher study as well as those in the Arnold and Brooks study made more incorrect inferences when presented with advance organizers.

Another area of inquiry in auditory processing has been related to mnemonic or memory aids. Shellen (1974) investigated the effects of initial and concluding *summaries* as compared to no summaries, and the effects of mnemonic summaries as compared to traditional summaries. The summary group exceeded the non-summary group on a recall task. The mnemonic summary differed from the traditional only in that the alphabetical order (A, B, C, D, E, F, G) was stressed. Most readers will undoubtedly recall their own consternation when their spelling teacher mixed the order of the spelling list; order or knowledge of the number of items to be recalled appears to aid these and similar tasks.

It is important to differentiate recall from recognition tasks as found by Christie (1977). Christie also found in a comparison of an *intentional instructions* group (students were informed of a recall task) with an incidental instructions group (no forewarning of recall task) that the former group performed significantly better than the latter. The fourth-graders appeared to benefit more from the admonition that a recall task would follow than the first-graders. Shellen's (1975) experiment also confirmed that students recalled more when they were told that their school grades would be affected, but he did not find a difference between those who were made aware of testing as compared to those who were not so warned. A second finding by Shellen was that *interest* in the topic was significantly related to achievement but that it did not interact with the incentive condition. Shellen interpreted the latter finding to mean that "listening achievement scores obtained under test conditions may be more representative of normal listening behavior than was previously believed" (p. 17).

Another recent approach, a rather intriguing idea, was investigated by Benjamin (1972): How do students perceive *rhetorical questions?* Using college students, he found that they perceived the rhetorical questions to be the statement that the question implied. Can a question then be an accusation? Journalists and "hot line" investigative reporters often use rhetorical questions to their advantage (Griffith, 1980) and consequently this agent of oracy should be further explored.

Even some commercial materials produced in the 1970s recognized differences between hearing and listening (Bracken and Bridges, 1971). Among the exercises included are basics such as *tracking* and focusing; cognitive skills such as recognizing organizational patterns and relationships; and *speed speech* practice.

Another set of materials (Bracken and Hays, 1970) develops awareness of *pitch*, *volume*, *quality of sound*, and *rhythm* as well as other skills. Some attention is given to the role that *gestures* and *pictures* play in communication.

In summary, the reader may wish to review the list of *underlined* terms in this chapter to gain some notion of the range of auditory processing skills considered by researchers and practitioners. Some of these ideas will undoubtedly be further developed, others will prove to be dead ends.

EDUCATIONAL IMPLICATIONS

Perhaps the most important generalization emerging from the foregoing discussion about auditory processing is that *comprehension* may well be developed through auditory and through visual input. Models such as Mackworth's even suggest common meaning processing mechanisms.

A second observation is a corollary of the first: Layering on of auding instruction is probably not necessary. Making inferences and making comparisons likely involve the same processes whether the input is visual or auditory; hence they need not be taught twice, once in "listening" instruction and once in "reading" instruction. This is a good reason for integrating language instruction.

The neurophysiological aspects of hearing and the perceptual process of listening have probably not received a fair share of attention or it has not been recognized that these are basic to auding. However, some of the more recent commercial materials are beginning to incorporate training directed at these levels. The teaching of attending, mnemonics, and other aspects of auditory processing have been discussed previously.

Another critical feature of auditory processing that is gradually being accepted is the notion that it is part of a communication process and hence influenced by non-linguistic factors. Recent publications refer to the "new literacy" (Foster, 1979), "communicative competence" (Wood, 1977), or "nonverbal communication" (Wieman and Wieman, 1975). Because the person receiving a message is obviously influenced by the speaker's gaze, enthusiasm, gesticulations, content of message, and congruency among them, it seems wise not to try to separate these variables within the communications process.

Another profitable realization would be that spontaneous speech and written language that is read orally are not necessarily synonymous. Teachers and libraries should collect samples of real, live speech to be listened to by students. Alternatively, classes could engage in recording and building spontaneous speech libraries for their own use.

Because tapes and records of a variety of materials are available in most schools and because the processing of this information is time consuming, some experience with variable speed listening should be considered. Slower-than-normal rates have been shown to be efficacious for children with learning disabilities (Blosser, Weidner, and Dinero, 1976; McCroskey and Thompson, 1973); faster-than-normal rates may be useful in reducing study time (Woodcock and Clark, 1968) or improving reading speed (Neville, 1975); and two speeded presentations may be better than one slower presentation (Aiken, Thomas, and Shennum, 1975). The technology of compressing speech has been surprisingly well developed, especially for commercial education purposes, and these machines are within the affordable range for schools (e.g., Speech Controller from The Variable Speech Control Company, San Francisco, CA 94123, and other devices).

RESEARCH IMPLICATIONS

As stated earlier, auditory processing research in education is in its infancy and consequently validation work, even on its vocabulary, is necessary. Since auding includes hearing and listening, how can these be controlled?

Sticht, Beck, and Hauke (1974) list dozens of studies, few of which have equated reading and auding rates. Because rate affects comprehension, these studies must be interpreted carefully. Replicative studies would be useful.

Another aspect not often controlled is the type of comprehension assessed. Yet there are indications that recall and recognition require different cognitive processes (Shellen, 1975).

Much more developmental information about auditory processing, especially at the school-age level, is needed. Even Loban's (1976) longitudinal study of children from kindergarten through grade twelve does not report any useful numeric data about the children's auding ability.

Tests of auditory processing need to reflect those factors influencing this communication process. The effects of varying signal-to-noise ratios under actual classroom conditions need refining. How do gestures, facial expression, intonation, and enthusiasm interact in aiding or detracting from a message? Do tests of auditory processing reflect the content of the curriculum? How effective are aural-cloze tests? What is the relative importance of recognizing register and other paralinguistic features?

More transfer studies (auding to reading comprehension and vice versa) are needed.

Bibliographies of books containing natural or spontaneous speech would be a real help to the teacher.

Ethnographic studies of children and students engaged in communication but focusing on auditory processing could uncover useful information for educational purposes. As the adage goes: Nature gave us two ears and only one mouth so that we could listen [aud] twice as much as we speak!

FOR DISCUSSION

1. What is the relationship between auding and reading comprehension? What is the relationship between auding and productive language (speaking and writing)?
2. Why does Froese focus his chapter on continuous discourse rather than on isolated speech and word perception?
3. What "listening skills" do students come to school with and what can be done for students to increase listening ability?
4. What is the role of previous experiences in auding?
5. What is the role of motivation in auding?
6. Froese presents a model from Lundsteen whose purpose is to direct teachers' attention to aspects of listening that need to be covered in instruction. What areas are most often neglected and how can instruction be planned to meet student needs in those areas?
7. What is the purpose of a hierarchy of listening skills?
8. What kinds of materials are most appropriate for instruction in auding?

REFERENCES

Aiken, E. G., Thomas, B. S., and Shennum, W. A. Memory for a lecture: Effects of notes, lecture rate, and information density. *Journal of Educational Psychology*, 1975, *67*, 439–444.

Arnold, C. J., and Brooks, B. H. Influence of contextual organizing material on children's listening comprehension. *Journal of Educational Psychology*, 1976, *68*, 711–716.

Benjamin, R. L. The rhetorical question: Its perception by listeners. ERIC Document ED 085 777, 1972.

Bloom, B. S. (Ed.). *Taxonomy of educational objectives: Cognitive domain.* New York: McKay, 1956.

Blosser, J. L., Weidner, W. E., and Dinero, T. The effect of rate-controlled speech on the auditory receptive scores of children with normal and disordered language abilities. *Journal of Special Education*, 1976, *10*, 291–298.

Bracken, D. K., and Bridges, C. J. *Listening progress laboratory.* Toronto: Educational Progress Corporation, 1971.

Bracken, D. K., and Hays, J. H. *Listening skills program.* Willodale, Ont.: SRA, 1970.

Bransford, J., and Johnson, M. Contextual prerequisites for understanding: Some investigations of comprehension and recall. *Journal of Verbal Learning and Verbal Behavior*, 1972, *11*, 717–726.

Brown, D. P. *Auding as the primary language ability.* Unpublished doctoral dissertation, Stanford University, 1954.

Burdick, J., and Collins, P. *Listen and read.* Huntington, New York: EDL/McGraw-Hill, 1968.

Canada, R. M., and Lynch, M. L. Systems techniques applied to teaching listening skills. *Counselor Education and Supervision*, September 1975, *15*, 40–47.

Christie, D. J. Memory for prose: Development of mnemonic strategies and use of high order relations, 1977, ED 141 827m.

Christie, D. J., and Schumacher, G. M. Some conditions surrounding the effectiveness of advance organizers for children's retention of orally presented prose. *Journal of Reading Behavior*, 1976, *8*, 299–309.

Commission on the English Curriculum. *The English language arts*, New York: Appleton-Century-Croft, 1952.

Commission on the English Curriculum. *Language arts for today's children.* New York: A-C-C, 1954.

Davis, F. B. Research in comprehension in reading. *Reading Research Quarterly*, 1968, *3*, 499–545.

Devine, T. G. Listening: What do we know after fifty years of research and theorizing? *Journal of Reading*, 1978, *21*, 296–303.

Edmonton Public School System. *Listening and speaking objectives.* Edmonton, Alberta: Author, 1979.

Educational Progress Corporation *Listening Progress Laboratory.* Toronto: Author, 1971.

Flannegan, J. C, et al *Language arts behavioral objectives.* Palo Alto, California: Westinghouse Learning Press, 1971.

Foster, H. M. *The new literacy.* Urbana, Illinois: NCTE, 1979.

Friedman, P. G. *Listening process: Attention, understanding, evaluation.* Washington, D.C.: National Education Association, 1978.

Froese, V. Comprehension in reading. *Manitoba Journal of Education*, 1971, *7*, 37–44.

Gibson, E. J., and Levin, H. *The psychology of reading.* Cambridge, Massachusetts: MIT Press, 1975.

Griffith, T. Trial by interview. *Time*, January 21, 1980, 43.

Hedrick, D. L., and Kunze, L. H. Diotic listening in young children. *Perceptual and Motor Skills*, 1974, *38*, 591–598.

Kellogg, R. E. Listening. In P. Lamb (Ed.), *Guiding children's language learning.* Dubuque, Iowa: Brown, 1972.

Kintsch, W. *The representation of meaning in memory.* Hillsdale, New Jersey: Lawrence Erlbaum Associates, 1974.

Kintsch, W., and Kozminsky, E. Summarizing stories after reading and listening. *Journal of Educational Psychology*, 1977, *69*, 491–499.

Larson, G., and Petersen, B. Does noise limit the learning of young listeners? *Elementary School Journal*, 1978, *78*, 264–265.

Lazarus, A., and Knudson, R. *Selected objectives for the English language arts, grades 7–12.* Boston: Houghton Mifflin, 1967.

Lindsay, P. H., and Norman, D. A. *Human information processing.* New York: Academic Press, 1972.

Loban, W. *Language development: Kindergarten through grade twelve.* NCTE

Research Report. No. 18. Urbana, Illinois: National Council of Teachers of English, 1976.

Luderer, E. The effect of prefatory statements on the listening comprehension of fourth and fifth graders. ERIC Document ED 127 561, 1976.

Lundsteen, S. W. *Listening*. Urbana, Illinois: ERIC, NIE, and NCTE, 1979.

Massaro, D. W. (Ed.). *Understanding language: An information-processing analysis of speech perception, reading, and psycholinguistics*. New York: Academic Press, 1975.

McCroskey, R. L., and Thompson, N. W. Comprehension of rate controlled speech by children with specific learning disabilities. *Journal of Learning Disabilities*, 1973, *6*, 29–35.

McLeod, R. W. A comparison of listening comprehension levels in literary narrative, science, and social studies materials at the sixth grade. *Alberta Journal of Educational Research*, 1979, *20*, 178–185.

Neville, M. H. Effectiveness of rate of aural message on reading and listening. *Educational Research*, 1975, *18*, 37–43.

Phillips, P. P. *Speech and hearing problems in the classroom*. Lincoln, Nebraska: Cliff Notes, 1975.

Rankin, P. The importance of listening ability. *English Journal*, 1928, *17*, 623–630.

Riding, R. J., Van der Will, C., and Lambourne, R. D. The effect of syntactic structure and children's temporal ability on the comprehension of spoken prose. *Educational Review*, 1977, *29*, 285–298.

Royal Bank of Canada. *Monthly Letter No. 60*, January 1979.

Rumelhart, C. E. Notes on a schema for stories. In D. G. Brown and A. Collins (Eds.), *Representation and understanding: Studies in cognitive science*. New York: Academic Press, 1975.

Russell, D. H., and Russell, E. F. *Listening aids through the grades*. New York: Teachers College Press, 1959.

Shellen, W. N. The effects of message summaries on the immediate free recall of main points, 1974, ED 093 021.

Shellen, W. N. Measurement of listening achievement: The role of perceived interest and extrinsic incentives. ERIC Document ED 105 539, 1975.

Smith, F. *Understanding reading*. New York: Holt, Rinehart and Winston, 1971.

Spearritt, D. *Listening comprehension—A factorial analysis*. ACER Research Series No. 76, 1962.

Stein, N. L., and Glenn, C. G. *An analysis of story comprehension in elementary school children: A test of a schema*. ED 121 474, 1975, p. 20.

Sticht, T. G., Beck, L. J., and Hauke, R. N. *Auding and reading: A developmental model*. Alexandria, Virginia: Human Resources Research Organization, 1974.

Swinney, D. A., and Hakes, D. T. Effects of prior context upon lexical access during sentence comprehension. *Journal of Verbal Learning and Verbal Behavior*, 1976, *15*, 681–689.

Taylor, S. E. *Listening*. Washington, D.C.: NEA, 1964.

Thorn, E. A., and Richmond, M. I. *Listening strategies: An elephant named Godfrey*. Toronto: Gage, 1970.

Trabasso, T. Mental operations in language comprehension. In J. Carroll and R. O. Freedle (Eds.), *Language comprehension and the acquisition of knowledge*. Washington, D.C.: Winston, 1972.

Travers, R. M. W. *An introduction to educational research*. London: Collier-Macmillan, 1970.

Trubowitz, S. The listening teacher. *Childhood Education*, April/May 1975, *51*, 320.

Walker, L. A comparative study of selected reading and listening processes. *Reading Research Quarterly*, 1974–75, *10*, 255–257.

Weaver, W. W. A factor analysis of the cloze procedure and other measures of reading and language ability. In A. J. Kingston (Ed.), *Towards a psychology of reading and language*. Athens: University of Georgia Press, 1977.

Weaver, W. W., and Rutherford, W. L. A hierarchy of listening skills. *Elementary English*, 1974, *51*, 1146–1150.

Whitfield, I. C. *The auditory pathway*. London: Arnold, 1967.

Wieman, M. O., and Wieman, J. M. *Nonverbal communication in the elementary classroom*. Urbana, Illinois: NCTE, 1975.

Wilkinson, A., Stratta, L., and Dudley, P. *Learning through listening*. London: Macmillan, 1976.

Wilkinson, A., Stratta, L., and Dudley, P. *The quality of listening*. London: Macmillan, 1974.

Wilt, M. A study of teacher awareness of listening as a factor in elementary education. *Journal of Educational Research*, 1950, *43*, 626–636.

Winnipeg Tribune, December 26, 1979.

Wolvin, A. D., and Coakley, C. G. *Listening instruction*. Urbana, Ill.: ERIC and Communication Skills and Speech Association, 1979.

Wood, B. S. *Development of functional communication competencies: Pre k–grade 6*. Urbana, Illinois: NCTE, 1977.

Woodcock, R. W., and Clark, C. R. Comprehension of a narrative passage as a function of listening rate, recall period, and IQ: Nashville third and sixth grade study. ERIC Document ED 105 478, 1968.

PART II LITERACY

On the reading side, literacy covers what teachers call decoding and word recognition; and on the writing side, it covers the transcription skills of handwriting, spelling, and punctuation.

from Moffet, J. and Wagner, B. H. *Student-centered Language Arts and Reading, K-13*. Boston: Houghton Mifflin, 1976, p. 10.

Consider the question of literacy, teaching reading and writing; what is learning to read and to write? Fundamentally it is an extension of the functional potential of language.

from Halliday, M. A. K. *Language as Social Semiotic*. Baltimore: University Park Press, 1978, p. 57.

In developed societies literacy, the ability to read and to write, has been treated as a vitally important index of well being. The progress of developing societies is frequently measured by it; the achievement of universal literacy is a fundamental educational objective.

from Harpin, W. *The Second 'R'*. London: George Allen & Unwin, 1976, p. 21.

Like easel painting, the printed book added much to the new cult of individualism. The private, fixed point of view became possible and literacy conferred the power of detachment, non-involvement.

from McLuhan, M. *The Medium Is the Message*. New York: Bantam, 1967, p. 50.

8 Grammar and Teaching of Writing: Analysis versus Synthesis

Stanley B. Straw

The statement that language processing skills and language arts are highly related has become axiomatic, but as observed by Evanechko, Ollila, and Armstrong (1976): "... the specific nature of these relationships is not always clear" (p. 315). It has been hypothesized by psycholinguists that one of the reasons that strong relationships have been found to exist among the language arts is that certain basic and common psychological and linguistic competencies underlie the language processing constructs of listening, speaking, reading, and writing. That is to say, the four areas all depend on a common set of competencies or knowledge.

Goodman (1973) has identified these linguistic competencies as *graphophonic* knowledge (a combination of knowledge of both the phonological and graphic systems of the language and their correspondences), *syntactic* knowledge (knowledge of the grammatical rules of the language), and *semantic* knowledge (knowledge of the meanings capable of being encoded in language). Pearson and Johnson (1978) term these *phonological*, *syntactic*, and *semantic* knowledge. Writers have pointed out, as well, that none of these systems work independently, that they operate simultaneously and interdependently in such a way that the language user draws on all three in order to process language (Goodman, 1973; Smith, 1975; Pearson and Johnson, 1978).

The importance of syntactic knowledge has been thoroughly investigated in studies of productive language development (Strickland, 1962; Hunt, 1965b; Stewig and Lamb, 1973; Ciani, 1974; Pope, 1974; Loban, 1976), but it has not been as thoroughly investigated in receptive language. Psycholinguistic research in the four areas, nonetheless, has confirmed the importance of syntactic knowledge in all four language processing areas. Slobin (1966) among others (McNeil, 1970; Entwisle and Frasure, 1974; Lesgold, 1974) has identified the importance of syntactic knowledge in listening comprehension; Bormuth (1966), Denner (1970), Guthrie (1973), Shackford (1976), and Wisker (1976) have identified and studied the syntactic component in reading comprehension. In the areas of productive language, the importance of syntactic knowledge has been identified in oral language (O'Donnell, Griffin, and Norris, 1967; Fox, 1970; Baines, 1975; Ciani, 1976; Loban, 1976) and in written composition (Hunt, 1966; Biesbock, 1968; Golub and Fredrick, 1970).

Because syntactic knowledge or competence has been demonstrated to be an important underlying component of language, it would follow that instruction aimed at enhancing growth in syntactic competence ought also to enhance growth in listening, speaking, reading, and writing.

The purpose of this chapter is to investigate the literature on instruction aimed at increasing syntactic competence and to examine its effect on language performance. From this review, some suggestions are made as to the direction in which educators need to move both in the areas of research and curriculum development.

FORMAL GRAMMAR INSTRUCTION AND LANGUAGE GROWTH

Traditionally, instruction aimed at growth in syntactic competence has been in language analysis or language description, commonly termed *grammar study*, *formal grammar*, or simply *grammar*. Whether or not formal grammar *should* be taught has become, at times, an inflammatory issue. Perhaps part of this controversy can be attributed to a misunderstanding of the terms. To begin with, it should be pointed out what formal grammar instruction is *not*, as the term has been used by researchers in general. It is *not* instruction in usage, standard dialect, mechanics or writing conventions (such as punctuation, capitalization, etc.), courtesies in speech or writing, spelling, or handwriting. Historically, none of the researchers investigating the efficacy of formal grammar instruction has defined the term as any of these skills. Those skills are most often referred to in writing as "editorial skills" (Cooper and Odell, 1977).

What then is formal grammar? Formal grammar is usually referred to as the analysis and the study of the linguistic description of the syntax of the language. This would include study of the definitions and appropriate uses of form classes (parts of speech), study of the make up of constituent structures (words, phrases, clauses, etc.), identification and analysis of sentence patterns and phrase structure rules, identification of the structure of embedded clauses and sentences, identification of sentence types and transformations: totally, in fact, the study of the syntactic structure of the language, usually from an analytic point of view. Formal grammar study is essentially study about language and its structure (For further discussion of this issue see Chapter 9, Grammar: A Perspective.)

Primarily, grammar instruction in schools has been justified because it is believed that the study of the structure of language will positively affect growth in productive language, in particular, written composition. However, the efficacy of teaching formal grammar has been challenged. Braddock, Lloyd-Jones, and Schoer (1963) in their comprehensive review of research of written composition stated that "study after study based on objective testing . . . confirms that instruction in formal grammar has little or no effect on the quality of study compositions" (p. 37). They further reported studies, such as the one conducted by Harris in 1962, that measured the effect of formal grammar instruction on composition ability in students. Braddock, Lloyd-Jones, and Schoer stated:

> The conclusion can be stated in strong and unqualified terms: the teaching of grammar has a negligible or, because it usually displaces some instruction and practice in actual composition, even a harmful effect on the improvement of writing. (pp. 37–38)

The studies reported by Braddock, Lloyd-Jones, and Schoer were studies in which structural or traditional grammar was taught to children. When transformational-generative grammar appeared in the late 1950s, it was hypothesized that the results of previous studies showing that the teaching of grammar was not effective for enhancing writing performance could be attributed to the fact that inappropriate grammars were taught. A number of studies then appeared investigating the efficacy of teaching transformational-generative grammar to students.

Bateman and Zidonis (1966) designed and completed a 2-year study of the effects of generative grammar study on the writing of secondary students. They found that the generative grammar group did not differ significantly from the traditional grammar group in the number of words written, but did show significant improvement in other areas, such as structural complexity. However, the results of this study have been severely criticized. Mellon (1969) criticized the study because of inappropriate statistical analyses and pointed out that group differences could be attributed to the performance of four students in the generative grammar group. This study has also been severely criticized by O'Hare (1973) and by Combs (1975).

Other research has indicated that neither variety of grammar has a significant effect on language development. Davenport (1970) conducted an experiment similar to the Bateman and Zidonis study and found no statistically significant gains in writing behavior on the part of the generative grammar group over that of a group that studied traditional grammar. Fry (1971) conducted an experiment employing two different teaching methods along with the two different kinds of grammar content and found no significant differences due to either variable, either the kind of grammar taught (traditional or transformational), or the method of teaching (direct teacher instruction or computerized individualized instruction). Futhermore, there was no interaction between the two variables.

A recent study of the effect of grammar instruction on writing performance was reported by Elley, Barham, Lamb, and Wyllie (1976). They conducted a 3-year investigation of the effects of three different training programs: one in transformational grammar, one in traditional grammar, and one in which no grammar was taught at all but which employed instruction in reading and writing. Their conclusions were as follows:

> The main purpose of this investigation was to determine the direct effects of a study of transformational grammar on the language growth of secondary school pupils. The results presented show that the effects are negligible. Similarly, those pupils who studied a course containing elements of traditional grammar showed no measurable benefits. The RW [reading/writing] group, who studied no formal grammar for three years, demonstrated competence in writing and related language skills fully equal to that shown by the two grammar groups. . . . It is difficult to escape the conclusion that English grammar, whether traditional or transformational, has virtually no influence on the language growth of typical secondary school students. (pp. 17–18)

In conclusion, the research seems to support the notion that the teaching of grammar, that is, the study of language structure, has little or no value in enhancing or fostering language development.

The question could then be asked: If syntactic knowledge is a basic underlying competency for language performance, why does instruction teaching the rules of the language not affect performance in productive language? The answer to that question is, at least, two-fold.

To begin with, it would seem that teaching students the syntactic rules of the language is not, in fact, increasing their syntactic competence, because they have already mastered the rules, though not the terminology, that are the content of grammar instruction before they ever receive formal grammar instruction. Chomsky (1969) has noted that "a common assumption among students of child language has been that the child has mastered the syntax of his native language by about age 5" (p. 1). Carroll (1960) in an exhaustive review of the literature in language development concluded that "by the age of six, the average child has mastered nearly all of its [language's] common grammatical forms and constructions" (p. 745).

Further studies by Strickland (1962), Hunt (1965b), and Loban (1976) indicate that even though the syntax of students becomes increasingly more complex after grade three, few, if any, new rules or structures are learned. What seems to be happening is that students do not learn new rules but become more comfortable and adept at manipulating the language rules they already know. In that way, complexity in syntax is increased but new structures are not added to the child's syntactic repertoire. For example, on a very elementary level, every regular student can use nouns, verbs, prepositional phrases, adverbs, etc., long before teachers ever teach the students those terms. Learning the names of the terms does not increase the students' already sophisticated ability to manipulate the words either in receptive or productive language.

The second reason that students may not gain in language processing ability as a result of grammar instruction may be that, by definition, the study of language is an analytic activity, that is, the taking apart of sentences of the language. On the other hand, language use, as indicated by research in both receptive language (Bransford and Franks, 1971) and productive language (Dale, 1976), is a synthetic process. The learning of how to parse the language may be a totally different process, unrelated to effective use of language (Stein and Glenn, 1978).

THE ALTERNATIVE: SENTENCE MANIPULATION

In response to the seeming ineffectiveness of grammar instruction in enhancing language growth, researchers in the mid-sixties began to investigate alternatives to grammar that would build on students' tacit and intuitive knowledge of language and that would more closely resemble the synthetic nature of language processing. The instructional procedure that was developed was a kind of sentence manipulation termed *sentence-combining*. Stated simply, sentence-combining is instruction in taking two or more sentences, often simple or kernal sentences, and combining them into a single, more complex sentence. A comprehensive and insightful history of sentence-combining by Mellon (1979) appears in the recently published monograph from Miami (Ohio) University (Daiker, Kerek, and Morenberg, 1979).

Effects on Productive Language (Writing)

The research studies on the effect of sentence-combining over the past 15 years have been numerous, and the evidence about the effect of sentence-combining on language performance is compelling.

The first major study was conceptualized and carried out by Mellon (1969). He divided 247 seventh grade students into three groups. Each group was given a different kind of instruction: 1) sentence-combining instruction, 2) traditional grammar instruction, and 3) no instruction in written composition. Mellon found statistically significant growth in syntactic fluency for the sentence-combining group as measured by 12 indices of written syntactic complexity, including words per clause, clauses per T-unit, and words per T-unit. This growth was not evident in either of the other two treatment groups. In fact, the control (traditional grammar) and placebo groups' posttest and growth scores were "mutually indistinguishable" (p. 71). Not only did this study provide evidence that sentence-combining practice is effective in fostering and enhancing language development, but it also compiled further evidence about the ineffectiveness of instruction in traditional grammar. Mellon's final conclusions were:

> It should be remembered first of all that what each of the sentence-combining "problems" actually represents is one mature sentence entered upon the record of the student's total experience in language . . . its significance lies in its having demonstrated the following—systematic programs entailing a rhetorical, intensive, and specially planned experiencing of mature sentences will increase the rate at which the sentence structure of the student's own writing becomes more highly elaborated (or differentiated) and thus more mature. (p. 73)

The contention made here by Mellon is that sentence-combining practice affects the students' underlying linguistic knowledge and that underlying linguistic knowledge, in turn, is evident in their performance in written composition.

O'Hare (1973) also studied the effect of sentence-combining on student writing at the seventh grade level. He, like Mellon, found significant differences in the syntactic growth of the sentence-combining group over a control group that studied reading/writing units during the 9-month period. O'Hare's experimental group gains were statistically significant on all six of his measures of syntactic development and growth. The experimental group made a mean gain of more than 5 years (based on Hunt's 1966 norms) when words per T-unit were used as the measure of syntactic growth. Another finding of O'Hare's study was that the posttest compositions of the sentence-combining group were judged qualitatively superior to those of the control group.

Combs (1975), using sentence-combining exercises comparable to O'Hare's, found results similar to O'Hare's both on measures of syntactic complexity and syntactic maturity and also on writing quality. Combs' study differed from O'Hare's in that Combs had a shortened treatment period of 10 weeks as compared to the 9 months of instruction in the O'Hare study. Miller and Ney (1968) also found similar results with fourth grade students when sentence-combining exercises were presented orally rather than in written form.

In more than 30 studies, the conclusion was reached that sentence-combining had a significant effect on productive language growth. Gains in syntactic control and maturity have been found in a variety of areas: in instruction with differnt ethnic groups (Hunt and O'Donnell, 1970); with low and high ability students (Ofsa, 1974); with college students (Sipple, 1976); with secondary students (O'Hare, 1973; Combs, 1975; Ofsa, 1974); and with elementary students (Miller and Ney, 1968; Green, 1972; Perron, 1974). Gains have been reported whether the dependent measures have been a result of structural analysis (Crymes, 1971); judgments of quality (Combs, undated; O'Hare, 1973; Combs, 1975); or as a result of a T-unit analysis (Mellon, 1969; Hunt and O'Donnell, 1970; O'Hare, 1973; Ofsa, 1974); and, regardless of the pretest and posttest writing task (Cooper, 1971). Similar growth has been found as a result of sentence-combining instruction whether the exercises have been presented orally (Miller and Ney, 1968) or in written form (O'Hare, 1973; Perron, 1974; Combs, 1975). In the area of second language learning, sentence-combining has been shown to have a significant effect on students' language development. Akin (1976) found significant growth in English language students who were studying German as a second language. He reported significant growth on the part of the sentence-combining group over the control group in both oral and written language production in German. Similar results were reported with students learning English as a second language (Ross, 1972; Klassen, 1976).

Effects on Receptive Language (Reading and Listening)

Sentence-combining exercises and instruction have been shown to have a significant effect on the productive language development of students, as discussed in the preceding section. This effect has been hypothesized to occur primarily because sentence-combining affects the underlying linguistic knowledge and competence of students, particularly their syntactic knowledge.

Furthermore, the research literature contains a number of studies investigating the effect of sentence-combining instruction on reading comprehension achievement and on receptive language performance. The hypothesis underlying this research is that if sentence-combining activities affect the syntactic knowledge of students, which, in turn, affects their language production performance, and, if the same syntactic knowledge underlies the abilities of productive and receptive language, then it is reasonable to assume that sentence-combining activities would also affect performance in the areas of reading and listening comprehension.

Sternglass (1976) recommended that, because of the common underlying knowledge required for reading and writing, teachers provide students with opportunities to analyze increasingly complex sentences in reading at the same time they are learning to produce more complex sentences in writing. She also claimed:

> When the complexities of syntax interfere markedly with the processing of language, then a careful examination of these structures involved in reading can be helpful. When the reader has gained familiarity with particular complex syntactical structures (i.e., through sentence-combining activities), they will no longer slow him down in reading. . . . For the reinforcement of reading and activity of writing, students can be given simple kernal sentences which are easiest to read, in relative terms, and asked to combine them. Mutual reinforcement of complexity in reading and writing can then be produced simultaneously. . . . As students gain familiarity in the construction of unfamiliar sentence-types, their new knowledge will carry over to their reading of these sentence types. (pp. 6–8)

Sandra Stotsky (1975) in her comprehensive review of the sentence-combining research stated that "significant results [of the teaching in sentence-combining on written composition] from these programs have led some researchers to suggest that enhancing children's syntactic skills in writing may also improve reading comprehension" (p. 32). She further maintained:

> It is reasonable to assume that the child who understands how to compose a highly complex sentence also understands that sentence. It is therefore plausible to construe the sentence-combining exercises as one highly structured kind of writing activity which . . . may facilitate cognitive growth [ability to comprehend] as well. (p. 59)

Hunt and O'Donnell (1970) devised a sentence-combining program and studied its effect on measures of performance in reading and writing with two different ethnic groups. As in earlier studies, a significant gain was evident on measures of syntactic maturity in productive language. Results on the reading test indicated that the sentence-combining program significantly increased measured reading ability for the experimental group of black students over the control group of black students who did not receive sentence-combining training. However, the same effect was not evident when posttest scores for the white experimental and control groups were compared. Hunt and O'Donnell did not attempt to explain the interaction between ethnic affiliation and treatment, but they did question the sensitivity of the reading posttest in measuring reading comprehension growth.

Fisher (1973) instructed fifth, seventh, and ninth grade students in sentence-combining in order to measure the program's effect on reading comprehension ability as measured by alternative forms of the Stanford Paragraph Meaning Test and by cloze tests. When the scores of the two reading dependent measures were collapsed, he found a treatment effect

($p < 0.05$) in favor of the sentence-combining group over a control group who studied English literature and English usage.

Combs (1975), along with studying the effects of sentence-combining instruction on the syntactic maturity and quality of writing of seventh grade students, also studied the program's effect on reading performance. The Gates-MacGinitie Reading Test and an experimenter-constructed cloze test were used as measures of growth in reading ability. Combs reported his results on the Gates-MacGinitie as follows:

> The results measured by the *Gates-MacGinitie Reading Test* (GMT) are examined first. A *t*-test comparison on the mean change scores (pre-test to post-test) for the experimental and control groups produced significant results for both groups. (Rate—control $p < .05$; experimental, $p < .001$; comprehension, $p < .05$ for both groups). The level of significance was somewhat higher for the experimental group on the measures of reading rate than that for the control group. But the significant changes on the GMT comprehension measure were *negative* ones suggesting that the GMT comprehension subtest is not sensitive to the effect the treatment has on students receiving sentence-combining practice or that sentence-combining practice has no effect on students' reading comprehension. . . . At best, the effect of the combined results from the GMT are ambiguous. (pp. 80–81)

It is interesting but not very enlightening that both groups did significantly poorer on the GMT comprehension posttest than they did on the pretest.

The specially constructed reading measure in the Combs study was designed in a way that was intended to be more sensitive than the standardized test to syntactic gains encouraged by the treatment administered to the experimental group.

Combs' final conclusion regarding the effect of sentence-combining instruction on reading skills and comprehension are as follows:

> In summary, the assessment of results from the two reading measures in the present study is confusing, yet encouraging. The experimental and control groups both make significant gains in reading rate on both measures. Both show significant decreases in reading comprehension on the GMT. Either the treatments have no measurable effect on students' reading abilities or the three reading subtests (rate and comprehension subtests of the GMT and the rate subtest of the special reading measure) are not sensitive to treatment effects. The latter may well be the case since the comprehension subtest of the special reading measure registers a differential effect on the control and experimental treatments. (pp. 85–86)

After examination of Combs' results, it cannot be said that Combs' research has delivered a clear effect on reading comprehension resulting from instruction in sentence-combining (Graves, 1977).

Hughes (1975) tested the hypothesis that sentence-combining training significantly enhances reading comprehension by affecting increased syntactic fluency. He employed 24 seventh grade students as subjects.

The 12 students in each of the two groups were matched according to IQ and reading ability. The groups were matched according to IQ and reading ability. The experimental group received instruction and practice in sentence-combining, while the control group received practice in analyzing and writing newspaper articles. Treatment extented over 10 weeks, and the sentence-combining group worked exclusively with adjective embedding. The instruction was given to four entire classrooms at two different schools, although only 24 students' scores were analyzed.

Three tests of reading were administered to the subjects: a cloze test drawn from John F. Kennedy's *Profiles in Courage*, the rate and accuracy subtests of the Gates-MacGinitie Reading Test, and Goodman and Burke's Reading Miscue Inventory.

Hughes found no significant differences in the growth of the two groups on either the cloze test or the two subtests of the Gates-Mac-Ginitie. However, he did find significant differences on the grammatical strength section of the Miscue Inventory ($p < 0.01$). The mean gain on the grammatical strength test seems to support the hypothesis that sentence-combining training affects the linguistic or syntactic competence of language processors.

Levine (1976) used third grade students as subjects; the purposes of the study were:

1. to determine whether instruction in the manipulation of grammatical structures is related to reading comprehension;
2. to determine whether instruction in the manipulation of grammatical structures is related to written composition; and
3. to determine whether transformational sentence-combining is a linguistic skill common to both written composition and reading comprehension. (p. 6431-A)

Posttest reading comprehension measures included a standardized test—Stanford Achievement Test (*SAT*)—and a teacher-made cloze test. Instruction involved 96 sessions in sentence-combining. The results reported indicated a significant difference in reading comprehension as measured by the *SAT* in favor of the experimental group, but no differences were found on the cloze test. Levine claimed that these results warrant the conclusion that sentence-combining has a decided effect on reading comprehension.

The final study to be reviewed here was carried out by Straw (1978). Employing fourth grade students as subjects, he measured the effect of sentence-combining instruction over a textbook approach, taught over a 5-week period, on measures of both reading and listening comprehension. The analyses of his data indicated that sentence-combining significantly affected student performance on a cloze test of reading comprehension and on a standardized test of listening comprehension. This study is most convincing in that significant positive effects for the sentence-combining group were found in yet a different language comprehension mode—listening—further establishing that sentence-combining affects the syntactic competence of students.

The totality of the research in sentence-combining indicates that the activities in sentence manipulation, because they are based on and expand the language ability of students and because of the synthetic nature of the activities, significantly affect productive and receptive language growth. Such claims cannot be made or empirically substantiated for grammar instruction and study. These research conclusions lead this writer to recommend that sentence-combining instruction and practice be substituted for the bulk of grammar instruction received by students in most language arts curricula, or at least, that the practice which accompanies most grammar instructions be sentence-combining practice rather than in parsing or analyzing sentences.

SENTENCE-COMBINING AND CLASSROOM INSTRUCTION

Some of the limited controversy on sentence-combining has centered on whether or not sentence-combining is a "total program." Opponents of sentence-combining are quick to point out that it is only one approach and is not a complete language arts program. To this writer's knowledge, no one who is a proponent of sentence-combining has ever made this claim; in fact, proponents will be the first to admit that, although sentence-combining has been employed to teach a number of writing skills, it should not be substituted for the bulk of language arts activities. Strong (1973) states that his program is designed to be adjunct to a regular program, and O'Hare (1975) calls his program an elective course.

A number of published programs are available in sentence-combining, and teachers interested in employing this instructional technique are encouraged to examine one or more of these programs (Strong, 1973; O'Hare, 1975; Rippon and Meyers, 1979; Daiker, Kerek, and Morenberg, 1979; Strong, in press). As pointed out by Mellon (1979), a complete program in sentence-combining can accomplish a number of objectives of the composition or writing program in schools. Not only can sentence-combining increase the maturity of students' syntax, but sentence-combining exercises have been used to teach ". . . thematically, reference, cohesion, stylistic concordances, and the abstractive ideation created by parts functioning within wholes" (p. 7). It seems important, however, to point out that sentence-combining does not necessarily assist students in generating sound ideas for writing; what it can do is to aid students in handling and expressing ideas, whether their own or someone else's, better, more clearly, and more maturely.

Although this writer does not view sentence-combining as a total language arts curriculum, personal experience in working with teachers in developing sentence-combining programs has shown that in the hands of thoughtful teachers, sentence-combining can be employed to significantly aid students' growth in language performance, particularly in writing, and can be used to aid students, not only in developing more mature syntax, but also in developing maturity in those often elusive areas of organization, style, tone, point of view, cohesion, and theme.

Undoubtedly, the validity of the approach has been empirically established. John Mellon (1979) in his history of the sentence-combining movement has stated eloquently what most of those working in sentence-combining feel. It seems appropriate to conclude this review with his words:

> What I want to say now, to all teachers, is that sentence-combining is ready for classroom use. . . . [t]here is a time for caution and a time for action, and with sentence-combining, the time for action has arrived. . . . I don't know of any component in our arsenal of literacy-teaching methods that is better supported empirically than sentence-combining. At the risk of sounding like a sloganizer from the Sixties, the best advice I can give teachers today, relative to sentence-combining, is—Do it! (pp. 34–35)

This author can only concur.

FOR DISCUSSION

1. Straw develops a case for minimizing instruction in formal grammar in language arts curricula. Why has formal grammar not been shown to be an efficient means in assisting student development of language performance? Why is formal grammar still an aspect of the majority of language arts texts on the market?
2. Differentiate between formal grammar and editing skills.
3. Is there any reason to teach grammatical terminology?
4. Why does sentence-combining seem to be such a salient method of teaching language development?
5. How much sentence-combining instruction could be included in a language arts program without detracting from other essential elements?

REFERENCES

Akin, J. O. *Enhancing the syntactic fluency of beginning foreign language learners through sentence-combining practice.* Unpublished doctoral dissertation, University of Georgia, 1976.
Baines, H. V. H. *An assessment and comparison of syntactic complexity and*

word associations of good and poor readers in grades four, eight, and twelve. Unpublished doctoral disseration, University of Georgia, 1975.

Bateman, D., and Zidonis, F. *The effect of a study of transformational grammar on the writing of ninth and tenth graders.* NCTE Research Report No. 6. Champaign, Illinois: National Council of Teachers of English, 1966.

Biesbock, E. J. *The development and uses of a standardized instrument for measuring composition ability in young children (grades two and three).* Unpublished doctoral disseration, University of Georgia, 1968.

Bormuth, J. R. Readability: A new approach. *Reading Research Quarterly,* 1966, *1,* 79–132.

Braddock, R., Lloyd-Jones, R., and Schoer, L. *Research in written composition.* Champaign, Illinois: National Council of Teachers of English, 1963.

Bransford, J. C., and Franks, J. J. The abstraction of linguistic ideas. *Cognitive Psychology,* 1971, *2,* 331–350.

Carroll, J. B. Language development. In C. W. Harris (Ed.), *Encyclopedia of educational research.* New York: Macmillan, 1960.

Chomsky, C. *The acquisition of syntax in children from 5 to 10.* Research Monograph No. 57. Cambridge, Massachusetts: MIT Press, 1969.

Ciani, A. J. *Syntactic maturity and vocabulary diversity in the oral language of first, second, and third grade children.* Unpublished doctoral dissertation, Indiana University, 1974.

Ciani, A. J. Syntactic maturity and vocabulary diversity in the oral language of first, second, and third graders. *Research in the Teaching of English,* 1976, *10,* 150–156.

Combs, W. E. *Some further effects and implications of sentence-combining exercises for the secondary language art curriculum.* Unpublished doctoral dissertation, University of Minnesota, 1975.

Combs, W. E. *Sentence-combining persistence and its effect on students: Quality of writing.* Studies in Language Education No. 21, Department of Language Education. Athens: University of Georgia, undated.

Cooper, C. R. A no-grammar approach to sentence power: John C. Mellon's sentence-combining games. *California English Journal,* 1971, *7,* 35–40.

Cooper, C. R., and Odell, L. *Evaluating writing: Describing, measuring, judging.* Urbana, Illinois: National Council of Teachers of English, 1977.

Crymes, R. The relation of study about language to language performance with special reference to noninalization. *TESOL Quarterly,* 1971, *5,* 217–230.

Daiker, D. A., Kerek, A., and Morenberg, M. *Sentence-combining and the teaching of writing.* Akron: University of Akron Press, 1979.

Daiker, D. A., Kerek, A., and Morenberg, M. *The writer's options: College sentence-combining.* New York: Harper and Row, 1979.

Dale, P. S. *Langauge development: Structure and function.* New York: Holt, Rinehart, and Winston, (2nd ed.). 1976.

Davenport, H. D. *The effects of instruction in generative grammar on the writing ability of students in the ninth grade.* Unpublished doctoral dissertation, University of Tennessee, 1970.

Denner, B. Representational and syntactic competence of problem readers. *Child Development,* 1970, *41,* 881–887.

Elley, W. B., Barham, I. H., Lamb, H., and Wyllie, M. The role of grammar in a secondary school English curriculum. *Research in the Teaching of English,* 1976, *10,* 5–21.

Entwisle, D. R., and Frasure, N. E. A contradiction resolved: Children's processing of syntactic cues. *Development Psychology*, 1974, *10*, 852–57.

Evanechko, P., Ollila, L., and Armstong, R. An investigation of the relationships between children's performance in written language and their reading ability. *Research in the Teaching of English*, 1976, *9*, 315–325.

Fisher, K. D. *An investigation to determine if selected exercises in sentence-combining can improve reading and writing.* Unpublished doctoral dissertation, Indiana University, 1973.

Fox, S. E. *Syntactic maturity and vocabulary diversity in the oral language of kindergarten and primary school children.* Unpublished doctoral dissertation, Indiana University, 1970.

Fry, D. J. W. *The effects of transformational grammar upon the writing performance of students of low socioeconomic backgrounds.* Unpublished doctoral dissertation, Memphis State University, 1971.

Golub, L. S., and Fredrick, W. C. *Linguistic structures and deviations in children's writing sentences.* Technical Report No. 152. Madison: University of Wisconsin, 1970.

Goodman, K. S. Psycholinguistic universals in the reading process. In F. Smith (Ed.), *Psycholinguistics and reading.* New York: Holt, Rinehart and Winston, 1973.

Graves, D. H. Research for the classroom. Promising research studies. *Language Arts*, 1977, *54*, 453–458.

Green, E. A. *An experimental study of sentence-combining to improve syntactic fluency in fifth-grade children.* Unpublished doctoral dissertation, Northern llinois University, 1972.

Guthrie, J. Reading comprehension and syntactic responses in good and poor readers. *Journal of Educational Psychology*, 1973, *65*, 294–299.

Harris, R. J. *An experimental inquiry into the functions and values of formal grammar in the teaching of correct written English to children aged twelve to fourteen.* Unpublished doctoral dissertation, University of London, 1962.

Hughes, T. O. *Sentence-combining: A means of increasing reading comprehension.* Kalamazoo: Western Michigan University, Department of English, 1975.

Hunt, K. W. A synopsis of clause to sentence length factors. *English Journal*, 1965, *54*, 300–309 (a).

Hunt, K. W. *Grammatical structures written at three grade levels.* NCTE Research Report No. 3. Champaign, Illinois: National Council of Teachers of English, 1965 (b).

Hunt, K. W. Recent measures of syntactic development. *Elementary English*, 1966, *43*, 732–739.

Hunt, K. W., and O'Donnell, R. *An elementary school curriculum to develop better writing skills.* Tallahassee Florida State University. U.S. Office of Education Grant No. 4-9-08-903-0042-010, 1970.

Klassen, B. R. *Sentence-combining exercises as an aid to expediting syntactic fluency in learning English as a second language.* Unpublished doctoral dissertation, University of Minnesota, 1976.

Lesgold, A. M. Variability in children's comprehension of syntactic structures. *Journal of Educational Psychology*, 1074, *66*, 333–338.

Levine, S. S. *The effect of transformational sentence-combining exercises on the reading comprehension and written composition of third-grade children.* Unpublished doctoral dissertation, Hofstra University, 1976.

Loban, W. D. *Language development: Kindergarten through grade twelve.*

NCTE Research Report No. 18. Urbana, Illinois: National Council of Teachers of English, 1976.

McNeil, D. The development of language. In P. Mussen (Ed.), *Carmichael's handbook of child psychology*. New York: John Wiley and Sons, 1970.

Mellon, J. *Transformational sentence-combining: A method for enhancing the development of syntactic fluency in English composition*. NCTE Research No. 10. Urbana, Illinois: National Council of Teachers of English, 1969.

Mellon, J. C. Issues in the theory and practice of sentence-combining: A twenty-year perspective. In D. A. Daiker, A. Kerek, and M. Morenberg (Eds.), *Sentence-combining and the teaching of writing*. Akron, Ohio: University of Akron Press, 1979.

Miller, B. D., and Ney, J. W. The effect of systematic oral exercises on the writing of fourth-grade students. *Research in the Teaching of English*, 1968, *2*, 44–61.

O'Donnell, R. C., Griffin, W. J., & Norris, R. C. *Syntax of kindergarten and elementary school children: A transformational analysis*. Research Report No. 8. Champaign, Illinois: National Council of Teachers of English, 1967.

Ofsa, W. J. *An experiment in using research in composition in the training of teachers of English*. Unpublished doctoral dissertation, University of Illinois at Urbana-Champaign, 1974.

O'Hare, F. *Sentence-combining: Improving student writing without formal grammar instruction*. NCTE Research Report No. 15. Urbana, Illinois: National Council of Teachers of English, 1973.

O'Hare, F. *Sentencecraft: An elective course in writing*. Lexington, Massachusetts: Ginn and Company, 1975.

Pearson, P. D., and Johnson, D. D. *Teaching reading comprehension*. New York: Holt, Rinehart and Winston, 1978.

Perron, J. D. *An exploratory approach to extending the syntactic development of fourth-grade students through the use of sentence-combining methods*. Unpublished doctoral dissertation, Indiana University, 1974.

Pope, M. The syntax of fourth graders' narrative and explanatory speech. *Research in the Teaching of English*, 1974, *8*, 219–227.

Rippon, M., and Meyers, W. E. *Combining sentences*. New York: Harcourt, Brace, Jovanovich, 1979.

Ross, J. Controlled writing: A transformational approach. *Literacy Discussion*, 1972, *3*, 277–292.

Shackford, H. G. *Junior high school students' knowledge of grammatical structure and its relation to reading comprehension*. Unpublished doctoral dissertation, Boston University, 1976.

Sipple, J. A. W. *Some models for a multi-media English usage program*. Paper presented at the annual convention of the Conference on College Composition and Communication, Philadelphia, March 25–27, 1976.

Slobin, D. Grammatical transformations and sentence comprehension in childhood and adulthood. *Journal of Verbal Learning and Verbal Behavior*, 1966, *5*, 219–227.

Smith, F. *Comprehension and learning*. New York: Holt, Rinehart and Winston, 1975.

Stein, N., and Glenn, C. An analysis of story comprehension in elementary school children. In R. Freedle (Ed.), *Advances in discourse processing, Vol. II: New directions*. Norwood, New Jersey: Ablex, 1978.

Sternglass, M. S. Composition teacher as reading teacher: Linguistics is the bridge. (ERIC Document ED 120782, 1975)

Stewig, J. W., and Lamb, P. Elementary pupils' knowledge of the structure of American English and the relationship of such knowledge to the ability to use language effectively in composition. *Research in the Teaching of English*, 1973, *7*, 324–337.

Stotsky, S. L. Sentence-combining as a curricular activity: Its effect on written language development and reading comprehension. *Research in the Teaching of English*, 1975, *9*, 30–71.

Straw, S. B. *The effect of sentence-combining and sentence-reduction instructions on measures of syntactic fluency, reading comprehension and listening comprehension in fourth-grade students.* Unpublished doctoral dissertation, University of Minnesota, 1978.

Straw, S. B. Measuring the effect of sentence-combining instruction on reading comprehension. In D. A. Daiker, A. Kerek, and M. Morenberg (Eds.), *Sentence-combining and the teaching of writing.* Akron, Ohio: University of Akron Press, 1979.

Strickland, R. The language of elementary school children: Its relationship to the language of reading textbooks and the quality of reading of selected children. *Bulletin of the School of Education* (Bloomington Indiana University), 1962.

Strong, W. *Sentence combining: A composing book.* New York: Random House, 1973.

Strong, W. *Sentence combining and paragraph linking.* New York: Random House, in press.

Wisker, R. A. The effects of syntactic expectation during reading. *Journal of Educational Psychology*, 1976, *68*, 597–602.

9 | Grammar: A Perspective

John M. Kean

Continuing controversy about the role of grammar in the school curriculum is evidence of the health and vigor of the English discipline rather than the stimulus for cataclysmic changes in the way English educators treat the topic with their students. Yet the arguments sometimes seem equivalent to arguing about how many angels can fit on the head of a pin. The arguments about the role of grammar in the curriculum have existed for centuries among university faculty and even longer among those who would rule the world. And, since there were grammar schools during the Middle Ages and the Renaissance, its role then in the education of children was probably hotly debated. Even the Holy Roman Emperor and Shakespeare were not immune to discussions of grammar. In 1414, the Emperor is reputed to have said, "Ego sum rex Romanus et supra grammaticum." Shakespeare entered the fray with, "Thou hast most traitorously corrupted the youth of the realm in erecting a grammar school" (Henry VI, Part IV, vii 35). In 1838, educators at the Michigan Education Convention in Detroit were grappling with the ways that "the study of grammar can be more conducive than it is to the end of speaking and writing the English language with propriety" (Cubberley, 1934). The questions have remained the same. However, the research over the years to support the arguments has been limited when compared with other curriculum areas.

Sarah D'Eloia (1977) provided an appropriate epitaph for the study of grammar per se.

> Wherever it has been seriously researched, the analytical study of grammar has failed to produce significant results in student writing across the board—whether the result sought was improvement in the control of errors, increased sentence length, or increased variety of sentence structure; whether the students were in junior high school, high school, or college;

163

whether they came from privileged or under-privileged backgrounds; whether the grammar studied was traditional, structural, or transformational/generative. If there is one conclusion to be drawn which cuts across all the studies, it is this: the more time spent analyzing grammar, the less time spent writing; the less time spent writing, the less the improvement in the written product. (p. 1)

Although many teachers might agree with this statement, they would also find difficulty in responding to its implications. It is not easy to respond to because the very word "grammar" seems to have mystical qualities neither apparent to the senses nor obvious to the intelligence. The problem of deciding an appropriate role for grammar in school programs is, additionally, tied to a host of political, economic, psychological, sociological, and religious phenomena that at times make the situation almost hopeless. The debate about the sanctity of dialect, the relationships between jobs and language use, the dominance of masculinity in the language, the arguments about the interpretation of masculine pronouns in the Bible, the ideological debates about the thinking characteristics of individuals, groups, and cultures, and the ever present tendency by all cultural and economic subgroups to create their own argot seem to have forced many people to see grammar instruction as the only solution to all of the oral and written language problems of society. In fact, "there seems to be a general assumption among laymen that grammar is the critical mass in learning to write: and if not all teachers share that assumption, many partake of the misunderstanding of the word. Asked what she meant by 'language arts,' one elementary school teacher replied succinctly, 'Grammar!'" (Fadiman and Howard, 1979).

One can sympathize with this position. At about the time conscientious teachers have reached consensus on one definition or the complexities of one set of phenomena, they are presented with another set that strains the credibility English educators must have among themselves and with the various audiences that have to be dealt with, i.e., students, colleagues, administrators, researchers, and community.

At times it seems that if teachers would only teach grammar, all the problems of venereal disease, starvation, war, corruption, bureaucracy, and hatred would be solved. The problems are made even more complex by the advice, warnings, soothsayings, and conflicting testimony which seem to issue from the mouths of linguists, educators, rhetoricians, psychologists, and others who make pronouncements about language growth. Although they have learned more and more about how we communicate, piled theory upon theory, refined the levels of abstraction, and, indeed, the levels of grammar specification, they seem not to have provided an integrating theory or vehicle that would allow the practitioner who is trying to help students to write to make positive warranted decisions about intervention strategies. This is not to say that there is not information available that is useful, but that the load of information is now so heavy that it is difficult to pull it into the classroom.

DEFINITIONS

This chapter examines some recent research on grammar which provides positive direction to the search for a useful role for grammar in the teaching and learning of writing. But first it is necessary to establish some definitions because part of the problem in discussing grammar has been the failure to recognize that the word has different meanings in the minds of different people. This chapter provides three definitions of grammar. Three seems to be the minimum number necessary to talk about it, although other writers have provided five or even more, noting that "the term 'grammar' itself is something of a chameleon" (Weaver, 1979).

1. Grammar is a description of the expression system of the language and the ways in which the various grammatical elements (sounds, units of meaning, and construction) are arranged into communication units. Or, to put it another way, it is a description of the classes of words, their inflections, and their functions and relations in the sentence.
2. Grammar is a description of those grammatical elements which are to be preferred and those which are to be avoided. In other words it describes "good grammar" and "bad grammar"—that which is socially prestigious and that which is not. When used in reference to writing, it most often includes punctuation, spelling, and capitalization as well as word classes, inflections, and their functions and relationshps in sentences.
3. Grammar is that set of rules which the psycholinguists have suggested that a human intuitively develops and uses in order to communicate, i.e., "the abstract rules of linguistic knowledge that the speakers use in putting together the sentence in order to have it mean what the speaker intends" (Lance, 1977, p. 48).

Boercker (1975), Lance (1977) and Weaver (1979) have provided excellent discussions of grammar definitions which provide a basis for clarifying the possible meanings that the many audiences listed earlier may have.

REFLECTIONS ON RESEARCH IN GRAMMAR STUDY

Research dating back to at least 1902 has tried to establish a direct relationship between the study of grammar and students' growth in expressive ability, particularly in writing (Palmer, 1975). In one of the latest examinations of this research, Newkirk (1978) concluded that:

1. The term "formal instruction" is vague, seeming to apply to a wide range of practices, many of which have not been experimentally examined.
2. Correlations studies have come up with a wide range of correlations between grammar knowledge and writing ability.
3. The correlation technique, because it does not examine causality, can provide no information about the effects of grammar instruction.
4. There is no evidence that grammar, as it is traditionally taught, has a noticeable effect on writing improvement. Yet it should be noted that few of the accepted practices in the teaching of writing have been experimentally validated.
5. Although there have been a great many studies of the relationship of grammar instruction to writing, few meet the minimal requirement for experimental research.
6. The few long term studies that do meet the criteria for an experimental study do not clearly establish the ineffectiveness of grammar instruction, nor do they clearly establish the superiority of alternate direct methods for teaching error avoidance.
7. There is evidence that younger secondary students and students of average and below average intelligence have difficulty learning grammar as it is traditionally taught.
8. Studies have concentrated on the relationship of grammar instruction to error-avoidance. Few have dealt with the possible relationship of grammar instruction to sentence construction and writing style. (pp. 17–18)

Earlier in this chapter, D'Eloia's conclusions were suggested as an epitaph for the *formal* study of grammar, but even after being embalmed by linguists and formally laid out in its coffin for interment, grammar has a way of sitting up, calling for a sip of water to restore its strength, and returning as lively as a 10-year-old child to his/her verbal rounds.[1] Obviously, "grammar" is not dead even though "formal grammar" may be. Newkirk's summary suggests that much remains to be done. The next section of this chapter presents some statements about grammar in the schools and describes some research which can provide direction to our efforts to find an appropriate role for grammar in school programs.

---

[1] I borrowed this delightful phraseology with slight modification from Willard R. Espy's foreward to Susan Kelz Sperling's *Poplollies and Bellibones: A Celebration of Lost Words*, New York: Penguin Books, 1977. He was, of course, talking about an authoritative necrology of words presumed dead.

Flawed Reasoning from the Past

Grammar instruction has always been a standard feature of academic schooling. Much of this instruction has sprung from an image of what schooling ought to be and of the roles that we construct for ourselves in the schools. The image, of course, was never quite consistent with reality. There were numerous reasons for this. Our imperfect understanding of the rules of living language led us to believe that if we taught everyone a set of rules for language, everyone would speak and write the same way—not that everyone would have the same style, but that they would follow the same usage rules. We ignored the culture of the community and glorified the culture of the school and created confusion in the minds of students about the relationship between standard edited English, their own community, and the broader community. It was as if the football coach were to say, "Learn these plays and you will be a good football player," and then proceeded to teach more and more plays, without any insistence upon practice or without ever offering the opportunity to play the game for real. We overplayed the delayed gratification or the delayed payoff by spending more time on the rules and dry-lab diagramming than we did on writing. We also assumed that all students would profit from the same kind of instruction and be able to transfer the skill to the real world. Grammar was often taught with contrived examples in highly ritualistic, isolated ceremonies that bore no resemblance at all to the functional use of such information in real communication situations.

Carpenters and electricians are taught to read blueprints so that they can duplicate an engineer's or architect's ideas about the construction of a building. Engineers, architects, and managers are taught to draw blueprints, i.e., diagrams, as a useful way to convey an idea about projects infinitely more useful to the carpenter than if the projects had to be described in words. In no case did architects learn to draw blueprints to increase the likelihood of their developing the style of a Frank Lloyd Wright or a Buckminster Fuller. They learned to develop them to convey their own ideas to builders. The sentence diagram, be it a traditional diagram of the forties and fifties or the tree diagram of the sixties and seventies, does not help language learners to write sentences (i.e., build structures); it only enables them to draws diagrams. True, there were some learners who did profit from this particular way of abstracting language, but they were clearly in the minority. Teaching students to analyze language has often been compared to teaching mechanics how a motor works so that they will be better prepared to understand what goes wrong with the motor. The analogy is unfortunate, because the mechanic might better be compared with the English teacher, copy editor, or one who makes language his business, while the writer of language might better be compared with the driver of the vehicle.

Student writers must have an understanding of grammar that is equivalent to the drivers' knowledge of their vehicles and how to use them. The drivers of bicycles, mopeds, motorcycles, cars, trucks, or buses need to know something in common, i.e., rules of the road, mapreading, steering, but they need to know many different things depending upon the function of their vehicles, i.e., ways to conserve gas, noises that signal potential mechanical problems, what the flashing red light on the dashboard means, and simple repair techniques such as how to change a fuse. Student writers need to learn how to write for different audiences and for different purposes, which is analogous to learning how to drive differently on the freeway or on a residential street. More basically, they need to know how to punctuate (obey stop signs and road signs).

Grammar Needed to Take Tests?

Of course, when one set of reasons for including analytical grammar in the curriculum is shown to be false, another set is added. It is still believed that grammar terminology and analytic skills such as diagramming are needed because students will be taking a standardized test for which such information is necessary. Sutton (1976) examined 11 leading standardized tests which tested language skill directly or featured a section on English, verbal ability, or the like in order to determine how much grammar terminology was required to respond to test items. "The tests examined were among the most frequently used today and represent what a college-bound student might well encounter from middle school through college admission" (p. 37). The knowledge of the terminology of grammar required on seven of the tests was zero, while for three of the tests it was 1.8%, 1.9% and 3.4% of the content, respectively. One test required grammatical terminology in 24% of its items. He concluded that "grammar terminology per se is a very minor aspect of standardized tests in English. The major testing concerns seem to feel that this terminology is not necessary for college work nor for determining general language ability" (p. 40).

Sutton went on to make several statements which are pertinent to this discussion:

> I am well aware of the school of thought which holds that constant drill on grammar terminology, diagramming sentences, etc., will produce effective communicators. These persons, one suspects because *they* were taught that way, insist on bringing this highly specialized terminology into the English classroom. It is as inappropriate as supposing that one can't become a first rate driver unless he knows the names of all of the parts of an automobile engine. The facts are clear. There is no evidence to support the notion that

knowledge of grammar terminology aids one in being a better writer, reader, speaker, or listener. (p. 40)

Teach Grammar from the Student's Perspective

We all use grammar and we all have an intuitive grasp of its rules within the confines of the communication needs within our own community. The teacher's task is to help students understand and improve their own grammar with a minimal amount of interference with their communication and without inhibiting their desire to communicate. Many complex decisions are required of the teacher to do this, and these decisions generally need to be directed to individual children rather than to groups of children. The teacher needs to know when to intervene, when to teach, and when not to. The teacher needs to know what will have a chance of working and what will not. For example, young children acquiring basic grammar rules may frequently use incorrect verb forms, e.g., "taked" for "took," substituting a regular form when no regular verb form exists. Generally, this simply means that the child is developing and testing rules. A teacher might well decide not to interfere in this rule formation, noting that the child will likely change the form quickly anyway. Alternately, the teacher might decide to model the correct form by using it in conversations with the child. In other words, the teacher needs to examine the situation from the child's perspective. Mistakes in grammar generally do have explanations and it is the explanation which should govern the decision about what the teacher should do to help the child to change or improve.

Teachers, then, need to make decisions about what, when, where, and how to correct language. But they also need to make decisions about when, where, and how to help children improve immature syntax—language that is essentially correct by adult norms but that is not as effective or as powerful as it could be. The two types of decisions are not mutually exclusive, because as the children attempt to use increasingly complex language constructions, the chances of their making errors also increase. In varying degrees, this is true whether one is talking about subject-verb agreement, spelling, punctuation, or other grammatical elements. At one level it is true that one can assume that students should have learned concept "X" before they got to grade level "Y," but that does not account for all the intervening variables that might have prevented the students from practicing and thus internalizing the skill. Thus, students may have been taught something about anaphoric relations between words or groups of words at the fifth grade, but if they did not write passages that encouraged appropriate use of pronouns, it is difficult to expect them to be able to use them correctly at the ninth grade level.

When to Teach What?

Marzano and DiStefano (1978) analyzed 750 compositions, randomly selected from National Assessment of Education Progress essays written by 9-, 13-, and 17-year-olds, to determine the skills that go into the writing of a good composition. The essays were first rated high, medium, and low in quality. Forty-three different indices reported or hypothesized to have a relationship with composition quality were then identified from a survey of past research and were applied to each of the sample compositions. Analysis of the results led to the identification of five composing skills related to writing quality: modifications within sentences, subordination between sentences, sentence sense, grammar and usage, and vocabulary.

The analysis of grammar and usage skills provides some suggestions for determining the role of grammar in school programs, particularly about a hierarchy of skills and the complexity of the task of deciding what is to be taught at a grade level. Some examples from the numerous findings of this study are included to illuminate the problems in determining what should be emphasized at different instructional levels. Marzano and DiStefano found that error measures of spelling and run-ons were a factor in quality at all ages, but that fragments, agreement errors, and tense errors were related to quality for 17-year-olds only. Measures of verb complexity were related to quality at the 9-year-old level. Capitalization and punctuation were not related to quality at any level.

In their discussion of two of the five skills, Marzano and DiStefano took special note of some of the problems inherent in setting up a sequence of grammar skills. Although run-ons were a factor at all levels, fragments did not become an issue until high school. Younger students did use fragments, but it was not until high school that their compositions became long enough for the frequency of fragments to affect quality. Spelling was a factor at all levels, but subject/verb, pronoun/antecedent, and tense agreement did not become issues until later:

> This is not to say that elementary students do not make errors in tense or agreement. At the elementary level compositions contain sentences whose structures are simple enough that subject/verb, pronoun/antecedent problems rarely arise. For example, a common cause of agreement problems between subject and verb occurs when there are intervening phrases between subject and the verb. Consider the following agreement error:
>
> The *pep talks* given to the team by the coach *was* very useful.
>
> The subject (pep talks) which is plural and the verb (was) which is singular should agree but the intervening phrase, "given to the team by the coach," has probably made the writer confused as to the subject of the sentence. Since elementary school students write few intervening phrases, there is less occasion for subject/verb agreement errors to arise. (p. 15)

They recommend that specifics such as "subject/verb agreement, pronoun, antecedent and tense agreement should not be overemphasized at the elementary level, but should receive considerable attention from junior high on" (p. 19).

Interrelationship of Ideas and Expression Marzano and DiStefano's study reinforces the statement made earlier in this chapter that mistakes do have a reason. From the example presented above, it can be seen that the elementary teacher ought not be blamed for many of the errors that occur at the high school level because such errors are as much a product of the level of writing being attempted as they are the product of the language rules that the student has internalized.

Richard Lloyd-Jones makes the argument forcefully in "The Politics of Research into the Teaching of Composition" (1977):

> The public—including professors of various academic subjects—often confuses ignorance of the subject with the inability to handle language. It is easier to blame a badly written examination or paper on the writing than on ignorance of the subject which the professor is supposed to be teaching . . . Even more frustrating is the fact that as one's intellectual reach is extended, one's once-adequate writing is no longer sufficient. The larger one's experience, the more the old skills with language have to be reworked to fit new circumstances . . . To some extent, confusing prose is a sign of active engagement with new ideas as opposed to routine regurgitation through the pen of what is stuffed into the ear. . . . [Writing] is not an activity which one masters once and for all. . . . Only our naivete—the ignorance of what we supposedly taught—would lead anyone to imagine that a 17-year-old would know whatever one will have to know about writing or that any person always writes well. (pp. 219–220)

Lloyd-Jones' observation coupled with the research suggests clearly that all phases of the task are interrelated. Information as well as language maturity level and time affect the product that a student provides.

Grammar and Learning How to Write

If we accept the notion that grammar study should be subordinated to the elimination of error, then we further need to accept several other notions. First, grammar instruction must be tied to the errors the students are making or are *likely to make*, given the kind of writing that they are expected to do. Second, if grammar study is to be effective, writing assignments need to be structured. Third, if grammar is to be improved, then all phases of the writing task need to be given attention, from prewriting to editing.

Several types of prewriting activities have been consistently supported by the research literature (Gentry, 1978). Miller and Ney (1968) reported that systematic oral language exercises have been efffective with students:

1. Students who participated in systematic oral language exercises wrote with greater freedom and facility.
2. Experimental subjects who practiced certain structures in their oral and written forms used these structures significantly more often than did control subjects.
3. Students who practiced putting together sentences in oral and written forms so that simple sentences were changed to complex structures used a greater number of complex sentences. (pp. 60–61)

Reading to students and simply providing them the opportunity to talk about and through a subject before writing about it has also been effective (Blake, 1971).

At the other end of the continuum, rewriting and editing, there seems not to have been much research, although Emig (1971), in speaking of the implications of her research on the composing processes of twelfth graders, makes a very strong statement about both the definition of revision and the time devoted to it: "At the other end of the process, revision is lost, not only because it is too narrowly defined but because, again, no time is provided for any major reformulation or reconceptualization" (p. 99). More research needs to be focused on this part of the writing process.

An entirely separate, but supportive line of research has been suggested by Falk (1979). She reviewed language acquisition research and argued that much can be learned about learning to write by implication from what has been learned about children's oral language acquisition. Two basic assumptions underlie her argument:

1. Writing, as the written representation of language, and speech, as the oral representative of language, are different but co-equal concrete means to express language. Therefore, whatever is known about the learning of oral language production (i.e., learning to talk) will have implications for the learning of written language production (i.e., learning to write). Both are instances of language acquisition.
2. The fundamental capacities of human beings for acquiring language do not change in any significant qualitative manner as they mature (i.e., the language learning abilities of chilren and adults are essentially the same). Therefore, whatever is known about how children acquire language will have implications for understanding how adults acquire language. (p. 437)

Falk suggests that children and adults learning to write need the same freedom to hypothesize and experiment as young children have when they are learning to talk. She argues against highly structured writing assignments that limit creativity and hence normal language growth. Just as children learn by experimenting that there are exceptions to rules for forming past tenses of verbs, so they can also learn the rules for punctuation. In normal language production, there is the possibility of error:

For example, a student who has overgeneralized the placement of commas and who always uses them with relative clauses, as in *Men, who hunt, are cruel*, will learn far more quickly about comma placement in restrictive and non-restrictive relative clauses if misunderstood by readers than if subjected to a set of exercises or punctuation rules. (p. 442)

Writing: Communication or Exercise? Falk's suggestions make sense, but only in an environment where writing is done for real audiences and for significant purposes. This idea is not new, but it seems rarely to have been practiced in mainstream educational settings. The opportunity to write for one's peers, younger children, adults, or whomever has not been provided to most students. Schools have been and continue to be seen as places where one can short-circuit natural growth through drill and exercise and expect feedback from a skilled writing instructor. The situation is almost "Catch 22." Teachers believe that their own feedback is necessary for student writers to grow. However, there are too many students and too little time for teachers to provide constructive feedback on compositions, so they do not assign much writing. Writing is not assigned, so writers cannot practice the craft. Time that might have been devoted to writing is used in other assignments; therefore, the students cannot even choose to spend their instructional time writing. When writing is requested, time is rarely provided for students to discuss the content prior to the writing in spite of research supporting such discussions. Further, the students are seldom provided the opportunity or shown how to revise or edit what they have written. Instead, even the kindest of teachers provides feedback like this:

> You have dealt with the *meanings* of the novel quite well—good understanding and substantiation most of the time. One major problem, however, [name of student deleted], is that your sentence structure really presents difficulty. You should take time to go to the Writing Lab to rectify your writing problem—for future classes and papers. Unfortunately it has affected your grade on the paper (as it must) and probably will continue to do on future writings [*sic*].[2]

On an 8-page typed paper, the teacher had found four comma faults, three fragments, and several awkward sentences. The feedback was counterproductive. The message was confusing and neatly got the teacher out of doing anything about the student's "problem." In other words, expert feedback does not necessarily help the student to improve the writing. The real value of writing was also missed because there was no useful audience. If the student had dealt with the meaning of the novel well, how much more useful would have been the opportunity to share this

---

[2] This example comes from a college freshman's paper, 1979. Its origin shall remain anonymous.

information with peers in the class. This sharing could have provided useful dialogue among students as well as aid them in understanding how one can use papers as a basis for dialogue.

Alternatively, the paper or selected parts could also have been shared as part of a classroom editing group exercise. This process, although not yet researched extensively, has generated enthusiasm among those teachers who have tried it. The process has been used from elementary schools through graduate school with good effect. The peer editing group not only provides peer support, but also ties the editing to a distinct audience over a long enough period of time to permit the student writer to make predictions about the audience and about the language that will most effectively communicate with that audience.

IMPLICATIONS FOR TEACHING

The focus of this chapter is on the pragmatic treatment of grammar in school programs, based on the assumption that grammar study should be subordinate to and in support of helping students develop writing skills. For this to happen, there first has to be a writing program within which grammar study can function as a support. There has been strong professional backing and appropriate definition given to the effort to develop writing programs, but the public still seems more interested in supporting grammar than it does writing. Teachers must make every effort to help the public put grammar into some kind of perspective. Professional organizations have begun to provide information to support this political effort, but they do not have the access to local communities and parents that teachers do through their local English councils and educational associations. The National Council of Teachers of English has made available numerous documents particularly through its SLATE (Support for Learning and Teaching of English) Newsletter. The Newsletter provided an excellent definition of writing in the *Standards for Basic Skills Writing Programs* (1979), which can serve as the basis for a program.

> Writing is the process of selecting, combining, arranging and developing ideas in effective sentences, paragraphs, and often longer units of discourse. The process requires the writer to cope with a number of variables: *method of development* (narrating, explaining, describing, reporting, persuading); *tone* (from personal to quite formal); *form* (from a limerick to a formal letter to a long research report); *purpose* (from discovering and expressing personal feelings and values to conducting the impersonal "business" of everyday life); *possible audiences* (oneself, classmates, a teacher, "the world"). Learning to write and to write increasingly well involves developing increasing skill and sensitivity in selecting from and combining these variables to shape particular messages. It also involves learning to conform to convention of the printed language appropriate to the age of the writer and to the form, purpose and tone of the message. (p. 1)

Given this definition and given the supporting criteria for a writing program identified in the Newsletter, it should be possible to put grammar into some kind of perspective and to dispel many of the myths that surround grammar. The public will always, it seems, prefer the second definition given earlier in this chapter, i.e., grammar is a description of those grammatical elements which are to be preferred and those which are to be avoided. The definition includes such items as punctuation, spelling, and capitalization as well as word class, inflections, and their functions and relationships in sentences.

However, we need to educate both ourselves and the public about the most effective ways to improve grammar. Grammar study should be incorporated within the writing program rather than taught separately. It should be taught on a need-to-know basis when the writing that students are doing calls for it. It should be taught using as little terminology as is absolutely possible. Provisions should be made for students to learn "correct" grammar from attempting and failing to communicate rather than through drill and exercises. Drills and workbook exercises, when used, should focus on sentence building and sentence-combining exercises (discussed in Chapter 8) rather than on analytical reviews of conventional rules. At times, grammar should not be taught at all but allowed to develop as the students test out their own hypotheses about what works and what does not. This procedure can work only in situations where the opportunity to write is very frequent. There is no real definition of frequent, but it seems clear at least by analogy that one cannot refine skills by practicing every other week. Physical fitness experts now tell adults that they cannot keep their bodies in shape unless they exercise at least 3 times a week. They are also told that they need to exercise every other day, not 3 times at the end of the week, and clearly not all week once a month. Shorter, regular opportunities to write are probably much more productive than the massive burst of energy required to produce a term paper once a semester. This is not to say that sixth graders or college freshmen should not write research papers, but that such efforts should be controlled and developed within the capabilities of the student and with due regard to the actual purpose of the writing program.

IMPLICATIONS FOR RESEARCH

This chapter discusses several areas that provide possibilities for research. Too often we have attempted research on writing with all of the fervor of a used vacuum cleaner salesman demonstrating how well his machine will pick up lint from the mattress pad, forgetting that we really wanted a machine that would pick dirt off the floor. Perhaps what is needed in research in this area is a *Consumer's Report* on research findings to remind us about priorities. At times the research that we seem to need on effective grammar instruction does not seem to fit the research methodology we know how to use. The results have at best been discouraging.

A recent example of an effort to improve writing in schools is the Bay Area Writing Project supported by the National Endowment for the Humanities and designed to provide teachers themselves with writing experiences as well as with the latest research and best practice information. The project is designed to help teachers teach other teachers about writing as well as to improve the teaching of writing in their own classrooms. Michael Scriven (1979), evaluation director for the project, has reported that most teachers felt that participation affected their teaching substantially and beneficially and that it produced changes in their teaching methods, especially activities, use of a wide range of techniques, and use of peer feedback. However, when the writing of participants' students was compared before and after participation, and with that of students of a comparison group of teachers, no consistent patterns were found. Scriven speculated that this might have been "due to the already superior quality of the Invitational (and comparison) teachers, which would leave little room for improvement, or to several other methodological or logistical factors" (p. 7).

Falk (1979) in her speculations about language acquisition and the teaching of writing suggests that "some of the factors important to the successful teaching and learning of writing may never by feasible objects of controlled experimental study" (pp. 445–447).

But even with such cautions, and with Newkirk's summary of research problems as a backdrop, it still seems appropriate to proceed with research. The work of Marzano and DiStefano is exciting and with the availability of the National Assessment of Educational Progress essay deserves to be extended. Marzano and DiStefano have not exhausted the composition skills related to grammar and usage that we need to know more about if we are to have the proper information upon which to base our decisions concerning what skills are appropriate in what depth for what age levels. However, their work has certainly extended our knowledge beyond the common sense hierarchy upon which we have based decisions in the past.

Falk's suggestions, too, should be followed up and her assumptions put to the test. The parallels between *natural* oral language development and *natural* writing development need much more attention. Perhaps, as Falk suggests, controlled experimental studies are not appropriate, but the case study method used regularly in oral language development studies and the ethnographic methods for studying writing certainly should lend themselves to exploration of these relationships. Studies which examine the effects of real audiences and peer editing on student writing are well within our research capabilities. Although some of our colleagues are fond of saying that case studies are out of vogue except as ways to identify variables for *real* research, it may very well be that we are only beginning to identify the variables, be they grammar, vocabulary, literary background, experience, or methodology, that do affect writing improvement.

There are other areas for research related to writing generally and grammar specifically. Lloyd-Jones' work on the politics of research on composition needs elaboration. We have never examined carefully the ideology—the social-political, economic forces—that control both the research questions we ask or the objectives we set for language growth in either speaking or writing. True, the profession has addressed this question in a careful manner in monographs like the *Students' Right to Their Own Language* (Committee on College Composition and Communication, 1974). But this statement has not been accepted by either the laymen who set policy for schools or the researchers who conduct applied research studies on school-based speaking and writing programs.

Additionally, we need to know much more than we now know about parental and peer influence on both motivation for and the production of writing. It seems that little has been done on the rhetoric of back-to-basics movements and their relationship to real problems in schools, whether those relate to grammar or to mathematics.

There are enough significant findings in the research literature to support the contention that direct manipulation of words in specific exercises such as sentence-combining is effective as an aid to writing, but this work needs both to be extended and replicated in many settings. The same is true of research related to other prewriting activities like discussions and reviews. Too often prewriting is thought of as preparation *for* rather than part *of* the writing process. There are also culture and age differences which may be very important in the selection of prewriting activities. Additionally, we need to know much more about which types of prereading activities are appropriate for which kinds of writing. Most studies of writing processes, whether focused on grammar or on any other writing component, have been tied to descriptive writing *or* narrative writing *or* persuasive writing *or* expository writing *or* poetry. Most of the conclusions from studies have been generalized (albeit not by the researchers themselves) to all types of writing, with writing becoming very amorphous in the process.

CONCLUSION

The controversy continues but there are hopeful signs. Some researchers have moved out in exciting new directions and some myths may soon be disputed. Consensus on some general principles has been long in coming. The prestigious Council for Basic Education seems willing to support less formal grammar study. Fadiman and Howard, in their work *Empty Pages: A Search for Writing Competence in School and Society* (1979), which the Council for Basic Education supported, say, "it is essential that the students really understand that competent writing is not possible if, for example, subject and verb disagree in number." However, they believe that "this understanding can be achieved without recourse to much formal grammatical drill, analysis, or rule memorizing" (p. 65). There will always be tension between grammar study and writing for it is difficult always to keep the main goal—improvement of writing—in mind. Perhaps Higginson in his 1890 Preface to Emily Dickinson's *Poems* expresses it best: "When a thought takes one's breath away, a lesson on grammar seems an impertinence."

ACKNOWLEDGMENTS

The author is indebted to Irene Diamond, Wisconsin Writing Project Co-coordinator, University of Wisconsin—Madison, and to Joan Hagen, Assistant Professor of Elementary Education, University of Wisconsin—Whitewater, for their helpful comments on the various drafts of this chapter.

FOR DISCUSSION

1. Kean identifies a high correlation between grammar knowledge and writing ability. If instruction in formal grammar does not significantly affect writing ability, why or how is this the case?
2. Kean discusses teachers' corrections of children's language. What are some situations in which correction is appropriate? What are some situations when correction is detrimental or inappropriate?
3. Kean discusses particular elements of writing that affect the quality of student composition at particular levels. How could these elements be appropriately sequenced in a writing or composition program? Would the sequence be the same for all students?
4. Are Kean's conclusions opposed to Straw's in Chapter 8?
5. Kean states that a support system such as grammar can only be taught in the context of a writing program. What implications does this have for classroom teachers at all levels?

REFERENCES

Blake, H. E. Written composition in English primary schools. *Elementary English*, October 1971, *48*, 605–615.
Boercker, M. S. *What every single teacher should know about language . . . but may not*. Clarksville, Tennessee: Queen City Publishers, 1975.

Committee on College Composition and Communication Language Statement. Students' right to Their Own Language. *College Composition and Communication*, Fall 1974, *25*, 1–32.

Cubberley, E. P. *Readings in public education in the United States*. New York: Houghton Mifflin, 1934.

D'Eloia, S. The uses—and limits—of grammar. *Journal of Basic Writing*, Spring-Summer 1977, *1*(3), 1–48.

Emig, J. *The composing process of twelfth graders*. Urbana, Illinois: National Council of Teachers of English, 1971.

Fadiman, C., and Howard, J. *Empty pages: A search for writing competence in school and society*. Belmont, California: Fearon Pitman Publishers, Inc., in association with the Council for Basic Education, 1979.

Falk, J. S. Language acquisition and the teaching and learning of writing. *College English*, December 1979, *41*(4), 436–447.

Gentry, J. "The Second 'R' is Alive and Well." In H. G. Shane and J. Walden (Eds.), *Classroom-relevant research in the language arts*. Washington, D.C.: Association for Supervision and Curriculum Development, 1978.

Lance, D. M. What is "grammar"? *English Education*, Fall 1977, *9*(1), 43–49.

Lloyd-Jones, R. The politics of research into the teaching of composition. *College Composition and Communication*, October 1977, *28*, 218–222.

Marzano, R. J., and DiStefano, P. Five empirically based composition skills. ERIC Document Reproduction Service, ED 162 337, 1978.

Miller, B. D., and Ney, J. W. The effect of systematic oral exercises on the writing of fourth-grade students. *Research in the Teaching of English*, Spring 1968, *2*, 44–61.

National Council of Teachers of English. Standards for basic skills writing programs. *SLATE: Support for Learning and Teaching of English*, April 1979, *4*, No. 2.

Newkirk, T. Grammar instruction and writing: What does the research really prove?" ERIC Document Reproduction Service, ED 153 218, 1978.

Palmer, W. S. Research on grammar: A review of some pertinent investigations. *High School Journal*, March 1975, *58*(6), 252–58.

Scriven, M. Bay Area writing project evaluation summary of three studies. *The National Writing Project Network Newsletter*, March 1979, *2*(2), 7.

Sutton, G. A. Do we need to teach a grammar terminology? *English Journal*, December 1976, *75*(9), 37–40.

Weaver, C. *Grammar for teachers: Perspectives and definitions*. Urbana, Illinois: National Council of Teachers of English, 1979.

10 Assessment and Evaluation in Written Composition: A Commonsense Perspective

Stanley B. Straw

Investigators have attempted for decades to develop valid and reliable means of measuring and assessing growth and performance in writing. Interest in the area has received new impetus because of recent educational issues, including teacher accountability, the "back-to-basics" movement, and concern about dropping scores on college and university placement exams. These issues have made evaluation of student writing an important, and, at times, an inflammatory topic. In addition, educational practitioners, particularly classroom teachers, do not seem to be employing assessment methods much different than those used before researchers began in the 1930s to study scientifically and systematically the factors affecting the composing process and measures of writing performance. In fact, intuitive judgment seems to be the most widespread method of evaluation in writing (Diederich, 1974).

This state of affairs may indicate that all of our research has simply verified the appropriateness of the intuitive judgment employed by most teachers. On the other hand, it may also indicate that teachers are either not familiar with the research which has been done or that they find the instruments developed from the research too involved and awkward to be effectively employed on a regular basis in the classroom.

In this chapter, the major methods of assessment of students' composing performance that are in use today and the recent research in composition measurement are reviewed; implications of the current methodology and research for both practitioners and researchers are drawn. The foremost question addressed here is: Do the results of the recent research have any practical use on a day-to-day basis for the classroom teacher?

A number of purposes for assessing and evaluating student writing have been identified. A primary reason that has been stated by John

Maxwell (1975) is that "teachers of English and the language arts have always wanted to know the results of their teaching, to see if their efforts have done someone some good." This reason alone seems adequate for spending considerable time and energy on the search for valid and reliable means of assessing student writing. Furthermore, Cooper and Odell (1977) have identified additional purposes for and uses of student assessment. They have divided them into three major areas: administrative (predicting student grades, student placement, assignment of grades), instructional (diagnosis of writing, student feedback and guidance), and evaluation and research (measuring growth, determining the effectiveness of particular instructional programs, measuring group differences, describing writing performances, identification of variables affecting writing performance). All of the above are sound purposes and uses. However, it seems that two major questions involved with evaluation that are of perhaps the greatest importance for the classroom teacher are: *How can I identify my students' strengths and weaknesses in writing?* and *How can I determine if the instructional procedures I am employing are effective?* These are the issues addressed in this chapter.

MEASUREMENT IN WRITING: VALIDITY AND RELIABILITY

The state of the art in the assessment of writing skills and ability is vast and varied. This chapter is concerned with only the measurement of composition and the composing process, not with those areas that Cooper and Odell (1977) have referred to as "editorial skills." Editorial skills include " . . . choosing the best sentence, recognizing correct usage, punctuation, and capitalization" (p. viii). These skills do not lie within the domain of composition or the composing process and, although much work has been done in the area of the measurement of these skills, they have little or no relevance to the process of composing a piece of writing.

The words "valid" and "reliable" are used above in referring to measurement in writing. Because these terms are central to any discussion of assessment, they warrant further definition.

Validity refers to the soundness of an evaluation instrument in measuring what it is supposed to be measuring. Cooper and Odell (1977) explain validity in the following manner:

> If a measure or measurement scheme is valid, it does what we say it is doing. We want to insist on a careful distinction between *predictive validity* and two other kinds of validity, *content* and *construct validity*. If a measure has *predictive validity*, then it predicts performance at some time in the future or it correlates well with some criterion . . . If a measure has *content* validity, then it is an appropriate measure for a writing program. It actually measures what writers have been practicing in a writing course of program. If a measure has *construct validity*, then it actually measures the construct of interest, in this case, writing ability or writing performance. (pp. xi–xii)

Of primary interest here are two terms *content validity* and *construct validity*. A test of handwriting performance is not a valid measure of writing ability: it violates the concept of content validity because it does not measure performance in composing; it also violates the concept of construct validity because it does not measure the competencies needed by a student in order to accomplish the task of composing.

Test reliability, on the other hand, "is the degree to which a test is an accurate gauge of an individual's performance" (Purves et al., 1975). Reliability refers to the ability of a test to be accurate in the assessment of a person's ability or performance.

ELEMENTS OF THE WRITING PROCESS

Before we can quantify or describe student performance in written composition, the constructs underlying the process need to be identified, if possible, and considered. Three major areas that are consistently identified by students and teachers as affecting their judgments of composition quality are vocabulary features, syntactic features, and organizational and stylistic features. By the same token, these are the three areas often assessed by researchers attempting to measure student performance in composition.

However, as pointed out by Britton, Burgess, Martin, McLeod, and Rosen (1975), these attributes of a piece of writing are exactly that—attributes—and may be the result of a number of variables affecting or constructs underlying the writing process. Britton et al. further point out that competence in these areas interacts with other variables, such as purpose, function, and audience, when a writer produces a written work. A description of the writing process and the cognitive, social, and linguistic factors underlying competence, if indeed such a description is possible, is not within the scope of this chapter. However, it is important for the teacher of writing to be aware that student composition performance is always affected by a set of constructs and variables that are not evident in the composition product itself. Competence in vocabulary or syntax or organization may be reflected in a paper that is made up of "mature" vocabulary and syntax and "tight" organization. On the other hand, a composition weak in any or all of these areas *may not* indicate a lack of competence on the part of the student in these areas, but rather may be a result of any of a number of other factors which can affect writing performance. These factors include things as assignment variables, writing environment variables, cognitive development, student interests and feelings, and perception of audience (Braddock, Lloyd-Jones, and Schoer, 1963; Crowhurst, 1978) By the same token, a composition which is the sum of "mature" vocabulary plus "mature" syntax, plus "tight" organization may not be evaluated as a mature or high quality composition. Therefore, the areas of writing performance that are usually measured are, in fact, indices—indicators—of a writer's competence in writing and, as such, cannot be assumed to measure completely the psychological constructs underlying the writing process itself.

In fact, one of the reasons that measurement in writing has been described as "barely emerging from the state of alchemy" (Hunt, 1966) may be that a cohesive, exact, and generally accepted description of the writing process has not yet been developed. Therefore, we are still measuring the product, that is, the performance, not the process or the competence. On the other hand, the reliability of the measures and assessment procedures described in this chapter has been investigated and assessed and the measures and assessment procedures have been shown to have validity at least in terms of being indices of writing performance, if not descriptions of competence.

VOCABULARY

Extent of Vocabulary Knowledge

Perhaps the most obvious index of writing performance is a writer's knowledge and use of vocabulary. Competency in vocabulary maturity, control or precision and variety (Neilsen, 1977) have been shown to significantly affect raters' perceptions of writing quality. Classic studies in vocabulary point that growth in vocabulary is significantly related to language ability (Bolton, 1954; Vineyard and Massey, 1957). Objective measures of vocabulary growth, whether that growth is measured in terms of word frequency, word depth or complexity, or maturity, correlate highly with measures of performance in language. However, performance on a recognition test of word meanings does not necessarily determine performance in vocabulary use in writing. Objective tests of vocabulary, though they possess predictive validity for writing performance, have low content validity because these objective tests are primarily reading, not writing measures. The fact that a student can recognize a word and identify its synonym or definition from a set of foils does not mean that that same student is capable of or comfortable in using that word in a written composition. It takes a much greater control of vocabulary to employ a word in a productive task, such as writing, than in a receptive task, such as listening or reading (Singleton, 1960). Furthermore, such tests only *sample* a student's vocabulary knowledge; they do not test either the depth or breadth of his knowledge of words.

It seems obvious, then, that objective tests of receptive (usually reading) vocabulary knowledge, although they may predict a student's vocabulary control, do not give the investigator any substantial information about a student's ability to use vocabulary in a writing task.

The alternative to the objective task is that of counting and classifying the vocabulary used by students in actual writing tasks. The validity of such measures seems obvious, but the task of collecting such data is both time consuming and laborious. Furthermore, a student's performance on a free-write task will supply the investigator with a very limited sample of a student's ability to employ vocabulary. In addition, numerous other variables such as topic familiarity, audience perception, and assignment significantly affect a student's performance in vocabulary within a particular free-write situation (Finn, 1977).

For decades researchers have been attempting to assess the size of students' writing vocabularies based on the students' own writing. Estimates range from 2,500 to 23,750 words for first grade students to 25,000 to 136,500 for twelfth grade students (Smith, 1941; Rinsland, 1945; Singleton, 1960; Lorge and Chall, 1963), depending on the criteria employed for word knowledge and on the definition of the term *word*. Unfortunately, many of these studies have focused on spelling performance as the criterion of word knowledge and have not dealt with either word maturity or appropriateness of word choice.

Vocabulary Maturity

The studies discussed above do not define for us what maturity in writing is or how that relates to quality in written composition. Maturity in writing vocabulary has been defined in a number of different ways. One approach defines vocabulary maturity in terms of type/token ratios, that is, the ratio of the number of different words used in a composition to the number of total words used. This ratio is often referred to as "vocabulary diversity" (Fox, 1972). Research in oral language (Fox, 1972; Dahl, 1975; Hopkins, 1976) indicates that as children grow older, they use a greater proportion of different words to the total number of words spoken, that is, the use of vocabulary becomes more diverse. The assumption underlying this type of measure is that as students become more adept at vocabulary use, they use words with greater precision, and, therefore, use more specific words (and less frequent words) for concepts. The less mature student, having a limited number of available vocabulary items, will use the same word for a multiplicity of concepts, whereas the more mature student will use a greater number of different words to express ideas. This type of measure further assumes that the more mature student has more precise concepts and conceptual relations to encode in language.

The data on the usefulness of the type/token ratio in written language are not at this point convincing. Although the underlying assumption seems logical—that as a student becomes more mature in writing, the diversity of the student's vocabulary will be greater—there is limited empirical evidence to substantiate the assumption. Knapp (1972), in an exploratory study, did not find a significant growth in vocabulary diversity among students at the fourth, at the eight, and at the eleventh grades, although Slotnick (1972) reports diversity in vocabulary and word choice to be highly related to composition quality.

Intuitively, it would seem that diversity in word choice would affect raters' perceptions of style and variety, and, therefore, would be related to quality. However, no solid and convincing evidence seems to be available to justify type/token ratio as a reliable measure of vocabulary maturity in writing.

Another way in which vocabulary maturity in writing has been assessed is through frequency counts. Classic studies of the frequency of the appearance of words in published materials have led researchers to hypothesize that, as a student matures in writing, the student's use of less frequent words will be greater (Rinsland, 1945; Wesman and Seashore, 1949; Hildreth, 1953; Cherry, 1957; Zipf, 1965). These investigations assume that word difficulty or maturity is synonymous with word frequency in print. That may be a fallacious assumption in that, again, audience perception, purpose for writing, and topic can significantly affect a student's choice of vocabulary (Finn, 1977).

Two studies have attempted to control for these variables. The first, by Neilsen (1977), asked teachers to choose between synonyms the word they felt to be more mature. In all cases, the less frequent synonym was chosen as the more mature vocabulary item. She further found that maturity of vocabulary as identified in this manner significantly affected teachers' ratings of the quality of compositions.

Finn (1977), on the other hand, analyzed the word choices of students after eliminating words that were topic specific and a set of words that he identified as being low frequency but which did not indicate maturity (such as slang words, contractions, and proper nouns). He found that the adjusted word frequency count could be applied as an objective measure of writing maturity.

In addition, an interesting study reported by Page (1968) found that average word length in letters correlated at a 0.51 level with composition quality and that the standard deviation of word length (a measure of the variety or variance of word length) correlated with quality at a 0.53 level. This would indicate that as students mature in writing, they use a greater number of longer words. Since word length and frequency are highly correlated negatively, there is some indication that frequency and word length are limited indices of writing maturity.

Undoubtedly, as students grow in their ability to write, their ability to use more mature vocabulary more appropriately also grows (Diederich, 1962; Fosvedt, 1965). However, as can be seen from the studies presented here, the definition of mature word choice has not yet been agreed upon by teachers and investigators and the collection of data is both time consuming and, without computer assistance, tedious. It is questionable, therefore, whether any of the methods reviewed here have any practical usefulness on an ongoing basis for the classroom teacher.

SYNTACTIC COMPLEXITY AND MATURITY

Another area that has been investigated extensively as an index of writing maturity is the syntax used by students in compositions. Hunt (1966) points out the following:

> Any teacher of English can tell a fourth-grade theme from a twelfth-grade theme . . . [H]e could tell the average fourth-grade theme from the average eighth-grade theme. Just how would he detect the difference? For one thing he would rely on word choice. The vocabulary of the average eighth grader is measurably different from that of the average fourth grader. But also the teacher would feel that some of the sentence structures used by the eighth grader were too mature to be used by the fourth grader. (p. 732)

Two analyses, *syntactic complexity* and *syntactic maturity*, have primarily been used as indices of growth in syntax. Syntactic complexity has caused a great deal of confusion and, as Neilsen (1977) has pointed out:

> No precise definition of syntactic complexity appears in the literature. However, the consensus of most researchers . . . using the same or similar terms (e.g., syntactic fluency, structural complexity), is that syntactic complexity reflects length of independent clauses, amount of subordination, range of sentence patterns, number of sentence-embedding (or sentence-combining), transformations (cluster size), and depth of these transformations. (p. 3)

A closer look at the term and its use indicates that syntactic complexity is an attribute or set of attributes associated with text and not with the person producing or processing language. Bormuth (1966) defines syntactic complexity in terms of 64 different variables based on "parts of speech" and 48 "form class and traditional type variables" (p. 115). However, syntactic complexity refers primarily to the linguistic description of the syntax of the language. Even though the linguistic descriptions may be the most complete and accurate descriptions of syntactic complexity, because they lack psychological validity (Winterowd, 1976), they seem to be inappropriate measures of development in writing competence or performance. Furthermore, there is no evidence that syntactic complexity correlates highly with writing quality (Christensen, 1968).

The syntactic growth or maturity of a person differs markedly from the concept of syntactic complexity. Syntactic growth refers to the attributes of the person using language, not to the text itself. It applies to the language user and his ability to process syntax, either receptively (as in listening and reading) or productively (as in speaking or writing). Syntactic maturity in receptive language refers to the growth in the ability of a person to process and understand more syntactically complex material, closely parallels increases in syntactic complexity, and is related to the concepts of readability and comprehensibility of material (Bormuth, 1966; Fry, 1968; Harris, 1974; Klare, 1975; Raygor, 1976). On the other hand, in productive language, syntactic maturity refers to the growth of a person in expressing language that more nearly approximates the adult model (Smith, 1974). Here is a very basic difference between the concepts of syntactic growth in receptive and productive language. As growth occurs in receptive syntactic ability, the language user is able to process and understand more complex syntax; on the other hand, as growth occurs in producitve syntactic ability, the language produced by the language user approaches the adult syntactic model, which may or may not be more syntactically complex (Smith, 1974).

Measures of Syntactic Maturity

Over the past 50 years, a number of different measures of syntactic growth or maturity in productive language have been developed. Unfortunately, most of these have been descriptions of syntactic complexity, not syntactic control or maturity.

The first problem in developing an appropriate index of syntactic maturity in writing is the definition of a mature style (Christensen, 1968). Because the definition of syntactic maturity is the development toward the superior adult model, it would seem appropriate that the first step in developing an index of development would be the identification of the features that delineate "mature" writing, or of those features that correlate highly with perceived writing quality.

Mean Sentence Length   The first measure to be used as an index of syntactic development was mean sentence length, which was employed as one of the measures of maturity in nearly every study between 1930 and 1960 (Lull, 1929; Seegers, 1933; Frogner, 1933; Davis, 1937; Anderson, 1937; Heider and Heider, 1940; Anastasi and D'Angelo, 1952; McCarthy, 1954). However, soon after researchers began using mean sentence length as an index of syntactic maturity, they realized that alone, at least, it was an inappropriate and invalid measure of syntactic growth (LaBrant, 1933; Seegers, 1933; Anderson, 1937). Features such as run-on sentences and sentence fragments could affect a student's mean sentence length, though they were not indicative of syntactic control. Therefore, Seegers also employed, along with mean sentence length, the frequency of certain types of dependent clauses (substantive clauses, conditional clauses, clauses of manner, cause clauses, adjective clauses, time clauses, and miscellaneous clauses) and the ratio of dependent clauses to independent clauses. Frogner (1933) used percentages of certain types of sentences (simple, complex, compound, compound-complex, sentences with dependent clauses) to all sentences as a measure of growth in the syntax of children's writing. She also employed negative measures of growth such as the percentages of sentence fragments, run-on sentences, and awkward complex sentences. Anderson (1937) used a pronoun index, while Heider and Heider (1940) measured 19 different structural features including kinds of sentences, amount and kind of subordination, number of prepositional phrases and infinitives, types of connectives used, word order, and elliptical forms. Davis (1941) employed measures of sentence length, position of subordinate clauses, use of finite verbs and verbals, use of expressive connectives, as well as a subordination index.

However, like mean sentence length, these structural linguistic measures soon came under severe criticism (Anderson, 1937). Even though these measures were descriptive of some of the features of growth in syntax, their usefulness as indices of writing performance was questionable. In addition, an examination of McCarthy's (1954) tables of results of research prior to 1954 indicates that reliability of these measures is questionable and that they did not necessarily indicate growth in writing. Even though these structural analyses of sentences did not seem sensitive or reliable measures of syntactic maturity, they were not abandoned as indices until the appearance of transformational-generative grammar in the late fifties and early sixties.

With the appearance of Chomsky's transformational grammar (1957), these traditional or structural analyses were set aside, and attempts were made to develop from the new grammar appropriate indices of development.

Hunt's T-unit   Loban (1963), in his attempt to follow the language development of students from kindergarten to twelfth grade, developed the first truly innovative and usable index of maturity based on what he called the "communication unit." Loban (1976) has defined his communication unit structurally as "each independent clause with its modifiers" (p. 9). Loban's index of maturity was the average number of words per communication unit. This is essentially the same index developed by Hunt (1965b) and termed the "minimal terminal unit" or "T-unit." Besides the T-unit, Hunt and Loban have also employed a subordination index (dividing the total number of clauses, both subordinate and main, by the number of main clauses), as well as the mean clause length. Hunt (1965a) has made the following statement referring to these factors:

> ... the T-unit length is probably a better index of grade level [maturity] than any other indexes evaluated. Sentence length is the poorest index. Subordination ratio [# of main clauses/# of total clauses] is somewhat better. Mean clause length is still better, and mean T-unit length is at least as good as any, and apparently, the best of all. (p. 306)

This opinion is obviously supported by many current researchers because the T-unit and mean clause length have been used as the primary indices of language development in the major studies of syntactic maturity within the past 10 years (Hunt, 1965b; Mellon, 1969; O'Hare, 1973; Smith, 1974; Richardson, Calnan, Essen, and Lambert, 1975; Combs, 1976; Loban, 1976). In fact, Neilsen (1977) observes that even though Hunt's T-unit may be a gross measure of development, it is presently the most widely used single index of syntactic growth and development. Furthermore, O'Donnell, Griffin, and Norris (1967) have concluded that "mean length of T-units has a special claim to consideration as a simple, objective, valid indicator of development in syntactic control." It further has the advantage that since it has been used so widely as an index of maturity, approximate norms for levels of development have been identified. In addition, Stotsky (1975) points out:

> With the development of Hunt's units of analysis, reliable techniques for measuring syntactic growth from grade to grade and between ability groups have become available. Moreover, both Hunt's works have provided normative data in terms of specific averages for his indices of syntactic growth and for the developing frequency of occurrence of specific syntactic structures both in free writing and on a controlled instrument. (p. 47)

On the other hand, Hunt's T-unit has been attacked on several points. Christensen (1968) claims that longer clauses and T-units are not the mark of a mature style. He states:

> A mature style must say much in little, agreed, but a mature style must be easy to decode. The long clause is not the mark of a mature style but of an inept style—the easy writing that's curst hard reading. The real problem in writing is to reconcile these two seeming opposites—to pack much into little, but to pack it so it can be easily unpacked. It can be done. A mature style is one that does it. (p. 577)

Furthermore, Christensen analyzed what he felt to be truly mature writing and found that there was little difference between the words per T-units or words per clause of an "inept" style and the "truly mature" style.

Related to Christensen's criticism, O'Donnell (1968) has pointed out:

Although it is evident that clause length, T-unit length, and number of clauses per T-unit increase with advance in grade, there are not data to show how consistently these indexes measure the structural complexity of an individual student's writing in various situations. (p. 6)

In addition, O'Donnell (1976) points out that:

Another limitation, obvious to anyone who has attempted to analyze the structure of children's language, lies in the fact that indices based on mean length of syntactic units do not discriminate among the various ways length can be achieved. (p. 33)

The research on the effect of increasing mean T-unit length on rater's judgments of quality is inconsistent. Neilsen (1977) found no significant effect, while O'Hare (1973) did, and Crowhurst (1978) found differential effect dependent on the purpose of the writing assignment and the perceived audience.

Three Recent Measures   Three other measures have been suggested recently, two of which show some promise in terms of increased validity of an index.

The first, suggested by Williams and Naremore (1969) is based on Bernstein's (1962, 1964) elaborated and restricted codes. Because of the questionable validity of Bernstein's analysis, this index seems to lack validity itself. Furthermore, the analysis seems to be based on a traditional grammar model of compound/complex sentences that is reminiscent of analyses done prior to 1960. This particular index has not appeared in the literature since 1969 and was not reviewed by O'Donnell (1976) in his latest review of measures of syntactic maturity. Given its underlying assumptions, it is probably of questionable usefulness.

The second index was developed by Endicott (1973) in an attempt to develop a "psycholinguistically" valid measure of syntactic maturity. Endicott claims that the theoretical model underlying his measure is a "transformational and morphemic analysis of language. The transformational·model is one provided by Chomsky. The morphemic model is the one generally accepted by linguists today" (p. 5). (Endicott gives no reference to support his statement about acceptance of the morphemic model.) Endicott considers the manipulation of transformations and morphemic synthesis as phases of mental operations. While the index *may* be based on a valid psychological memory model, the measure needs to be refined before it can be useful. In the first place, Endicott's definition of "co-memes" is unclear and difficult to analyze. Second, as pointed out by O'Donnell (1976), there may be much disagreement among researchers using the scale, severely limiting its reliability in the hands of different users. In addition, it seems possible that two sentences, one of which is obviously more complex and mature than the other, may receive the same score on the index.

The third recent index that has been developed was designed by Golub and Kidder (1974). The purpose of their scale was twofold: to develop a measure that pointed to "specific, teachable linguistic structures which are likely to make a difference in the syntactic density of what a growing child or student reads or writes" (p. 1128), and a measure that could be processed on a computer. Golub and Kidder claim that their index (called the Syntactic Density Score or SDS) "goes beyond the simple word count and takes into account uses of complex verb phrase expansions, use of some advanced structures of time, and reductions of embedding that take the form of prepositional phrases" (p. 1130). The SDS includes the following: 1) words per T-unit, 2) subordinate clauses per T-unit, 3) mean main clause word length, 4) mean subordinate clause word length, 5) number of modals (will, shall, can, may . . .), 6) number of "be" and "have" forms in the auxilliary, 7) number of prepositional phrases, 8) number of possessive nouns and pronouns, 9) number of adverbs of time, and 10) number of gerunds, participles, and unbound modifiers. Each of these elements is weighted, then scores are added together and a grade level assigned for the sum. It seems unclear from the article how Golub and Kidder arrived at the weighting of each of these elements or at the grade level norms.

O'Donnell (1976) reports that the SDS has "considerable capacity to discriminate among types of structures, and it appears to have been developed by empirical procedures. The items included, however, have a high degree of redundancy in what they measure" (p. 37). In the same article, O'Donnell wonders if a less complex measure (such as number of words per T-unit) might not be an equally reliable measure and more easily applied to language samples. Nonetheless, it seems that the SDS has a good deal of construct validity and needs to be tested for reliability and ease of use (particularly since a computer program has been developed for the index). No research has been reported on the relationship of language growth or writing maturity and the SDS.

Areas for Further Research   One of the major problems of research in syntactic development has been that a valid, reliable measure of syntactic maturity has not yet been developed. While the instruments we now have available are able to give a developmental score (usually a grade level), these measures, such as clause length and the T-unit, are gross indices of growth. Furthermore, they are unable to identify the features of discourse that determine growth and maturity. They tell us that T-units and clauses get longer as language develops, but they do not tell us why the T-units and clauses get longer nor how to plan instruction for furthering syntactic development. Furthermore, the premise that "longer is more mature" is uncomfortable, as has been pointed out by Christensen (1968).

In this author's opinion two major needs exist for research in the area of measuring syntactic maturity:

1. To develop a concise description of the features most often associated with the adult model or the mature style. Until the model has been adequately defined, it will be impossible to adequately judge growth toward that model.
2. To develop an index of growth with corresponding norms that will give a measure of maturity and identify those features of the adult model that are or are not present (and, ideally, to what degree) in the writing of language users.

A final problem of the measures reviewed above is the difficulty in the use of any of these measures. While it seems possible to employ a computer to analyze the syntactic features of students' writing, these resources are not available to the average classroom teacher. To analyze linguistically students' compositions on anything like a regular basis becomes an impossible task, with questionable returns in terms of individual composition assessment and student growth.

ORGANIZATIONAL AND STYLISTIC FEATURES: QUALITY JUDGMENTS

While it is impossible to separate vocabulary and syntax from organization, style, or quality, these areas seem to have been traditionally evaluated in a very different manner than the evaluation of either vocabulary or syntactic development. Primarily, the evaluation instruments developed to assess organization, style, and/or quality have fallen into two categories: holistic judgments and analytic scales, both admittedly subjective evaluations. However, the fact that they are subjective does not imply that they cannot be either valid or reliable.

Holistic Judgments

Holistic judgments fall into the two subcategories of essay scales (a series of complete pieces arranged according to quality) and general impression marking (the assignment of a single score to a paper based on a rater's intuitive judgment of quality).

In essay scales, the raters are acquainted with a series of complete pieces on a particular topic that have been assigned particular ratings by "expert" raters. At one end of the continuum is an exemplary paper and at the other end is a severely deficient one. The other example pieces are spread between the two extremes. The rater then is asked to match the paper that is being graded with the one it is most nearly like in terms of quality and to assign it the same numerical score. A number of such scales are available: an expository scale developed by the California Association of Teachers of English (Nail et al., 1960), one developed for "imaginative writing" by the London Association for the Teaching of English (Martin et al., 1975), the Smith scale for elementary letter writing (Smith, 1969). In order for such scales to be used, however, the raters must be trained in or very familiar with the essays within the scale. Cooper (1977) points out that the use of essay scales in research has dropped from 30 to 40 years ago; this may be that since many other factors affect the quality of a composition (perceived audience, purpose, student background, etc.), the validity and reliability of such scales for assessing assignments that deviate in the least from the standard pieces may be weak. Cooper further suggests, however, that teachers may wish to develop their own scales based on the assignments given in their own classes in order to be consistent in their ratings of their own students. However, this would necessitate the teacher having and being familiar with eight to ten sample papers for every writing assignment given over the school term or year. It would also limit the assignments a teacher could give to students to the ones that were scaled, and the teacher would be unable to deviate from the original or standard instructions in any way if valid scores were to be assigned to the papers.

The second means of holistic judgment grading is probably the one most used in schools now: general impression marking. Cooper (1977) describes general impression marking as follows: "General impression marking is the simplest of the procedures in . . . holistic evaluation. It requires no detailed discussion of features and no summing of scores given to separate features. The rater simply scores the paper by deciding where the paper fits within the range of papers produced for that assignment or occasion" (pp. 11–12).

One of the major problems in this type of assessment is its reliability. The score that one rater gives a particular paper may differ markedly from the score another rater gives the same paper because each rater may be attending to very different aspects of the writer's performance. Diederich (1974) reports a research study in which 60 raters evaluated the same set of papers. He reports a median correlation of 0.31 among the raters' judgments. He attributes this low correlation (he insists on a correlation of 0.80 as a minimum for reliability) to the fact that each rater was *primarily* interested in different attributes of the paper. Some raters were most influenced by ideas, while others attended mostly to usage, sentence structure, punctuation, and spelling; still others attended primarily to organization, or diction, or flavor. Obviously, if different graders attend to different features, then agreement among raters will be difficult to attain as will any reliability of grading. It is also possible that a single rater may at one time be attending to one set of features and at another time to a different set of features. These problems, however, are fairly easily overcome if raters can come to agreement on a standard set of criteria for judging compositions (Cooper, 1977; Diederich, 1974).

Because a very complete and competent discussion of holistic evaluation has recently been published (Cooper, 1977; Lloyd-Jones, 1977), some less popular procedures of or additional problems involved in holistic grading are not presented here. However, it seems appropriate to mention some implications of the procedures for classroom teachers. The first is that there is reason to believe that holistic evaluation, the same type of evaluation used by most classroom teachers now, can be a valid and reliable means of assessing students' writing if the teacher establishes *a priori* and follows closely a reasonable set of criteria by which to evaluate student writing. Furthermore, a teacher's evaluation needs to be periodically compared to another rater's evaluations *based on the same criteria* in order to ensure fairness and consistency in evaluation.

Analytic Scales

One way in which the teacher may determine a set of evaluation criteria is by employing an analytic scale, which is closely related to holistic evaluation. Essentially, an analytic scale is a set of qualities that may be applied to a particular type of writing with points assigned for each quality. One of the simplest scales available is the Sager Writing Scale (CWRS), which is intended for use with intermediate and junior high school students (Fagan, Cooper, and Jensen, 1975). The CWRS has four scales (vocabulary, elaboration, organization, and structure) with four ratings possible on each scale (0, poor; 1, fair; 2, good; 3, excellent). Reliability for three raters is reported to be 0.97. Fagan, Cooper, and Jensen (1975) report a number of other scales: The ETS Composition Scales (useful for expository writing), the Glazer Narrative Composition Scale (useful for narrative writing), the Schroeder Composition Scale (also useful for narrative writing), and the Literary Rating Scale (useful for fictional stories).

Analytic scales are useful in that they focus the rater's attention on particular qualities of writing. Cooper (1977) points out, however, that like most procedures of evaluating student writing, analytic scales "are not sensitive to the variations in purpose, speaker role, and conception of audience" (p. 14). Furthermore, as anyone who has ever used an analytic scale can testify, at times the scale does not list qualities that seem important; as a result, a weak paper when analyzed may receive a higher score than the rater feels is appropriate, or a strong paper may have weaknesses that show up on the analytic scale but that do not seem as important as rated when the composition is viewed as a whole. (This last criticism of analytic scales will be answered when further research has been done on identifying those variables that affect writing performance, enabling most of the salient features of a piece of writing to be included on the scale.) Nonetheless, the interrater reliability of analytic scales is high (0.80 or above), and the scales do serve to focus the rater on qualities usually identified as important in composition quality (Fagan, Cooper, and Jensen, 1975; Cooper, 1977).

One final word about analytic scales which is important is that teachers can easily design their own analytic scales so that they can achieve greater consistency and reliability in their own evaluations of student writing. Again, Cooper's article (1977) on holistic evaluation describes a strong and meaningful method of how to develop such a scale.

A POSSIBLE EVALUATION PROGRAM

Throughout this chapter, an effort has been made to keep as the primary focus the question of how what we know about evaluation relates to day-to-day assessment in the classroom and what it means for the classroom teacher. In one sense, what is presented here reaffirms for teachers what they have been doing all along. Primarily, teachers have employed holistic grading procedures in evaluating student themes and that seems to be the most efficient and realistic approach to take. In another sense, however, the foregoing discussion points up some problems of which teachers may not be aware, e.g., the need for criteria in assessing writing; the effect of purpose, mode, audience, speaker role, and other such variables on student compositions; the existence of some objective measures of structure and word choice; the need for periodic colleague rating of student papers. It seems that the general approach used by most teachers is valid. What is needed now appears to be a refinement and, perhaps, an expansion of that approach, so that teachers can be assured of the reliability and validity of their own intuitive judgments.

After this admittedly incomplete and cursory description of some evaluation techniques in written composition, it seems appropriate to suggest what a reasonable and appropriate program of evaluation might be for the teacher of written composition at any level. If teachers want to know the effect of their own teaching; if they want to know the areas of strengths and weaknesses of their students; and, if they want to be able to predict the performance of their students, then a beginning-of-the-year assessment in written composition seems mandatory. That pre-instruction assessment would best be done by having students write two papers. If possible, these should be written on two different days. Two papers are required in order to control for situational factors which can affect student performance (see Braddock, Lloyd-Jones, and Schoer, 1963; or Diederich, 1974 for complete discussions of multiple writing assignments). These two essays should be identified by number rather than be name so that the raters can maintain objectivity in the assessment. The two assignments should also be identical in terms of mode, audience, speaker's role, and purpose in order to control for the effects of these variables on the writing performance.

These two essays should then be analyzed using a number of different techniques:

1. Vocabulary: probably the nouns, verbs, and adjectives (at least) should be examined closely for maturity of word choice using whatever method the teacher feels is appropriate.
2. Syntax: the essays should be analyzed using a T-unit analysis (see Hunt, 1977, for a complete description) in order to assess the syntactic maturity of the student.
3. Organization and style: a holistic method or an analytic scale should be employed to assess the general quality of the composition. This should be done by at least two raters (the classroom teacher and perhaps a colleague). Criteria should be established to gain reliability between the two raters.

These three analyses will give the teacher a global assessment of each student's performance in the three major areas of written composition. The teacher should file these scores away after looking for general trends in the class. At the end of the term or year, exactly the same procedure should be followed as a post-instruction assessment. The difference between the pre- and posttest should give the teacher an appropriate gauge of each student's progress.

The question now can be asked: What is to be done for the rest of the time? Paul Diederich (1974) outlines a logical and astute answer to that question. He states:

> During my twenty-five years at the Educational Testing Service, one of my principal duties has been consulting . . . on problems of measurement, grading, record-keeping, and reporting. I have had to visit more classes than I care to remember, and my predominant impression has been that these classes are fantastically over-evaluated. . . . Fewer and better measures at longer intervals of time are enough to show students, their parents, and their teachers how they are doing. At other times, teachers should be free to devote their whole minds to teaching and students to learning. (pp. 2–5)

How should students, then, be evaluated? Between the pre- and posttests suggested above, the teacher will be teaching particular aspects of composition and the students will be writing. But detailed evaluation of each composition seems time consuming and often more harmful than helpful (Diederich, 1974). Student compositions should, of course, be read, but it seems that improvement is best encouraged by a few marginal comments, mostly positive (Diederich, 1965), with a final comment on how the student might improve his next composition, usually related to the instruction that immediately preceded the writing assignment. In this way, the teacher focuses on the student's strengths in writing and then focuses the student's attention on one or two ways in which to improve on the next composition. If the student received a close examination and detailed comment on every "error" in the paper, without solid advice on how to improve each one of those errors, then the student will neither focus on the most important areas which need improvement nor have any substantive direction in how to improve.

The close testing done at the begining and end of the term should give teachers adequate direction for assigning grades; it will also indicate growth for each student over time and will eliminate the need to assign a grade to each composition and then laboriously average a whole string of composition grades. The abbreviated, formative evaluations, by the same token, will assist students in focusing on their major problems in order to improve their own composition performance and eliminate a lot of tedious marking for the teacher.

The state of the art in composition is still in its infancy as is the state of evaluation and assessment in composition. Much work needs to be done toward developing valid, reliable instruments for assessing student progress and growth in writing. On the other hand, what is now available can be of tremendous worth to the classroom teacher of composition and can assist students to grow in their writing ability.

FOR DISCUSSION

1. Why has Straw entitled his chapter "A Commonsense Perspective"?
2. What are the prerequisites if a teacher is to implement the kind of evaluation program suggested by Straw?
3. How can a teacher best assess student knowledge of vocabulary in different kinds of writing situations?
4. What effect can pre-writing instruction have on the measures of writing performance in students?
5. What constitutes maturity in writing? Does Straw cover all of those areas?
6. How can a teacher, when evaluating student writing, control for variables such as purpose, audience, situation, mode of discourse, etc.?
7. How can a teacher justify to an administrator or to parents the kind of assessment program suggested by Straw?

REFERENCES

Anastasi, A., and D'Angelo, R. A comparison of Negro and white preschool children in language development and Goodenough Draw-a-Man IQ. *The Pedagogical Seminar and Journal of Genetic Psychology*, 1952, *81*, 147–165.

Anderson, J. E. An evaluation of various indices of linguistic development. *Child Development*, 1937, *8*, 62–68.

Bernstein, B. Social class, linguistic codes and grammatical elements. *Language and Speech*, 1962, *5*, 221–240.

Bernstein, B. Elaborated and restricted codes: Their social origins and some consequences. In J. Gumperz and D. Hymes (Eds.), *The Ethnography of Communication*, American Anthropologist Special Publication, 1964, *6*.

Bolton, F. B. Predictive value of the Columbia and Michigan vocabulary tests for academic achievement. *Peabody Journal of Education*, 1954, *32*, 9–21.

Bormuth, J. R. Readability: A new approach. *Reading Research Quarterly*, 1966, *1*, 79–132.

Braddock, R., Lloyd-Jones, R., and Schoer, L. *Research in written composition*. Champaign, Illinois: National Council of Teachers of English, 1963.

Britton, J., Burgess, T., Martin, N., McLeod, A., and Rosen, H. *The development of writing abilities (11–18)*. Schools Council Research Studies, 1975.

Cherry, C. *On human communication: A review, a survey, and a criticism*. Cambridge, Massachusetts: MIT Press, 1957.

Chomsky, N. *Syntactic structures*. The Hague: Mouton and Co., 1957.

Christensen, F. E. The problem of defining a mature style. *English Journal*, 1968, *57*, 572–579.

Combs, W. Further effects of sentence-combining practice on writing ability. *Research in the Teaching of English*, 1976, *10*, 137–149.

Cooper, C. R. Holistic evaluation of writing. In C. R. Cooper and L. Odell (Eds.), *Evaluating writing*. Urbana, Illinois: National Council of Teachers of English, 1977.

Cooper, C. R., and Odell, L. (Eds.). *Evaluating writing: Describing, measuring, judging*. Urbana, Illinois: National Council of Teachers of English, 1977.

Crowhurst, M. *The effect of audience and mode of discourse on the syntactic complexity of the writing of sixth and tenth graders*. Unpublished doctoral dissertation, University of Minnesota, 1978.

Dahl, S. S. *An identification of language variables related to success in begining reading*. Unpublished doctoral dissertation, University of Wisconsin-Madison, 1975.

Davis, E. A. Mean sentence length compared with long and short sentences as a reliable measure of language development. *Child Development*, 1937, *8*, 69–79.

Davis, E. A. The location of the subordinate clause in oral and written language. *Child Development*, 1941, *12*, 333–338.

Diederich, P. B. *Definition of ratings on the ETS composition scale*. Educational Testing Service, 1962.

Diederich, P. B. In praise of praise. In Sister M. Judine (Ed.), *A guide for evaluating student composition*. Champaign, Illinois: National Council of Teachers of English, 1965.

Diederich, P. B. *Measuring growth in English*. Urbana, Illinois: National Council of Teachers of English, 1974.

Endicott, A. L. A proposed scale for syntactic density. *Research in the Teaching of English*, 1973, *7*, 5–12.

Fagan, W. T., Cooper, C. R., and Jensen, J. M. (Eds.). *Measures for research and evaluation in the English language arts.* Urbana, Illinois: National Council of Teachers of English, 1975.

Finn, P. J. Computer-aided description of mature word choices in writing. In C. R. Cooper and L. Odell (Eds.), *Evaluating writing: Describing, measuring, judging.* Urbana, Illinois: National Council of Teachers of English, 1977.

Fosvedt, D. R. Criteria for the evaluation of English compositions. *Journal of Educational Research,* 1965, *3,* 108–112.

Fox, S. E. Syntactic maturity and vocabulary diversity in the oral language of kindergarten and primary school children. *Elementary English,* 1972, *49,* 489–496.

Frogner, E. Problems of sentence structure in pupils' themes. *English Journal,* 1933, *22,* 742–749.

Fry, E. A readability formula that saves time. *Journal of Reading,* 1968, *11,* 513–516.

Golub, L., and Kidder, C. Syntactic density and the computer. *Elementary English,* 1974, *51,* 1128–1131.

Harris, A. J. Some new developments on readability. Paper presented at Fifth IRA World Congress on Reading. Vienna, Austria, August 13, 1974.

Heider, F. K., and Heider, G. M. A comparison of sentence structure of deaf and hearing children. *Psychological Monographs,* 1940, *52,* 42–103.

Hildreth, G. Inter-grade comparisons of word frequencies in children's writing. *Journal of Educational Psychology,* 1953, *44,* 429–434.

Hopkins, C. J. *An investigation of the relationship of selected oral language measures and first-grade reading achievement.* Unpublished doctoral dissertation, Purdue University, 1976.

Hunt, K. W. A synopsis of clause to sentence length factors. *English Journal,* 1965, *54,* 300–309. (a)

Hunt, K. W. *Grammatical structures written at three grade levels.* NCTE Research Report No. 3. Champaign, Illinois: National Council of Teachers of English, 1965. (b)

Hunt, K. W. Recent measures of syntactic development. *Elementary English,* 1966, *43,* 732–739.

Hunt, K. W. Early blooming and late blooming syntactic structures. In C. R. Cooper and L. Odell (Eds.), *Evaluating writing: Describing, measuring, judging.* Urbana, Illinois: National Council of Teachers of English, 1977.

Klare, G. R. *Readability: A new look.* Paper presented at the National Reading Conference, St. Petersburg, Florida, December, 1975.

Knapp, T. R. *Essay topics and modes, and their effects on student prose.* Unpublished paper, University of Rochester, 1972.

LaBrant, L. A study of certain language developments of children in grades 4–12 inclusive. *Genetic Psychology Monographs,* 1933, *14,* 387–491.

Lloyd-Jones, R. Primary trait scoring. In C. R. Cooper and L. Odell (Eds.), *Evaluating writing: Describing, measuring, judging.* Urbana, Illinois: National Council of Teachers of English, 1977.

Loban, W. D. *The language of elementary school children.* NCTE Research Report No. 1. Champaign, Illinois: National Council of Teachers of English, 1963.

Loban, W. *Language development: Kindergarten through grades twelve.* NCTE Research Report No. 18. Urbana, Illinois: National Council of Teachers of English, 1976.

Lorge, I., and Chall, J. Estimating the size of vocabularies of children and adults:

An analysis of methodological issues. *Journal of Experimental Education*, 1963, *32*, 147–157.

Lull, H. C. The speaking and writing abilities of intermediate grade pupils. *Journal of Educational Research*, 1929, *20*, 73–77.

Martin, N. C., et al. *Assessing compositions*. Glasgow: Bloekie, 1965.

Maxwell, J. C. *Introduction to common sense and testing in English*. Urbana, Illinois: National Council of Teachers of English, 1975.

McCarthy, D. A. Language development in children. In L. Carmichael (Ed)., *Manual of child psychology*. New York: John Wiley & Sons, 1954.

Mellon, J. C. *Transformational sentence-combining: A method of enhancing the development of syntactic fluency in English composition*. NCTE Research Report No. 10. Champaign-Urbana, Illinois: National Council of Teachers of English, 1969.

Nail, P., et al. *A scale for evaluation of high school student essays*. Urbana, Illinois: National Council of Teachers of English, 1960.

Neilsen, L. *The effect of headed nominal complexity and vocabulary on qualitative judgments of written composition*. Unpublished masters thesis, University of Minnesota, 1977.

O'Donnell, R. *An objective measure of structural complexity in children's writing*. Unpublished paper delivered at the American Educational Research Association, 1968.

O'Donnell, R. C. A critique of some indices of syntactic maturity. *Research in the Teaching of English*, 1976, *10*, 31–38.

O'Donnell, R. C., Griffin, W. J., and Norris, R. C. *Syntax of kindergarten and elementary school children: A transformational analysis*. NCTE Research Report No. 8. Urbana, Illinois: National Council of Teachers of English, 1967.

O'Hare, F. *Sentence combining: Improving student writing without formal grammar instruction*. NCTE Research Report No. 15. Urbana, Illinois: National Council of Teachers of English, 1973.

Page, E. B. The use of the computer in analyzing student essays. *International Review of Education*, 1968, *14*, 210–225.

Purves, A. C., et al. *Common sense and the teaching of English*. Urbana, Illinois: National Council of Teachers of English, 1975.

Raygor, A. L. The Raygor Readability Estimate: A quick and easy way to determine difficulty. Paper presented at the National Reading Conference, Atlanta, Georgia, December 7, 1976.

Richardson, K., Calnan, M., Essen, J., and Lambert, L. The linguistic maturity of 11-year-olds: Some analysis of the written compositions of children in the National Child Development Study. *Journal of Child Language*, 1976, *3*, 99–115.

Rinsland, H. D. *A basic vocabulary of elementary school children*. New York: Macmillan, 1945.

Seegers, J. C. Form of discourse and sentence structure. *Elementary English Reviews*, 1933, *10*, 51–54.

Singleton, C. M. Vocabulary development for the mature student. In National Reading Conference Ninth Yearbook, *Research and evaluation in college reading*. Fort Worth: Texas Christian University Press, 1960, 72–87.

Slotnick, H. B. Toward a theory of computer essay grading. *Journal of Educational Measurement*, 1972, *9*, 253–263.

Smith, M. K. Measurement of the size of general English vocabulary through the elementary grades and high school. *Genetic Psychology Monographs*, 1941, *24*, 311–345.

Smith, V. H. Measuring teacher judgment in the evaluation of written composition. *Research in the Teaching of English*, 1969, *3*, 181–195.

Smith, W. L. Syntactic recoding of passages written at three levels of complexity. *Journal of Experimental Education*, 1974, *43*, 66–72.

Stotsky, S. L. Sentence-combining as a curricular activity: Its effect on written language development and reading comprehension. *Research in the Teaching of English*, 1975, *9*, 30–71.

Vineyard, E. E., and Massey, H. The interrelationship of certain linguistic skills and their relationship with scholastic achievement when intelligence is ruled constant. *Journal of Educational Psychology*, 1957, *48*, 279–286.

Wesman, A. G., and Seashore, H. G. Frequency versus complexity of words in verbal measurement. *Journal of Educational Psychology*, 1949, *40*, 395–404.

Williams, F., and Naremore, R. C. Social class differences in children's syntactic performance: A quantitative analysis of field study data. *Journal of Speech and Hearing Research*, 1969, *12*, 778–793.

Winterowd, W. R. Linguistics and composition. In G. Tate (Ed.), *Teaching composition: 10 bibliographic essays*. Fort Worth: Texas Christian University Press, 1976.

Zipf, G. K. *Human behavior and the principle of least effort: An introduction to human ecology*. New York: Hafner, 1965.

11 | The Language Base of Spelling

Richard E. Hodges

In the August 1979 issue of *Saturday Review* there appeared the following advertisement:

> UNFORTUNATE TYPOGRAPHICAL ERROR has resulted in unusable mammoth banner 10 ft. wide by 135 ft. long, ordered originally at a cost of $65,000 for entrance of Ft. Worth, Texas airport. Banner now reads, "Welcome to Fort Werth." Bids invited. SR Box M.B.

This whimsical ad lightheartedly but vividly illustrates the value that society places on correct spelling. Spelling competence is considered an important component of general literacy. Poor spellers are commonly regarded as inadequately educated and, in more extreme instances, they find that employment opportunities can be hindered. Because of this social stigma, persons with spelling difficulties will sometimes go to great lengths to disguise their problem by writing so poorly that their handwriting cannot be read, by not writing at all, and by dismissing spelling as a trivial matter in any case. Given its social status, spelling instruction maintains a modest though permanent place in the language arts curiculum, at least through the elementary school years, because it is in schools that one is supposed to learn to spell.

While the processes of learning to read and to write justifiably command a greater amount of the attention of researchers and curriculum specialists, interest in the nature and development of spelling abilities has a long tradition in the language arts literature. Paradoxically, however, increasing amounts of knowledge about the nature of English orthography and how it is learned have not made a significant impact on actual classroom practices in teaching spelling. A cursory visit to classrooms will reveal that many teachers teach this tool subject in a manner that conventional wisdom has traditionally dictated—as a low-order psychomotor skill subject that is believed to be acquired by memorization, drill, and weekly testing.

The purpose, then, of this chapter is to review the current state of knowledge about English spelling and its acquisition and to pose a framework for considering how spelling might be taught, while at the same time indicating areas in which further study seems warranted. To accomplish this purpose, the chapter provides: 1) historical perspective of the nature, acquisition, and teaching of English spelling, 2) some contemporary views of English orthography and its acquisition, 3) a framework for formulating a spelling curriculum, 4) some suggestions of how spelling might be taught, and 5) some possible areas for further research.

Each of these topics, of course, could readily be developed in greater depth than present space permits. However, the ensuing discussion should reveal for the reader that, contrary to conventional wisdom, learning to spell is a highly sophisticated intellectual activity about which emerging theory and research findings can provide important insights into human language learning in general and into spelling instruction in particular.

A HISTORICAL PERSPECTIVE OF SPELLING INSTRUCTION

An ability to spell correctly has been valued throughout the Western world from ancient times to the present (Hodges, 1977). Not only is poor spelling thought to impede written communication, but proper spelling is regarded as an indication of good scholarly habits. While the existence of spelling in the school curriculum has historical roots, spelling instruction also is based on assumptions about the nature of English orthography and the nature of human learning. A brief historical review of these assumptions helps shed light upon current instructional practices.

Theories of the Nature of English Orthography

Theories are symbolic constructions which serve to explain the world in which we live. Theories provide frameworks in which facts can be organized and which give credence to practice. English orthography also can be set in theoretical frameworks, whose suppositions have important consequences for how the subject has been, or might be, taught. Historically, English spelling can be described in terms of three theoretical contexts: 1) the orthography is largely irrational and governed by few, if any, principles, 2) the orthography is at least partially systematic, and 3) the orthography is almost optimally systematic for its purposes in written communication.

An Irrational Orthography   All writing systems are ways of recording language so that humans can communicate over time and distance.

Unlike spoken language (prior to the development of radios and other electronic devices which record speech), writing enables communications to be preserved for future use and to be sent beyond the limits of the human voice. Because of the closely connected functions of speech and writing, and because writing is a fairly recent event in the history of humankind, writing has commonly been regarded as a surrogate of speech and therefore based upon it. That this may not necessarily be the case can be seen in writing systems, such as in the Chinese language, in which *ideographs* relate to meaning rather than directly to phonology. English orthography, on the other hand, has ordinarily been classified as an *alphabetic* writing system in which graphic characters—alphabet letters—correspond to English speech sounds—or phonemes—ideally in a one-to-one, or isomorphic, match. The problem of English spelling, say its detractors, is that orthography has strayed from this principle to the extent that few if any reliable sound-letter relationships remain (Hodges, 1964). The late Sir James Pitman (1969), one of the foremost spelling reformers of this century, once remarked:

> Alphabetic writing is, essentially, a visual codification of speech. Its sequence of characters enables a relationship to be established between words that are written or printed and words that are spoken, between the visual capacities of the reader and his auditory oral capacities . . . In the case of the English language the connection between the visual symbols and spoken words is unfortunately very imperfect and misleading. The true alphabetic principle is applied only partially. . . . Unlike, say, Finnish, Italian, or Spanish, most English printed words are not spelled as they are pronounced. They represent sounds which we would be horrified to utter. We spell for the eye and hand rather than for the ear and tongue. (p. 40)

The consequence of this view of English spelling has given rise to spelling reform movements both in England and in the United States and to such pedagogical solutions as ITA, in which a seemingly deficient alphabet is augmented with additional graphic symbols in order to bring about a one-to-one correspondence between sound and letter. The so-called "whole word" method of reading has also been seen as a means of circumventing the seeming difficulties in learning our "unphonetic" language.

A Partially Systematic Orthography With the development of descriptive linguistics as a science early in this century, more detailed views of English orthography became possible. Linguists, in seeking to describe living spoken languages in terms of their structural features, posited that writing systems could be described in the same way, since writing reflected speech. Therefore, because spoken language can be described in terms of words (morphemes), syllables, and phonemes, so also can orthographies, with English spelling being classified as an *alpha-*

betic writing system. In this view, the unit of analysis is the *phoneme* and its graphic counterpart, the *grapheme*.

Many early linguists also held a glum view of the English writing system, albeit on apparently scientific grounds. In their view, the alphabetic nature of English orthography suffers because spoken language is vibrant and changing, while writing is static and unchanging. With words borrowed from other languages further compounding the problem, our writing system may "delight the historian, but to the person who must learn to match the spelling with the sounds he has used since childhood, mastering English spelling is a time-consuming and frustrating task" (Kurath, 1964).

The main practical distinction between the linguists and the spelling reformers lay in their solution to the problem in reading and spelling instruction. The linguists proposed that the systematic properties that do pertain in the orthography be utilized in learning to read and spell; the reformers saw few if any properties that were worth applying. As is seen later in this chapter, the descriptive viewpoint led to some important studies to determine the orthographic "fit" between English speech sounds and letters.

The structure of English orthography can, however, be analyzed not merely in terms of sound-letter correspondences as its primary unit, but in terms of patterns of spellings within words. Employing the *word* as the analytic unit, English spelling, it is asserted, tends to use a single combination of letters to represent a given word (morpheme) and disregards all but the most gross phonemic differences between words with the same semantic identity, as for example, *sane-sanity* (Francis, 1958). Thus, the writing system is not a simple alphabetic orthography, but one with complex relationships between graphic symbols and oral language. Other studies of the structure of English spelling that were based on this rationale are discussed later in this chapter.

A Nearly Optimal Orthography   A view of English spelling as a system which represents morphemes or words also pertains to the way in which generative transformationalists describe the orthography. In *The Sound Pattern of English*, Chomsky and Halle (1968) assert that the English writing system is designed for readers who know their language and for whom a knowledge of *phonetic* differences among words is already a part of their phonological competence. The power of the orthography, then, lies in its disregard for irrelevant phonetic differences and its focus on retaining the graphic identity of semantically related words. These *lexical* spellings therefore move away from direct phonetic representation and toward semantic representation, despite variations in how semantically related words might be pronounced. *Words that are the same (semantically) look the same*, thereby allowing the proficient reader to focus on meaning rather than on pronunciation, while in phonetic transcription they would look quite different.

While this viewpoint favors the *reader* of English, it may be argued that difficulties are still posed for the *writer* of English who, if competent in the production of written language, must be able to spell correctly both semantically related and unrelated words. As Frank Smith (1975) has noted, the orthography is something of a compromise for readers and writers, in which phonetic relationships favor the speller, while lexical relationships favor the reader. Yet, the postulation of a rule-governed writing system is of crucial importance to the matter of spelling instruction which is discussed shortly.

The Nature of Spelling Ability

The structure of English orthography is an essential factor when considering how spelling might be taught. A second essential factor concerns how correct spelling is believed to be learned. How, then, has the nature of spelling ability been regarded in the past? The answer to this question helps to shed light on traditional instructional practices in the teaching of spelling.

Learning theory in the seventeenth and eighteenth centuries was largely the province of philosophers who attempted to describe relationships between the mind and knowledge. These philosophical positions underlay schooling in England and in colonial America. With the development of anatomical and physiological studies, however, psychological speculations about learning began to be developed. One such theoretical rumination that influenced schooling was that of the German physician, Joseph Gall (1758–1828) who developed the science of *phrenology*, popularly known as "faculty psychology." According to Gall and his followers, discrete psychological functions (faculties) were localized in specific small parts of the brain, verbal memory, for example, being located directly behind the eyes. (Gall proposed that protruding eyes was an indication of good verbal memory!) Gall subsequently identified 27 faculties controlling cognitive and emotional behavior, with verbal memory—the faculty of attending to and distinguishing words and recollections of words—the faculty of greatest importance in learning to spell and to read.

While phrenology was subsequently discredited (although the localization of brain functions has become a major variable in current neurophysiological research), it had a large lay appeal and eighteenth and nineteenth century spelling instruction was firmly based on the notion that faculties, like muscles, were trained and strengthened through hard work and drill. As a result, compilers of spelling books paid little heed to the usefulness of words and, instead, selected words on the basis of their potential to foster verbal memory. A popular speller of the period, both in England and in American, was Dilworth's *A New Guide to the English Tongue*, which included words such as *Nebuzaradum*, *Abelbethmaleah*, *Compostella*, and *Thyatria*. Young "scholars" traversed the English lexicon from A to Z. Said one man in recalling his spelling lessons in the early 1800s:

> To teach spelling, a lesson was assigned, consisting of a certain number of columns arranged in alphabetical order, as the words of our spelling books usually are, which the pupil was requested to study over and over, until he could recollect them from memory. None of them were ever defined for him; nor was he requested or encouraged to seek for definitions for himself. In this manner, one word suggested by association, the next; the second, the third, and so on. No faculty was called into exercise but the memory. . . . (Alcott, 1831)

Throughout much of the nineteenth century, diligence, hard work, and external motivation were hallmarks of spelling instruction, even with a shift away from faculty psychology and the alphabet method to a form of gestalt psychology and a "whole word" approach in the mid-1800s. Spelling ability was believed to be the consequence of either inborn ability or hard work, a view of the nature of spelling ability that still widely exists today.

But, with the rise of Social Darwinism, there also arose a growing interest in applying scientific method in solving educational problems. Accompanying this movement was a deep interest in and application of the new psychology of behaviorism. For scholars and others who were interested in spelling instruction in the early twentieth century, the principles of behaviorism, with habit formation the basis of learning, showed great promise in making spelling instruction more effective in its outcome and more economical in time. Spelling instruction moved away from drill on words to strengthen the mind toward drill on words needed in writing. Horn (1919), one of the foremost spelling researchers of the first half of this century, declared:

> Efficiency in teaching is to be increased by a specific attack on the individual words to be learned. This is in line with the whole tendency in modern experimental education, a tendency which has been well outlined by Thorndike in his discussion of specific bonds. . . . (p. 56)

The behaviorist's view of the nature of spelling ability has undoubtedly dominated over other psychological theories applied to spelling instruction in the twentieth century. However, the second half of this century has been marked by significant advances in our understanding of human learning in general and of the acquisition of spelling ability in particular. Two such advances, among others, warrant special attention. First, there are the insights into human intellectual development emanating from the work of the Swiss psychologist, Jean Piaget, and others, whose theoretical orientation provides a means to consider spelling ability as a *developmental* process in which the young learner is actively involved in his own intellectual development. A second major advance concerns a growing knowledge about general language acquisition which provides powerful new ways to examine the nature of spelling ability as a part of language learning.

Before looking at the implications of these advances for spelling instruction, however, we first need to review briefly how spelling has been taught in order to set the stage for an exploration of how spelling *might* be taught in the light of contemporary views and knowledge of language and of learning.

Teaching Spelling   It has been seen that learning to spell has been thought of as a relatively lower-order psychomotor skill whose mastery is gained through memorization, hard work, and diligence for the great majority of spellers not gifted with an inborn spelling ability. Or, so the conventional wisdom goes.

Spelling instruction has long been a handmaiden of the teaching of reading. From colonial days well into the nineteenth century, the alphabet method was the principal instructional approach (Towery, 1971; Hodges, 1977), a method in which children first learned the names and order of the alphabet letters and then letter combinations such as *ab*, *eb*, etc. In some respects, this method of reading and spelling instruction was a kind of "phonics" approach, with roots burrowing through the sands of time to ancient Greece and Rome.

Early spelling books contained more than lessons in spelling words, however. They also included moral precepts and religious teachings, as well as instruction in reading, grammar, and arithmetic.

Although most compilers of spelling books agreed with Noah Webster (1831) that "letters are the marks of sounds," there were some noted dissidents. Horace Mann, the Massachusetts Secretary of Education in the 1830s and 1840s, was influential in changing the course of spelling instruction when he advocated using a "whole word" approach following his visit to European schools. His proposal promoted visual learning as the basis of spelling instruction.

An emphasis on visual memory in spelling instruction does not stem only from learning theory, however. It will be recalled that at least since the tenth century, English spelling has been largely regarded as a chaotic, unpredictable association of letters with sounds.

Spelling research and curriculum development in the first half of the present century was largely dominated by researchers and curriculum specialists who held English orthography in low regard and for whom learning to spell was a matter of memorization and establishing efficient study habits. Hillerich as recently as 1977 advocated this traditional position on English spelling:

> Whether one looks at the research on language itself or the research on the effects of teaching generalizations to children, the obvious conclusion is that no one can develop generalizations that will assure correct spelling of a word that has not been examined specifically for spelling. . . . If all the teacher is interested in is teaching spelling, there is not need for any spelling book. All that teacher needs is a good word list, developed through a pretest with immediate correction by the child, followed by instruction on the study method. . . . (p. 302).

At the heart of the issue of how spelling should be taught, then, lies the efficacy of the English writing system. A belief that English spelling is erratic leads to the inevitable conclusion that learning to spell requires that words be learned as discrete items. A belief that English spelling is systematic leads to the conclusion that learning to spell involves learning generalizations about how words are spelled. As a consequence, much spelling research has focused on word selection and teaching method, including such methodological practices as teaching "hard spots" in words, word grouping, test-study versus study-test, and list versus context techniques (Sherwin, 1969).

A CONTEMPORARY PERSPECTIVE OF SPELLING INSTRUCTION

Two lines of inquiry have guided spelling studies in the past decade. The first line of inquiry concerns the extent to which English spelling is or is not systematic; the second line of inquiry concerns the extent to which individuals who are learning to spell do so systematically. Both areas—linguistic and psychological—have far-reaching implications for spelling instruction.

The Linguistics of Spelling

Both linguists and educationists who are interested in English orthography have undertaken analyses of its structural characteristics. Robert Hall, Jr. (1961) examined English spelling in terms of the "fit" between phoneme and grapheme. He concluded that the spellings of words can be classified as "regular," "semiregular," and "irregular" and he proposed that spelling and reading programs should begin with "regular" spellings and gradually introduce students to words with less regular spellings.

A thorough analysis of sound-letter relationships in English spelling was carried out by Paul Hanna and his colleagues at Stanford University (Hanna et al., 1966). The researchers used computer technology to analyze the spellings of over 17,000 words with regard to phoneme-grapheme correspondences in various positions in the syllables of the words. The number of *different* spellings of each phoneme in the corpus was counted and a percentage was derived to determine the "regularity" of the spelling of each phoneme. Any spelling which occurred 80% or more of the time in the 17,000 words was considered to be a predictable spelling of a given speech sound. Using these data, the researchers developed a computer program which attempted to spell the 17,000 words on the basis of predictable phoneme-grapheme correspondences. The computer correctly spelled about 50% of the words, with an additional 37% of the words misspelled with only one incorrect match of a grapheme to a phoneme. Moreover, an examination of misspelled words revealed that most misspellings could be accounted for when morphological and etymological factors were considered. The researchers concluded that, far from being capricious, English orthography is substantially more systematic than is commonly regarded and that the results of the study had important implications for spelling curricula.

The Standford Spelling Project drew considerable attention, both favorable and unfavorable. Some educators have criticized the study on the grounds that only 50% of the corpus could be correctly spelled even after the application of complex "rules," hardly a reassuring statistic, they claimed, for persons learning to spell (Hillerich, 1977; Mazurkiewicz, 1978). These critics overlooked the fact that, had morphological information (mainly affixation principles) been added to the computer program, over 85% of the 17,000 words would have been correctly spelled. Thus, while the narrow focus on phoneme-grapheme correspondences had delimited a broader look at English orthography, the study intimated that, at more complex levels, the orthography is considerably systematic.

Linguists' criticisms were more substantive in pointing out that the most serious flaw of the research was its focus on sound-letter correspondences as the unit of analysis instead of on the *words* in which they occur (Roberts, 1967; Venezky, 1970). They pointed out that English orthography is *both* phonemically and morphemically based and that any classification of English spellings must take these levels into account.

Possibly the foremost study in the late 1960s that sought to examine English spelling with the *word* as the analytic unit was that of Richard Venezky (1967). Venezky was primarily interested in the reading process, and his research explored the predicting of the pronunciation of written words on the basis of phonemic and morphophonemic factors. Analyzing some 20,000 words in the Thorndike-Lorge word lists in terms of these factors, Venezky (1970) established that English spelling patterns in words could be classified according to the following taxonomy:

I.   Predictable: patterns that can be predicted on the basis of regular graphemic, morphemic, or phonemic features of the words or sentences in which they occur.

    A.   Invariant: patterns that admit no (or very few) variations or exceptions.

    B.   Variant: patterns that have predictable variations or exceptions. (Variant patterns could be divided further on the basis of the features needed to predict each pattern.)

II.   Unpredictable: all patterns that do not fit into category I above.

    A.   Affix aided: patterns that could be derived by relating the words to one of its prefixed or suffixed forms, for example, *sign*, *signal*.

    B.   High frequency: occurs frequently (frequently enough to allow an association group to be profitably employed in teaching).

    C.   Low frequency: occurs too infrequently to merit the formation of an association group. (p. 41)

The significance of Venezky's work lies in his clarification of the complex nature of English orthography, whose structure can be understood only when factors more complex than phoneme-grapheme correspondences are taken into consideration, an orthography in which phonological and morphological relationships play a crucial role.

A recognition that writing is *more* than simply a means of representing speech led other linguists to explore English spelling at deeper levels (Reed, 1965; Smith, 1968; Gleitman and Rozin, 1977).

As has been seen, Chomsky and Halle (1968) saw English spelling as being even more systematic, as viewed from the standpoint of generative-transformational theory. It must be emphasized, however, that Chomsky and Halle do not claim that the orthography is isomorphic with the surface phonology of the language—with phonemes—but that underlying *lexical representations* can be mapped to speech or to writing on the basis of an individual's intuitive knowledge of a complex set of phonological and lexical factors.

The theoretical base underlying Chomsky's work marks a watershed in studies of orthography because it not only imposes linguistic order to the English writing system, but also assigns a psychological reality to orthographic structure. In doing so, a shift of research focus was made from the orthography to the learner.

The Psychology of Spelling

It is important to point out that the logic of a subject as formulated by scholars may not be the logic that is applied by a learner of that subject. Linguistic formulations of English orthography are not "context-free," but are influenced by the tools and processes used by linguists in their theoretical work. Thus, the concept of *phoneme* that is central in the phonology of descriptive linguistics is not important in generative-transformational linguistics where the phoneme is regarded as little more than a methodological artifact that is unsubstantiated in the phonological reality of English speakers. In short, different theoretical views of the writing system are constrained by those theories to include and exclude certain features.

A critical question, then, is what is the *learner's* linguistic knowledge of English spelling? The question is not a trivial one; most of the studies of how spelling is learned have not taken into consideration how learners view the orthography, but have dealt with such factors as learning rates and perceptual processes which shed light on the learning process but little on the learning of English spelling. Spelling researchers during the 1970s who consider *both* the orthography and the learner are beginning to provide substantial insight about learning to spell.

Spelling as a psycholinguistic process can be examined in a number of ways: from the vantage point of the young child who is initially encountering the orthography; by analyzing the spellings of older, more accomplished users of written English; by comparing good spellers with poor ones; or by studying persons with severe spelling problems. These approaches share a common supposition: that correctly spelled words yield little information, but that deviations from standard orthography can provide valuable information about the spelling process.

The first major step in this direction was Charles Read's study of preschool children's spelling attempts, a study that has precipitated a series of additional explorations in which researchers look for developmental characteristics in young children's acquisition of knowledge about English spelling on the basis of their spelling errors, or, in Read's terms, their *invented spellings* (Read, 1971, 1975a, 1975b). An analysis of these invented spellings yields valuable information on how *children* see relationships between English phonology and orthography.

Read's study involved approximately twenty preschoolers who learned the alphabet letter names, were taught that a letter may spell a phone or phones in its name, e.g., A = /ey/; B = /biy/, and then were asked to spell words by arranging alphabet blocks. However, because many speech sounds cannot be spelled by letter names, the children had to make choices in spelling the words: they could, for example, give up trying to spell; invent new symbols; ask for help; or attempt to spell the sound on the basis of a spelling they already knew. Read's subjects mainly used the latter two strategies.

Read found clear evidence that, even at an early age, children detect phonetic relationships represented in the writing system. All of Read's subjects, with some minor variations, appeared to invent similar spellings which reflected certain judgments they held in common about English speech sounds and their graphic representations. Clearly, these preschoolers knew a system of phonetic relationships which they had not directly been taught and which they used in spelling words. In fact, most adults would probably not recognize many of the phonetic judgments that the children made in their invented spellings.

Read's study underscored two very important points about the acquisition of spelling ability. First, children are not *tabula rasa* upon which nothing about phonetic characteristics underlying English spelling has been written. Read's children (and others we will look at shortly) demonstrated a surprisingly detailed, but intuitive, knowledge of English phonology. Second, children make judgments that are *qualitatively* different from those of adults about relationships between phonology and English spelling. Children, in fact, recognize phonetic relationships that are not generally accessible to adults. Both spoken and written language acquisition are *developmental* processes, a finding reaffirmed in Read's later study of kindergarten–second graders' judgments concerning pronunciations of real and nonsense words (Read, 1975a).

Carol Chomsky's (1971) examination of young children's spellings in "open" classrooms likewise demonstrated some of the principal spelling features commonly used by children in their early encounters with English spelling. Some of the principal features she noted were:

1. Words close to English spelling (those containing "long" vowels) are the easiest to identify:

   BOT = BOAT   JMEZ = JIMMIES   FEL = FEEL
   TIGR = TIGER

2. L and R function syllabically, with no vowel letter at all:

   FRN = FERN   GRL = GIRL   LITL = LITTLE
   KLR = COLOR

3. Other than long vowels are often omitted in children's early writing:

   DG = DOG   MN = MAN   KBE = CUBBY

4. Nasals before consonants are customarily omitted:

   WOT = WON'T   PLAT = PLANT   BOPY = BUMPY
   NUBRS = NUMBERS

5. CHR and JR are commonly used in place of TR and DR:

   CHRAN = TRAIN   JRAGIN = DRAGON
   CHRIBLS = TROUBLES

6. Letters are sometimes used according to their full pronounced names:

   THAQ = THANK   104
   YOU   YL = WHILE   R = ARE   U = YOU
   CRIT = KARATE

The next set of studies in which early developmental stages in learning to spell have been examined are those of E. Henderson and his associates at the University of Virginia. Extending Read's work, these researchers examined children's creative writings in order to identify error *types* which might indicate a developmental progression in spelling acquisition.

One of the first studies was that of Beers and Henderson (1977) in which they collected writing samples of first graders in a language experience classroom over a 6-month period. Like Read, they found that children's growing awareness of English spelling is not simply one of knowledge of phoneme-grapheme correspondences, but of a combination of phonological and syntactic information. Beers and Henderson identified three apparently invariant stages in young children's spelling strategies, regardless of when a child begins to write. These strategies included:

1. A letter-name strategy in which articulatory features are used to determine a letter for a sound (e.g., *gat* = *gate*).
2. A refinement of vowel spellings, in which alphabet letters are used to represent sounds rather than being regarded as sounds themselves.
3. An assimilation of information beyond purely phonetic information, as in the use of the final *e* marker (*gate* = *gate*), and using morphological information to form endings, as *-ing*.

Beers and Henderson's young spellers were not deficient in phonetic knowledge, but they did lack underlying concepts about *words* which precluded them from using language features in their attempts to spell, as, for example, morphological information.

In a later study, Beers, Beers, and Grant (1977) examined the kinds of errors made when nearly 200 children in grades one through four were asked to spell five high frequency words (*hat, bed, stick, gate, ride*) and five low frequency words (*sap, speak, wit, drape, spike*). Again, Beers and his colleagues found that children systematically develop their own spelling strategies as they learn to write, in this instance an initial reliance on a letter name strategy (*gat* for *gate, drap* for *drape*), next adding an incorrect vowel letter after a correct one (*hait* for *hat, riad* for *ride*), and then incorrectly substituting a short vowel for another one (*spik* for *speak*). Moreover, when faced with spelling an unknown word, the children tended to revert to primitive spelling strategies, as in using letter names for spelling.

Gentry's (1978) study of the spelling strategies used by first and second grade children in learning to write has added still further information about developmental stages in spelling. Examining these children's spellings, Gentry enumerated five spelling strategies used by his subjects as they progressed toward correctly spelled words: 1) a *deviant* strategy in which a child demonstrates an awareness of print and attempts to *approximate* writing by randomly using real letters and Arabic numerals approximating real letter forms, repeating letter sequences, and writing from right to left; 2) a *prephonetic* strategy in which a rudimentary phonetic system begins to emerge, often spelling a word with the correct beginning and/or ending consonant sound; 3) a *phonetic* strategy in which essential phonetic elements for representing surface structure of the phonology are present even though the letters used are wrong (as had Read's subjects); 4) a *transitional* strategy in which spelling *looks* like an English word, with correct letter sequences and use of markers; and 5) a *correct* strategy in which the speller produces a word in standard orthography. Some examples of these strategies are:

CORRECT	TRANSITIONAL	PHONETIC	PREPHONETIC	DEVIANT
CHIRP	CHRIP	CHRP	J	IMMPMPT
PURRED	PURD	PRD	P	BDRNMPM
TYPE	TIPE	TIP	TP	BRNBMM
TROUBLE	TRUBAL	CHUBRL	T	PMIMRN

The developmental progression in learning to spell thus suggests that, like other intellectual processes, the acquisition of spelling ability is possibly governed by general developmental factors, a possibility into which J. Zutell inquired (1979). He examined the spelling of 60 first through fourth graders, correlating their spelling performance with a battery of Piagetian tasks for the purpose of investigating general relationships between cognitive development and word knowledge. The subjects spelled words that were selected on the basis of some phonetic or graphic factor, e.g., lax vowel, tense markers, consonant doubling, and vowel extension. As Zutell expected, he found that spelling strategies became more sophisticated with higher grade level, with the vowel extension strategy, e.g., *explain-explanation*, least understood by the younger children. Significant correlations were found between the use of such strategies and preoperational and operational stages as measured on a set of Piagetian tasks. In sum, the development of spelling ability appeared to evolve from a correlation of both *cognitive and linguistic processes*.

Bearing in mind Read's observation that young children's spelling strategies are different than those of accomplished spellers, let us now briefly explore the spelling strategies of older students, an area of spelling ability which presently has had little systematic examination on psycholinguistic grounds. Templeton (1979) presented 12 real English words and 12 pseudowords to 60 sixth, eighth, and tenth graders and asked them to form their derivations, e.g., *contrite* + *ion* = _____, *urban* + *ity* = _____, *deplore* + *ic* = _____, under two conditions: seeing a base word and a suffix and forming the derivation, and seeing only the suffix while having the base word pronounced. Templeton found all age groups better able to form derivatives when students could see the base and suffix. They were also better able to spell correctly the derived forms than to pronounce them correctly. In addition, when words were presented visually in a syntactic environment, correct spelling of derivations improved. Templeton's experiment demonstrated an important factor: the more information concerning word structure to which students are sensitive, the more sophisticated and adaptive will be their interaction with printed language. In brief, as individuals get older and have increased interactions with written language, they are better able to induce from our essentially stable writing system spelling strategies in *groups* of words, associated on the basis of shared phonological, morphological, and syntactic features.

An ongoing study of regional "spelling-bee" champions in which the author has been involved over the past few years provides additional evidence to support the contention that accomplished spellers do not merely rely on phoneme-grapheme correspondences to spell words about which they are uncertain. On the contrary, good spellers appear to draw their information from a full reservoir of knowledge about spoken and written language structures in attempting to spell unfamiliar words. These "spelling-bee" contestants, ages 10 to 14, consistently demonstrate a use of semantic, syntactic, morphological, and phonological information in their spelling, relying on phoneme-grapheme strategies only when all other clues do not elicit from memory the particular word in question. These, and other good spellers, appear to have a knowledge of written language in general that goes far beyond their memory of words learned in spelling lists.

Why, then, are some good readers poor spellers, while good spellers are almost invariably good readers? Several studies conducted by Frith (1978a) of 20 12-year-olds provide a picture of good spellers and readers who have abilities to relate print to meaning as well as to sound, while good readers who spell poorly are weak in relating print to sound. This weakness appears not so much to be a lack of ability, but an avoidance or lack of preference for doing so. Good spellers seem to be equally adept at converting print to meaning and sound.

Frith (1978b) has also provided a lucid disussion of the problems involved in determining causal factors in spelling difficulty. Positing that spelling problems can result from underlying perceptual and linguistic difficulties, Frith contends that spelling instruction that is based only on sound-letter relationships is incomplete:

> Spelling need not be taught as some sort of faulty transcription from sound, but as making transparent underlying grammatical and lexical condi-

tions. English orthography reflects knowledge sometimes on the level of sound and sometimes on the level of meaning or syntax. Therefore, children learning to spell take longer than they would using a writing system that was based on sound only. However, the time is not wasted. They learn much about the English language, its history, its provenance from older languages, the underlying roots of words, derivations of meanings, and syntactic forms. Hence, there are compensations for the effort involved in learning to spell. (p. 280)

We have attempted thus far to show that learning to spell is a complex undertaking, that it is developmental in nature, and that it involves acquiring and applying knowledge of both spoken and written language. This view of the spelling process is considerably removed from the view in which spelling is regarded as a low-order memory activity in which *habits* rather than knowledge form the base of a spelling curriculum.

A PSYCHOLINGUISTIC
FRAMEWORK FOR SPELLING INSTRUCTION

Our thesis is that spelling is a language-based, cognitive process. This process develops over time from one's interactions with written language, from which is derived a functional knowledge of the English writing system. This is not to imply that direct spelling instruction does not nor cannot contribute to the development of spelling ability; rather, our thesis serves to focus on the learner's own active involvement in acquiring a facility in producing correctly spelled words.

A system or structure, it will be recalled, is an organization of some pattern of events into an understandable framework. Because human beings are pattern-seeking creatures, we are obliged to try to make sense out of what William James called the "kaleidoscopic flux of confusion" into which we are born. Concept formation thus is a kind of system building in which one experiences, identifies, and classifies recurring events in life, thereby giving structure to an otherwise chaotic environment.

As we have seen, language is also systematic and, in an effort to explain this fundamental part of human behavior, linguists devise theories and conduct research in the laboratory of real life as well as in simulated settings. However, it is important to observe that, in a very pragmatic sense, linguists do not need to tell us that language is systematic because each of us already knows that, having intuitively discovered this primary fact in the first few years of life. Language *must* be systematic or else its oral form of expression could not be learned naturally over the short span of time in which most young children accomplish this feat. Language acquisition is indeed one of humankind's marvels and mysteries, the secrets of which have yet to be fully unfolded.

Just as learning to talk involves a child's actively identifying, classifying, and applying recurring language patterns, i.e., phonology, grammar, and a lexicon in relation to meaning, learning to write also involves acquiring a knowledge of recurring patterns, i.e., generalizations or "rules," that relate spoken with written language and patterns contained in written language itself. Where does English orthography fit into language acquisition? An orthography, it will be recalled, is not merely speech written down. Congenitally deaf persons, after all, do learn to spell and to write. *Speech and writing are different but co-equal representations of language.* In English and other languages that employ alphabetically-based orthographies, an orthography *links* speech with writing. This view of the orthography in relation to language can be graphically illustrated:

Through orthography, spoken and written language are closely related, not simply at a superficial level of spelling-sound correspondence (Smith, 1975), but primarily at the lexical level. The *word* is the natural unit of study in the spelling process, and, as the diagram suggests, with both spoken and written words sharing common linguistic properties.

Orthographic words can be analyzed in many contexts: in terms of the sounds and graphemes of which they are comprised and of the relationships among those sounds and graphemes; in terms of morphological and syntactic properties; with respect to their historical developments; and, ultimately, regarding the meanings imbued to them. Word study *over time* engages the learner at all levels of language. There are no crash courses in learning to spell, for the acquisition of spelling ability is a developmental process.

In this developmental perspective, general intellectual processes develop over time, subject to the constraints of a biological timetable and experience. As Piaget and others have shown, the young child is not a miniature adult, but an individual who is searching for and organizing cues that enables sense to be made of the environment according to the child's level of cognitive development. The many child language studies show us that it is a child's great propensity to generate, to analogize, to look for regularities, to seek and to *create* order in his language.

For most individuals, the writing system is a part of that environment, and it, too, becomes a phenomenon to be made sense of. Excluding such highly routinized spellings as one's name, spelling involves the cognitive processing of information about spoken and written expressions of language and their interrelatedness. From this information, the learner generates hypotheses about how language becomes expressed in writing. Thus, the young child (as in Read's and others studies) "spells" words on the basis of the limited information that he or she possesses about the interrelationships between speech and orthography, between phonetic knowledge and letter names. Children's invented spellings are indeed vivid testimony of human intellectual capacities to make order out of the world around us.

A child's spelling errors are mistakes only in terms of adult norms and a standard orthography. In the child's terms, these errors are representations of a developing knowledge of linguistic/orthographic reality. The same can also be said about the spelling errors of most individuals, both children and adults, because an individual's spelling errors are literally *graphic* expressions of that person's knowledge of linguistic/orthographic reality. *There are few random spelling errors in an individual's writing.* Each of us develops over time a "cognitive map" of the orthography which we use to guide us over the orthographic terrain. Accomplished spellers, as do accomplished readers, utilize cues from all levels of written language—graphic, phonetic, morphophonemic, lexical, syntactic, and semantic. Spelling is not a unitary ability; it involves the processing of information from different levels of language. A word such as *phthalocyanine* is hard to spell (other than to chemists or paint manufacturers, perhaps) because of its rarity, morphemic structure, length, unpredictability of its graphemes, and its pronunciation.

Teaching Spelling

An effective educative environment for spelling study is one in which students are most likely to learn the regularities, patterns, and "rules" that constitute English spelling. No packaged spelling program by itself will accomplish this. A spelling curriculum can set the stage and point the direction for the child's involvement with written language. But, in a very real sense, one learns to spell through an ongoing interaction with written language. Just as one learns to talk by talking and learns to read by reading, one learns to spell by spelling, and that occurs at *every instance* in which one engages in the writing act. Learning to spell is not the exclusive domain of formal spelling instruction.

What, then, are some working principles to guide curriculum development in spelling? While not inclusive, a few fundamental principles emerge from our growing insights about the nature of English spelling and its acquisition. Among these principles are the following.

Spelling Is Interrelated with Speech and Other Aspects of Written Language   Spelling has the particular function of representing language graphically through some physical means such as handwriting and forms a link between oral and written expressions of language. Learning to spell is a complex enough task to warrant formal study, but its relationship to written language generally should also be recognized. Spelling instruction needs to provide pupils with opportunities to use emerging spelling skills in written contexts.

The Logic of a Subject and the Logic of Learning the Subject Are Not Necessarily the Same   While the linguistic structure of spelling has been fairly well established, it does not necessarily follow that *individuals* learn to spell in the same logical order that a linguistic analysis follows. Learning to spell does not proceed in a piecemeal fashion of learning about one aspect of the orthography and then another. Learning to spell involves becoming acquainted with the *total* framework of the orthography, how sound-letter relationships, letter sequences, word-building properties, and so on are interrelated.

While youngsters who are just beginning to study spelling do need to have a thorough understanding of the phonetic base of spelling, instruction ought continually to illuminate and to foster an understanding of all the structural elements of the orthography. Spelling should not attend only to sound-letter relationships, but should present spelling as an integrated system which is a part of written language. Spelling experiences should be arranged in a manner that proceeds from simple to complex relationships and from concrete to abstract concepts in ways that are appropriate to levels of child development, with adequate provisions for reviewing and applying prior knowledge.

Some Aspects of Learning to Spell Are Unique to This Subject   Learning to spell adds another dimension to the general language learning process, namely, that of gaining an understanding of a *graphic* communication system and how that system relates to oral forms of expression. In this process, both visual and auditory abilities are called upon, as well as the tactile and muscular abilities (haptical) that are involved in writing. Spelling is a multisensory process.

While most individuals are likely to use all these sensory modes in learning to spell, it would not be correct to conclude that they are equally employed in the same ways by all persons. For some persons, greater use is made of the visual properties of words than of their auditory properties in learning to spell, while the reverse is true for others. Spelling instruction should provide for individual learning styles and rates through the use of a variety of instructional media and approaches.

Language Learning Is a Natural and Active Process   Our present understanding of how children learn oral and written language indicates that such learning takes place through an active exploration of the linguistic environment. While it is true that young children acquire some knowledge about language by being told, the bulk of their linguistic information comes from situations where they explore language and discover clues about the basic patterns and principles of which it is comprised.

The cognitive processes that occur in learning to speak are also applied in learning about written language. Developing spelling ability involves an active participation in discovering the important patterns and principles that govern the writing system and using this information in new writing situations. Spelling instruction ought to capitalize on children's natural and active inquisitiveness about language by enabling them to explore and to discover how the writing system works and by providing numerous opportunities for them to try out their knowledge in new situations that reinforce their growing spelling skills.

Spelling Should Be Taught in the Context of Language Study   Spelling is a *language-based* activity. It employs essentially the same intellectual processes and rests upon essentially the same linguistic properties that other language behavior uses. Teaching spelling as a low-order memorization skill fails to recognize that, in the process of developing spelling ability, individuals draw upon knowledge of many aspects of language—sounds, word-building principles, word meanings. Spelling instruction should provide pupils with an understanding of the ways in which their general knowledge of language relates particularly to spelling, and how this knowledge can be used to develop spelling ability.

Continuous Evaluation Is Essential to Spelling Growth   Learning takes place when there are opportunities to get feedback on one's behavior. We need to know the consequences of our actions in order to improve upon them. We learn from making mistakes and correcting them.

This observation is particularly relevant for the teaching of spelling. Growth in spelling ability develops in conjunction with observing and checking one's spelling attempts and in correcting those attempts to correspond to standard orthography. Simply correcting errors is not sufficient, however. Analyzing the errors that one makes to determine the *causes* for them provides knowledge that can be used in spelling other words. An ability to distinguish correct spellings from incorrect ones and to correct *both* the mistakes and their causes is a crucial part of spelling ability. Spelling instruction needs to provide opportunities for pupils *and teachers* to assess students' progress toward a full understanding of standard orthography.

A SUMMARY AND SOME RESEARCH DIRECTIONS

We have attempted to demonstrate in this chapter that to regard spelling ability as a low-order psychomotor skill acquired through memorization and drill is to disregard its underlying complexity. The acquisition of a functional knowledge of the English writing system and its relationship to language, it has been argued, places spelling study in a much larger and richer context—the context of language itself. When seen in this context, much past spelling research which has largely been concerned with *methodological* issues such as test-study versus study-test approaches, list versus context methods, and syllabication as an instructional method has at best only superficially helped to explain the nature of spelling ability and the consequences of such knowledge for the language arts curriculum and instruction. Much like John Godfrey Saxe's (1884) six blind men of Indostan who, on the basis of touching different parts of the animal's body, arrived at very different conclusions about how the elephant must look, and who then

> . . . Disputed loud and long,
> Each in his own opinion
>   Exceeding stiff and strong,
> Though each was partly in the right,
>   And all were in the wrong!

Spelling ability, too, has been commonly viewed in a piecemeal, unrelated manner. However, the disciplines of linguistics, psychology, and the interdisciplinary field of psycholinguistics now provide a theoretical framework in which to describe the spelling process and to gauge the development of spelling ability.

There are, of course, many substantive unresolved issues which this chapter may have triggered in the reader's mind. For one, the question of general written language acquisition and the place of spelling in the context of learning both the substance and norms of English writing have only recently been given attention approaching that given to oral language development. For another, while insights about initial spelling development of young learners are emerging and some attention is now being given to the spelling processes of older, more accomplished learners, there is a need to explore further the *contiguity* of the development of spelling ability.

Of a more specific nature, schemes for classifying spelling errors which are now emanating from a psycholinguistic perspective need to be expanded to account for errors at more complex levels of English orthography, classifications that will help to clarify how older individuals apply other aspects of linguistic knowledge in spelling words, as, for example, morphemic and syntactic knowledge. A qualitative analysis of spelling errors would be useful in determining the causes of spelling problems. The development of some form of diagnostic spelling test is dependent, however, upon the validity of our theories of the development of spelling ability and of English orthography (Frith, 1978b).

With respect to curriculum research, there is much yet to be done in exploring the scope and sequence for spelling study, taking into account what is known about the developmental nature of spelling acquisition and the nature of English orthography. There is also a need to explore the interrelationships between formal spelling study and other curricular areas in which students interact with and use written language, not only in other language arts subjects, but in all subject fields in which writing is a part of the instructional process. Likewise, instruction warrants a closer examination in light of emerging insights about the development of spelling ability and about the writing system. The ultimate aim is the development of a spelling curriculum (whether a discrete program or embedded in other language arts areas) which is linguistically, psychologically, and instructionally valid.

Spelling as a subject of research or curricular study is one of those paradoxical subjects in which the high social value placed upon correct spelling has not commonly been paralleled by an equally high interest among researchers and curriculum specialists. However, when spelling research is placed within the broader contexts of language structure and learning, it can provide important insights into human behavior. Likewise, when spelling as a curricular question is placed within the broader contexts of the development of written language competence, it merits greater attention than has customarily been given to it by curriculum specialists. While it is true that poor spelling ability is not a terminal disease, it does diminish the speller's status and the value of his written efforts. Other than as a collector's item, how much would *you* bid on a banner reading "Welcome to Fort Werth"?

FOR DISCUSSION

1. Hodges states that learning to read and to write have commanded greater attention among researchers and curriculum specialists than has spelling. Is the same true with textbooks and teachers? Why or why not?

2. Differentiate between the acts of decoding letters into sounds and the encoding of sounds into letters (spelling)? What implications does that difference have in instruction and/or integration of reading and spelling programs?

3. How do Hodges' comments on children's knowledge of phoneme-grapheme relationships compare with Bewell and Straw's on metalinguistic awareness?

4. What is the utility of spelling words orally? Does this require different competencies that spelling words on paper in list form or in real writing situations? Why or why not?

5. Linguists have hypothesized that as children learn language, they completely reconstruct the grammar of their native tongue. What

similarities does this hypothesis have to the hypotheses presented by Hodges?

6. Should spelling be taught separately from other language areas or should it be integrated? How could integration take place without stifling a student's spontaneous expression?

REFERENCES

Alcott, W. A. History of a common school from 1801 to 1831. *American Annals of Education*, November 1831, 509.

Beers, J. W., Beers, C. S., and Grant, K. The logic behind children's spelling. *The Elementary School Journal*, January 1977, *77*, 238–242.

Beers, J. W., and Henderson, E. H. A study of developing orthographic concepts among first graders. *Research in the Teaching of English*, Fall, 1977, *4*, 133–148.

Chomsky, C. Reading, writing, and phonology. *Harvard Educational Review*, May 1970, *40*, 287–309.

Chomsky, C. Invented spelling in the open classroom. *Word*, 1971, *27*, 1–3.

Chomsky, N., and Halle, M. *The sound pattern of English*. New York: Harper and Row, 1968.

Francis, W. N. *The structure of American English*. New York: Ronald Press, 1958. (See Chapter 9, "Writing It Down: Graphics.")

Frith, U. From print to meaning and from print to sound, or how to read without knowing how to spell. *Visible Language*, Winter 1978, *12*, 43–54. (a)

Frith, U. Spelling difficulties: An annotation. *Journal of Child Psychology and Psychiatry*, July 1978, *19*, 279–85. (b)

Gentry, J. R. Early spelling strategies. *The Elementary School Journal*, November 1978, *79*, 88–92.

Gleitman, L. R., and Rozin, P. The structure and acquisition of reading 1: Relations between orthographics and the structure of language. In A. S. Reber and D. L. Scarborough (Eds.), *Toward a psychology of reading: The proceedings of the CUNY conference*. Hillsdale, New Jersey: Lawrence Erlbaum Associates, 1977.

Hall, R. A., Jr. *Sound and spelling in English*. Philadelphia: Chilton Company, 1961.

Hanna, P. R., Hanna, J. S., Hodges, R. E., and Rudorf, E. H. *Phoneme-grapheme correspondences as cues to spelling improvement*. Washington, D.C.: U.S. Government Printing Office, U.S. Office of Education, 1966.

Hillerich, R. L. Let's teach spelling—not phonetic misspelling. *Language Arts*, March 1977, *54*, 301–307.

Hodges, R. E. A short history of spelling reforms in the United States. *Phi Delta Kappan*, April 1964, *45*, 330–332.

Hodges, R. E. In Adam's fall: A brief history of spelling instruction in the United States. In H. A. Robinson (Ed.), *Reading and writing instruction in the United States: Historical trends*. Urbana, Illinois, and Newark, Delaware: ERIC Clearinghous on Reading and Communication Skills and International Reading Association, 1977.

Horn, E. Principles of method in teaching spelling, as derived from scientific investigation. In G. M. Whipple (Ed.), *Fourth report of the Committee on Economy of Time in Education*, Eighteenth Yearbook of the National Society for the Study of Education. Bloomington, Illinois: Public School Publishing Co., 1919.

Kurath, H. *A phonology and prosody of modern English*. Ann Arbor: University of Michigan Press, 1964.

Mazurkiewicz, A. J. Phoneme-grapheme correspondences as cues to spelling improvements: A further appraisal. *Reading World*, March 1978, *17*, 190–196.

Pitman, J., and St. John, J. *Alphabets and reading: The initial teaching alphabet*. London: Pitman and Sons, 1969.

Read, C. Pre-school children's knowledge of English phonology. *Harvard Educational Review*, February 1971, *41*, 1–34.

Read, C. Children's judgments of phonetic similarities in relation to English spelling. *Language Learning*, June 1973, *23*, 17–38.

Read, C. *Children's categorization of speech sounds in English*. National Council of Teachers of English Research Report No. 17. Urbana, Illinois: National Council of Teachers of English, 1975. (a)

Read, C. Lessons to be learned from the preschool orthographer, In E. H. Lenneberg and E. Lenneberg (Eds.), *Foundations of language development: A multidisciplinary approach* (Vol. 2), New York: Academic Press, 1975. (b)

Reed, D. W. A theory of language, speech, and writing. *Elementary English*, December 1965, *42*, 845–851.

Roberts, A. H. Roundtable review: A review by a specialist in the uses of computers in linguistic research. *Research in the Teaching of English*, Fall 1967, *1*, 291–207.

Saturday Review. August 4, 1979, 59.

Saxe, J. G. The blind men and the elephants. *The poems of John Godfrey Saxe*. Boston: Houghton Mifflin, 1884.

Sherwin, S. J. Eggys, egges, eyren: the problem of spelling. In. S. J. Sherwin, *Four problems in teaching English: A critique of research*, pp. 29–108. Scranton Pennsylvania: International Textbook Company, 1969.

Smith, F. The relationship between spoken and written language. In E. H. Lenneberg and E. Lenneberg (Eds.), *Foundations of language development: A multidisciplinary approach* (Vol. 2). New York: Academic Press, 1975.

Smith, H. L., Jr. *English morphophonics: Implications for the teaching of literacy* (Monograph No. 10). Syracuse: New York State English Council, 1968.

Templeton, S. Spelling first, sound later: The relationship between orthography and high order phonological knowledge in older students. *Research in the Teaching of English*, October 1979, *13*, 255–264.

Towery, G. M. *A history of spelling instruction in America*. Unpublished doctoral dissertation, Florida State University, 1971.

Venezky, R. L. English orthography: Its graphical structure and its relation to sound. *Reading Research Quarterly*, Spring 1967, *2*, 75–105.

Venezky, R. L. Regularity in reading and spelling. In H. Levin and J. Williams (Eds.), *Basic studies in reading*. New York: Basic Books, 1970.

Webster, N. *The American spelling book*. Middletown, Connecticut: William H. Niles, 1831, p. 19. Facsimile edition of *Noah Webster's American spelling book*. New York: Bureau of Publications, Teachers College, Columbia University, 1962.

Zutell, J. Some psycholinguistic perspectives on children's spelling. *Language Arts*. October 1978, *55*, 844–850.

Zutell, J. Spelling strategies of primary school children and their relationships to Piaget's concept of decentration. *Research in the Teaching of English*, February 1979, *13*, 69–80.

12 Handwriting: Practice, Pragmatism, and Progress

Victor Froese

The purpose of this chapter is to identify ways in which the teaching and learning of handwriting in schools (and beyond) has been conditioned by common practice, pragmatism, and, somewhat less, by research. More specifically the chapter deals with problems with handwriting, developmental aspects of handwriting, uses of psychographology, and aspects of letter formation. Because most of these topics pertain both to right- and left-handed writers, the left-handed writer is not dealt with separately in this chapter (see Enstrom, 1964, and Howell, 1978, for a brief review).

The following position statements reflect the author's interpretation of the literature:

1. There is still no generally accepted definition of "legibility."
2. Handwriting instruction has changed very little over the past 60 years.
3. Transition from manuscript to cursive (if necessary at all) should be an individual matter.
4. Evaluation of handwriting is still largely unresolved.
5. Research on letter forms and the uniqueness of letters is still lacking.

Finally, an attempt will be made to synthesize the findings discussed and suggest some practical and research applications.

GENERAL OBSERVATIONS

It should be noted that a number of overviews in the field of handwriting exist (National Conference on Research in English, 1966; Andersen, 1968; Ebel, 1969; Askov, Otto, and Askov, 1970; Shane, Walden, and Green, 1971; Suen, 1975; Brown, 1977; Graves; 1978; Shane and Walden, 1978). These reviews cover the field over the seven decades of this century quite thoroughly. What must be remembered is that these references are often bibliographic rather than critical analyses, yet it is easy to confound these two categories. Furthermore, a few "giants" of handwriting dominated the field and thereby injected, whether intentionally or not, considerable bias into the literature. Occasionally, even somewhat misleading information is repeated as a result. The writer discovered, for example, that three different reviews stated in very similar terminology that "Berry, in a study employing Italic writing with students in grades one through eight, reported that papers improved in legibility and appearance" (Andersen, 1966b). Unfortunately, the Berry reference is not a "study" in even loose usage of that term; it is simply a testimonial, stating opinion. When mixed in with reputable studies, this type of review can present a far more complete picture of handwriting research than actually exists.

A second caution in considering handwriting research must also be noted. It is easy to lose perspective with regard to how handwriting fits into the total language arts picture. That is, handwriting is a tool but one with limited utility. For example, Templin (1963) found that adults used handwriting for making out checks, for social correspondence, for filling in forms, and for preparing shopping lists. Elementary teachers in Wilt's (1950) study estimated that children spent 17% of their school time in writing, thereby ranking it fourth after reading, speaking, and listening. The caution expressed in this paragraph is perhaps best summarized be Krathwohl (1963) in his comments at the Invitational Conference on Research in Handwriting at the University of Wisconsin: "We get overly concerned . . . with form, and not with the language or with the idea that is being communicated." He goes on to suggest that an ideal method for teaching handwriting would be one which least interferes with self-expression, results in accurate perception, provides the least interference with other learning, provides for rapid communication, is physiologically realistic, and is amenable to realistic motivation. If one keeps these suggestions in mind, one can more objectively interpret handwriting research.

A final caution is best stated in Tabachnick's (1963) words: "We cannot use a report about what is 'most practised' to tell us about what is 'best practised'."

REVIEW OF THE LITERATURE

Legibility

To date there still appears to be no generally accepted definition of "legibility." Studies often define operationally what is meant—for example, Quant (1946) defines it as readability as measured by eye-movement photography. Others interpret legibility in terms of speed of tachistoscopic recognition, reading errors, speed of reading, or in terms of quality judgments on an arbitrary scale. Groff (1975) somewhat caustically states that "legibility seems deliberately defined in a circuitous manner so as to make this evasion [stating what constitutes legibility] possible. That is, a synonym for legibility usually is offered as its definition, rather than any exact description of its outer dimensions."

It is generally conceded (Andersen, 1966a) that Freeman in 1915 developed the first scale utilizing five factors of legibility: letter form, uniformity of slant, uniformity of alignment of letters, quality of line, and spacing between letters and words. These factors are stressed in most language arts textbooks today even though Freeman revised his scale (in 1953) to use general excellence only and not the five factors separately.

Freeman's factors were not empirically validated and there is no reason to believe that they are equally important. In fact, Quant (1946) found alignment and weight of line not to be significantly related to legibility and found letter formation to be the most important single factor. But Quant warned that "no one characteristic of handwriting exists separately from other characteristics, but they are interrelated in the handwriting process." Andersen (1969) on the other hand, found that the "more legible the sample, the larger the writing." Size, within certain limitations, may consequently be another factor to consider. Obviously there are several research questions still to be investigated; these are enumerated in a later section.

To complicate (or to simplify?) the issue, not all letters cause equal legibility difficulties. Horton (1970) found that only six letters (*h*, *i*, *k*, *p*, *z*, *r*) accounted for 30% of illegibilities in the writing of sixth graders studied, and the letter *r* accounted for 12% of the illegibilities all by itself. From Horton's research we can learn that illegibilities are not evenly distributed. For teaching purposes, it would be a great help to know where difficulties are likely to occur and which letters to emphasize in what is already a tight teaching schedule.

Assuming that some form of handwriting will be with us for some time, how can students and teachers be assisted in evaluating it in order to make it legible? Harris and Herrick (1963) found that evaluation of their own writing by slow-learning students was significantly different from that of average and bright students as well as from that of adult placement. The authors also suggested that models of handwriting may not be as effective as we would like them to be because children have difficulty judging what is different about the "aspired to" models. These findings may have implications for current teaching practices.

Rate and Speed

Another dimension of handwriting appearing in the literature is that of writing rate or speed. Andersen (1968) states that "the research shows no evidence to support the view that speed is a significant feature of handwriting." On the other hand, Harris and Rarick (1963) found a moderately high inverse rank order correlation of -0.55 between legibility and time. However, in another study Harris and Rarick (1955) state that the "speed of writing is a relative and highly individual matter." A clue to this puzzle may lie in the purpose for writing and the length of sample examined, that is, speed may not be a significant problem when writing one sentence (the ubiquitous "The quick brown fox"), but it may affect legibility after 15 or 30 minutes of continuous writing. The amount of writing experience may also be important. Templin (1963) did find females' writing to become less legible with writing quantity, but the opposite effect held true for males.

Groff (1961) in fact has criticized the conditions Ayres used for gathering writing rate data. Presumably memorized passages could be written faster than unfamiliar ones. Consequently, Groff had intermediate grade students write the three beginning sentences from the Gettysburg Address under different conditions, which he maintained more nearly approached natural handwriting conditions. The speeds obtained were about 20 words per minute slower at each grade level than those suggested by Ayres.

Manuscript and Cursive

A further crucial consideration requires attention—whether the writing is manuscript or cursive. Proponents of one writing method usually criticize the other with regard to its speed or lack of speed. While no conclusive evidence appears in the literature, Hildreth's (1948) work suggests some answers. She had eighth graders who had been taught only cursive or only manuscript make a series of connected and unconnected strokes. While she found a negligible difference in rate of strokes for manuscript and cursive writers, she did find significant differences in rate of joined and unjoined strokes (in favor of unjoined). This finding was interpreted as favoring manuscript (unjoined) writing.

Perhaps because Freeman's "quality of line" has been interpreted in terms of pressure applied to the writing instrument or to the writing surface, this matter has been under considerable investigation. Harris and Rarick (1955) did a rather thorough investigation of the issue using GSR and EMG measures and concluded that "great differences in average writing pressure exist in adults ... Furthermore, since such differences appear to have but little relationship to the legibility of the handwriting, it would seem that teachers should not expect each pupil to write with equally light or heavy pressure." An essentially similar conclusion had been reached by Quant (1946).

Utility of Handwriting

The utility of handwriting has already been alluded to with respect to its inclusion in the curriculum. Groff (1975) predicts that "handwriting legibility will continue to decline, a fall-off that could have some positive side effects, nonetheless." He speculates that illegible handwriting may speed up technological development of speech-to-print recordings, notetaking machines, and the introduction of typewriting. If nothing else, Groff's comments lead to a reexamination of the usefulness of handwriting. If legibility is at issue, then Quant's (1946) study shows that handwriting is less legible than printed (typewritten) material. Templin's (1963) work also sheds some light on the legibility of the handwriting of various occupational groups. From legibility ratings she ranked the occupations from best to poorest: bookkeepers, elementary teachers, high school teachers, physicians, and college professors.

Another issue related to the utility of handwriting hinges on its relationship to beginning reading instruction. Do manuscript and cursive writing contribute to or hinder reading instruction? Voorhis (1931) compared first graders' reading abilities after being taught either cursive or manuscript writing and found that "the manuscript group scored significantly higher than the cursive group in every case." Campbell (1973) investigated the effect of typewriting on reading acquisition of learning disabled children and found that the typewriting group made more progress than the handwriting group. It was suggested that typing required a lower level of psychomotor development.

Teachers' Perceptions

A final point to be discussed in this section deals with the role of teachers' perceptions in evaluating handwritten work. Marschall and Powers (1969) varied both writing (typed; neatly, fairly, and poorly written) and type of error (no error, spelling error, grammatical error) and found that "prospective teachers are influenced by the quality of composition and the writing neatness of an essay response, even when they are given explicit directions to grade on content alone in accordance with an outline of derived content." Somewhat surprisingly, they found the raters to prefer neat handwriting over typewritten essays. Marschall and Powers' work is supported by Briggs (1970) who obtained similar results. One wonders whether teacher biases can be minimized through instruction or through a confrontation with results like those found by these authors since Depillo (1970) found no differences in ratings when creativity was controlled.

Alphabet Models

Another unresolved issue revolves around the letter form agreement in commercially produced writing systems. In a national survey, Herrick and Okado (1963) found that 82% of all school systems reporting indicated that they used a commercial system of handwriting as a basis for their program of handwriting instruction and that 19 commercial systems account for 97% of the commercial materials used. In an earlier study comparing five commercial systems (The Committee for Research in Handwriting, 1951), considerable differences were found in both the manuscript letters, e.g., seven uppercase y's; five lowercase w's and the cursive letters, e.g., ten uppercase f's; three or four lowercase d, k, p, x's). Obviously many discrepancies cause difficulties for students; this may be a signal that more study is needed to establish efficient and legible forms (discussed in more detail in a later section).

A second alternative to the traditional manuscript alphabet has been Enstrom's (1966) slant print as a transitional step to cursive writing.

The third alternative is a simplified script based on the Danish system (Mullins et al. 1972). It minimizes differences between manuscript and cursive writing, eliminates unnecessary loops, strokes, and flourishes, begins all initial letters with downstrokes, is slightly sloping, and eliminates all penlifts within words.

The fact that all these procedures coexist perhaps is a sign of tolerance for a possible change if a sound system can be devised. Quant (1946) suggested that "from the point of view of legibility, this emphasis on simplifying letter forms is correct." In 1968, Andersen again stated that "both researchers and general public have expressed concern for the development of a system of simplified letter form."

One other influence is worthy of mention although its impact is still minor, that is, the interest in calligraphy (Vandervoort, 1970; Diaco, 1971). While the term may refer to the art of fine handwriting in general, often it refers to some form of italic script used originally for writing manuscripts. Often the Chancery alphabet is identified specifically. While many good sources of information are available (Benson, 1959; Reynolds, 1969; Gourdie, 1976) no systematic research could be located on the efficiency of this approach.

Readiness and Transition Time

One of the arguments for the current method of handwriting instruction (beginning with manuscript, then changing to cursive) is that the manuscript form is easier to learn and easier to write (Voorhis, 1931). However, these claims are speculative and have not been adequately documented. In fact, the two above claims together approximate what Furner (1969) has called perceptual-motor learning. Furner found in her doctoral dissertation study that "first graders who used a problem approach [e.g. verbalizing of descriptions to guide practice] performed significantly better than those using a commercial approach." These findings, however, simply argue for a perceptual-motor rather than a strictly motor learning approach, but they do not shed light on the ease of learning manuscript writing.

Although "handwriting readiness," like reading readiness, has come into vogue in the late 1960s (King, 1968; Allen and Wright, 1975), most articles are pragmatic rather than empirical. More convincing is the work of Niedermeyer (1973), who taught kindergarten children of various innercity and suburban schools the letters and numerals. Her tryout groups (experimental subjects) scored significantly better than her comparison groups in terms of letter and numeral legibility. The conclusion reached was that there appeared to be no reason to delay systematic printing instruction, that there were no large socioeconomic or ethnic differences, and that a positive attitude toward school (attitude was assessed via structured interview) was generated.

While the Niedermeyer study dealt with manuscript writing, several studies in the field of learning disabilities appear to favor cursive writing from the beginning. Early et al. (1976) favor cursive writing because fewer reversals and transposition errors occur. But the evidence is hardly convincing and they admit that certain teacher, school, and pupil variables were not controlled. Mullins et al. (1972) have proposed a simplified script which might be helpful to learning disabled children (and normal children as well!) but no evidence was quoted.

Since there appear to be few physiological reasons to hamper writing—whether manuscript or cursive—the readiness issue seems rather inconsequential. Most first grade children can apparently learn either method, especially when good teaching procedures are employed.

If a change from manuscript to cursive is made (a development only 50 years old), the transition time needs consideration. To answer the question, Enstrom (1966) asked teachers in 329 school districts in six states when the transition was made. He found a range of from beginning of grade two to third grade, but the majority (57.7%) made the transition from manuscript to cursive by the 18th week of second grade. These teachers were reported by the author to have free decision-making power in this matter. Otto and Rarick (1969) made a post hoc study of fourth and fifth graders making the transition at four different times of the year (2;1, 2;2, 3;1, 3;2) and found significant transition time effect using analysis of variance procedures, but only for the 2;2 and 3;2 groups. They concluded that the program was more important than the transition time.

Several alternatives to the traditional (since the 1920s) procedure of following manuscript with cursive writing have been proposed. Several authors support only manuscript writing without a transfer to cursive. Plattor and Woestehoff (1971) found that "children's ability to read cursive writing is dependent upon their ability to read manuscript style. . . . The evidence of a growing body of comparative data would seem to support the introduction of manuscript as the writing style in the primary grades and its maintenance throughout children's educational careers."

It appears that *one* transition time would not be appropriate but that, instead, individual readiness should be the deciding factor if a transition is made.

Letter Forms

Basic to the improvement of any handwriting mode should be an analysis of its forms, joining strokes, criterial features, and difficult spots. While Newland (1932) discovered that only 14 forms of illegibility accounted for 50% of all elementary and high school illegibilities, this fact is seldom used in handwriting instruction. It should, however, be noted that the Newland study does not consider the frequency of the occurrence of letters. The four letters (*a, e, r, t*) contributing most to illegibility are also among the most frequently occurring letters—an effect which tends to overestimate the importance of these particular letters.

In the 1950s comparisons among commercial handwriting methods (The Committee for Research in Handwriting, 1951) resulted in many differences being noted. The question as to which forms are most efficient appears to be overridden by convention and preference.

Not until the 1960s did an order of difficulty for manuscript letters appear in the literature. Lewis and Lewis (1964) investigated the relative difficulty of the 52 letter forms in the manuscript alphabet for first graders and found lowercase letters (like *q, g, p, y, j, m, k*) and uppercase letters (like *U, G, R, Y, M, S*) to be the most difficult ones.

One of the most intriguing projects reported is a factor analysis study of the Swedish alphabet to discover the multidimensional similarity of letters. The Swedish alphabet is similar to the English alphabet except that it does not contain a *w* and has three additional symbols (*å, ä, ö*). Kuennapas and Janson (1969) found nine factors: vertical linearity, roundness, parallel vertical linearity, vertical linearity with dot, roundness attached to vertical linearity, vertical linearity with crossness, roundness attached to a hook, angularity upward, and zigzaggedness. The authors provide tables indicating which letters load on particular factors, the kind of information which could profitably be used in devising easily perceptible letter forms or in modifying present letter forms. Such information would be invaluable if it were available for cursive writing as well.

One other development of relevance to this chapter and to letter formation is Callewaert's (1963) "round handwriting." Callewaert, a physician, suggests placing the writing instrument between the index and middle finger and thereby likening the movement to "two cranks and two connecting-rods, perfectly adaptable to curves and loops." Claims are also made for this method being physiologically more sound in that it permits relaxation of the hand and facilitates the backward cursive movement. Otto et al. (1966) evaluated Callewaert's modified grip with college students. Although the students preferred the traditional grip in terms of comfort and produced more legible writing with it, they adapted quickly. The speed of letter formation with the modified grip was as good as with the traditional grip even though the students had had no previous training. It appears that Callewaert's grip deserves further attention, especially with younger subjects or with subjects who may have coordination difficulties.

Psychographology

A number of studies in the last decade deal with the application of psychology to handwriting analysis and hence the resulting derivative, psychographology, and its counterpart, graphotherapy (King, 1976; McCutcheon, 1978). Zweigenhaft (1970), for example, found a 50% increase in signature size from several months before earning a Ph.D. to 4 years after.

Holder (1969), Tenaglia (1973), Solomon (1978), and Gilbertson (1980) deal with the analysis of encoded behaviors such as fears, temperament, concentration, artistic talents, feelings about others, and feelings about self. The emphasis is on assisting the teacher or parent to understand the various manifestations of the child's or student's handwriting and using these findings to understand the child or to be warned of various personality changes. For example, retracements of letters (*m, n*) may signal a fear of change, looped letters (*d, t*) may indicate sensitivity to criticism. Clusters of various characteristics lead to the identification of personality types—versatile, introvert, egotistic, etc.

Developmental characteristics of handwriting were discussed by de Ajuriaguerra and Auzias (1975). Of special note is the description of spatial awareness and its relationship to Piagetian principles.

If handwriting is encoded behavior, then one might well ask the question: Can changing handwriting practices affect personality or self-concept? Some affirmative evidence may be found. Stoller (1973) found a definite relationship between handwriting change and improved self-concept in fourth graders. A 6-week program resulted in significantly improved handwriting and self-concept.

EDUCATIONAL IMPLICATIONS

In this section and in the following section, Research Implications, the five position statements stated at the beginning of this chapter are discussed in more detail. As the reader will discover, educational implications based on interpreted research will often result in further researchable questions and vice versa.

First, one must conclude that an adequate definition of legibility is still not available. While most commercial systems use Freeman's five factors (letter forms, uniformity of slant, uniformity of alignment of letters, quality of line, and spacing between letters and words) he himself revised his scale to use "general excellence" only. If "legibility" is defined as "general excellence" then we have not progressed in our understanding of this concept.

However, a composite of several research findings does suggest some useful guidelines. Quant (1946) found alignment and weight of line not to be significantly related to legibility but found *letter formation* to be the most important single factor. Andersen (1969) found that the *larger* the writing (within limits), the more legible it was. Furthermore, Horton (1970) found that only six *letters* (*h*, *i*, *k*, *p*, *z*, *r*) accounted for 30% of illegibilities in the sixth graders studied. And Harris and Rarick (1963) found a -0.55 rank order correlation between legibility and time. That is, the *faster* one writes, the less legibile it becomes.

To summarize, reasonably good evidence exists to support the consideration of letter formation, size, and appropriate rate. One could consider *joining* and *spacing* to be related to letter formation within words. Slant and alignment are not closely related to legibility per se, but uniformity of slant and alignment add to the aesthetic effect of handwriting.

Some useful sources of teacher information on handwriting (although not necessarily based on the findings discussed above) may be found in Markoff (1976) and Marcus (1977).

The second position statement indicated that emphasis on handwriting was cyclical but that it has changed little. That parents' and teachers' perception of handwriting has changed little over the last decade is documented by Sloan and Triplett (1977) and Renaud and Groff (1966). Research on the best transition time indicates that when the transition is made is less important than what is offered in the instructional program

(Otto and Rarick, 1969). Considerable differences were found in both the manuscript and cursive alphabets of commerical systems.

There appear to be few, if any, physiological reasons to hamper writing—whether manuscript or cursive. The current practice of introducing manuscript writing in the first grade is approximately 50 years old and continues to be the predominant modus operandi.

A further position was taken with respect to the need to change from manuscript to cursive writing and whether an optimum transition may be pinpointed. Plattor and Woestehoff (1971) state that the evidence of a growing body of comparative data seemed to suggest the maintenance of manuscript writing throughout a child's educational career. Otto and Rarick's (1969) research indicated that the program was more important than the transition time. In a 1979 study of the writing (composition and mechanics) of children in grades 3, 6, 9, and 12 in the Province of Manitoba, it was found that a sizeable number of twelfth graders spontaneously wrote their essays in manuscript form.

The fourth position stated that the procedures for evaluating handwriting were largely unresolved. In some ways evaluation is dependent on a clarification of the legibility issue, that is, it is dependent on identifying the key components of legibility. However, evaluation may be global as well. Essentially, that is the method used by writing scales as proposed by Noble (1965), Ayres (1957), Freeman (1959), and West (1957). Writing samples are judged against criterion samples. The use of writing scales is not particularly helpful for the teacher except perhaps in assigning grades. For diagnostic purposes a finer system of analysis is necessary. Perhaps this is the reason for the findings by Addy and Wylie (1973) that 70% of all schools surveyed evaluated handwriting on the basis of teacher observation rather than on a standardized writing scale.

To overcome some of the limitations of standardized handwriting scales it is possible to adapt the scaling idea to more localized conditions and obtain diagnostic information as well. A teacher or group of teachers collect many samples of handwriting for each grade level and then sort them in to several categories of global legibility, i.e., excellent, very good, good, fair, poor). From each category, one or two representative samples are mounted as the models to be used for comparison. For each level, a range of attributes (uniformity of slant and size, letter formation, alignment, etc.) may be illustrated. The teacher then assigns a value of 5 to 1 for each attribute and compiles the total score for an overall rating.

The fifth position statement implied that the research on letter forms and the perceptual uniqueness of letters is still lacking. As stated previously, the question as to which letter forms are most efficient and readable is overridden by convention rather than by research. The most innovative work was undertaken by Kuennapas and Janson (1969) who factor analyzed the multidimensional similarity of letters, thereby isolating nine factors. Studies by Gibson and Levin (1976) also help to clarify the discriminating features of letters.

Quant (1946), Andersen (1968), and Askov, Otto, and Askov (1970) have all similarly concluded that letter forms might profitably be simplified without loss of legibility.

The modified scripts of Minkoff (1975), Mullins et al. (1972), and Thurber (1978) are in fact compromises between cursive and manuscript writing.

In light of the foregoing evidence the most practical advice for the teacher is to organize the capital and small letters into groups with similar characteristics (see Markoff, 1976, for example) for teaching purposes and to eliminate unnecessary strokes, retracings, and frills.

RESEARCH IMPLICATIONS

As expressed earlier, much handwriting research is circular and tautological, and what is "most practiced" is not necessarily what is "best practiced."

Clarification is needed on a number of important issues such as the following:

1. What is the relative importance of the five factors of legibility as proposed by Freeman? How should they be weighted in a scoring system?
2. What is the effect of handwriting on composing and on spelling? What are the interrelationships among these three variables?
3. What emotional impact does the transition from manuscript to cursive have on the young student? Which emotional or personality changes are detectable through psychographology? Can this type of information be used profitably for teaching purposes?
4. What are the distinctive features of letters that make them readable or legible? How can ease or difficulty of letter recognition be quantified?
5. Can the perceptual and the motor aspects of handwriting be separated experimentally? How does verbalization assist the motor act of handwriting?
6. Is an interactive effect produced by modifying the script and modifying the grip?
7. How do junior and senior high school students respond to the maintenance of manuscript writing?
8. Does the teaching of calligraphic skills enhance interest in handwrit-

ing? Does it produce better handwriting in general? Does it result in enhanced self-concept?

9. Can a study of notetaking behaviors provide clues to efficient letter formation and ligatures? Is an efficient alphabet also more readable?

SUMMARY AND COMMENTS

This chapter attempts to survey handwriting research and practice over the past 60 years (approximately 1920 to 1979). This span marks the period in America since manuscript writing was introduced from England.

The review was directed by the author's questions regarding the role of handwriting in our society and schools, by questions regarding the evaluation of handwriting in other than traditional ways, and by an interest in developing an efficient, empirically based, and utilitarian handwriting system.

Much handwriting research, such as that on scaling, has been tautological, because it is based on current commercial materials. Yet other basic questions, such as defining legibility, have not been resolved although they are essential for meaningful progress. The field has been considerably hampered by the mentality expressed so well by Otto and Andersen (1969): "There seems to be more interest in finding out what is being done and in telling people what they should be doing than in testing hypotheses or creating new ones." Interestingly enough, the useful research in handwriting has been spread throughout the 60 year period discussed in this paper and is not concentrated in the most recent decade only (as advancements in technology might suggest).

The most promising findings, from the author's viewpoint, have been the research and survey work on the difficulty of manuscript and cursive letters, the development of cardinal handwriting scales, the work on modified grips, the factor analysis of criterial aspects of letters, and the construction of modified scripts.

While research in handwriting is at a rather low ebb and educators are rather disinterested in the matter, perhaps it is a period of indecision before some more decisive developments. Manuscript writing was a new development in the 1920s and within a few decades it was used in the majority of schools—by 1962, in 86% of the nation's schools (Herrick and Okada, 1963).

FOR DISCUSSION

1. Froese states that, as yet, there is no definition of legibility. If this is the case, how can teachers effectively evaluate student performance or growth in handwriting?

2. Of what use are scales in evaluating legibility in connected discourse?
3. What should be the objective or goals of a handwriting program in schools?
4. Should handwriting instruction be extended into secondary school? Why or why not?
5. What is the justification for teaching manuscript handwriting before cursive writing? Is that position valid?
6. Does the fact that nearly all children receive beginning handwriting instruction at the same time, regardless of their readiness level, account for differences in handwriting ability later? What constitutes readiness for handwriting instruction? Are there identifiable differences between boys and girls?
7. What are some ways teachers can improve their own instructional procedures in handwriting?

REFERENCES

Addy, P., and Wylie, R. E. The "right" way to write. *Childhood Education*, February 1973, *49*, 253–259.

Allen, E. G., and Wright, J. P. Ready to write! *Elementary School Journal*, April 1975, *75*, 430–435.

Andersen, D. W. Handwriting research: Movement and quality. *Research on handwriting and spelling*. NCTE, 1966, 14. (a)

Andersen, D. W. Handwriting research: style and practice. *Research in handwriting and spelling*. NCTE, 1966, 21. (b)

Andersen, D. W. *Teaching handwriting*. Washington, D.C.: NEA, 1968.

Andersen, D. W. What makes writing legible? *Elementary School Journal*, April 1969, *69*, 365–369.

Askov, E., Otto, W., and Askov, W. A decade of research in handwriting: progress and prospect. *Journal of Educational Research*, November 1970, *64*, 99–111.

Ayres' handwriting scale. New York: Noble and Noble, 1957.

Benson, J. H. *The first writing book*. New Haven, Connecticut: Yale University Press, 1959.

Briggs, D. The influence of handwriting on assessment. *Educational Research*, November 1970, *13*, 50–55.

Brown, G. State of the art in handwriting, ERIC Document ED 147826, 1977.

Callewaert, H. For easy and legible handwriting. In V. E. Harrick (Ed.), *New horizons for research in handwriting*. Madison: University of Wisconsin Press, 1963.

Campbell, D. D. Typewriting contrasted with handwriting: A circumvention study of learning-disabled children. *Journal of Special Education*, Summer 1973, *7*, 155–168.

The Committee for Research in Handwriting. *Handwriting in Wisconsin: A survey of elementary school practices*. Madison: University of Wisconsin, 1951.

de Ajuriaguerra, J., and Auzias, M. Preconditions for the development of writing in the child. In E. Lenneberg and E. Lenneberg (eds.), *Foundations of Language Development*, Vol. 2. New York: Academic Press, 1975.

Depillo, N. C. *The influence of handwriting upon teacher's evaluation of children's creative stories.* Unpublished doctorial dissertation, University of Wisconsin, 1970.

Diaco, R. Calligraphy, art education. ERIC Document ED 071977, 1971.

Early, G. H., Nelson, D. A., Kleber D. J., Treegoob, M., Huffman, E., and Cass, C. Cursive handwriting, reading, and spelling achievement. *Academic Therapy*, Fall 1976, *12*, 67–73.

Ebel, R. L. (Ed.). *Encyclopedia of educational research.* New York: Macmillan, 1969.

Enstrom, E. A. Research in teaching the left-handed. *Instructor*, October 1964, *74*, 44, 46, 104.

Enstrom, E. A. The acceptance of slant print. *Elementary English*, April 1966, *43*, 409–412.

Freeman, F. N. A new handwriting scale. *Elementary School Journal*, January 1959, *59*, 218–221.

Furner, B. A. The perceptual-motor nature of learning in handwriting. *Elementary English*, November 1969, *46*, 886–894.

Gibson, E. T., and Levin, H. *The psychology of reading.* Cambridge, Mass.: The MIT Press, 1976, p. 16.

Gilbertson, B. Your handwriting is you. In C. Hobson (ed.), *Resourcebook.* Toronto: Special Interest Magazines, 1980, 32–34.

Gourdie, T. *Italic handwriting.* New York: Pentalic, 1976.

Graves, P. H. Research update: Handwriting is for writing. *Language Arts*, March 1978, *5*, 393–389.

Groff, P. J. New speeds of handwriting. *Elementary English*, December 1961, *38*, 564–565.

Groff, P. J. The future of legibility. *Elementary English*, February 1975, *52*, 205–220.

Harris, T. L., and Herrick, V. E. Children's perception of the handwriting task. In V. E. Herrick (Ed.), *New horizons for research in handwriting.* Madison: University of Wisconsin Press, 1963, pp. 159–179.

Harris, T. L., and Rarick, G. L. *Pressure patterns in handwriting.* Madison: University of Wisconsin, 1955.

Harris, T. L. and Rarick, G. L. Physiological and motor correlates of handwriting legibility. In V. E. Herrick (Ed.), *New horizons for research in handwriting.* Madison: University of Wisconsin Press, 1963, pp. 58–87.

Herrick, V. E., and Okado, N. The present scene: Practices in the teaching of handwriting in the United States—1960. In V. E. Herrick (Ed.), *New horizons for research in handwriting.* Madison: University of Wisconsin Press, 1963, pp. 17–32.

Hildreth, G. Comparative speed of joined and unjoined writing strokes. *Journal of Educational Psychology*, February 1948, *36*, 91–102.

Holder, R. *You can analyze handwriting.* New York: Signet, 1969.

Horton, L. W. Illegibilities in the cursive handwriting of ninth-graders. *Elementary School Journal*, May 1970, *70*, 446–450.

Howell, H. Write on, you sinistrals. *Language Arts*, 1978, *55*, 852–856.

King, F. M. Readiness for handwriting. *Elementary English*, February 1968, *45*, 201–203.

King, L. W. Evaluating sexual behavior from writing characteristics. ERIC Document ED 161057, 1976.

Krathwohl, D. R. Proposals of consultants for the improvement of research in handwriting. In V. E. Herrick (Ed.), *New horizons for research in handwriting.* Madison: University of Wisconsin Press, 1963, pp. 246–251.

Kuennapas, T., and Janson, A. Multidimensional similarities of letters. *Perception and Motor Skills,* 1969, *28,* 3–12.

Lewis, E. R., and Lewis, H. P. Which manuscript letters are hard for first graders? *Elementary English,* December 1964, *41,* 855–858.

Marcus, M. *Diagnostic teaching of language arts.* New York: John Wiley and Sons, 1977.

Markoff, A. M. *Teaching low-achieving children reading, spelling and handwriting.* Springfield, Illinois: Charles C Thomas, 1976.

Marschall, J. C., and Powers, J. M. Writing neatness, composition errors, and essay grades. *Journal of Educational Measurement,* Summer 1969, *6,* 72–101.

McCutcheon, L. Mental health and the measurement of self-disclosure. ERIC Document ED 166566, 1978.

Minkoff, H. Teaching the transition form print to script analytically. *Elementary English,* February 1975, *52,* 203–204.

Mullins, J., Joseph, F., Turner, C., Zawadzki, R., and Saltzman, L. A handwriting model for children with learning disabilities. *Journal of Learning Disabilities,* May 1972, *5,* 58–63.

Niedermeyer, F. C. Kindergarteners learn to write. *Elementary School Journal,* December 1973, *74,* 130–135.

Newland, T. E. An analytical study of the development of illegibilities in handwriting from the lower grades to adulthood. *Journal of Educational Research,* December 1932, *26,* 249–258.

Noble's handwriting scale. New York: Noble and Noble, 1965.

Otto, W., and Andersen, D. W. Handwriting. In R. L. Ebel (Ed.), *Encyclopedia of educational research.* New York: Macmillan, 1969.

Otto, W., and Rarick, G. L. Effect of time of transition from manuscript to cursive writing upon subsequent performance in handwriting, spelling, and reading. *Journal of Educational Research,* January 1969, *62,* 211–216.

Otto, W., Rarick, G. L., Armstrong, J., and Koepke, M. Evaluation of a modified grip in handwriting. *Perception and Motor Skills,* February 1966, *22,* 310.

Plattor, E. E., and Woestehoff, E. S. Toward a singular style of instruction in handwriting. *Elementary English,* December 1971, *48,* 1009–1011.

Quant, L. Factors affecting the legibility of handwriting. *Journal of Experimental Education,* June 1946, *14,* 279–316.

Renaud, A. J., and Groff, P. J. Parent opinion about handwriting style. *Elementary English,* December 1966, *43,* 873–878.

Reynolds, R. L. *Italic calligraphy and handwriting.* New York: Pentalic, 1969.

Shane, H. G., and Walden, J. *Classroom-relevant research in the language arts.* Washington, D.C. Association for Supervision of Curriculum Development, NEA, 1978.

Shane, H. G., Walden, J., and Green, R. *Interpreting language arts research for the teacher.* Washington, D.C.: Association for Supervision of Curriculum Development, NEA, 1971.

Sloan, C. A., and Triplett, D. Parents' and teachers' perceptions of handwriting. ERIC Document ED 155723, 1977.

Solomon, S. *Knowing your child through his handwriting and drawing.* New York: Crown Publishers, 1978.

Stoller, R. J. Can self-concept be improved in a group of children by changing certain handwriting strokes in their writing? ERIC Document ED 147 820, 1973. (Based on doctoral dissertation, Walden University.)

Suen, C. Y. Handwriting education in Canada. *Saskatchewan Journal of Educational Research and Development*, Spring 1975, *5*, 46–52.

Tabachnick, B. R. Discussion of Paper I (Herrick and Okada). In V. E. Herrick (Ed.), *New horizons for research in handwriting*. Madison: University of Wisconsin Press, 1963, p. 33.

Templin, E. M. The legibility of adult manuscript, cursive, or manuscript-cursive handwriting styles. In V. E. Herrick (Ed.), *New horizons for research in handwriting*. Madison: University of Wisconsin Press, 1963, pp. 185–199.

Tenaglia, R. Graphotherapy: Aiding children's personality development. *Elementary English*, 1973, *5*, 775–778.

Thurber, D. N. *O'Nealian handwriting*. Glenview, Illinois: Scott, Foresman, 1978.

Vandervoort, P. Calligraphy in the curriculum. *School Arts*, 1970, *70*, 34–36.

Voorhis, T. G. *The relative merits of cursive and manuscript writing*. New York: Teachers College, Columbia University, 1931.

West, P. V. *American handwriting scale*. New York: Palmer, 1957.

Wilt, M. E. A study of teaching awareness of listening as a factor in elementary education. *Journal of Educational Research*, April 1950, *43*, 626–636.

Zweigenhaft, R. L. Signature size: A key to status awareness. *Journal of Social Psychology*, 1970, *81*, 49–54.

13 How Children Recognize Words in Print

Timothy C. Standal

The importance of word recognition to fluent reading seems to be both controversial and little understood; perhaps it is a matter of definition. Some write as though word recognition were the sum total of reading. It is not. Some write as though word recognition were only incidental to reading. It is not, or, at least, it is not in the sense sometimes conveyed.

The process by which people, not just children, recognize words in print is of interest to a range of professionals, including educators and psychologists. Some are interested in the process for what it can reveal about how human beings process information. Some are interested in the process for what it can reveal about strategies of instruction which improve upon those now used. This writer is interested in the topic for both reasons; however, the focus of this chapter is on what research suggests is necessary for good instruction. The point of view taken in this chapter is as follows.

Word recognition instruction is important because only those who can recognize words in print can hope to comprehend. Word recognition skills, though important, are "throw-away" skills. This is because fluent readers do not "decode" words in the sense of sounding them out. They rarely use those skills because most words they encounter they recognize (can pronounce and understand) almost instantly. But they needed the skills instruction in order to arrive at the point where the skills are no longer needed.

Word-recognition skill *does not* equal reading—it is a necessary prerequisite to reading, but it is not reading. Reading is much more. It is the ability to make judgments, inferences, and applications. It is for evoking laughter and tears. It is for evoking the "aha syndrome." (Aha! That's what I thought . . . Aha! I've felt just that way . . . Aha! So that's the answer. . . .) In short, pronunciation or recognition of words in print is not the point of reading; comprehension is the point of reading.

When fluent readers read, they only rarely come upon words that they do not recognize immediately. This may be less true in technical or study reading, and more true in general or entertainment reading. Nonetheless, even in fairly technical reading such as this chapter, there will be few, if any, words used which are not immediately recognized. Fluent readers, by definition, have large stocks of words that they can pronounce and understand very quickly.

The goal of all reading programs, stated or implied, is to increase the stock of sight words to the point where readers only rarely need to resort to other skills in order to "get" a word. This does not mean that words are, or should be, taught as whole units—the so-called look-and-say approach. It simply means, as stated above, that the hallmark of a fluent reader is the possession of a large stock of words that the reader recognizes at sight. Therefore, if the goal of reading instruction is the production of fluent readers, then a good part, if not all, of that goal is met by adding sufficiently to the store of words which the reader recognizes rapidly.

How do readers reach this level of rapid decoding skill? This is the difficult part. One of the most unfortunate trends in reading research has been to examine the behavior of skilled readers and, based upon what is found, to work backward from that in order to be able to suggest what should be taught or not taught to novice readers. This trend has given us such silliness as the suggestion that since fluent readers do not appear to use any systematic decoding skills, no systematic decoding skills should be taught (see, for example, Smith, 1971). Research that tells us what fluent readers do is useful in the present context because it can reveal stages of development of the skill of fluent reading. While the focus of this discussion will be on novice readers, some research that used fluent readers as subjects will be cited for purposes of comparison.

Before beginning that discussion, however, it should be noted that, for the present purpose, "recognizing words in print" does not mean learning word meanings. That is, of course, an important aspect of reading instruction; but, the fact is, most initial reading instruction is focused on teaching children to recognize in print words they already have in their speaking and listening vocabularies. Children come to the task of learning to read possessing a truly astonishing number of words and word meanings. The estimates of the size of the average 6-year-old's listening and speaking vocabulary range from 2,500 to 17,000 words (see Burmeister, 1978). So children learning to read are not (for the most part and with some notable exceptions to be discussed) learning words in the sense of learning meanings for words; they are learning techniques of recognition. Good reading instruction is designed to build on extant listening and speaking vocabulary. This brings up a related point: for students who are learning to read in a language other than their native language, there is a dual problem—they are learning word meanings and techniques for recognizing words in print at the same time. This problem, ignored for so long, is beginning to get the attention it deserves. Nonetheless, such students are beyond the scope of the present discussion, which focuses on the novice, non-handicapped child learning to read in his native language—in this case, English.

LEARNING TO READ IN ONE'S NATIVE LANGUAGE

Word recognition research has a long and rich history. As long ago as 1886 it was found that a letter in a word is more easily and quickly identified than a letter in a string of letters (Cattel, 1886). This "word superiority effect," as it came to be known, has been examined and re-examined from, it seems, every possible theoretical perspective. The original findings, nearly 100 years old now, have been consistently replicated. This is certainly not the oldest example of research into how people recognize words in print, but it does serve to demonstrate how long the phenomenon of instant word recognition has fascinated psychologists and educational researchers.

What do we know today about how children recognize words in print? It appears we know a great deal. In the rather brief review which follows, some classic findings and some recent findings are cited. Although this research is thought to be representative, it is by no means exhaustive.

The estimates of the size of a child's listening and speaking vocabulary at age 6, the age at which reading instruction typically commences, range from 2,500 to 17,000 words, as noted previously. The range is so wide because the number derived is dependent upon which words are counted. For example, almost every 6-year-old has the words *stop*, *stopped*, and *stopping* in his listening and speaking vocabulary. Are those three different words, or are they variations of a single word? It is easy to see that the counting procedure decided upon will have a tremendous effect on the final count. In any event, as stated earlier, children do acquire a genuinely astonishing number of words in their first 6 years.

Not only do they come to the task of learning to read with a large vocabulary, they also come to the task with an almost fully-formed syntactic system. That is, they are able to recognize most allowable word sequences of the English language. Still, in spite of their amazing linguistic accomplishments, they may not have acquired all the words they need in order to begin learning how to read. Blachowicz (1978), citing an extensive body of research, comments on the problems children experience with the very words that are essential to word recognition instruction. For example, children at the beginning stages of reading instruction may not know the meanings of essential terms such as *letter*, *word*, *sentence*, or *number*, that is, they may not have these words in their oral language or listening and speaking vocabularies. Functors, the glue words of the language, such as *of, to, from, the, a*, etc., seem to pose particular problems because children are often not able to separate them from content words (words such as *bush, home, car, truck*). It is easy to see that there may be great problems in teaching a child to recognize in print the word *car*, when the teacher is unaware that the child thinks of *the car* as one word instead of two. Simply stated, *the* is not, for the child, a word in spoken language; it is a part of a word. Thus, among the first tasks a child must accomplish in learning to recognize words in print, is to learn the terms used in explaining the task—the language of instruction (see Chapter 6 for a detailed account of metalinguistic awareness).

When a novice reader looks at a single word (assuming the child knows what a word is), where in the word is the critical information found? Do novice readers look at the whole word? Do they direct their attention to the word's configuration? Do they look left to right serially? Do they concentrate on the top half or the bottom half? Where do they direct their eyes? Marchbanks and Levin (1965), using novice and beginning readers as subjects, used 3- and 5-letter synthetic words in order to determine the relative importance of the various letters and overall word shapes as cues to word recognition. It was found that, overall, the most important cues are initial letter, final letter, and then (in the case of the 5-letter words), medial letters. The shape of the word was consistently the least important cue.

Rayner and Hagelberg (1975), however, using a slightly different conception of what contributes to word shape, found that first graders relied heavily on the first letter and the overall word shape when the stimulus was fairly simple (trigrams). In this delayed-match-to-sample task, the choices included trigrams that maintained the shape of the sample stimulus by inclusion of visually-confusable letters. For the 5-letter stimuli (quingrams), the overall shape for the first graders was not a potent cue. For kindergarten subjects in this series of experiments, no consistent pattern of preference was shown, except that on the quingrams the first letter seemed the most important cue.

RECOGNITION OF WORDS IN
ISOLATION AND IN MEANINGFUL CONTEXT

The growth in sophistication of word recognition strategies is very rapid. It appears that children advance from being uncertain about what a word is (either in print or spoken language), to using processing techniques very similar to those used by adult fluent readers. Although researchers have documented in many different ways this increase in word recognition sophistication, only two broad categories of research are considered here: the recognition of words in isolation and the recognition of words in meaningful contexts.

"Real world" reading is, of course, done almost exclusively in context. About the only time adults read words in isolation is when they are reading a grocery list and, even then, the fact of the words appearing on a special list provides a kind of context. So, if reading is not reading words in isolation, why conduct research on words in isolation? The reason is relatively simple. The best research controls as many variables as possible. Researching words in isolation is simply "cleaner," experimentally; it is more controlled. Nonetheless, it is a limitation on the generalizability of the findings, a limitation of which every researcher cited here is well aware.

How quickly do children begin to be aware of the orthography of their language? How much experience and instruction (which is, after all, only a subset of experience) do they require before they can recognize what is a "legal" string of letters (glamp), and what is an "illegal" string of letters (mpagl) in English?

Juola et al. (1978) used a search task that involved deciding whether or not a target letter was present in a word, an orthographically regular pseudoword, or a non-word (letter strings which did not follow English orthographical conventions, e.g., *sdowr*). They used as subjects kindergartners, second graders, fourth graders, and college students. For all but the kindergarten subjects, responses to the search task were generally fastest for words, next fastest for pseudowords, and slowest for non-words. Kindergarten subjects showed no such preferences based upon display type. These findings suggest that even relatively unskilled readers (second graders) have already begun to internalize, to some degree, the orthographic patterns of English. That internalization appears to be a function of exposure through specific instruction and general experience. The authors state that, "although the rate at which visual information is processed continues to increase beyond the fourth-grade, the cognitive processes involved in rapidly recognizing words and searching them for specific letters appear to be functionally equivalent for adults and for children who have been reading only about two years." Santa (1976–77) reports similar findings. In her research there was found a strong developmental trend indicating that children become " . . . more flexible in their levels of analysis as they become more skilled readers."

As noted earlier, "real world" reading is almost exclusively reading in context. When the behavior of young readers reading in context is examined, what is found? Not surprisingly, when the factor being considered is word recognition, the findings are very similar to findings on words in isolation. But, of course, the kind of context provided has an effect, too. For example, Klein (1976) demonstrated that ability to use context in a word boundary task is a function of both maturity of the reader and level of complexity of the stimulus material. The simpler material was deemed to have greater contextual constraints and, therefore, was easier. The word boundary task, in this case, was placing slashes between words on a page of connected discourse where all the letters of all the words were one space apart. There were two levels of syntactic complexity, simple and complex.

This developmental ability to utilize context in word recognition has been found by other researchers and is, in fact, an integral part of many models and theories of the reading process. For example, Samuels et al. (1978) suggest, along with Klein, that the processing of printed material is developmental and that it proceeds from component processing to holistic processing. This means that even at the beginning stages of acquisition of the skill of reading, the reader is, as Cunningham (1975–76) asserts, searching for the largest manageable unit of information. It is merely that that unit, at the beginning stage, is more than likely a single letter, while at the later stages it may be (as Samuels et al. suggest) holistic, that is, at the level of immediate, whole-word recognition referred to at the beginning of this chapter. Cunningham was interested in the question of whether progress to the larger units of information can be hastened through instruction. She developed strategies for teaching second graders with poor recognition skills to compare larger units of words they knew at sight with words they did not know. This task required, essentially, the readers asking themselves, "What is there in this new word that is similar to one of the words I already know?" Even though the instruction was limited to a 2-week period, the experimental subjects were found to be significantly better able to pronounce new words.

The consideration here of word recognition in isolation and in context, without regard to the kinds of words being recognized, is by design. There is no way that all the factors of potential importance to word recognition could be covered within the scope of this chapter. Nonetheless, some of those other variables at least need to be acknowledged. For example, Richards (1976) compared the effects of abstractness or concreteness of words on the time it took subjects to recognize them. Similarly, Hargis and Gickling (1978) compared the effects of high-imagery and low-imagery words on recognition time. These are merely two examples of the sort of variables that might be included in word recognition research.

However, it seems that similar results are found, regardless of which variables are considered and regardless of whether they are considered on words in isolation or on words in some kind of context. Children at the beginning stages of learning to read pay attention to single letters, to the initial letter within a word, and then to the final letter. As they are instructed and as they gain experience, they begin to make more use of predictable letter clusters (*th*, *ch*, *ck*, *sl*, *ea*, for example) and common spelling patterns (*and*, *ate*, *ight*, etc.): they also learn to better utilize the information provided by context.

With the exception of Rayner and Hagelberg (1975), no study in this section mentioned the dominant mode of instruction for the subjects used in the study. Since more than half of the material cited is from psychological journals rather than from educational journals, perhaps the mode of previous instruction was never considered. Maybe psychologists have evidence to suggest that mode of instruction has little to do with stages of acquisition of the skill of reading, or perhaps they merely assume it. Perhaps they are right; we do not presume to know. Nonetheless, it seems somehow sensible to assume that a child from a program of early, intensive phonics instruction would behave differently from a child taught in a language experience program which is, after all, a kind of whole-word approach. Let that lack of identification of dominant mode of instruction serve as an overall limitation on the generalizability of the findings of the various studies here cited.

IMPLICATIONS FOR INSTRUCTION

Just on the basis of the studies discussed, what implications are there for classroom practitioners, regardless of the method of instruction they use?

The first is obvious. Children need direct instruction in the vocabulary of instruction. Teachers of beginning readers must be certain that the terms they use are understood by the children they teach. This means that all students must know what a letter is and, indeed, must know all the letters of the alphabet. It means that all children must know what a word is and what a sentence is. In the writer's opinion, this is best accomplished by having the children's own utterances represented in print. Once that is done, it is a simple matter to show what a word *in print* is. (In the stream of speech, word boundaries are difficult or impossible to identify; this is probably why children new to words in print do not know what a word is.) It is easy to see that a common exercise, such as the one that asks children to "circle the word that names the picture," is wellnigh impossible if the student does not know what a word is. The same advice—direct instruction—applies to any term used in instruction that a child might not know or might not recognize in an instructional context. After all, to the child whose parent might be a lawyer or criminal, the word "sentence" is likely to have a meaning far different from the one intended when the word was used in reading instruction.

Second, word shape alone does not seem to be a useful word recognition tool for beginning readers. Not only do children not choose to use it on their own, but a few minutes spent examining a list of typical first grade words will reveal a great many with the same overall configurations. There is useful information in word shape and, at least from the research of Rayner and Hagelberg, it appears that fluent readers do use that information. It is, however, beyond the developmental level of beginning readers and should not be taught as a word recognition technique.

Third, since word recognition develops from smaller to larger units, teachers should provide a large amount of practice with words that contain predictable spelling patterns and teach as whole units, or "sight words," those words that have unusual or infrequent letter combinations. This should not be construed as endorsement of the so-called linguistic approach that offers only regular spelling patterns, nor should it be construed as an endorsement of a "whole-word" or "look-say" approach that teaches reading as if there were no letter-sound correspondences. It is an endorsement of an eclectic approach which assumes that some techniques are better for some instruction and other techniques are better for other instruction. What is "best" depends upon the word the child is being taught to recognize in print, e.g., flash cards to teach instant recognition of whole words that have infrequent or unusual letter combinations; phonogram or "word family" (*ate*, *eat*, and *ight*) instruction for those "regularly" spelled words.

Fourth, the role which context plays in the recognition of a single word depends on the strength of the context (see, for example, Pearson & Studt, 1975; Froese, 1977), the level of sophistication of the reader, and the word itself. In fact, there is relatively little known about how these factors interact. Nonetheless, the real-world reading that people do is seldom, if ever, done on words in isolation. Words in isolation carry very little meaning. Think, for example, of how many different contexts you could build for the word *step* in order to give it different meanings. In addition, English is a positional language. There is a great deal of difference between *housecat* and *cathouse*. For these reasons, if for no others, as much word recognition instruction as possible should be in meaningful contexts. This means, for example, that words taught as whole units (the look-say approach) should be included in meaningful phrases or short sentences for flash-card review. Or, if teaching a phonics generalization, include examples in phrases or short sentences. Meaning, though not the focus of this chapter, is important and meaning resides in context.

SUGGESTIONS FOR RESEARCH

There is probably no universal agreement about any topic or question related to reading, either as a psychological phenomenon or as an educational concern. But there may be nearly universal agreement about one thing: There is no one best way to teach reading to all students. Of course, there are always a few zealots who advocate a particular method as the answer; however, for the most part, the search for the single best method has been abandoned, probably at least partly as a result of the first grade studies (Bond and Dykstra, 1967) which found no one method clearly superior to the others. Thus, the classic question, "Which one is best?" has been replaced by other, perhaps more modest, questions: When should some form of systematic word recognition be taught and how much emphasis should it receive? (Not, it will be noticed, *should* systematic skills be taught, but *when* and *how much* should be taught.) The questions are answered differently depending on who is responding to them. That is probably as it should be.

In any area of concern as complex as reading, we would all do well to cultivate a great anxiety in the face of "revealed" truth which is widely accepted. That unlikely acceptance would signal an end to the active questioning which is essential to the continued growth of any field. Thus, the writer having offered his version of the truth of word recognition, cautions against accepting uncritically *anyone's* version of the truth. Be demanding. Be active questioners. Be sensible. The people for whom you work, your students, small as they are, deserve nothing less.

FOR DISCUSSION

1. If a child does not have a word in his listening/speaking vocabulary, should he be taught to recognize that word in print? What implications does this have for the presentation of "new words" prior to a reading lesson? How can a teacher be assured that students have words in their listening/speaking vocabulary?
2. Differentiate between functors and content words. Should they be taught in the same manner? Why or why not?
3. How do Standal's comments about "words" and "context" compare with those made by Bewell and Straw (Chapter 6)? By Hodges (Chapter 11)? By Aulls (Chapter 15)?
4. Standal states that the level of abstractness of a word can affect a student's ability to recognize that word in print. Why would this be the case?

REFERENCES

Blachowicz, C. L. Z. Metalinguistic awareness and the beginning reader. *The Reading Teacher*, May 1978, *31*(8), 875–876.

Bond, G. L., and Dykstra, R. The cooperative research program in first grade reading instruction. *Reading Research Quarterly*, 1967, *II*(4), 5–142.

Burmeister, L. E. *Reading strategies for middle and secondary school teachers* (2nd ed.). Reading, Massachusetts: Addison-Wesley, 1978.

Cattel, J. M. The time it takes to see and name objects. *Mind*, 1886, (No. 11), 63–65.

Cunningham, P. M. Investigating a synthesized theory of word identification. *Reading Research Quarterly*, 1975–76, *11*(2), 127–143.

Froese, V. *The quality, direction and distance of within sentence contextual constraints*. Unpublished doctoral dissertation, University of Minnesota, 1977.

Golinkoff, R. M., and Rosinski, R. R. Decoding, semantic processing, and reading comprehension skill. *Child Development*, 1976, *47*, 252–258.

Hargis, C. H., and Gickling, E. E. The function of imagery in word recognition development. *The Reading Teacher*, May 1978, *31*(8), 870–874.

Johnston, J. C. A test of the sophisticated guessing theory of word perception. *Cognitive Psychology*, 1978, *10*, 123–153.

Juola, J. F., Schadler, M., Chabot, R. J., and McCaughey, M. W. The development of visual information processing skills related to reading. *Journal of Experimental Child Psychology*, 1978, *25*, 459–476.

Klein, H. A. The role of material level on the development of word identification. *The Journal of Psychology*, 1976, *94*, 225–232.

Marchbanks, G., and Levin, H. Cues by which children recognize words. *Journal of Educational Psychology*, 1965, *56*, 57–61.

Pearson, P. D., and Studt, A. Effects of word frequency and contextual richness on children's word identification abilities. *Journal of Educational Psychology*, March 1975, *6*(1), 89–95.

Rayner, K., and Hagelberg, E. M. Word recognition cues for beginning and skilled readers. *Journal of Experimental Psychology*, 1975, *20*, 444–455.

Rayner, K., and Posnansky, C. Stages of processing in word identification. *Journal of Experimental Psychology: General*, 1978, *107*(1), 64–80.

Richards, L. G. Concreteness as a variable in word recognition. *American Journal of Psychology*, December, 1976, *89*(4), 707–718.

Richards, L. G., and Heller, F. P. Recognition thresholds as a function of word length. *American Journal of Psychology*, V. 89, no. 3, September 1976, *89*(3), 455–466.

Samuels, S. J., DaBerge, D., and Bremer, C. D. Units of word recognition: Evidence for developmental changes. *Journal of Verbal Learning and Verbal Behavior*, 1978, *17*, 715–720.

Santa, C. M. Spelling patterns and the development of flexible word recognition strategies. *Reading Research Quarterly*, V. 12, no. 2, 1976–77, *12*(2), 125–144.

Smith, F. *Understanding reading: A psycholinguistic analysis of reading and learning to read*. New York: Holt, Rinehart and Winston, 1971.

14 | A Decade of Research in Reading Comprehension

P. David Pearson

When the history of reading is written for the last half of the twentieth century, the decade of the seventies will be remembered for many things, but none more important than the fact that it marked the beginning of an era when the field turned its interests, concerns, and intellectual muscle to issues of reading comprehension.

This paper traces the development of the comprehension movement. First, the scene is set at the beginning of the decade by a delineation of the strands of research and theory that characterized our knowledge base about reading comprehension at that time. Second, the paradigm shifts that have occurred in the seventies are discussed, and an attempt is made to identify sources of influence behind the shifts. Third, the question of progress is evaluated: What do we know now that we did not know in 1970? Fourth, some speculation is made about the decade of the eighties as to the research strands and instructional practices that seem to follow from the traditions established in the seventies.

THE SCENE IN 1970

In 1970, our knowledge of reading comprehension was fairly well defined by four research strands: readability, the cloze procedure, factor analytic studies, and, the child-bride of the field, psycholinguistics.

Readability research, by that time, had a history of 35 to 40 years, stemming back to Gray and Leary (1935) and Lorge (1939) in the early thirties, carried on by Flesch (1948) into the forties and George Klare (1963) into the fifties and sixties. Basically what the research told us was that long words and long complex sentences were hard to understand, but we were not sure why. We did not know whether long words and sentences were causative of or merely symptomatic of content that was hard to read for other reasons, such as concept density.

The cloze technique had been with us for a decade and a half. Taylor (1954), Rankin (1965), and Bormuth (1967) had used it to great advantage in refining research in comprehension and readability. If nothing else, we knew that we had a good dependent variable for measuring comprehension: it was objective (it did not depend on a test writer's judgment about what questions were important to ask), easy to score, and highly reliable.

It is probably fair to say that Davis (1944) made factor analysis studies of reading comprehension respectable. Between 1944 and 1969 several important factor analytic studies of reading comprehension all shared the common purpose of isolating independent components of reading comprehension, and all found that whatever host of allegedly independent components they started with reduced to a few statistically independent factors, such as a word difficulty factor and a reasoning factor.

If readability, cloze, and factor analytic studies represented the conventional wisdom concerning reading comprehension, then psycholinguistics was the hope of the future. Simons' (1971) review of reading comprehension reflected this hope. After reviewing and discussing the conventional perspectives on reading comprehension, Simons raised the banner of transformational grammar as the hope and guiding light of the future.

Psycholinguistics had tremendous appeal, especially to young researchers looking for a perspective that would set them apart from the conventional wisdom. Part of its appeal stemmed from the impact that Chomsky's (1957) views had on the psychology of language in the decade of the sixties. Based upon studies like those of Miller and Isard (1963), Mehler (1963), Gough (1965), and Slobin (1966), there was a genuine feeling that behavioristic views of language development and processing would have to be supplanted with views that were both nativistic and cognitive in orientation. Furthermore, these research studies seemed to suggest that the transformational generative grammar created by Chomsky (1957) might actually serve as a model of human language processing. Thus, there was a ready-made theory waiting to be applied to reading comprehension. Third, psycholinguistics was appealing because it commanded academic respectability. There was something appealing about standing on the shoulders of the new psychology, working within a paradigm for which there was a model that made fairly precise predictions and actually had testable hypotheses.

Hence it was the beginning in the late sixties and extending into the mid-seventies, considerable empirical and theoretical work was completed within the psycholinguistic tradition. Surely the influence of psycholinguistics on reading is nowhere better demonstrated than in the work of Kenneth Goodman (1965) and Frank Smith (1971). For both Goodman and Smith, looking at reading from a psycholinguistic perspective meant (and still means) looking at reading in its natural state, as an application of a person's general cognitive and linguistic competence. It seems odd even to bring up their names in discussing the influence of psycholinguistics on comprehension research. The oddity stems from the fact that neither Goodman nor Smith distinguishes between reading and reading comprehension. Their failure to make the distinction is deliberate, and they would likely argue that reading is comprehending (or that reading without comprehending is not reading). The distinction that many of us make between word identification and comprehension would seem arbitrary to them.

For others, the influence of the psycholinguistic tradition, particularly the use of transformational-generative grammar as a psychological model, on views of reading comprehension was more direct and obvious. The work of Bormuth (1966, 1969), Bormuth, Manning, Carr, and Pearson (1971), Fagan (1971), and Pearson (1974–75) reveals a rather direct use of psycholinguistic notions in studying reading comprehension.

Such was the scene in the early seventies. The conventional modes of research, while still strong, were being challenged by the same phenomenon that had already proved so destructive to the traditional views in the psychology of language—psycholingusitics.

THE MID-SEVENTIES: A PERIOD OF RE-EXAMINATION

The motive force behind the shift from behavioristic to cognitive views of language comprehension in psychology was a linguist, Noam Chomsky. He exposed the prevailing views on the psychology of language for their gross inadequacies and provided an alternative model (transformational grammar) of language processing.

Fittingly, the motive force behind the exodus from a narrow psycholinguistic view based upon transformational grammars was another linguist, Charles Fillmore. In 1968, he published a paper that argued for a centuries-old case grammar approach to linguistic explanation. Case grammar was appealing to psychologists and educators who were experiencing great difficulty with models of comprehension based upon a transformational generative grammar.

Those very models that had seemed to be sensible and alluring only 5 years earlier were not standing the tests of empirical verification well at all. With its emphasis on transformations to realize a variety of surface structures from a single deep structure, the model had to stress an analytic view of comprehension. Yet researchers (e.g., Bransford and Franks, 1971) were collecting data that indicated that comprehension consisted of synthesis rather than analysis. Others (e.g., Sachs, 1967) found that comprehension and recognition memory seemed to be more sensitive to semantic rather than syntactic factors, contrary to the emphases in a transformational model. Still others, like Pearson (1974–1975), found that the predictions from a derivational theory of complexity, i.e., comprehension difficulty varies as a function of the number of transformations necessary to travel from surface to deep structure, were exactly the opposite of results obtained in several comprehension studies.

In such a milieu, something like Fillmore's case grammar was quite appealing; it emphasized synthesis rather than analysis, semantic rather than syntactic relations. In addition, case grammar allowed one to begin to examine relations that were obtained between linguistic ideas that crossed sentence boundaries.

The psycholinguistic tradition, based as it was on Chomsky's transformational grammar, had concentrated upon the sentence as the basic unit of analysis. Somewhere in the early to mid-seventies, the proposition replaced the sentence as the basic unit of analysis. Researchers in artificial intelligence began using it in the early seventies (Schank, 1973; Minsky, 1975). Lindsay and Norman (1972) discussed propositions in their experimental psychology textbook. Kintsch (1974), Rumelhart (1975), Frederiksen (1975), Thorndyke (1977), and Stein and Glenn (1977) were all using propositions to analyze recall protocols by the mid-seventies.

The proposition fit nicely with an emphasis on case grammar. Just as the verb was the center of a proposition (a proposition can be viewed as a predicate active or stative verb) and its arguments (nouns, adjectives, adverbs), so it is the central node with a case grammar passing of a sentence. All other form classes revolve around the verb. Also, many of the case relations in a case grammar are really relations among propositions (cause, condition, time, manner).

THE LATE SEVENTIES: A PERIOD OF FINE-TUNING

The changes incipient in the work of the mid-seventies have not been overturned in the late seventies; fine tuning more aptly describes what happened to the notions of case grammar and the proposition. Researchers have grappled with the general issue of how large bodies of information are structured. Furthermore, their concerns about structure have emphasized macro rather than microstructure, that is, they have been more concerned with the relations that obtain between whole episodes in stories or whole paragraphs or sections in exposition rather than between a verb and a noun or between two adjacent sentences.

Researchers tend to fall into two categories: those who have tried to characterize relations among ideas in texts and those who have tried to characterize relations among ideas stored in human memory. Neither group denies the importance or necessity of the other's work; each group has simply chosen to emphasize one area over the other. Hence, researchers like Rumelhart (1975), Stein and Glenn (1977), and Thorndyke (1977) have given us plausible macrostructures for narrative material in the form of story grammars. Researchers like Meyer (1975) or Halliday and Hasan (1976) have tried to provide more general structural accounts that would apply equally as well to expositions. Alternatively, the work of Schank (1973), Minsky (1975), Anderson (1977), and Rumelhart and Ortony (1977) has been more concerned with the structure of knowledge within the human processor itself. Still others, such as Kintsch (1974) or Frederiksen (1975) seem to be trying to provide a balanced emphasis on text and knowledge structure. These differences are more stylistic than categorical. All of the researchers are concerned with *human* information processing; they simply tend to emphasize different aspects of the processing. Therefore, those emphasizing the structure of the text are likely to emphasize something like the number of high level nodes within the story that were recalled. Conversely, those emphasizing the structure of the reader's knowledge are more likely to dwell upon something like non-textual inferences made during recall or how a reader's prior knowledge determines aspects of the text that will be remembered.

Why have these new perspectives taken hold? What do they provide that our simpler schemes of a decade ago did not? Basically, they have stood two tests: 1) they provide for the investigation of problems not easily conceptualized under older schemes, and 2) they provide a better account of the available data. On the first point, take the issue of inference. Until schema theory (Rumelhart and Ortony, 1977; Anderson, 1977) came along, there was no general framework available for explaining how readers could encode so many intrusions (non-textual items) into their recall protocols. On the second point, the case of story grammars is illuminating: What children and adults tend to recall from stories does seem to be directly related to the height of an idea in the hierarchical parsing of a story specified by a story grammar (Stein and Glenn, 1977; Thorndyke, 1977).

What have we learned in the decade of the seventies that we did not know when it began? First, comprehension is an active, syntactic process rather than a passive, analytic process. The reader counts at least as much as the text, if not more so. Second, knowledge is structured. Rather than a list of propositions, what we seem to have in our heads is a highly embedded network of concepts and events. These concepts and events are layered in such a way that certain abstract structures seem to predispose us to drawing as many inferences about what must have been on the page as to recalling precisely what was there. Inferences, at all stages of development, are a necessary fact of life in understanding comprehension and memory. Furthermore, our inclination to draw inferences is a function of the amount of data presented, the structure of that data, the demands of the comprehension probe, and our perception of what we are supposed to do.

Just as important as what we have learned is what we have not. We have yet to prove certain things we would like to prove, for example, that comprehension can be taught directly. If we could teach something that would influence comprehension, what would it be? Content? Skills? Syntactic structures? Schemata? We can infer that practice helps; kids who go to school probably comprehend better than those who do not go to school. But we really do not know what comprehension instruction is (see Durkin, 1978–79).

SOME RUMINATIONS ABOUT THE NEXT DECADE

Let me speculate about what I might say were I to write this chapter in 1990 rather than 1980. (It is always easier to discuss the future than the past. One is not bound by the taint of data.)

Schema-theory will still be around, but much of its glamour will have worn off (or wrinkled away). We will know much more about the *components* of schemata—the nature of variables and constants and *processes* like schema instantiation, schema generalization, and schema specialization, and about the nature of hierarchical embedding of schemata, one within the other. Educational practice will change as we begin to speculate about the implication derivable from existing research and theory and as we begin to conduct real instructional studies on *teaching* reading comprehension.

First, the research on children's comprehension of story structure will convince us to give children real stories to read from the outset of grade one. Such stories will be highly predictable in terms of their conformity to canonical story schemata. We will continue to recognize that the need to control vocabulary in the earliest of stories makes it difficult for writers to create well-formed stories. Nonetheless, we will become convinced that it is these young children who need story predictability the most.

Second, teachers will realize that if they want students to "get the author's message," they will be well advised to model for students to practice discovering it on their own. They should be cautioned, however, that not all reading has as its purpose "getting the author's message"; sometimes students need to read to update their own knowledge, in which case they are probably better off working within their own schema rather than an author's (Spiro, 1977).

Third, some of us will have completed practical studies within a schema-theoretic point of view. We will have discovered that teacher intervention in the form of full-blown concept development activities aid comprehension of subsequently read text. We will find that text written with lots of examples and good analogies helps develop concepts in content area reading better than watered-down text written to ease the readability load. These new texts—and these new perspectives on readability—will aid comprehension precisely because they will allow readers to make clearer connections between text and prior knowledge, as represented in schemata.

Some will look at this "new" research and these "new" recommendations and accuse us of re-inventing the wheel, of casting "old wine in new bottles." To them I would say, perhaps; but the *appelation controllé* is better. Before, all we knew is that the wine came from France and looked red. Now we know that it is from the fourth vineyard of Chateaux Giscours in the Commune Labarde in the Haut-Medoc area of the Bordeaux region. At least we ought to be more discriminating consumers.

Readability research will continue in two divergent directions. Some will continue the tradition of finding that longer and more complex words or sentences are part and parcel of content that is more difficult to understand. And they will build even better computer programs, with a greater number of computer-analyzed texts, so that teachers, including college reading professors, can pick the easiest books of all. I would not be at all surprised to see an article suggesting that if we stick with an N-V-N sentence structure and a corpus of 200 lexical items known by 88% of fifth grade students, then 82% of junior high students will be able to understand a chapter on the Civil War.

In this regard, I am reminded of a quote from Samuel Johnson:

> He that thinks with more extant than another will want words of larger meaning; he that thinks with more subtlety will seek for terms of more nice discrimination. . . . Yet vanity inclines us to find faults anywhere rather than in ourselves. He that reads and grows no wiser seldom suspects his own deficiency but complains of hard words and obscure sentences and asks why books are written which cannot be understood? (*The Idler*, No. 20)

Others will strike off in new directions. Some will go beyond the word and the sentence to look at variables like schema integrity, schema-cohesion, or schema-expansion with a passage. They will discover that these variables have an effect that interacts with word and sentence difficulty: difficult words and sentences can not only be tolerated but can be helpful if the relations among concepts in the passage are well articulated. In fact, they will discover that such articulation occasionally demands word and sentence complexity.

There will be new factor-analytic studies. However, the studies will differ from those of earlier generations because the test items will represent new and different domains. For example, instead of items testing vocabulary, main idea, sequence and cause-effect, the text items will derive from propositional relations among text segments in, for example, a case grammar analysis of discourse.

I am sure there will be other lines of research and speculation in this next decade, ones that have not occurred to me and would not until I saw them. But such is the nature of our academic cycles. Each generation must push its own paradigm to the limits of its parameters until the paradigm collapses, making way for a new world view. Thus, our fate is to prepare for our own destruction, so that future generations will regard our work with the same disdain that we afford our predecessors.

FOR DISCUSSION

1. Pearson implies that comprehension is a synthetic process. Explain how understanding of an author's message needs to be synthesized by the reader rather than analyzed. How does this relate to Straw's comments on writing in Chapter 8?
2. Differentiate between surface structure and deep meaning structure. Which is most important in comprehension (see Froese, Chapter 7)? In written composition? In spelling (see Hodges, Chapter 11)? In word recognition (see Standal, Chapter 13)?
3. How would Pearson react to a skills development model of reading comprehension?
4. Why has reading comprehension as discussed here been neglected in reading instruction? How does this relate to the difference between micro and macrostructure?

REFERENCES

Anderson, R. The notion of schemata and the educational enterprise. In R. C. Anderson, J. R. Spiro, and W. E. Montague (Eds.), *Schooling and the acquisition of knowledge*. Hillsdale, New Jersey: Lawrence Erlbaum Associates, 1977.

Bormuth, J. R. Readability: A new approach. *Reading Research Quarterly*, 1966, *1*, 79–132.

Bormuth, J. R. *Implications and use of cloze procedure in the evaluation of instructional programs* (Occasional Rep. No. 3). Los Angeles: University of California, Center for the Study of Evaluation Instructional Programs, 1967.

Bormuth, J. R. An operational definition of comprehension instruction. In K. S. Goodman and J. F. Fleming (Eds.), *Psycholinguistics and the teaching of reading*. Newark, Delaware: International Reading Association, 1969.

Bormuth, J. R., Manning, J. C., Carr, J. W., and Pearson, P. D. Children's comprehension of between- and within-sentence syntactic structures. *Journal of Educational Psychology*, 1971, *61*, 349–357.

Bransford, J. D., and Franks, J. J. The abstraction of linguistic ideas. *Cognitive Psychology*, 1971, *2*, 331–350.

Chomsky, N. *Syntactic structures*. The Hague: Mouton, 1957.

Davis, F. B. Fundamental factors of comprehension in reading. *Pschometrika*, 1944, *9*, 185–197.

Durkin, D. What classroom observations reveal about reading comprehension instruction. *Reading Research Quarterly*, 1978–79, *14*, 481–533.

Fagan, W. T. Transformations and comprehension. *The Reading Teacher*, 1971, *25*, 169–172.

Fillmore, C. J. The case for case. In E. Bach and R. Harms (Eds.), *Universals in linguistic theory*. New York: Holt, Rinehart & Winston, 1968.

Flesch, R. F. A new readability yardstick. *Journal of Applied Psychology*, 1948, *32*, 221–233.

Frederiksen, C. H. Representing logical and semantic structure of knowledge acquired from discourse. *Cognitive Psychology*, 1975, *7*, 371–458.

Goodman, K. S. A linguistic study of cues and miscues in reading. *Elementary English*, 1965, *42*, 639–643.

Gough, P. B. Grammatical transformations and speed of understanding. *Journal of Verbal Learning and Verbal Behavior*, 1965, *4*, 107–111.

Gray, W. S., and Leary, B. E. *What makes a book readable . . . : An initial study*. Chicago, The University of Chicago Press, 1935.

Halliday, M. A. K., and Hasan, R. *Cohesion in English*. London: Longman, 1976.

Kintsch, W. *The representation of meaning in memory*. Hillsdale, New Jersey: Lawrence Erlbaum Associates, 1974.

Klare, G. *The measurement of readability*. Ames: Iowa State University Press, 1963.

Lindsay, P., and Norman, D. *Human information processing*. New York: Academic Press, 1972.

Lorge, I. Predicting reading difficulty of selections for children. *Elementary English Review*, 1939, *16*, 229–233.

Mehler, J. Some effects of grammatical transformations on the recall of English sentences. *Journal of Verbal Learning and Verbal Behavior*, 1963, *2*, 346–351.

Meyer, B. J. F. *The organization of prose and its effects on memory*. Amsterdam: North-Holland Publishing, 1975.

Miller, G. A., and Isard, S. Some perceptual consequences of linguistic rules. *Journal of Verbal Learning and Verbal Behavior*, 1963, *2*, 217–228.

Minsky, M. A framework for representing knowledge. In P. Winston (Ed.), *The psychology of computer vision*. New York: McGraw Hill, 1975.

Pearson, P. D. The effects of grammatical complexity on children's comprehension, recall, and conception of certain semantic relations. *Reading Research Quarterly*, 1974–75, *10*, 155–192.

Rankin, E. Cloze procedure—a survey of research. *Yearbook of the South West Reading Conference*, 1965, *14*, 133–148.

Rumelhart, D. E. Notes on a schema for stories. In D. G. Bobrow and A. M. Collins (Eds.), *Representation and understanding: Studies in cognitive science*. New York: Academic Press, 1975.

Rumelhart, D. E., and Ortony, A. The representation of owledge and memory. In R. C. Anderson, R. J. Spiro, and W. E. Montague (Eds.), *Schooling and the acquistion of knowledge.* Hillsdale, New Jersey: Lawrence Erlbaum Associates, 1977.

Sachs, J. S. Recognition memory for syntactic and semantic aspects of connected discourse. *Perception and Psychophysics*, 1967, *2*, 437–442.

Schank, R. C. Identification of conceptualizations underlying natural language. In R. C. Schank and K. M. Colby (Eds.), *Computer models of thoughts and language.* San Francisco: Freeman, 1973.

Simons, H. D. Reading comprehension: The need for a new perspective. *Reading Research Quarterly*, 1971, *5*, 338–363.

Slobin, D. T. Grammatical transformations and sentence comprehension in childhood and adulthood. *Journal of Verbal Learning and Verbal Behavior*, 1966, *5*, 219–227.

Smith, F. *Understanding reading: A psycholinguistic analysis of reading and learning to read.* New York: Holt, Rinehart and Winston, 1971.

Spiro, R. Remembering information from text: The "state of schema" approach. In R. C. Anderson, R. Spiro, and W. Montague (Eds.), *Schooling and the acquisition of knowledge.* Hillsdale, New Jersey: Lawrence Erlbaum Associates, 1977.

Stein, N. L., and Glenn, C. G. *A developmental study of children's construction of stories.* Paper presented at the SRCD meetings, New Orleans, March 17–20, 1977.

Taylor, W. *Application of "cloze" and entropy measures to the study of contextual constraint in samples of continuous prose.* Unpublished doctoral dissertation, University of Illinois, Urbana-Champaign, 1954.

Thorndyke, P. W. Cognitive structures in comprehension and memory of narrative discourse. *Cognitive Psychology*, 1977, *9*, 77–110.

15 | The Nature and Function of Context during Reading and Writing

Mark Aulls

Over the years the concept of context has played an important role in the study and teaching of reading. Reading educators and researchers have predominantly used the concept of context to account for how readers: 1) predict sounds represented by graphic symbols, 2) predict words, and 3) derive the meaning of words. In addition, studies of the reader's use of context has predominantly been confined to the sentence. This is a useful but relatively narrow conceptualization of the reader's use of context. In order to explain through meaning representation texts longer than a sentence or to explain the extent of contextual resources used by humans in expressing meaning as text or acquiring meaning from longer discourse, it is necessary to reconceptualize the nature of context.

In virtually all senses the nature and function of context is inseparable from human experience, thought, and language. Anything which surrounds or influences human activity may be referred to as context. Two essential attributes to context are: 1) it must be relational in nature, and 2) it functions as something which effects any specific activity which entails acquiring, organizing, or using knowledge.

As the preceding concept of context applies to the cognitive activities of reading and writing, it may be used to account for how graphic symbols represent or cue meaning. It may be used to refer to sources of knowledge originating from the author/reader which surround or influence the expression or acquisition of meaning. Any linguistic units preceding or following a single word, phrase sentence, or series of sentences may influence the reader/author's construction or reconstruction of meaning. Those linguistic units or sources of knowledge which can be shown empirically to specifically and consistently influence the processes of constructing or reconstructing meaning may be considered as "contextual constraints."

There has been little or no attention given to types of knowledge and strategies which may serve as common sources of context that readers and writers use to construct meaning. If individuals who engage in both reading and writing do draw upon common contexts and are able to benefit from them, then the common knowledge and strategies learned through one activity should be applicable to and assist meaning construction in the other. From the author's point of view, this is an intriguing hypothesis which has considerable implications for future research and instruction.

In order to draw inferences about ways to instructionally influence the reader's or writer's use of different sources of context, one must first be able to specify probable context cues, observable contextual constraints, or cognitive sources of context and their influence on specific aspects of reading or writing. Thus, this chapter is organized to review the parameters for depicting the nature of contexts available to readers and writers, to summarize many of the influences contextual constraints appear to have on meaning acquisition or expression, and to then hypothesize a tentative model of those sources of context which serve to relate (as well as distinguish) the process of reading and writing. What the author views to be the most relevant instructional implications and some of the possible avenues for future research will conclude the chapter.

A REVIEW OF THE LITERATURE

How Context Functions in Reading Sentences

Prior to the 1970s, reading educators and most psychologists typically viewed the function of context to be within the sentence. This viewpoint undoubtedly originated from two sources. First, the most generally accepted model viewed reading as a global skill made up of subskills. The dominant linguistic competence theory (Chomsky and Halle, 1968) assumed that the sentence was the central underlying unit of language. Hence, studies of reading prior to 1970 naturally focused on the sentence as the largest of unit of meaning. One of the most important subskills was believed to be the reader's ability to use linguistic cues within the sentence to derive the meaning for a word or to predict words while reading each sentence. The term "context clues" was used to describe semantic or syntactic information units within a one or two sentence boundary, which the reader could use as an aid to derive the full sound-symbol correspondence of a word whose correspondences were not automatically predicted or as an aid to inferring the most probable meaning of a word as it was used by the author.

The following list of context clues represents a relatively inclusive description of those which have repeatedly been found to be a positive influence on getting word meaning or predicting words among both young and older readers in studies undertaken between 1928 and 1969 (Eckert, 1928; Elivian, 1938; Gibbons, 1940; McCullough, 1945; Seeman, 1944; Seibert, 1945; McKee, 1948; Burgard, 1950; White, 1950; Stearns, 1954; Spache and Berg, 1955; Deighton, 1959; Hafner, 1965; Dulin, 1968; Quealy, 1969; Rankin and Overholser, 1969):

1. Familiar expressions: I don't think our horse has a *ghost of a chance* to come in first at the derby.
2. Cause-effect: If you put the pan on the fire for too long, it will be *summota*.
3. Words in a series (or groupings): I went to the market for bread, meat, and *zalk*.
4. Contrast: I wonder whether the money given to us will be a blessing or a *foge*.
5. Modifying phrases and clauses (or grammatical phrase): The small *harpin* sailed into the harbor softly.
6. Apposition: The native believed the *gops*, or evil spirits, lived beyond the river.
7. Definition (or direct explanation): A *gespikin* is a musical instrument.
8. Description: A *quatz* has a rind: It is small, orange, and tastes slightly acidic.
9. Comparison: The *gumps* in the park are not like our maples because they are taller.
10. Restatement: The truck came to a *blatz* halt; it suddenly stopped.
11. Example: *Nacatucks* are smarter than most breeds of horses.

During the decade between 1960 and 1970 psychologists and psycholinguists also studied the nature of context as it applied within sentence contextual constraints. Generally these studies attempted rather tightly controlled experiments to determine what linguistic constraints operated that might independently or jointly influence the prediction of word units and word groups as well as the derivation of word meaning. The results of these studies tend to provide more specific insights than the context clue studies into the relative influence of underlying syntactic and semantic variables on reading sentences. Among the large number of findings reported are the following:

1. Position of a word influences accuracy in its predictability and text segments following a word tend to have greater constraint than preceding segments (Aborn, Rubenstein, and Sterling, 1959).

2. The grammatical class of a word influences its predictability with greater variability occurring for verbs and nouns in most studies (Bradley, 1968; Bhooma, 1969).
3. The syntactic patterns within which a word occurs influences its predictability, with some patterns having more consistent effects than others (Miller, 1962; Slobin, 1966).
4. The organization of words into groups is determined by syntactic constraints and the unit of meaning processed during reading is closer to a phrase or clause than a word unit as reading becomes faster and more efficient (Schlesinger, 1968; Levin and Turner, 1968; Resnick, 1970).
5. While syntactic constraints do influence the reader's ability to predict words and group words into meaning units, understanding sentences appears to be most predominantly a function of semantic variables. Thus, accurate and rapid syntactic access does not necessarily assure accurate acquisition of meaning. Some essential contexts are semantically richer than others in aiding readers to predict and get access to word meanings as well as to the meaning of word groups such as metaphors (Danks, 1969; Danks and Glucksberg, 1970; Bransford and Johnson, 1972; Ortony, Schallert, Reynolds, and Antos, 1978).

Results like those listed served to a large extent as a basis for reading educators and researchers in the late 1960s and early 1970s to gain a fresh perspective into the importance of syntactic patterns and semantic relationships among word concepts as *generalizable* underlying contextual constraints which influence the processing and understanding of any sentence or the word units and word groups comprising a sentence.

In the late 1960s and early 1970s a new, alternative approach toward studying the function of syntactic and semantic cues within a sentence emerged. The alternative was to assess the reader's "use" of general grapho-phomene, syntactic, and semantic cues within a sentence. In turn, this led to the study of strategies like predicting, sampling, self-correcting, and confirming prediction, which the reader might use to access or integrate context cues (Goodman, 1967; Smith, 1973, 1977; Goodman and Burke, 1973; Goodman and Goodman, 1977). Rather than teaching pupils to recognize specific contextual clues, the alternative was to emphasize ways of combining the major linguistic cues available in sentences. Hence, although it was recognized that sentences vary widely in contextual constraint, the more important issue was to determine how readers vary in their ability to access and integrate the grapho-phonemic, syntactic, and semantic cues available in order to process the meaning of a sentence.

How Context Functions in Reading Texts

Since the 1970s the study of the nature and function of context has been expanded beyond the sentence level to include between-sentence contextual constraints. The contributions to this shift came from the fields of psycholinguistics, semantics, and sociolinguistics. Linguists such as Grimes (1968), Van Dijk (1973), and Halliday and Hasan (1976) have proposed text grammars for envisioning how text statements are linked together to refer to one another and to afford contextual or semantic networks which readers use to weave together the authors' meanings in a cohesive manner.

Halliday and Hasan (1976) in their seminal work, *Cohesion in English*, use the word *text* to refer to any passage of whatever length that forms a unified whole. A text has texture in the sense that it functions as a unity with respect to its environment. It is a unit of meaning (a semantic unit), not a unit of form. Text is not a structural unit. It does have structure in the sense of unifying relationships among meanings. It is realized by sentences, but it does not consist of sentences. Text must have cohesion in the sense that interpretation of some element in the discourse is dependent on that of another. The one presupposes the other in the sense that it cannot be effectively decoded except by recourse to it. Cohesively related items are represented by recourse to it. Cohesion exists where interpretation of any item in the discourse requires making reference to some other item in the discourse. Thus, the guiding principle in language is that more general meanings are expressed through the grammar and the more specific meanings through the vocabulary. Cohesive relations fit into this same overall pattern. Text may also be thought of as a continuum of meanings-in-context. Within a text, the meaning of each sentence depends on its environment, including cohesive relations with other sentences.

The empirical reasons for developing text grammars (as opposed to sentence grammars) to study meaning representation was persuasively and carefully explicated by Tuin A. Van Dijk in 1973. The following list of reasons has stood the test of time and his theoretical linguistic arguments for text grammars have contributed much to advances in the development of text grammars:

a) The observable manifestations of language as a psychological and social system, viz. utterances, are tokens of texts rather than tokens of sentences.
b) Native speakers are able to process (produce, receive, interpret) such utterances as coherent wholes and not merely as a sequence of (unrelated) sentences.
c) Native speakers are able to recognize different types of relations between the sentences constituting the text of which the discourse is a

performance realization. This fact enables them to differentiate between grammatical and less grammatical texts.

d) Native speakers are able to recognize different relations between discourse which do not directly depend on the respective sentence structures alone: paraphrases, abstracts, question/answer, intertextual reference, etc.

e) Native speakers do not process discourses verbatim, e.g. by literal recall and by programming sentence structures, but by the formation of (underlying) macro-structures. [Structures which underlie the set of semantic representation of the sentences of text which are themselves semantic.] (p. 37)

In short, the study of texts through text grammars attempts to assess text as a unit in its own right and not merely as collection of sentences. This assumes that the text, not the sentence, is considered as the basic underlying unit of utterance. And in this sense, text grammars go beyond the principles of transformational generative grammar set out by Chomsky and Halle (1968). Furthermore, they redefine and broaden the conceptual framework for depicting context.

Cognitive psychologists interested in reading, as one aspect of cognition, have carried out experiments based on linguists' descriptions of text grammar. Many of these studies clearly provide results which suggest that the reader uses text level contextual constraints in order to access meaning at a variety of levels, including individual word meanings. The following results are representative of the range of text level contextual constraints or cues which readers appear to use in order to perform different types of comprehension acts:

1. The reader uses propositions (the internal representation of a sentence which expresses the relationships that exist among a sentence's concepts) to organize memory of text information (Kintsch, 1974; Kintsch et al., 1974).

2. The reader uses story grammar (an abstract knowledge of how stories mean) to anticipate and reconstruct story events (Stein and Glenn, 1977; Warren, Nicholas, and Trabasso, 1977).

3. The reader uses anaphora (the use of preceding referents to clarify the meaning of pronouns, proverbs, ellipses and the like) to weave together statements (Richek, 1977; Barnitz, 1979).

4. The reader's ability to classify text statements into major and minor meaning units as well as relevant and irrelevant meaning units changes as a function of years of schooling (Brown and Smiley, 1977).

5. The reader uses higher level propositions to infer lower level propositions and vice versa (Meyer, 1975, 1977; Meyer, Brandt, and Bluth, 1978).

6. The reader uses large text segments to interpret metaphors which in

limited contexts, such as a sentence, could not be understood (Ortony, Schallert, Reynolds, and Antos, 1978).

7. The reader's ability to fill in meaning *gaps* (segments of text information which cannot be related to preceding or following information and therefore must be derived from the surrounding context) as text is read increases with changes in general cognitive growth and world knowledge (Brown, 1975).

8. Readers in the middle grades do not appear to benefit equally from the text level contextual cues provided in expository and narrative genres (Brazee, 1976).

The pedagogical implications of findings like the ones reported are considerably different from those of the past which have conceptualized context as restricted to the sentence level. Conceptualizing the use of context as solely a matter of using sentence information to determine a word meaning precludes the development of instructional methods and materials that facilitate or model how the reader might link together sentences, propositions, and macrostructures in processing text meanings. In addition, the sole use of sentence unit contexts for instructional exercises implies that reading is only a forward-moving, sentence-by-sentence process. It may also imply that good readers do not go backward and do not go forward beyond the sentence being processed when a meaning gap occurs. Of course, this is quite contrary to what good readers actually do.

Other examples of unnecessarily delimiting context to the sentence level are also important. Published reading programs do not yet provide systematic instruction in the use of anaphora to guide readers in drawing inferences between sentences or in reconstructing dialogue or actions whose meaning depends on who did what to whom. Very few reading programs recognize that the main idea and superordinate topic are different information units or that the organization or cohesion of exposition is dependent on main idea structures, while narration simply does not entail the use of such structures. This undoubtedly leads to great confusion among students when asked on the one hand to identify the main idea of a story and on the other to identify the main idea of an expository paragraph. These tasks require very different knowledge. In addition, almost all instructional programs which do purport to teach children to identify main ideas in reality only test whether they can be identified (Jolly, 1967). Finally the reader's ability to follow, assimilate, and remember text information is highly related to knowledge of how propositions, anaphoric references, and other redundancy features of context within lengthy texts may be related to one another during reading.

From quite a different perspective, some psycholinguistic researchers have demonstrated that access to text cues within the sentence must eventually become highly automatic and integrated in order to read fast, to maintain an optimum capacity for predicting what will come next, for confirming the meaning relationship between prior information and incoming information, and for self-correcting the important distortions, gaps, or miscues during cumulative, sentence-by-sentence processing. Each of these sentence level strategies emphasize that reading is a constructive and cumulative process. This implies that they cannot be learned outside the context of reading whole text as opposed to reading exercises which present one or two sentences as the unit for comprehension instruction (Goodman and Goodman, 1977; Smith, 1977).

A second implication of viewing context as operating across text is the importance of introducing both younger and older readers to strategies for reconstructing as well as constructing information while reading longer text segments. Reconstruction occurs when the reader finds that the evolving meaning does not correspond to new incoming information or when the reader attempts to put in his own words what the writer did or did not explicitly state in the text or when the reader has too many information gaps occurring and loses the gist of the author's message, etc. Thus, reconstruction most often entails backward contextual inferences and rereading. In contrast, construction is primarily a forward-moving process and entails predictions (forward inferences) and gap-filling based on prior knowledge of the content being read. Knowledge and the use of both construction and reconstruction strategies give the most effective text meaning access.

Teaching students to use context is a matter of properly representing the nature of context cues as they operate both within and between sentences. It is equally a matter of not ignoring the importance of teaching readers strategies for how to get meaning access from text level contextual constraints. Appropriate strategies for reading most forms of discourse can only be learned from using complete texts. Finally, it may be the case that a reader must be exposed to a variety of text genre in order to obtain the number of strategies necessary to fluently acquire meaning from a broad variety of texts. For example, front page news articles do not employ the same organizational structure as a newspaper editorial, and both are quite different in structural organization than poetry. The truly literate reader has learned to select and monitor reading strategies which are most relevant to particular types of genre. Basal reader programs represent over 90% of the material used to teach reading comprehension, and they tend to primarily use narrative stories. Therefore, it appears likely that basal reader programs may not provide the variety of text that can help children develop the strategies needed to use context to read exposition.

THE NATURE OF CONTEXT AS IT APPLIES TO WRITING

The nature of context as it applies to writing any form of discourse has hardly been broached. This does not mean that the topic has no theoretical or practical value. The study of writing as a phenomenon has only very recently become a topic of inquiry by researchers, and the treatment of this topic represents the breaking of new ground. The process of writing at the very least entails first thinking about a topic, deciding how to express one's thoughts, setting down one's thoughts as text, and working with the text as well as one's thoughts to create a complete and final representation of what one wishes to say. Unlike the reader, the author does not begin constructing meaning from a complete printed text but from his own thoughts. However, as soon as thoughts are transformed into printed text, the author creates a tentative printed linguistic context which must follow the tacit grammar underlying any sentence or text. Whatever semantic revisions the author makes in the drafts (or temporary printed context) used to represent meanings, the necessity to observe principles of text cohesion remains. In this sense, the printed text places constraints on the process of writing which the author experiences. The extent to which various elements of the accumulating printed context interact with and constrain the author's creation of meaning has not been explored. However, informal observation clearly suggests, that during the original drafting of a text, the greater the attention an author gives to aspects of the surface structure such as spelling, within sentence syntax, word usage, etc., the less attention he can give to relating ideas in a cohesive group. Hence the features of accumulating text which the author gives most attention to represent sources of contextual constraint on the production of the complete message at any point in its construction. This naturally raises the question of what strategies for drafting a message appear to be more associated with successful writers when compared to poor writers.

The following strategies have been reported to be used by good writers and contrast to the writing strategies of poor writers (Donelson, 1967; Emig, 1971; Stallard, 1974; Graves, 1975).

1. Good older writers are less concerned than poor writers with mechanics and are more concerned with organizational aspects of composing.
2. Good older writers spend more time than poor writers on completing

writing assignments and engage in prewriting (rehearsal of thoughts about a topic) and rewriting.

3. Good older writers exhibit more attention than poor writers to paragraph development in writing essays.

4. Good younger and older writers are more reflective during writing, which often is followed by revisions. Older writers tend to adjust larger units of writing than younger writers. In contrast, poorer writers are more reactive than reflective, with fewer adjustments during writing. Adjustments or revisions are predominantly at the word level.

5. Good younger and older writers have a better sense of audience than poor writers. However, young writers appear to take considerable time to come to gain a sense of audience in guiding their writing strategies.

6. Young good writers give examples and use reasons in evaluating their own writing while poor writers appear only to be able to react affectively.

In a very important sense, to fully depict the parameters of context which surround and influence the process of writing, one must consider the contributions of world knowledge and metacognition to the activity of writing. World knowledge refers to all the information and concepts an individual derives from everyday events, reading, and exposure to media. Metacognition refers to knowledge of one's own knowledge, understanding of means and goal relationships, and sensitivity to the need for strategies to monitor one's use of knowledge within the context of a specific activity such as reading or writing.

Research on reading comprehension has compiled considerable evidence for the importance of world knowledge and metacognition in acquiring meaning from text. Some research is available to suggest the importance of each source of knowledge as contexts which influence the completeness and quality of the writing process as well as writing products. One example suggesting the importance of world knowledge is that early primary grade children write more and better quality text when world knowledge of a topic is substantial (Graves, 1979). Children given topics to write on produced less and lower quality writing than those who chose their own topic or were given a series of topics to choose from. An example supporting the importance of available metacognitive strategies is found in research reported by Graves (1979) and by Sowers (1979). First graders simply do not revise what they write, even when the text does not make sense. However, with ample opportunity to write, first graders do begin to internalize and use the question, "What will happen next?" to guide their construction of stories. In contrast, one study of older children who were taught metacognitive strategies to revise or reconstruct as they wrote essays found that text cohesion and overall quality were significantly improved (Schiff, 1978).

The study of context as it applies to constructing and reconstructing meaning during the writing process is in its infancy. However, the preceding studies strongly suggest that educational methods devised to teach writing will directly benefit from further research in this area.

A TENTATIVE MODEL DEPICTING
CONTEXT SHARED BY READERS/AUTHORS

Implications for Research and Instruction

The literature review has consistently implied that knowledge of the world and knowledge of text structures at and beyond the sentence level may influence the reading and writing process. Furthermore, it has been implied that the reader/writer changes in terms of the extent of knowledge of text, of reading, and of writing, as well as the ways in which this knowledge is applied during reading and writing. In other words, the reader/writer develops more and qualitatively different strategies for writing and reading. However, research says very little about how growth in knowledge and strategies occurs. Furthermore no distinction is made between the specific forms of knowledge and strategies used in writing and those used in reading or vice versa.

Advances in research on reading and writing instruction and in research on the nature of the potential relationships between the phenomena of reading and writing will only be accidental until models are generated to depict how they may be related as processes. Figure 1 represents a preliminary metaphor for describing how reading and writing may be related as processes; it is presented in order to establish a framework for generating instructional and research implications which merit pursuit in the near future.

The first fundamental assumption about the processes used by the reader/author is that the types of text available to a person as a reader are also available to a person as a writer. This does not mean that conscious access to all forms of text knowledge during both processes is equally available. This is partly due to differences in the course of the development of strategies by a person as a reader and as a writer. It is also due to the fact that the role of the reader is to get meaning while the role of the writer is to produce meaning. Hence, the role perspectives are different in the same sense that a waitress possesses a different script for events in a restaurant than a regular customer has for those events.

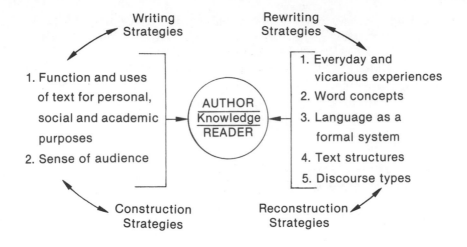

Figure 1. The interactive nature of the use of knowledge potentially acquired through reading and writing.

The second fundamental assumption is that opportunities to speak, read, and write will vary markedly among individuals due to differences in the cultural, social, local community, family, and school contexts in which each individual lives. The only possible neutralizer of these differences, aside from personal desire, may be the media of television and film. However, the individual's choices of how often and what TV programs and films to watch is again influenced by factors similar to those which influence opportunities to speak, read, and write. Obviously the same influences affect variations in the course of the patterns of development in the acquisition of mature reading and writing.

The critical feature of the model in Figure 1 is the reciprocal relationship depicted between writing and reading construction strategies and rewriting and reading reconstruction strategies. The term *writing strategies* refers to forming the structure of a message, making language choices during the process of filling in the structure sentence-by-sentence, and using language that is appropriate to interconnect substructures of the message as well as to communicate what the author wants the audience to understand. Throughout the process of writing it is assumed that the writer has some sense of topic or story and the knowledge necessary to develop it in a relatively fluent manner. During writing, the author is not in the role of reader because the author is primarily attending to the act of forming at least the gist of the meaning which will ultimately be found as a complete message. The writing process must be relatively fluent to allow the author to stay in conscious control of ideas being put on paper and the relationship among the ideas to be expressed.

The term *reading construction strategies* refers to the use of text redundancy cues (grapho-phonemic, syntactic, and semantic) to construct the author's meanings through prediction, organization, and filling information gaps through prior knowledge of the world. Construction entails a highly interactive and cummulative buildup of contextual constraints through which incoming meaning is sampled, confirmed, rejected, and/or rechecked. For mature readers this is a highly fluent series of events with few interruptions.

For young readers the process of construction is less fluent, not as rapid, and with a greater probability for interventions or distortions to occur in the buildup of the total message as it is stored in memory.

The term *rewriting* refers to strategies used by the author for assessing and/or reformulating what has been written as text. The text may not reflect all that the author intends to say or wants to say. However, it will be a text in the sense that it has some properties of wholeness or cohesion. Assessing a text entails judging its surface structure sentence-by-sentence as well as the connectedness of the sentences within the completed text. Reorganization refers to semantic changes in the original message or attempting to write entire text segments again because the author is still not clear about what he wants to say or because he thinks it will not communicate what he wants to say to a particular audience.

Obviously rewriting begins when the author reads and/or rereads his own work as a reader who attempts to construct the text meaning. How the author shifts his perspective from generating meaning to constructing meaning has never been studied empirically. However, it is likely that during rewriting the author uses strategies like the reader uses to reconstruct a text as opposed to constructing it. Somehow the author must obtain a different perspective into the meaning of what has been written as text as opposed to what he intended the text to mean. Hence, rewriting requires metacognitive strategies that spell out the structure selected to form the text content, the options for language choices given the intended audience, and the constraints of the overall discourse structure. Constraints allow the author as reader to judge the differences between the expected and obtained relationships among the preceding aspects of a message. Also they allow the author as reader to make decisions about what to do next.

The term *reading reconstruction strategies* refers to what the reader does to draw overt inferences between statements, paragraphs, episodes, etc. explicitly or implicitly stated in the text by the author. Reconstruction entails what the reader does to resolve ambiguity in a text or to refocus on the content of a text segment which cannot be readily retrieved. Finally, reconstruction occurs when the reader searches for text information which may be the source of a point in the text where the reader believes that the author has not made sense or when the reader is consciously aware that he misinterpreted something earlier in the text and the misinterpretation is the source of the present meaning conflict. The process of reconstruction is characterized by backward inferences and rereading texts' segments preceding the last point in which processing occurred. To successfully draw backward inferences, resolve ambiguity, resolve false presuppositions, and fully retrieve information, the reader must know where to look in the text, what to look for, and how to judge whether reconstruction of meaning is adequate to preserve the author's intended meaning.

The model predicts that the knowledge necessary to carry out rewriting and reading reconstruction acts are highly related. Furthermore, many of the strategies entailed to successfully rewrite a text are transferable to successful reconstruction of meaning and better comprehension during the reading of what an unavailable author intended as meaning. The most relevant knowledge sources are knowledge of acceptable text structures necessary to signal redundancy and referent relationships among concepts such as anaphora and propositions. In addition, the reader/author must be knowledgeable of the acceptable functions of specific types of discourse forms in a variety of genre. The most relevant strategies are backward inferences.

The model also predicts that similar types of knowledge are used for construction during reading and for writing. Scripts, frames, word concepts, and knowledge of the native language as a formal system make the construction of sentences possible during writing and enable prediction and sampling to occur during reading. In writing they allow the author to say the same thing someone else has said in different words. Especially good writers develop strategies from these sources of knowledge to say the same thing someone else has said, but to say it more efficiently or more effectively. In reading the strategies developed from these knowledge sources allow some readers to be better predictors than others and to read more rapidly with good comprehension.

The final prediction made by the model in Figure 1 is that only by reading broadly across genres does one become intimately conversant with the varied functions and uses of text. To some extent this prepares the reader as author to express himself in writing through forms of discourse which are appropriate to personal, social, and academic forms of expression. In addition, the reader comes to understand different types of audiences by sampling different types of discourse. This has some effect on the sense of audience the individual develops as a writer.

Given the basic components of the preceding model and the assumed relationships, the following statements represent arguments regarding the function of contexts which relate reading and writing and the influence of instructional contexts which surround reading and writing:

I. The function of contexts that related reading and writing
   A. Advances in the ease and accuracy of integrating syntactic and semantic information during the reading and writing of sentences is most positively influenced by regular opportunities for children to read and write their own spoken language.
   B. The knowledge needed to comprehend and write narrative text is not highly related to the comprehension and writing of expository text. The nature, function, and text structure of exposition is sufficiently different from narration that the reader/writer's knowledge of one will have little transfer to his knowledge of the other. Therefore, reading and writing instructional contexts must be designed to teach children the unique text structures and strategies (construction and reconstruction) appropriate to fostering meaning acquisition from both narration and exposition.
   C. Advances in the understanding of different types of discourse structures and their uses will have a positive relationship to meaning reconstruction in reading and improved cohesiveness in rewriting text.
II. The influence of instructional contexts that surround reading and writing
   A. The greater the amount of attention given by pupils and teachers to the process of reading and writing, the greater the likelihood of increases in reading, comprehension, and cohesive writing.
   B. Improvement in comprehending discourse is significantly related to the provision for an instructional environment in which equal opportunity is provided to learn its major structures through both reading and writing activities.

Implications for Reading and Writing

The nature of the instructional content surrounding reading and writing in the classroom is derived from the interaction between what the teacher does to expose children to text, and what children do with text created by others or with texts they create themselves.

If children are given little or no opportunity to regularly and actively participate in reading and writing, it follows that they will not learn much about how texts vary and what types of discourse options are available for expressing themselves through text. Reading and writing programs that place children in passive roles (filling in work sheets, responding to linguistic units outside the boundaries of text, and having little or no choice in the selection of the text they read or write) foster passive rather than active participation in exploring the contextual hookups between the reader's world knowledge and the redundancies provided by cohesive texts. Passive roles tend to preclude rather than foster reading comprehension and writing growth. On the other hand, reading and writing programs that foster active participation in discovering the relationship between knowledge of the world and the linguistic cues which provide for text cohesion place children in three roles: 1) generating texts to be read from their own language experiences, 2) responding to the relationships among grapho-phoneme, syntactic, and semantic cues within the context of meaningful text, and 3) having a variety of choices when selecting texts to be read which are written by others.

From the preceding viewpoint, reading and writing programs that focus on subskills are more likely to allow a teacher to put children in a passive learning role than are language-based programs such as one of the variations of the language experience program, a literature-based program, or a program that attempts to fully integrate speaking, listening, reading, and writing through performance (reader's theater, choral reading, song, pantomime, drama, reporting, researching, debate, making super 8 films, bookmaking, and videotape productions).

The teacher should play a dual role in an instructional environment which integrates reading and writing. First, the teacher must figure out what properties of text to highlight as the most important cues for the reader/writer to attend to and learn. Second, the teacher must create methods to guide the learners to develop strategies for combining their knowledge of text cues or structures in order to consciously access text meaning or form meaning as text. This dual role is quite different from one of a manager or a checker of student's responses to paper and pencil exercises and tests (Durkin, 1978). In the former case, teaching is designing and modeling; in the latter case, it is administering and evaluating.

What types of instructional methods adhere to the principle of active student involvement, learning about text structure, and developing strategies to consciously organize text as reader or writer? One example of a reading method and one of a writing method will be provided to suggest methods which can be employed.

Reading Method   Suppose that a teacher was interested in teaching children to employ two simple metacognitive strategies in order to aid them in constructing meaning as they read. Undoubtedly, young readers will face numerous interruptions in processing sentences due to unfamiliar graphic-to-sound correspondences for word units or to unfamiliar word meanings. If the reader cannot handle such interruptions in a manner that preserves the syntactic and/or semantic structure of a sentence, then gaps will occur in the construction of text meaning. The teacher must think of a way to actively involve students in predicting meaning under the preceding conditions and in monitoring their predictions.

One way of doing this is to prepare oral cloze exercises based on complete and cohesive passages or stories. The oral cloze method requires the teacher to read a text aloud and to stop at selected points during reading. The students must silently follow the text read aloud by the teacher and predict what word unit comes next. The teacher interacts with the children by asking whether or not each of their predictions sounds like language (preserves the author's syntactic structures) and makes sense (preserves the possible meanings allowed by the author's text up to the point of prediction). The children respond to the teacher's questions by explaining their choices or by making a new prediction. The teacher carefully structures the lesson by selecting words to delete which highlight either structure words (articles, conjunctions, prepositions, pronouns, or adverbs) or content words (nouns, verbs, adjectives, or adverbs). The teacher is also careful only to make deletions where prior context provides adequate information for making predictions. During the period when children are attempting to determine whether or not a prediction fulfills the criterion of preserving a sentence that sounds like language and/or that makes sense, the teacher is careful to allow but at the same time make overt predictions that make sense on the basis of the children's world knowledge and/or what has been explicitly stated in the text itself. The teacher is also careful to show the criterion that reading further aids in confirming their predictions when prior context is insufficient for confirmation. This reading method actively involves students, highlights specific types of text structure cues, and teaches students the strategy of self-monitoring predictions on the basis of whether they sound like language and make sense.

Writing Methods   Two writing methods adhering to the preceding three principles are the conference method and the simple structure method. The conference method was developed by Graves (1975) and is used to facilitate essay writing. The object is to allow a student to discover his own essay topic, to acquire sufficient background knowledge to write an essay on the selected topic, and to guide the writer through four or more successive drafts which include the phases of writing and rewriting. The teacher does this through short conferences of no more than 5 minutes duration which support the child in selecting a topic, delimiting what to say about it, organizing what is to be said, and revising how it is said in a manner that leads to a cohesive text which speaks to the writer's audience.

The intent of the second method, the simple structure method (Aulls, 1978), is to provide a model of a particular discourse structure (such as blank verse, the fable, a description, or a dialogue) which the children can fill in from their own reservoir of experiences and ultimately have many opportunities to work with for the purposes of personal expression or to write on a particular topic in a particular way for a particular audience. The steps of the method are quite simple: 1) the teacher provides a completed example of the structure to be explored, 2) the children and the teacher work together to fill in an incomplete structure, and 3) the children select a topic through which to reproduce the structure for themselves. This method can be applied to all types of poetry, rounds, stories, jokes, methods of recording advertisements, outlining, expository paragraphs, and descriptions. An example of each step is provided in Figure 2 for a cinquain, which is a specific type of blank verse poetic structure.

Like the reading method discussed above, this simple structure writing method puts the child in a highly active role as author, highlights specific structural cues for organizing text, and suggests strategies as they are needed to fill in and/or fill out meaning as text.

One final issue merits consideration. What types of text should children be exposed to as writers and readers in the primary and middle grades? From the author's view children at all levels of the elementary school should be read to and should read and simultaneously listen to or silently read a broad variety of narrative and expository material. In the primary grades, the language experience approach to reading and writing is probably the most effective approach (Braun and Froese, 1977). But instruction should include regularly being read to aloud and silently reading self-selected texts. In the middle grades, regular writing and reading of both narrative and expository discourse should be encouraged within a performance-oriented context. A performance context is a situation when reading leads to choral reading, making books to be read, reader's theater, slide-tape shows, radio theater, plays, and videotaped weekly news broadcasts. It emphasizes the personal, social, and academic situations and audiences within which reading and writing function in the society.

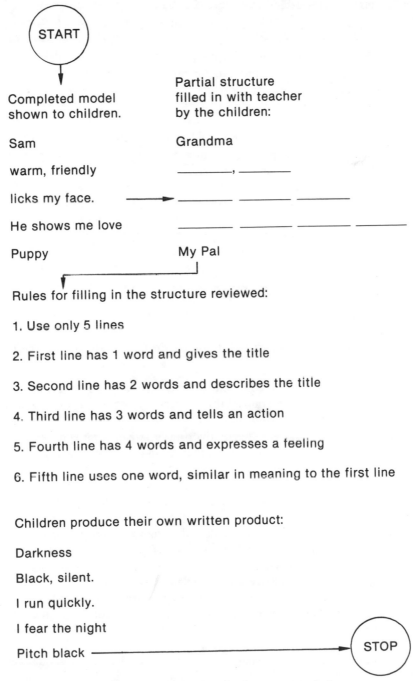

Figure 2.   The steps of the simple structure method.

Implications for Research

The nature and function of context as it relates to the process of reading and writing and teaching reading and writing represents a vast new area for empirical research. Prior research on context as it applies to reading has shifted from sentence units to longer text units. Theories of text grammar are only just beginning to be applied as frameworks for empirically testing aspects of reading comprehension. At the present time, they have not been applied at all to devising research on the phenomenon of writing. Fragments of research exist on the aspects of the instructional contexts which facilitate more, better quality, and greater variety of types of written expression. Research on instructional contexts which influence the qualitative and quantitative aspects of reading comprehension have little to say about stages of development and specific methods of instruction. On the other hand, a good deal has been learned about the nature of the reading phenomenon through systematic investigations of subskills, process, and reading comprehension models. The outcome has been a clearer understanding of what experience the reader brings as context to the printed page and what properties of text structure influence a variety of measures of reading comprehension such as free recall, prediction, backward inferences, judgments, and interpretation of metaphor.

Perhaps some of the more important research questions which are relevant to defining the function of context in both reading and writing are:

1. What levels of knowledge about the structure of texts derived through reading are transferable to the activities of writing and rewriting?
2. How can one validate the distinction between strategies used to construct a text and reconstruct a text during reading or writing?
3. Do children learn to more successfully monitor surface structure errors in writing through proofreading their own writing drafts in teams than by having the teacher proofread each writing sample they produce?
4. In what specific ways is a reader able to vary the use of reading strategies to comprehend different types of discourse such as a newspaper editorial or a poem?
5. What kinds of knowledge about the text structure of narration are not applicable to cohesively writing and comprehending exposition?
6. What changes occur as children progress from becoming acquainted with print as writers to the acquisition of relatively mature stages of writing?
7. What changes occur as children progress from becoming acquainted

with print as readers to the acquisition of relatively mature stages of reading comprehension?

In conclusion, the major purpose of this chapter has been to review the nature and function of sources of knowledge which serve as candidates for depicting the influence of context on reading, on writing, and on learning to read and to write.

The research reviewed has identified some interesting findings regarding what qualities of context apply during reading, but little empirical research has been done on the nature of context as it applies to writing. Furthermore, the research on instructional contexts which influence reading comprehension appears to be more limited than that for writing. However, some evidence was found to suggest that reading instructional practices may have an influence on writing and writing instruction may be related to certain aspects of improvement in reading comprehension.

The author's viewpoint is that reading and writing do share many similar forms of cognitive and linguistic knowledge and may involve related strategies. This was argued to be especially true for the strategies entailed in reconstruction and rewriting. If the preceding assumptions prove to be valid, then it follows that many practices in teaching writing should have a positive relationship to certain aspects of comprehending text. Finally, the most important implication for future research on reading and writing is the desirability of studying both processes simultaneously in order to map out the extent to which the knowledge and strategies used by the reader are related to those needed by the writer.

FOR DISCUSSION

1. Relate Aulls' comments on context to Pearson's on schema theory.
2. Differentiate between the context of written material and the context of the language processor (either psychological or environmental context).
3. What is the difference between sentence grammar and text grammar? How do they interact?
4. Pearson refers to reading as an interactive process. In what ways does Aulls perceive writing as an interactive process?
5. Aulls lists some differences between good and poor writers. What are the implications of these differences for the development of an effective writing program?
6. Since reading and writing are both dependent on similar competencies, why is the good reader not necessarily a mature writer? How could the two competencies be more effectively integrated?

7. How can a teacher develop an instructional context that will harbor and develop abilities in both reading and writing?

REFERENCES

Aborn, M., Rubenstein, H., and Sterling, T. D. Sources of contextual constraint upon words in sentences. *Journal of Experimental Psychology*, 1959, *57*, 171–180.

Aulls, M. V. *Developmental and remedial reading in the middle grades*. Boston: Allyn and Bacon Company, 1978.

Barnitz, J. Reading comprehension of pronoun-referent structures by children in grades two, four and six. *Technical Report No. 117*. Champaign—Urbana, Illinois: Center for the Study of Reading, March 1979.

Bhooma, V. K. *The effects of selected blackout conditions on reading test item responses*. Unpublished doctoral dissertation, University of Georgia, 1969.

Bradley, M. *Effects on reading tests on deletions of selected grammatical categories*. Unpublished doctoral dissertation, University of Georgia, 1968.

Bransford, J. D., and Johnson, M. K. Contextual prerequisites for understanding: Some investigations of comprehension and recall. *Journal of Verbal Learning and Verbal Behavior*, 1972, *11*, 717–726.

Braun, C., and Froese, V. *An experience based approach to language and reading*. Baltimore: University Park Press, 1977.

Brazee, P. *A qualitative and quantitative description of eighth grade students' oral reading in both narrative and expository materials*. Unpublished dissertation, University of Colorado, 1976.

Brown, A. L. Recognition, reconstruction, and recall of narrative sequences by preoperational children. *Child Development*, 1975, *46*, 156–166.

Brown, A. L., and Smiley, S. S. Rating the importance of structural units of prose passages: A problem of metacognitive development. *Child Development*, 1977, *48*, 1–8.

Burgard, J. F. *An investigation of the abilities of fifth and sixth grade pupils to derive word meanings from context in silent reading*. Unpublished masters thesis, School of Education, Boston University, 1950.

Chomsky, N., and Halle, M. *The sound pattern of English*. New York: Harper and Row, 1968.

Clay, M. M. A syntactic analysis of reading errors. *Journal of Verbal Learning and Verbal Behavior*, 1968, *7*, 434–438.

Danks, J. H. Grammaticalness and meaningfulness in the comprehension of sentences. *Journal of Verbal Learning and Verbal Behavior*, 1969, *8*, 687–696.

Danks, J. H., and Glucksberg, S. Psychological scaling of linguistics properties. *Language and Speech*, 1970, *13*, 118–140.

Deighton, L. C. *Vocabulary development in the classroom*. New York: Bureau of Publications, Teachers College, Columbia University, 1959.

Donelson, D. L. Variables distinguishing between effective and ineffective writers in the 10th grade. *Journal of Experimental Education*, 1967, Summer 1967, *35*(4), 37–41.

Dulin, K. *The role of contextual clues in the acquisition of specific reading vocabulary*. Unpublished doctoral dissertation, University of Washington, 1968.

Durkin, D. What classroom observations reveal about reading comprehension instruction. *Technical Report No. 106.* Champaign-Urbana, Illinois: Center for the Study of Reading, October 1978.

Eckert, M. M. *The effect of context on comprehension words.* Unpublished masters thesis, The University of Pittsburgh, 1928.

Elivian, J. Word perception and word meaning in silent reading in the intermediate grades. *Education*, 1938, *59*, 51–56

Emig, J. *The composing process of twelfth graders.* Urbana, Illinois: National Council of Teachers of English, 1971.

Gibbons, H. The ability of college freshmen to construct the meaning of a strange word from the context in which it appears. *Journal of Experimental Education*, 1940, *9*, 29–33.

Goodman, K. S., and Burke, C. L. *Theoretically based studies of patterns of miscues in oral reading performance, final report.* Detroit: Wayne State University, 1973. (ERIC Document Reproduction Service No. ED 079708)

Goodman, K. S., and Goodman, Y. M. Learning about psycholinguistic processes by analyzing oral reading. *Harvard Educational Review*, 1977, *47*, 317–333.

Goodman, Y. M. *A psycholinguistic description of oral reading phenomena in selected young beginning readers.* Unpublished doctoral dissertation, Wayne State University, 1967.

Graves, D. H. An examination of the writing process of seven year old children. *Research in the Teaching of English*, 1975, *9*(3), 227–242.

Graves, D. H. What children show us about revision. *Language Arts*, 1979, *56*(3), 312–319.

Graves, D. H. *The growth development of first grade writers.* Unpublished paper, presented at Canadian Council Teachers of English Conference, Ottawa, Canada, May 1979.

Grimes, J. E. *The thread of discourse.* Cornell University, 1968. (ERIC Document Report Service No. 019669)

Hafner, L. E. A one-month experiment in teaching context aids in the fifth grade. *Journal of Educational Research*, 1965, *58*, 472–474.

Halliday, M. A., and Hasan, R. *Cohesion in English.* London: Longman Group Ltd, 1976.

Jolly, H. B. Determining main ideas: Basic study skills. In L. E. Hafner (Ed.), *Improving reading in the secondary schools.* New York: Macmillan, 1967.

Kintsch, W. *The representation of meaning in memory.* Hillsdale, New Jersey: Lawrence Erlbaum Associates, 1974.

Kintsch, W., Kozminsky, E., Streby, W. J., and Keeman, J. M. Comprehension and recall of text as a function of content variables. *Journal of Verbal Learning and Verbal Behavior*, 1974, *14*, 196–214.

Levin, H., and Turner, A. Sentence structure and the eyes voice span. In H. Levin and E. J. Gibson (Eds.), *The analysis of reading skill* (Final Report Project No. 5–1213, from Cornell University to U.S. Office of Education). December 1968.

McCullough, C. M. The recognition of context clues in reading. *Elementary English*, 1945, *22*, 1–8.

McKee, P. *The teaching of reading.* Boston: Houghton Mifflin, 1948.

Meyer, B. J. Identification of the structure of prose and its implications for the study of reading and memory. *Journal of Reading Behavior*, 1975, *7*, 7–47.

Meyer, B. J. What is remembered from prose? A function of passage structure.

In R. Freedle (Ed.), *Discourse production and comprehension* (Vol. 1). Norwood, New Jersey: Ablex, 1977.

Meyer, B., Brandt, D., and Bluth, G. *Use of author's textual schema. Key for ninth grader's comprehension.* Unpublished paper presented at the American Educational Research Association Convention, Toronto, Canada, March 1978.

Miller, G. A. Some psychological studies of grammar. *American Psychologist*, 1962, *19*, 748–762.

Ortony, A., Schallert, D. L., Reynolds, R., and Antos, S. J. Interpreting metaphors and idioms: Some effects of context on comprehension. *Journal of Verbal Learning and Verbal Behavior*, 1978, *17*, 465–477.

Quealy, R. J. Senior high school students' use of contextual aids in reading. *Reading Research Quarterly*, 1969, *4*, 514–533.

Rankin, E. F., and Overholser, B. M. Reactions of intermediate grade children to contextual clues. *Journal of Reading Behavior*, 1969, *1*, 50–73.

Resnick, L. B. Relations between perceptual and syntactic control in oral reading. *Journal of Educational Psychology*, 1970, *61*, 382–385.

Richek, M. A. Reading comprehension of anaphoric forms in varying contexts. *Reading Research Quarterly*, 1977, *12*, 145–165.

Schiff, P. M. Problem solving and the composition model: Reorganization, manipulation, analysis. *Research in the Teaching of English*, 1978, *12*(3), 203–210.

Schlesinger, I. M. *Sentence structure and the reading process.* The Hague: Mouton, 1968.

Schwart, D., Sparkman, J., and Deese, J. The process of understanding and judgements of comprehensibility. *Journal of Verbal Learning and Verbal Behavior*, 1970, *9*, 87–93.

Seeman, J. *Extent to which junior high pupils can derive meanings of difficult words through the use of context.* Unpublished masters thesis, University of Maryland, 1944.

Seibert, L. C. A study of the practice of word guessing word meanings from a context. *Modern Language Journal*, 1945, *29*, 296–322.

Slobin, D. I. Grammatical transformation and sentence comprehension in childhood and adulthood. *Journal of Verbal Learning and Verbal Behavior*, 1966, *5*, 219–227.

Smith, F. *Psycholinguistics and reading.* New York: Holt, Rinehart and Winston, 1973.

Smith, F. Making sense of reading and of reading instruction. *Harvard Educational Review*, 1977, *47*, 386–395.

Sowers, S. *A six year old's writing process: The first half of first grade.* Unpublished paper, University of New Hampshire, 1979.

Spache, G., and Berg, P. *The art of efficient reading.* New York: Macmillan, 1955.

Stallard, C. K. An analysis of the writing behavior of good student writers. *Research in the Teaching of English*, 1974, *8*(2), 206–219.

Stearns, G. B. *The construction and evaluation of a test designed to measure the ability of high school pupils to understand word meanings through the use of context.* Unpublished doctoral dissertation, School of Education, Boston University, 1954.

Stein, N. L., and Glenn, G. G. An analysis of story comprehension in elementary school children. In R. Freedle (Ed.), *Multidisciplinary approaches to discourse comprehension.* Hillsdale, New Jersey: Ablex, 1977.

Van Dijk, T. A. Models for text grammars. *Linguistics*, 1973, *105*, 36–68.

Warren, W. H., Nicholas, D. W., and Trabasso, T. Event chains and inferences in understanding narratives. In R. Freedle (Ed.), *New directions in discourse processing* (Vol. 2). Norwood, New Jersey: Ablex, 1977.

White, L. M. *The ability of fifth grade pupils to get word meaning from context.* Unpublished masters thesis, School of Education, Boston University, 1950.

16 Comparative Reading

John Downing

This chapter takes a somewhat different direction from those that have preceded it in this volume. Instead of focusing on a particular topic or problem in language education, it reviews research that has a special type of perspective—a cross-cultural perspective—for looking at all kinds of problems in literacy instruction. Why is a cross-cultural perspective useful? How can studying reading in different languages and varying cultures help one to understand reading in one's own language and community? What knowledge of the learning-to-read process has accrued thus far from comparative reading studies? These are the questions that this chapter tries to answer.

The chief goal of comparative reading is to achieve a better theoretical and practical understanding of the fundamental psychological processes of literacy behavior, both in their learning and in their developed functioning. This goal can be pursued in many ways. Its application is obvious in large-scale cross-national surveys of achievements in reading such as the International Association for the Evaluation of Educational Achievement (IEA) study reported by Thorndike (1973). But this cross-cultural research approach is being developed in other important, though less obvious, ways. Some interesting comparative reading studies have been done on a small scale and some have been conducted inside a single country, comparing different cultural and linguistic groups. Whether the comparative reading research takes place within one country or across national boundaries is not important. *The essence of comparative reading studies is that they compare the reading behaviors of people in different cultures and in varying languages in ways that will reveal the fundamental processes of reading and writing and the ways in which these develop.*

MAJOR TYPES OF COMPARATIVE READING RESEARCH

The term *comparative reading* has been used for this type of research since the late 1960s (Downing, 1969). However, the concept of improving our understanding of reading by comparing its functioning in different languages and cultures predates the coining of the term.

International Compilations of Professional Wisdom

The pioneering study of this type was conducted for UNESCO by Gray (1953). He reviewed instructional materials for teaching literacy from various countries together with published reports on their effects. In addition, he used mailed questionnaires and informal personal interviews conducted during his visits to several countries. The only empirical data that Gray collected were on eye movements in reading for fourteen languages.

Gray's aim was practical. He tried to collect a consensus of world-wide wisdom on reading instruction that would be especially useful in developing or "Third World" countries. Gray stated his aim as follows:

1. To provide actual and potential leaders with as clear an outlook as possible on the problem of world literacy in its varied aspects, with special reference to the most effective methods of teaching reading and writing.
2. To provide guidance and concrete suggestions that will enable leaders to develop literacy programmes in harmony with these general facts and principles, and adapted to local needs.
3. To define the nature of the unsolved problems that should be studied in order to promote literacy throughout the world, and to consider means of solving them. (pp. 11–12)

However, Gray did make some theoretical pronouncements. From his cross-language eye movement research and a review of some other studies he concluded that "These studies demonstrate that the general nature of the reading act is essentially the same among all mature readers" (pp. 59–60). It is very important to note that Gray is referring to *mature readers*. It cannot be assumed from Gray's finding that learning to read proceeds in an identical manner in all languages. Even if the mature skill of reading is similar in all languages, it does not necessarily follow that the learning-to-read process is likewise completely identical. It is a well-established finding of psychological research that the processes in any complex skill such as reading are quite different in beginners and mature performers (Downing and Leong, in press).

In fact, Gray's data do not entirely support his claim. He admitted that "the number of words per regression reveals striking differences among languages" (p. 58), but he attempted to explain these differences as being due to individual differences in "immaturity," "type of training," and "perceptual habits" (p. 59). This issue remains the chief problem for comparative reading research: Are there any features in the manner in which children learn to read that are universal? We will return to this paramount problem later in this chapter. Gray's enterprise was based on his faith that the process *is* universal and that, therefore, the wisdom of reading specialists is transferable from one language environment to another.

The revised edition of Gray's book included a chapter by Staiger (1969) which reviewed events and publications in the field that had emerged since Gray's original work. Although this review was internationally comprehensive, it did not alter Gray's original position.

A number of minor surveys similar to Gray's were conducted at about the same period. These are reviewed elsewhere (Downing, 1973, pp. 65–67).

Cross-national Achievement Studies

A more empirical approach has been taken in some studies that have attempted to compare the reading achievements of different nations. Unfortunately, to date, none of these studies has been very successful in obtaining valid data for such cross-national comparisons. It is difficult to control the many variables that influence the acquisition of reading skill, but it is infinitely more difficult to control them in an international investigation because of the wide range of variations in schooling from one country to another. Nevertheless, the chief value of the studies that have been completed thus far is that they have demonstrated that objective comparisons between different countries are within our grasp. Their second value has been in discovering the methodological pitfalls in designing cross-national achievement studies that need to be avoided in future research of this kind.

The best known cross-national studies of reading achievement are the two conducted by the IEA (International Educational Achievements) group.

The first IEA study was reported by Foshay et al. (1962). Reading comprehension achievements of 13-year-olds in twelve countries were tested—Belgium, England, Finland, France, Germany, Israel, Poland, Scotland, Sweden, Switzerland, the United States, and Yugoslavia. The report claimed that "the universality of the reading task is affirmed" (p. 39), but, because only one age level toward the end of schooling was tested, the data cannot tell us anything about the really interesting problem of universals in the *learning task* in different languages and cultures. This investigation ran into several other methodological snags. The sampling design broke down and the authors of the report on the study admit serious limitations in the representativeness of the national samples. Translation of some items from one language to another produced errors, although the authors felt that they were not serious. These and other difficulties are reviewed in detail elsewhere (Downing, 1973, pp. 43–50).

The second IEA cross-national survey of reading comprehension was reported by Thorndike (1973). The fourteen countries participating were Belgium, Chile, England, Finland, Hungary, India, Iran, Israel, Italy, Netherlands, New Zealand, Scotland, Sweden, and the United States. This study has been reviewed in detail by Downing and Dalrymple-Alford (1974–1975). Although the second IEA survey included a number of improvements in design, it still contained several methodological weaknesses that raised grave doubts about its findings. The overgeneralized conclusion of the survey that home background is more important than schooling was certainly not justified by the data.

A less ambitious cross-national study conducted earlier by Pidgeon (1958) was more successful than either of the two IEA surveys. Pidgeon compared reading comprehension attainments of 11-year-olds in England and Wales with those of 11-year-old children in Queensland, Australia. His research design is a model of scientific rigor for comparative reading research. Pidgeon's stratified random sampling technique was especially effective. His most interesting finding was the wider range of reading scores in England and Wales as compared with Australia. Pidgeon's study also has been reviewed in detail elsewhere (Downing, 1973, pp. 39–43). There is little doubt that it provides the best model for this type of study to date. Even so, Pidgeon's study suffers from the same major flaw that made the two IEA surveys so unproductive. All three studies had no guiding theoretical basis or general logical framework, and hence no hypotheses. Their findings are *post hoc* speculations about the data that happened to result from tests that were administered without any particular research question in mind.

It is doubtful whether such purposeless international surveys of reading achievements need to be conducted again. Their reports, nevertheless, are valuable as a source of information on the problems and pitfalls of conducting objective international research that does have a clear aim.

Open-ended Exploratory Studies

In a new field of research it is often advisable to begin with open-ended methods that postpone the making of hypotheses until a wide range of *natural phenomena* has been examined. If questions or hypotheses are developed too early, the important variables may be overlooked. This was the thinking behind the first comparative reading study conducted by Downing (1973).

In this study, fourteen countries were selected as representing important cultural and linguistic differences in reading education. For example, India and Germany provided economic and cultural contrasts. The U.S.S.R., Great Britain, and Israel have different alphabets. The United States and Finland exemplified the contrast between irregular and regular grapheme-phoneme relations in languages coded with the roman alphabet. Japan and Hong Kong provided examples of syllabic and logographic writing systems to be compared with the alphabet systems. France and Denmark have quite different educational patterns. Other aspects of culture and language were represented in Argentina, Norway, and Sweden. One or two specialists in the study of reading were commissioned to write a descriptive account of literacy learning in the particular country of which they had special knowledge. Guidelines for these observers were minimal to allow them freedom to express spontaneously what were considered to be important aspects of reading education in the country described. The original national reports were published in one volume with a theoretical analysis and commentary.

Numerous hypotheses arose as the outcome of these exploratory comparisons. Most of these hypotheses await further research. It is impossible to do justice here to the 600 pages of the original report, but the most fruitful approach would seem to be to take one example of the hypotheses derived from the exploratory open-ended study and to pursue it by more rigorous testing methods.

Testing a Specific Hypothesis by Comparative Reading Research

Downing's first exploratory survey (1973) threw doubts on several popular generalizations about learning to read. One of these unexpected results was that the patterns of sex differences in reading attainments vary from one country to another. In the primary grades in the United States, on the average, girls make better progress in reading than do boys. This is well established in American research. But in several of the other countries studied, boys have more success than girls. Hence, because it is unlikely that the genetic makeup of America children is different from that of, say, German children, a cultural hypothesis may be appropriate. In other words, in the United States boys may detect that being good at reading is the cultural expectation for girls, and, as a consequence, they may develop a sex-role standard of giving less attention to reading instruction.

Downing et al. (1979) measured cultural expectations and sex-role standards about reading in Canada, Denmark, England, Finland, Israel, Japan, and the United States. A picture test showing various activities and objects, including reading and books, was administered in each country to six subsamples that approximated the following levels: students in grades one, four, eight, and twelve, college students, and adults. The subjects had to ascribe the activity or object as being more appropriate for either a boy or a girl. The results were consistent with the hypothesis that cultural expectations and sex-role standards about reading are congruent within one country but that they differ between countries. In particular, boys in Canada and the United States seem to learn rapidly to perceive reading as a feminine activity. This is not universal in all countries. For example, Danish and Japanese males at all ages in this study consistently viewed reading as acceptable masculine behavior. R. Valtin (personal communication, 1979), using the same test, found that German males also view reading as masculine.

This research on sex-role standards in reading demonstrates the potential value of comparative reading research. Without these cross-cultural comparisons, the belief that sex differences in reading attainments are caused by innate biological differences in the brains of boys and girls would remain unchallenged.

KEY PROBLEMS FOR FUTURE INQUIRY

To develop the concepts needed for the study of any discipline, one must get behind the immediately observable concrete examples to a higher level of abstraction. The same is true in the study of the reading and learning-to-read processes. It is virtually impossible to even begin to understand the psychology of the reading act until one is able to view these processes in the abstract, detached from their concrete and specific manifestations in one's own language. This is the central goal of comparative reading studies: to get behind the immediately observable manifestations of printed or written text and its interpretation by readers in order to discover the universal psychological characteristics of reading and learning to read. Claims that the final outcome is the same in all languages and cultures do not help our understanding of these processes. In contrast, by studying reading and reading acquisition in quite different languages and cultures, side by side, we can isolate those characteristics that they have in common and thus arrive at the true universals of reading. This work has barely begun. But previous studies indicate three potentially fruitful areas for future investigation. Figure 1 shows how these three areas of comparative studies may reveal universal psychological factors in the development of reading skill. In all languages and cultures the learner is in the same situation, that is, in all languages and cultures there are: 1) certain *features of spoken and written language* that are the raw data on the basis of which the learner can reason about the task of acquiring the skill of reading; 2) *certain social mores about*

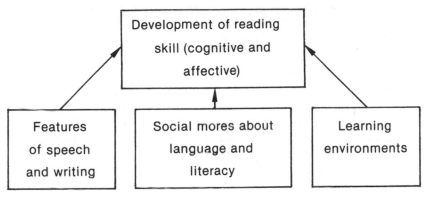

Figure 1.   The universal situation of the literacy learner.

language and literacy that influence the learner's attitude toward this task; and 3) *several environments* which contain factors that may support or hamper the development of reading skill.

Features of Spoken and Written Language

There is considerable research evidence that children's understanding of metalinguistic concepts and their awareness of features of speech and text is significantly related to their achievements in learning to read. Downing (1979) has reviewed this evidence at length elsewhere. Vernon's (1957) survey of research on the causes of reading disability led her to conclude that "the fundamental and basic characteristic of reading disability appears to be cognitive confusion" (p. 71). She also referred to reading disability as a failure in the development of reasoning. More recently, Vernon (1971) has again emphasized the importance of "conceptual reasoning" (p. 79) and "intelligent comprehension" (p. 82) in the acquisition of reading skill. This is the cognitive aspect referred to in the upper box in Figure 1. The child needs concepts of linguistic features in order to think about the tasks of reading instruction. Research has shown that most children enter these tasks with few if any of the necessary concepts. They have to work their way out of this initial cognitive confusion into increasing cognitive clarity in order to understand reading instruction.

The research referred to above has been done in several countries, including Russia, Sweden, Britain, Canada, and the United States. For instance, the concept of "a word" in speech is not understood by school beginners in any of these countries, in any of the languages involved. Luria's (1946) "glass theory" explains this:

> While actively using grammatical speech and signifying with words the appropriate objects and actions, the child is still not able to make the word and verbal relations an object of his consciousness. In this period a word

may be used but not noticed by the child, and it frequently seems like a glass window through which the child looks at the surrounding world without making the word itself an object of his consciousness and without suspecting that it has its own existence, its own structural features. (p. 61)

These studies of metalinguistic awareness have not been comparative. Although the fact that several different languages have been involved in the separate studies suggests that the child's development of concepts of features of speech and writing are a universal prerequisite for the acquisition of reading skill, comparative research might illuminate this problem very effectively. Languages differ quite markedly in their writing systems. Some critical hypotheses could be tested by appropriate comparative research. For example, one would predict that the relationship between the development of the concepts of "phoneme" and "syllable" and attainments in reading would be quite different for children whose native language is Japanese and for those whose language is English. The phoneme unit is not represented in the Japanese writing system whereas it is in written English. Also, the syllable unit is the smallest phonological element represented in Japanese writing, but it has no individual visible unity in the English writing system. Comparative reading research might clarify problems of this type much more effectively than studies within a single language community.

Social Mores about Language and Literacy

This is a much cloudier area of reading research. Sociologists and anthropologists have shown that folkways, beliefs, and attitudes can have an important influence on the development of skills, yet most reading specialists have paid them scant attention.

Earlier in this chapter, the research that indicated that patterns of sex differences in reading attainment may arise from social attitudes toward the femininity or masculinity of reading is summarized. The results of Downing's original (1973) comparative reading survey suggested several other hypotheses about the way in which the mores of a society may be a powerful variable in the learning-to-read process. There are two avenues for research which might clear up some of the fuzziness in this area.

First, it would be valuable to determine the impact on reading achievements of the esteem that different cultural groups accord to literacy. Downing's exploratory study (1973) found that countries vary in this respect. In several countries, reading instruction seemed to be given a rather low priority, while in others reading was of the utmost importance. In Denmark, Norway, and Sweden, for example, reading instruction is not a major concern in the early years. Reading instruction begins at age 7 and a calm and cautious introduction is thought to be appropriate. In contrast, in countries like the United States and Japan reading instruction begins earlier and there are many signs of deep concern that children succeed well in this task. It seems likely that these cultural priorities are detected by children and that they influence their attitudes toward reading and learning how to read. Comparative research might clarify this problem and indicate universal relationships between the learning-to-read process and the value placed on literacy by the adults surrounding the child.

A second avenue for research on social mores that seems likely to throw light on a universal problem in literacy development would be on the question of social attitudes toward languages and dialects. In particular, how does the learner's attitude toward the language of initial literacy instruction influence his or her progress in learning to read? That attitudes make an important difference is indicated by two contrasting studies.

Österberg (1961) compared an experimental group of children taught to read in the Piteå dialect of Swedish with a control group of children in the same dialect area who were taught to read in standard Swedish. The group taught in the dialect quickly got ahead of the standard language group during the initial period of instruction. Moreover, by the end of the year the dialect group was reading standard Swedish better than the control group that had received its instruction only in standard Swedish. But, when Stewart (1969, 1975) attempted the same experiment with a black American dialect, it was a total failure. The chief difference in these two studies seems to have been in the dialect speakers' attitudes toward their own speech. Whereas the children and parents in Piteå, Sweden valued their own dialect positively as a vehicle for literacy, the black American children and parents disparaged their own mother tongue in the context of literacy.

Comparative reading research that includes measures of attitudes toward the language of literacy instruction might clarify this question of the extent to which such linguistic attitudes influence progress in the acquisition of reading skill. It seems likely to be a universal factor in the process of learning to read.

Learning Environments

Here is an area of comparative reading study that holds great promise. There exists a wide variety of differences in children's home and school environments from one culture to another. Many of these differences represent environmental factors that are of interest to reading educators but about which the research conclusions are often equivocal. The possibilities for comparative studies of environmental factors are so vast that it is difficult to select one for special mention.

One environmentally determined feature of the child's experience in learning to read is the age fixed on by a country for the child's introduction to reading instruction. It is age 5 in Britain, Hong King, and Israel; age 6 in Canada and the United States; age 7 in Denmark, Finland, Norway, Sweden, and the U.S.S.R., and so on. Actually, one must be cautious about these legal ages because children often start reading instruction earlier in some other way which may be overlooked. For example, at least 75% of the children in Moscow attend kindergarten before age 7 and some simple instruction in literacy begins there.

The possibility that one could determine the magic moment or best age for beginning reading by comparing reading attainments in different countries with different school beginning ages is deceptively attractive. It soon becomes apparent that there are far too many other variables that influence reading achievement. Nevertheless, this does not mean that such a project must be abandoned. What is wrong with the simplistic notion of relating starting age to reading attainment is that the latter is too gross and insensitive a measure of the effects of the former.

Because a study of the effects of the age of beginning instruction on the acquisition of reading skill poses so many problems many reading educators have turned their backs on the question. However, careful attention to a detailed analysis of the aspects of the task that may be influenced by age might produce a design for a comparative reading investigation that would turn poorly charted notions of reading readiness into a precisely mapped area. We need to look very carefully at the literature of developmental psychology and relate it to an analysis of the cognitive demands of the learning-to-read process. From these considerations, hypotheses about specific cognitive operations in reading that may be influenced by the age of the learner could be derived and tested in comparative reading research.

IMPLICATIONS OF COMPARATIVE READING STUDIES

Comparative reading is such a new area of study that it is rather difficult, as yet, to draw from it detailed conclusions that have practical implications for reading instruction. However, there is clear evidence that practical outcomes will result from future expansions of comparative reading research. Already the main benefit of this type of study is apparent. It removes our ethnocentric and linguacentric blinkers. We no longer approach the study of how children learn to read with prejudgments based on the assumption that reading instruction as we know it in our own society represents a universal human situation. Two typical examples of the new insight gained from studying reading in other countries have been mentioned in this chapter.

As we have seen, sex differences in reading achievement follow different patterns from one country to another. Also, we reviewed research that showed that attitudes toward boys' reading and girls' reading vary from country to country. It seems likely, therefore, that the poorer average reading achievement of boys in North America is caused by the lower expectations of American and Canadian adults. This causal connection has been shown by three American studies. Palardy (1969) found that first grade boys whose teachers believed that boys are less successful than girls in learning to read in fact achieved more poorly in reading than first grade boys whose teachers believed that boys are as successful as girls in learning to read. Also Mazurkiewicz (1960) reported that the reading attainments of a sample of eleventh grade boys were superior for those male students who considered reading to be masculine than for those male students who perceived reading as being feminine. More recently, Dwyer (1974) found that sex-role attitudes contributed significant variance to reading test scores. Hence, it would seem that the reading achievement of boys in North America is adversely affected by the fatalistic assumption that boys are just naturally prone to having trouble learning to read. This example shows how comparative reading studies may cause us to question our own cultural assumptions and try new approaches to old problems. Thus, comparative studies of differences in reading behavior, because they hold up for scrutiny different approaches to common phenomena, reveal that what some assume to be "universal" in nature may actually be unique to a given cultural milieu.

Another of the studies cited earlier in this chapter provided an example of how comparisons sometimes reveal remarkably similar problems from one country to another. Österberg's (1961) Swedish dialect experiment shows how the mismatch between the language of the child and the language of reading instruction causes confusion in the pupil's mind when he or she is trying to understand basic linguistic concepts used in reasoning about speech and writing. When the mismatch was removed in Österberg's experimental group, the children could more readily comprehend their tasks in learning to read. Further evidence that mismatch between the child's language and the language of instruction causes retardation in the development of reading skill has been obtained in several other countries: Canada (Downing, 1978), Greece (Charis, 1976), Ireland (Macnamara, 1966), Mexico (Modiano, 1968), and Uruguay (Garcia de Lorenzo, 1975). In this case, one must search for theoretical hypotheses and practical strategies to cope with what seems to be an important universal phenomenon in learning to read. The retardation found in these studies of language mismatch suggests that a universal feature of learning to read is the learner's efforts to comprehend reading instruction on the basis of his or her past experience of his or her own language. From the practical point of view, the universality of the difficulty caused by language mismatch alerts educators to the hazards of such bilingual situations and calls for consideration of special teaching strategies.

In such ways comparative reading studies help to close off the blind alleys in our thinking about how children learn to read. By steering clear of idiosyncrasies, we can focus on the universally important factors in reading instruction.

How can educators become better acquainted with reading in other countries? Unfortunately, at the present time very few college courses are available on comparative reading. Most of those that are known to this author are graduate courses on the general topic of comparative reading. However, this topic may sometimes be included in a course on cultural foundations of reading. Instructors and students have made favorable comments on the outcomes of comparative reading courses. The commonly recognized main value of such courses is that the study of reading in other countries with different cultural customs and languages helps students to recognize more clearly the important variables in reading development *in their own country and language.*

Ideally a comparative reading course should have a fieldwork component. Students learn more from making comparisons for themselves as they observe schools, teachers, and pupils in cultural and linguistic settings that are different from their own. One American university has created an annual Comparative Reading Institute. In the first Institute, as well as in course work on reading education in Denmark, students had a substantial fieldwork experience in Danish public schools and related institutions. The second Institute made an intensive study of bilingual situations in Wales, and the third Institute is planned for Hong Kong which has some remarkable linguistic and cultural contrasts for American students to study.

Sometimes economic circumstances make such overseas fieldwork unfeasible for students. However, comparative studies in the field may be possible in the local environment if some variations in culture and language are available, as is often the case. For example, this author was able to include a fieldwork component in the comparative reading course he conducted recently at a university in Finland, where different cultural groups existed in the area. Similarly, in Canada and in the United States there is no shortage of opportunities for local fieldwork on cultural and linguistic minority groups.

In graduate studies and research, comparative reading can be a powerful stimulus to the professional development of students and scholars in reading. Therefore, it is not surprising that the potential development of comparative studies is currently the charge of one

International Reading Association committee. In 1976 IRA set up the Comparative Reading Committee with Eve Malmquist in the chair. The charges of this committee include considering the development of college courses on comparative reading and the locating of academic resources for its study. The committee's report will be of great interest to those who have already begun to explore this exciting new field of study.

FOR DISCUSSION

1. If the general nature of mature reading is essentially the same across cultures, then how is it that the learning-to-read process is different?
2. Does the nature of the educational system in different countries account for the wider range of scores found among countries? What factors could account for these findings?
3. What factors could account for differences in results found in different countries, such as differences among sexes in the United States and in Germany?
4. What major assumptions about the learning-to-read process can be drawn from Downing's article and model?

REFERENCES

Charis, C. P. The problem of bilingualism in modern Greek education. *Comparative Education Review*, 1976, *20*, 216–219.

Downing, J. Comparative reading: A method of research and study in reading. In J. A. Figurel (Ed.), *Reading and realism*. Newark, Delaware: IRA, 1969.

Downing, J. *Comparative reading*. New York: Macmillan, 1973. Reissued Ann Arbor, Michigan: University Microfilms International, 1979.

Downing, J. Strategies of bilingual teaching. *International Review of Education*, 1978, *24*, 329–346.

Downing, J. *Reading and reasoning*. New York: Springer, 1979.

Downing, J., and Dalrymple-Alford, E. C. A methodological critique of the 1973 IEA survey of reading comprehension education in fifteen countries. *Reading Research Quarterly*, 1974–1975, *10*, 212–227.

Downing, J., et al. A cross-national survey of cultural expectations and sex-role standards in reading. *Journal of Research in Reading*, 1979, *2*, 8–23.

Downing, J., and Leong, C. K. *Psychology of reading*. New York: Macmillan, In press.

Dwyer, C. A. Influences of children's sex role standards on reading and arithmetic achievement. *Journal of Educational Psychology*, 1974, *66*, 811–816.

Foshay, A. W. et al. *Educational achievements of thirteen-year-olds in twelve countries*. Hamburg, Germany: UNESCO Institute for Education, 1962.

Garcia de Lorenzo, M. E. Frontier dialect: A challenge to education. *Reading Teacher*, 1975, *28*, 653–658.

Gray, W. S. *The teaching of reading and writing*. Paris: UNESCO, 1953.

Luria, A. R. [On the pathology of grammatical operations.] *Izvestija APN RSFSR*, No. 17, 1946.

Macnamara, J. *Bilingualism and primary education.* Edinburgh, Scotland: Edinburgh University Press, 1966.

Mazurkiewicz, A. J. Social-cultural influences and reading. *Journal of Developmental Reading*, 1960, *3*, 254–263.

Modiano, N. National or mother language in beginning reading: A comparative study. *Research in the Teaching of English*, 1968, *2*, 32–43.

Österberg, T. *Bilingualism and the first school language.* Umeå, Sweden: Västerbottens Tryckeri, AB, 1961.

Palardy, J. M. What teachers believe—what children achieve. *Elementary School Journal*, 1969, *69*, 370–374.

Pidgeon, D. A. A comparative study of basic attainments. *Educational Research*, 1958, *1*, 50–68.

Staiger, R. C. Developments in reading and literacy education: 1956–1967. In W. S. Gray, *The teaching of reading and writing* (2nd ed.). Paris: UNESCO, 1969.

Stewart, W. A. On the use of Negro dialect in the teaching of reading. In J. C. Baratz and R. W. Shuy (Eds.), *Teaching black children to read.* Washington, D.C.: Center for Applied Linguistics, 1969.

Stewart, W. A. Teaching blacks to read against their will. In P. A. Luelsdorff (Ed.), *Linguistic perspectives on black English.* Regensburg, Germany: Verlag Hans Carl, 1975.

Thorndike, R. L. *Reading comprehension education in fifteen countries.* New York: Wiley, 1973.

Vernon, M. D. *Backwardness in reading.* London: Cambridge University Press, 1957.

Vernon, M. D. *Reading and its difficulties.* London: Cambridge University Press, 1971.

INDEX